W9-AQI-783

DATE DUE

MR 15 '12			
AP 1-2 '12			
NY 10 '12			

Rethinking Europe's Future

Rethinking Europe's Future

David P. Calleo

A Century Foundation Book

PRINCETON UNIVERSITY PRESS

PRINCETON AND OXFORD

The Century Foundation, formerly the Twentieth Century Fund, sponsors and supervises timely analyses of economic policy, foreign affairs, and domestic political issues. Not-for-profit and nonpartisan, it was founded in 1919 and endowed by Edward A. Filene.

Copyright © 2001 by The Century Foundation
Published by Princeton University Press, 41 William Street,
Princeton, New Jersey 08540
In the United Kingdom: Princeton University Press, 3 Market Place, Woodstock,
Oxfordshire OX20 1SY
All Rights Reserved

Library of Congress Cataloging-in-Publication Data
Calleo, David P., 1934–
Rethinking Europe's future / David P. Calleo.
p.   cm.
"A Century Foundation book."
Includes bibliographical references and index.
ISBN 0-691-09081-5 (cl. : alk. paper)
1. Post-communism—Europe. 2. European Union. 3. Europe—Economic integration.
4. Security, International. 5. Nationalism—Europe. 6. International relations.
7. Europe—Foreign relations—1989– I. Title.

D2009.C35 2001
320.94—dc21   2001035079

British Library Cataloging-in-Publication data is available

This book has been composed in Times Roman

Printed on acid-free paper. ∞

www.pup.princeton.edu

Printed in the United States of America

10 9 8 7 6 5 4 3

For Avis

Contents

PART THREE   *The New Europe*

Acknowledgments

A BOOK like this needs considerable help and is therefore the occasion for much well-deserved gratitude. To begin with, I thank The Century Foundation for its wise counsel and warm support, and I also thank two other lively and civilized institutions—the Centre d'Etudes des Relations Internationales (CERI) at the Institut d'Etudes Politiques in Paris and the Institut Universitaire des Hautes Etudes Internationales in Geneva. Both provided much needed opportunities for distance and fresh reflection.

My own institution—SAIS (The Johns Hopkins University Paul H. Nitze School of Advanced International Studies)—has been stimulating and supporting my writing for over thirty years. As usual, this book has drawn an excellent group of researchers and critics from among my students. I should particularly like to thank Christopher Chivvis, Anja Dalgard-Nielsen, Andrew Davies, Walter Ferrara, Cole Frates, Robert Heilman, Davis Hodge, Ethan Ilzetzki, Markus Jelitto, Thomas Kenyon, Richard Koe, Janis Lazda, and Alexander Ruck-Keene.

Several old friends and colleagues have given the book critical but sympathetic readings. I am particularly grateful to Fouad Ajami, Dana Allin, Charles Doran, Erik Jones, Thomas Keaney, André Liebich, Michael Mandelbaum, Judith Paulus, Benjamin Rowland, Robert Skidelsky, Michael Stürmer, Stephen Szabo, Jenonne Walker, and Lanxin Xiang.

Foreword

SINCE the colonization of the Americas, the history of the new world has been intertwined with that of the old. During the period from the War of Independence until the twentieth century, the United States fought a war with the United Kingdom, engaged in something quite close to an undeclared naval war with France, and conducted a far-flung conflict with Spain. In addition, through much of the nineteenth century, the rapidly growing American nation looked to Europe for both capital and markets. In the twentieth century, continuing American involvement with Europe led to massive participation in both World War I and World War II, as well as the Cold War. Taken together, these events transformed the American nation in ways that are still central to its national character.

For most Americans most of the time, however, even major occurrences in the international arena are seen as interruptions—distractions from the business of getting on with one's own life and dealing with the many issues that are an inevitable by-product of living in a dynamic nation such as the United States. Since the completion of the recent decennial census, for example, the American news media have been transfixed by the changes in demographics revealed by the new data, with little or no attention to comparative information about how the composition of the globe and the populations of other important nations also are changing. This sort of self-absorption is actually typical of the United States and often characterizes its politics. It would be a mistake, nonetheless, to assume that U.S. citizens, regardless of their preferences, are not becoming increasingly sophisticated about such things as the rapid globalization of commerce and extensive ways in which everyday life is touched by these changing patterns of trade and finance.

In Western Europe, the alterations in politics and economics that have occurred over the past two decades are even more a part of the lives of average citizens. Historic forces have been redirected toward new ends. Military rivalries have given way to supranational political structures; contests for territory have been replaced by economic inte-

gration on an unprecedented scale. The European Union is something
new under the sun—and given the ties that continue to bind the
United States and these nations, something that, in the long run, is
sure to have great significance for every American.

In that context, the Trustees of The Century Foundation were de-
lighted to have the opportunity to renew our collaboration with David
Calleo, Dean Acheson Professor and director of European Studies at
the Paul Nitze School of Advanced International Studies at The Johns
Hopkins University. As author of numerous important works of foreign policy and economic affairs, including *The Bankrupting of America: How the Federal Budget Is Impoverishing the Nation*, *The Future
of the Western Alliance*, and *The German Problem Reconsidered:
Germany and the World Order, 1870 to the Present*, Calleo brought
unusual qualifications to the task of explaining what is going in Europe and what this is likely to mean for the future of U.S.-European
relations.

The Foundation's association with Calleo includes the sponsorship
of *Beyond American Hegemony: The Future of the Western Alliance*,
which was published in 1987 to great praise; Paul Kennedy said in his
review in the *New York Times* that the book was "one that every
serious student of contemporary international affairs should read."
Unlike most works on international affairs published then, just before
the historic events in the Soviet Union began to unfold, Calleo's book
has stood the test of time extremely well. It not only was an important
contribution when it first appeared, but it remains very useful in understanding the possibilities for future American policy.

In the same way, *Rethinking Europe's Future* provides us with information we need moving forward, for we are living through an unusual era in terms of U.S. relations with the new Europe. Both sides,
in a sense, have the luxury of conducting policy in a way that toler-
ates continuing tension without dire consequences. What disagree-
ments there are usually can best be characterized as the kind that
occur among old friends or even members of the same family. One
can scarcely imagine the argument intensifying enough to result in a
fundamental division. Still, the future is unknowable. And, as Calleo
points out, the movement toward European integration, whatever
bumps are encountered along the way, has powerful momentum. The

European Union continues to grow stronger, deeper, and wider—and will increasingly include territories formerly dominated by the Soviet Union. In the context of European history, the process is of awesome importance, but this fact is sometimes lost on casual American observers whose eyes tend to glaze over at the sight of yet another story about the often rather pedestrian, day-to-day details of building a single market and a multistate union. This book helps to place those events in a meaningful context.

Over the years, David Calleo has made great contributions to our understanding of America's place in the world. His study of European political and economic integration will prove invaluable as we try to look toward how American policy should be shaped in the second post–Cold War decade. On behalf of The Century Foundation, I thank him for his work on this important and difficult subject.

Richard C. Leone, President
The Century Foundation
June 2001

Rethinking Europe's Future

Old Europe and New Europe

EUROPE BEGAN the twentieth century as the world's leading region. By the middle of the century it was devastated and occupied. By the end it was once more prosperous and free. Given Europe's roller-coaster ride through the past century, no one can predict with much assurance what its fate will be in the new. There are too many un-predictable elements. Europe has volatile neighbors to the east and south, including giant, foundering Russia. Old Balkan quarrels have revived in savage warfare. Security still depends heavily on the United States, whose own agenda is uncertain and disoriented. And prosperity hinges on a world economy shaken by seismic changes not necessarily favorable to Europe. True, Europe's old nation states have left the twentieth century tied into a union that promises a better fu-ture. But that union is now embarked upon bold but hazardous experi-ments with monetary integration and territorial expansion. Its com-plex institutions are overstretched and need fundamental reforms. Meanwhile, ancient national rivalries smolder among the partners. With so many contingent uncertainties, even the most knowledgeable predictions must rely heavily on historical imagination and intuition, and ultimately on faith.

Nonetheless, decisions are made and policies go forward. We are in one of those watersheds in history where present choices may deter-mine the course of events for a long time to come. Analysts must therefore try to make sense out of what is going on. Even if they cannot reliably predict the future, they can at least hope to move more consciously through the swirling events that are shaping it. This means not only analyzing current events but trying to determine an appropriate historical and theoretical framework for considering them. Finding such a framework after the Cold War means reprogramming our imaginations—transforming our visions and goals to suit a differ-ent reality. This rejuvenating of the public imagination is a vital col-lective task, where scholars, journalists, and artists, along with politicians, bureaucrats, and political activists in general, have their roles. This book is one attempt to contribute. Its title—*Rethinking Europe's Future*—suggests its approach.

BIPOLAR OBFUSCATION

Some thirty-five years ago, I made a similar attempt, in a book called *Europe's Future: The Grand Alternatives*. That book was somewhat unusual for the time in arguing that the European status quo of the Cold War, while already remarkably comfortable for the West, was more vulnerable to changes already occurring than many others thought—a view that I restated strongly in a subsequent book, *Beyond American Hegemony*, published in 1987.[1] Even at that late date, most analysts and practitioners continued to believe that radical changes lay well into the future.

The sudden retreat and unexpected collapse of the Soviet Union exploded the prevailing complacency but also encouraged some dangerous misconceptions. Cold Warriors—Marxists and anti-Marxists alike—had defined postwar history in a rather parochial and intellectual fashion—as a dramatic struggle between two opposing ideals: communism and capitalism. With the Soviet collapse and China apparently transforming itself rapidly into a market economy, the struggle seemed over. Liberal democratic capitalism had apparently won and was expected soon to predominate everywhere. As one famous article announced, it was therefore "the end of history."[2] The author, Francis Fukuyama, was doubtless too shrewd to take his celebrated aphorism too seriously. What had undoubtedly become obsolescent, however, was the postwar mind set that visualized history through a bipolar paradigm set by the Cold War. Indeed, that view had been out of date for a long time.

---

[1] David P. Calleo, *Europe's Future: The Grand Alternatives* (New York: Horizon Press, 1965), and *Beyond American Hegemony: The Future of the Western Alliance* (A Twentieth Century Fund Book; New York: Basic Books, 1987).

[2] Francis Fukuyama, "The End of History?" *The National Interest,* vol. 16 (Summer 1989), pp. 3–18, expanded in *The End of History and the Last Man* (New York: Free Press, 1992).

Throughout the Cold War many things were going on in the world that did not fit comfortably within the bipolar paradigm. As Europe lost its empires, Asia's giant countries—India and China—began transforming themselves into modern states: superpowers of the future. The Muslim world, more-or-less liberated from Western occupation, embarked on its own painful course toward modernization. Meanwhile, West European states achieved remarkable domestic transformations that greatly increased their economic weight and political stability. Japan followed a similar course in Asia and grew into an economic giant. Smaller countries in Asia began to follow. By 1989, all these changes together had constituted a major redistribution of economic strength within the capitalist world. Technology, meanwhile, was relentlessly bringing all parts of that world into more and more intimate contact—resulting in a heady mixture of confrontation and collaboration, loss and enrichment. These changes, which were going on throughout the Cold War, have of course continued after it. The fading of the bipolar perspective has made their significance more apparent.

HISTORY RESUMED: BACKWARD TO THE FUTURE

In trying to master the new era that is unfolding, intellectuals and policymakers search for new paradigms—to frame, order, and justify their ideas and projects, some new and some old. Seeking fresh guidance for the future inevitably prompts a new look at the past. In some respects, the new Europe after the Cold War is not unlike the old Europe before World War I. The old Europe had been plural and interdependent, with several interacting centers of power and an uneasy and shifting balance among them. Thus, the collapse of the rigid and insulated bipolar blocs seems not so much the end of traditional European history as its resumption, with the Cold War merely a frozen parenthesis.

A Europe returning to its normal history is not an altogether reassuring prospect. That history is long and bloody, and there is scarcely a single tranquil century in it. The first half of the twentieth century saw the disintegration of the Habsburg empire; the Soviet, Fascist,

3

and Nazi revolutions; the breakdown of the world economy; and two world wars of astonishing ferocity—an exceptionally violent period, even by Europe's normal standards. If the century's second half was comparatively stable, it is arguably because the Cold War between the superpowers deprived European states of a large measure of their independence.

POSTWAR EUROPE: DURABLE PROGRESS?

In the West, at least, postwar Europe had ample consolation for its geopolitical demotion. Thanks to the Atlantic Alliance, West Europeans enjoyed reliable protection, against not only the Soviets but also each other. And taking good advantage of a global *Pax Americana*, Western Europe grew collectively into the world's largest producer and consumer of goods and services.[3] Prosperity led to exceptional domestic stability and contentment. West European governments pioneered in developing the democratic welfare state and, with the Common Market, created a unique and highly successful regional structure for resolving national differences and concerting national policies. Thus, if the first half of the twentieth century was an exaggerated version of Europe's normal bellicose and self-destructive history, the second half was a prolonged departure from that history. The question is whether that departure can be prolonged, now that the Cold War occupation is over.

Europe's states have enjoyed long periods of stable progress and prosperity before. A relatively tranquil balance of power system lasted from Napoleon's defeat in 1815 until the mid-nineteenth century, when an explosion of nationalist revolutions inaugurated a new chain of major European wars, culminating in the Franco-Prussian War of 1870. Thereafter, despite the Great Depression of 1870–1896, the Boer War, the Russo-Japanese War, and various Balkan conflicts,

---

[3] Although the statistics change depending on factors such as exchange rates, most measurements showed Western Europe to be the biggest producer and consumer of goods and services by the end of the 1980s. The European members of the Organization for Economic Cooperation & Development (OECD) had a combined GDP (at 1990 price levels and exchange rates) of $7,240 billion, while the GDP of the United States stood at $5,554 billion.

Europe as a whole enjoyed a peaceful and prosperous interlude, until the great bloodbath that began in 1914 and recommenced in 1939. Should the long peace of the Cold War be seen as merely another transitory interlude? Or has there been a genuine mutation that allows us to imagine that Europe can now escape its normal historical alternation between peace and war?

One possible answer is that Europe's Cold War occupation is not over. Instead, a benevolent American protectorate has become a permanent feature of the European environment. The American protectorate, moreover, is now being gradually extended over many parts of the old Soviet Europe. So long as the protectorate remains intact, so, arguably, will the stability and prosperity that have grown up under it. But this is a vision of Europe's future that seems unrealistic for a variety of reasons. Although Western Europe and the United States may well remain military allies in the foreseeable future, Americans have grown relatively more concerned with their own economic, social, and political problems and less capable of managing other people's affairs. At the same time, the security problems of the new Pan-Europe are now more domestic and complex in character, more difficult and inappropriate for an outside power to manage. Moreover, the rapid rise of giant Asian powers suggests that the United States may need to grow more selective in its military commitments and will therefore demand more "burden-sharing" from the Europeans. Americans and Europeans, after all, are not only allies but also major economic competitors. And several European states are themselves major military powers. In the absence of any clear common threat, both Europeans and Americans themselves may grow progressively uneasy about continuing America's traditional postwar military hegemony over Europe. A new transatlantic relationship will have to be found, one in which Europe will depend more on its own indigenous forces, institutions, and balances.

Europe today, of course, seems very different from the Europe of 1914 or 1939. All the major Western states are democracies. War has supposedly become unthinkable among closely related democratic societies. But conflict has many forms and many ways to start. Interstate systems break down in different ways at different times. Democracies can be more fragile than they seem. Habits of violence spread. Confrontations can get out of control, and incidents can degenerate or be manipulated into wars, particularly after a long period of deteriorating relations. Today's difficult economic conditions, along with the disquieting surge of racist and ethnic violence in many European countries, suggest that the continent's peace and stability are not artless products of nature and should never be taken for granted.

Fortunately, West European states have used their long Cold War vacation to build a European Union that presumably compensates for diminishing American hegemony. That European Union has owed its postwar success to two critical factors: American support and a special relationship between France and Germany. Strong American support was particularly significant in the early days of Europe's fledgling community. A major school of American diplomacy regarded America's heavy postwar hegemonic role as transitory and looked forward to a more integrated Europe and a more equal transatlantic alliance. Such a Europe seemed a more reliable partner for sustaining the liberal global economy that Americans were hoping to build. Thus, American policy favored European integration in theory and never turned resolutely against it in practice.

The idea of constructing a pan-European confederacy around Franco-German partnership had its roots in the interwar period and revived strongly after World War II. The nascent partnership was the major political force behind the early institutions that began Europe's postwar process of integration, notably the European Coal and Steel Community of 1952 and the European Economic Community of 1958. In 1963, a treaty signed by Konrad Adenauer and Charles de Gaulle gave the partnership a formal institutional framework of its own. Thereafter it developed to include diplomatic and military cooperation and gradually became a sort of steering committee for the European Union as a whole. By the late 1980s, Franco-German partnership was well established, and Europe's unifying process seemed ready to accelerate on several fronts—commercial and monetary union, diplomatic coordination, even pooled military forces.

EUROPE CHALLENGED

The sudden collapse of Soviet power, starting in 1989, proved a major shock to West European integration. Without the Soviet empire and the Cold War, not only was America's future role uncertain, but Europe suddenly regained many of its traditional divisive problems. Reunited Germany was, once again, substantially bigger than its neighbors and more problematic internally. Europe's old German problem was threatening to revive. With Russia chaotic and the states of its old Central and East European empire in turmoil, Germans felt themselves pulled inexorably back to *Mitteleuropa*. Many analysts began to fear that the European Union would, after all, prove merely an epiphenomenon of the Cold War. Fortunately, Europe's postwar enthusiasm for union had deeper roots. While postwar integration was greatly facilitated by the exigencies of the Cold War, its real inspiration came from Europe's self-destructive experiences in the half-century before the Cold War began. Engaging France and Germany in a great cooperative project had seemed the best way to contain German power. But so long as the Cold War lasted, these long-term political goals of integration were more visionary than urgent. Containing Germany was hardly a pressing need while the country was partitioned and occupied. Preventing Europe's being dominated by outside powers was another of integration's long-term aims. But while Soviet forces remained in the middle of Germany, few West Europeans had any compelling desire to send the Americans away. Not until the Cold War system began to crumble did the European Union's long-term political and military goals grow immediate. With Germany reunited, the Soviets gone, and even the Americans withdrawing two-thirds of their troops, a renewed German problem began to seem possible. The European Union finally faced the challenge for which it was designed.

Europe's nation states reacted with apparent vigor—principally by more and more ambitious plans for their union. With the Maastricht Treaty of December 1991, West European governments committed themselves to press forward with commercial, monetary, diplomatic, and military integration. Thus "deepened," the restyled European Union planned to reach out to incorporate the newly liberated states of Central and Eastern Europe. The Union of Western Europe was to become the Union of Pan Europe.

Rapidly unfolding events soon called the Maastricht goals into question. An unusually severe recession seemed to underscore Europe's vulnerability in an increasingly competitive world economy. Unemployment reached levels not seen since the 1930s and showed no sign of rapid improvement. The German government's heavy borrowing to cover the costs of national reunification worsened the slump. Meanwhile, the Yugoslav crisis, which exploded in 1991, mocked European pretensions to diplomatic and military coordination. Popular opposition to Maastricht grew serious in several countries, including France. For the first time, the ideal of European union risked losing its popular mandate.[4] But despite discouraging experiences in the earlier 1990s, Europe's states pressed ahead with more and more ambitious plans for their Union. Hopes began to be fulfilled. Most notably, monetary union occurred on schedule in 1999. By the decade's end, even the perennial schemes for diplomatic and military cooperation seemed ready to take on real substance.

Viewed in longer perspective, considering the terrible decades of war, tyranny, and depression that followed after 1900, Europe's old nation states left the twentieth century in surprisingly good health. Their political economies, however troubled, nevertheless continued to blend prosperity, liberty, and security with success. They entered the new century having built a complex European Union that represented great progress toward resolving the old contradiction between sovereignty and interdependence. As neighboring nation states, they were preserving national consensus and self-determination while using their confederacy to harmonize their relationships, and thereby greatly increasing their own effectiveness. Their Union seemed a sort of Holy Roman Empire reborn—like its predecessor scarcely holy, hardly Roman, and not much of an empire. Rather, it was communitarian in spirit, Gothic in structure, and elected no emperor. But for all its messy diversity, it kept moving forward.

Europe entering the twenty-first century, however, has few reasons for complacency about its future. Current trends point toward a radi-

---

[4] The Danes narrowly rejected the Maastricht Treaty in the referendum of June 2, 1992 (50.3 percent against, 49.7 percent for), while the French accepted it by a narrow margin (51.04 percent for, 48.95 percent against). By December 1993, Eurobarometer polls showed support across the European Union for European integration down to 54 percent of those polled, from a post–Cold War high of 69 percent in 1991. "Eurobarometer: Opinion Poll Shows Drop in Support for EU Membership," *Europe Information Service European Report*, December 17, 1993, and *Europe Information Service European Report*, July 22, 1992.

cally different world system, where neither Europe's own comfortable position nor the continued predominance of Western power and values is assured. Demography alone compels apprehension.[5] The travails of Europe's eastern region and southern neighbors will threaten contagious disorder for the foreseeable future. And with the Soviet empire gone, Europe's Union confronts a pan-European reality, in itself a threat to the EU's own comfortable Western identity. The Western partners have to decide which Eurasian countries are in their union and which are not. Internally, they will have to extend their confederal institutions, already highly complex and delicately balanced, to a larger and more heterogenous membership. Satisfactory accommodations will have to be found for neighbors who remain outside. And new arrangements will be needed for security problems that are themselves greatly altered. This means recasting relationships with both Russia and America.

The Soviet demise is challenging to Europe in other respects. What, for example, does it imply for the future cohabitation of capitalism and nation states? Was the failure of Soviet collectivism also a decisive defeat for the communitarian varieties of capitalism widely practiced in postwar Europe? Was the collapse of the Soviet Union, in itself, a vindication of capitalism? Arguably, exposing the squalid bankruptcy of the Soviet model did little to discredit Marx's analysis of capitalism's own weaknesses. Instead, the decade following the Soviet collapse saw the return of a strong deflationary current in the world, despite America's own record prosperity. With one financial crisis following another, Europe's high unemployment, together with the severe disarray of Japanese and several other Asian capitalist

---

[5] World population is predicted to rise from its 1998 level of 5.9 billion to 8.9 billion in 2050; the European share of that population is expected to fall from 12.4 percent in 1998 to 7.0 percent in 2050. United Nations Department of Economic and Social Affairs, Population Division, *1998 Revision of World Population Estimates and Projections* <http://www.popin.org/pop1998/4.htm>. Chapter 13 explores some of the political and economic effects of such growth in non-European labor pools. For a discussion of Europe's demographic problems with its southern borders, see Jean-Claude Chesnais, "Le Crépuscule de l'Occident," *European Journal of Population*, vol. 12, no. 4 (1996), pp. 338ff., and *La Demographie* (Paris: Presses Universitaires de France, 1998).

economies, seemed to demonstrate the dangerous instability of capitalism, as well as the diminishing ability of national sovereignties to control it.

All rich countries, of course, face challenges arising from capitalism's rapid technological change and highly competitive global economy, but European states seem especially vulnerable. Europe's labor is the most expensive in the world, and its welfare systems are the most generous. Its investment in research and new technology lags behind that of the United States and Japan. The outrageous levels of unemployment that grew chronic in the 1990s have become a threat to fiscal, social, and political stability throughout the continent.[6]

EUROPE: THE NEW WORLD ORDER?

Whether Europe's states do succeed with their union is scarcely less important to others than to the Europeans themselves. A quarreling Europe has been a great burden to the rest of the world. Over the several decades of the Cold War, both the superpowers squandered untold resources on arms, not least because they believed, with ample evidence, that Europe was too dangerous to be left to its own devices. The Cold War was no doubt a monstrous solution to Europe's traditional problems, but it was better than another European war. Today, the new global challenges are such that the world really cannot afford the old Europe. In this century, Europe should take a leading part in global solutions rather than itself remain the principal global problem.

---

[6] In 1995, national R & D expenditures as a percentage of GDP were as follows: United States 2.52 percent; Japan 2.78 percent; Germany 2.28 percent; France 2.34 percent; the United Kingdom 2.05 percent, and Italy 1.14 percent. Hourly compensation costs for production workers in manufacturing in 1996, with the United States as 100, stood at Germany 180; France 109; the United Kingdom 80; and Italy 102. U.S. Bureau of the Census, *Statistical Abstract of the United States: 1998*, 118th edition (Washington, DC: U.S. Government Printing Office, 1998), pp. 612, 844. The average level of EU unemployment remained stubbornly fixed around the 10 percent mark throughout the 1990s, while France and Germany saw 12 percent unemployment by the middle of the decade. *OECD Economic Outlook June 1999* (Paris: Organization for Economic Cooperation and Development, 1999), p. 248. See below, chapter 12, for discussion.

It is therefore tempting to see a unifying Europe as the harbinger not only of a more plural world but also of one with better hopes for peaceful stability. In this vision, a strong, cohesive Europe joins in a rejuvenated alliance with America. Together, they embrace Russia in a larger pan-European system—not to make a common front against an alien non-Western world but to keep their own balance and their own relations in order across Europe and the Atlantic. Such a Europe becomes a model for reasonable behavior among states in other regions of the world—a *noyau dur* of enlightened rationality. This view presumes, however, that Europe will succeed with its confederal experiment, an outcome that Europe's history hardly allows us to take for granted.

And, of course, a European Union that does flourish in the twenty-first century will be a problem as well as a solution. It can scarcely avoid becoming a major new force in the world. Its very existence, coupled with the rise of Asian superpowers, should indicate a world system that is growing more plural. For those who have grown fond of the idea of a seamless global world, with only one superpower, this is a disquieting prospect. For Americans and Europeans alike, it raises issues that will need to be faced consciously and generously. Suppressed, they can easily poison transatlantic relations and, someday, shatter the West once more.

THE BOOK'S STRATEGY

Our inquiry into Europe's future looks to the basic questions about Europe's future: Will Europe, liberated from bipolar hegemony, continue the Cold War's positive experiment with integration, or will it return to the fissural tendencies that proved so self-destructive in the prewar past? And what will be the global consequences if Europe's integration does succeed? Answering these questions requires addressing some major historical issues. To begin with, what is the nature of Europe's long-standing self-destructive tendencies, and what lessons can we learn from studying their history? Second, what was the basic character of postwar Europe that permitted West European integration to go forward? More important, what dynamic ele-

11

ments remain from the postwar era to shape Europe's union in what now seems a very different regional and global setting? Addressing these questions gives the book its structure. The chapters that follow fall into three distinct but interdependent parts—each with a short introduction:

Part I, "Europe's Living History," looks at critical parts of modern Europe's long-standing historical legacy—in particular the rival interpretations and lessons of World War I, and, more generally, Europe's enduring system of nation states, with their symbiotic but uneasy relationship with capitalism.

Part II, "Legacies of the Cold War," focuses on what endures of postwar Europe, depicted as three overlapping, antagonistic, but interdependent "systems"—the bipolar strategic system, the European Union, and the global economy. The opening chapter considers the origins of each and its interdependence with the others. Subsequent chapters analyze each system's character, dynamics, and continuing influence.

Part III, "The New Europe," enters the postwar era. Succeeding chapters consider Maastricht and the European monetary union, "globalism" and European integration, the European Union's projects for enlargement and constitutional reform and for its own more autonomous collective security. A penultimate chapter considers models for a pan-European security system, with varying arrangements for Russia and America. The final chapter, "Europe in the New World Order," speculates on the probable role and character of the European Union, should it be a major power in the new century.

So broad a range of topics and disciplines is a challenge for the writer and the reader both. Europe, with all its rich diversity and vitality through the centuries, is in no way a simple subject. Its history is hardly a tidy collection of uncontested interpretations with clear lessons for the future. Certainly, no one should claim infallible powers for divining Europe's future. In 1900, who could have imagined what would follow over the next twenty years, let alone over the rest of the twentieth century? We can be certain, however, that what happens with Europe's confederal project will be one of the great issues for our present century. Modesty should not keep us from trying to imagine the future, or from studying history for inspiration to improve on it. At the very least, we should seek to understand what is happening to us and why. I have tried to write in this spirit. Failure may be inevitable, but I hope useful to others.

Selected Sources

History Resumed: Backward to the Future?

For differing arguments about the potential durability of peace in Europe after the end of the Cold War, see Michael Mandelbaum, *The Dawn of Peace in Europe* (New York: Twentieth Century Fund Press, 1996); John J. Mearsheimer, "Back to the Future: Instability in Europe After the Cold War," *International Security*, vol. 15, no. 1 (Summer 1990) and "The False Promise of International Institutions," Working Paper 10 (John M. Olin Institute for Strategic Studies, Harvard University, November 1994); and Kenneth N. Waltz, "The Emerging Structure of International Politics," *International Politics*, vol. 18, no. 1 (Fall 1993).

Fukuyama's thesis was echoed by others, with various national twists. See, in France, Jean-Marie Guéhenno and Victoria Elliot, "The End of the Nation State," *Political Studies*, vol. 45, no. 2, and, in Britain, Robert Cooper, *The Post-Modern State and the New World Order* (London: Demos, 1996). The apparent triumph of free-market capitalism did not, of course, convince everyone. Samuel Huntington, *The Clash of Civilizations and the Remaking of World Order* (New York: Simon & Schuster, 1996), set the tone for many debates of the late 1990s. For my reaction, see David P. Calleo, "A New Era of Overstretch? American Policy in Europe and Asia," *World Policy Journal*, vol. 15, no. 1 (Spring 1998), and "Restarting the Marxist Clock," *World Policy Journal*, vol. 13, no. 2 (Summer 1996).

Europe Challenged

Many saw the reunification of Germany as a major potential threat to peace in post–Cold War Europe. For my own contemporary analysis, see David P. Calleo, "German 'Reunification': An American View," *Die Zeit*, November 3, 1989, p. 7. Other works that deal with this

13

issue include Konrad Jarausch, *The Rush to German Unity* (New York: Oxford University Press, 1994); Tony Judt, *A Grand Illusion? An Essay on Europe* (New York: Hill & Wang, 1996); Peter Merkl, *German Unification in the European Context* (University Park: Pennsylvania State University Press, 1993); Stephen F. Szabo, *The Diplomacy of German Reunification* (New York: St. Martin's Press, 1992); Condoleeza Rice and Philip Zelikow, *Germany Unified and Europe Transformed* (Cambridge, Mass.: Harvard, 1995); and Dirk Verheyen and Christian Søe, *The Germans and Their Neighbors* (San Francisco: Westview Press, 1993), as well as several essays in David P. Calleo and Markus Jelitto, eds.,"The New Germany in the New Europe," *SAIS Review*, Special Issue (Fall 1995). For a longer-term perspective, see Wolfram F. Hanrieder, *Germany, America, Europe: Forty Years of German Foreign Policy* (New Haven: Yale University Press, 1989). For a good contemporary German analysis of how the end of bipolarity was seen as a threat to European unity, see Josef Joffe, "The New Europe: Yesterday's Ghosts," *Foreign Affairs*, vol. 72, no. 1 (1993). Among Europe's leaders, Margaret Thatcher justified her fears of Germany in *The Downing Street Years* (London: HarperCollins, 1993), pp. 792–798, while a retrospective summation of François Mitterrand's views can be found in his *De l'Allemagne, de la France* (Paris: Editions Odile Jacob, 1996). For the views of American leaders, see George Bush, *A World Transformed* (New York: Knopf, 1998), and James A. Baker, *The Politics of Diplomacy: Revolution, War and Peace, 1989–1992* (New York: Putnam, 1995).

Europe's Living History

INTRODUCTION: WARS, STATES, AND CAPITALISM

EUROPE'S PEOPLES have long histories, full of glories and horrors, about which they have deep memories. What Europeans imagine they want for their future generally reflects the lessons they believe they have learned from their past. A rich accumulation of theories competes to explain old misfortunes and how to avoid repeating them. Rethinking Europe's future thus requires reconsidering its past—in particular how Europeans have explained their self-destructive wars of the twentieth century and how they imagine they may escape such wars in the future.

More fundamentally, rethinking requires considering the nature of the two formulas that have set the framework for modern European history: the nation state and capitalism. Modern Europe was the breeding ground for both, and together they explain Europe's dynamic character and long ascendancy over the rest of the world. The nation state gave Europe an unrivaled capacity to legitimate its rulers and mobilize its populations; capitalism engendered Europe's remarkable economic, technological, and social progress. These two formulas, entwined, have also been full of internal and mutual contradictions that do much to explain the instability and violence of modern Europe. In particular, three paradoxes about nation states and capitalism are reflected across modern history. The first is the paradox of interdependent sovereignties: Europe's nation states strive by nature to be sovereign but in practice depend heavily on each other. The second is the paradox of nationalist capitalism: Capitalism, which depends on nation states, also tends to undermine them. And the third is the paradox of capitalist self-destruction: Capitalism, as it develops, tends to undermine itself. Trying to explain and resolve these paradoxes has generated a rich corpus of influential speculation, with rival solutions that continue to dominate pictures of Europe's past and plans for its future.

The next four chapters confront this theorizing about the past. Chapter 2 considers rival lessons about the two world wars of the twentieth century. Chapter 3 considers the origins of Europe's states and classic theories about how a system of such states should be managed. Chapter 4 considers the transition from absolute states to "communitarian" nation states and asks why the latter formula has proved so tenacious. An appendix provides a glossary of terms. Chapter 5 turns to some of the great modern analysts of capitalism and its troubled relations with the nation state. Taken together, the four chapters sketch a certain view of how modern European history has been unfolding. Informing that view is a methodological habit, learned long ago when I was an undergraduate at Yale: an interdisciplinary approach to history and political economy emphasizing the influence of competing ideas or ways of looking at the world.[1] Obviously, any quick survey of so vast and speculative a subject will be inadequate. The reader impatient to get on with contemporary problems may no doubt skip the whole section. For me, however, it is the overture that contains the themes for what follows.

---

[1] I majored in what was then the College's interdisciplinary honors program in the Humanities, History, the Arts and Letters. (H.A.L.) Among many gifted teachers, I was particularly influenced by three: Joseph Toy Curtiss, Lewis Perry Curtiss, and Frederick Watkins. Each had a powerful and highly disciplined sense for the interconnectedness of politics, literature, and the arts, entwined with the study of worldviews in the history of ideas. I later taught in H.A.L. and have always suspected that it was, in its day, the finest undergraduate major anywhere. My years in graduate school naturally added new influences, most notably Robert Dahl, Leonard Krieger, and Arnold Wolfers. Struggling to reconcile the fashionable methodologies of the social sciences with what I had learned in H.A.L. constituted, in itself, a major part of my education. The resulting methodological approach was elaborated at some length in my first book, *Coleridge and the Idea of the Nation State* (New Haven: Yale University Press, 1966), where I analyzed the influence of the Romantic worldview on the development of constitutional nation states.

Competing Lessons of World War I

THE VICTORS' VIEW

THE TWENTIETH CENTURY saw two spectacular breakdowns of the nation state system in Europe. In between was a breakdown of capitalism around the world. The failures were closely linked. Economic tension contributed greatly to Europe's interstate conflict, and the resulting wars were closely bound to the breakdown of its liberal capitalism. These great wars were, first and foremost, brutal collisions of the interests and ambitions of Europe's nation states. Twice in a century, those states allowed their political-economic differences and rival geopolitical visions to draw them into titanic struggles, whose destructiveness still stupefies the imagination. What explains so total a breakdown in the capacity of Europe's nation states to manage their relations? What did they themselves think they were doing? As might be expected, each nation tended to have its own explanation.

The most popular explanation has been to blame the world wars on German "aggression." Why the Germans should have grown so spectacularly aggressive has been the subject of a vast body of historical, cultural, sociological, and economic analysis. Germans themselves have been among the most enthusiastic and imaginative contributors. Given the horrors of the Nazi regime, the thesis of German guilt is hard to put aside. Whenever there is any temptation to do so, the barbarity of the Holocaust is there to bring wandering speculation back to order. Thus, the "German problem" occupies a special place in the Western political imagination. A German demon is forever waiting to break loose. Germany, it seems, is too big and dynamic to fit easily into a purely European frame. And it is too illiberal and volatile a society to be trusted.[1]

---

[1] Anyone interested in a more ample presentation of this analysis might consult my earlier book, *The German Problem Reconsidered: Germany & the World Order, 1870 to the Present* (New York: Cambridge University Press, 1978).

Mistrust of Germany seems particularly militant and long-lived among the British, where it mingles with pride in their own country's lonely heroism in the darkest days of World War II. For many, these feelings cluster around the figure of Winston Churchill, one of the twentieth century's most charismatic leaders. Churchill not only defied the Germans but also embraced the Americans. Churchill's lesson was that the survival of democratic freedom in Europe depended on an enduring Anglo-American alliance, the Atlantic vision that still exercises a powerful attraction for significant parts of European and American populations. But the consequences of the Grand Alliance were not altogether what Churchill had intended. As the war continued, Britain's own resources were more and more exhausted and the Americans grew more and more predominant. *Faute de mieux*, Churchill ended up as the apologist for American hegemony over Europe.

Churchill also popularized another lesson from World War II of more questionable value: the futility of "appeasement." This is a lesson that rests on a particular historical interpretation of World War II, one that blames Hitler's international rise on misguided Western efforts to meet Germany's complaints about its treatment after World War I. According to the antiappeasement thesis, if the Western powers had, early on, recognized Hitler as the embodiment of evil that he was and girded themselves to fight him, the war would have taken a very different course. As a broader lesson in statecraft, this Churchillian historical thesis has encouraged several dubious but popular postwar tendencies. These include a strong propensity to see world events in a Manichean fashion and to personalize and demonize international antagonisms. Foreign policy analysis becomes a perpetual search for new Hitlers. International morality is reduced merely to finding evil and standing up to it. Those inclined to conciliation and mutual adjustment are seen as misguided, if not morally deficient. All this fitted the early Cold War very well. Stalin was a plausible substitute for Hitler. The Allied war against Hitler became the Allied war against Stalin. Churchill himself helped to manipulate the transition. But as Churchill would very likely have been quick to see, this way of looking at things was not altogether adequate for the more complex world of detente and nascent multipolarity typical of the later Cold War.

Certainly it is not very useful in the increasingly plural and complex world that lies ahead.

In any event, so long as the bipolar Cold War lasted, blaming the world wars on Germany was a convenient thesis. A demonic Germany meant an intrinsically unstable Europe, a Europe that required an outside balancer. German guilt and exceptionalism thus became the justification for the bipolar occupation of Germany in particular and of Europe in general. Postwar Germans themselves accepted the analysis, even if they resisted its bipolar solution. Today, despite the Soviet collapse, apprehension of Germany's dark potential helps to perpetuate the North Atlantic Treaty Organization (NATO) and a continuing American hegemonic role in Europe. In a different way, it is also a major rationale for the European Union. As a thesis about modern European history, this analysis continues to weigh on the future.

But while blaming the twentieth century's world wars primarily on Germany's exceptional aggressiveness has been highly convenient, it is also a clearly inadequate view historically. Particularly dubious is the tendency to equate German behavior in World War II with German behavior in World War I. There exists, after all, a respectable historiographical defense of the German position in World War I. Over several decades of controversy, many non-German scholars have found elements of it highly convincing, and certainly essential for any just and balanced view. More to the point for our present purposes, critical elements of the German apology have been strongly influential in the postwar policies of the Europeans themselves.

Germany's Rival View

At the time the world wars broke out, official British and French apologists had no great intellectual difficulty agreeing on why they began: Germany was bidding for European hegemony. Both conflicts seemed to reflect the familiar pattern of previous hegemonic wars. United, the Germans were the continent's major power. As all modern European history appeared to demonstrate, it was only natural that Germany should seek hegemony and that the other powers should oppose it. By defending Europe's traditional balance of power, the

British and French believed they were defending their independence as well as guarding their empires.[2]

But the Imperial Germans also maintained they were waging war for defensive purposes. They were protecting their national unity from the wrath of the French, they said, who were determined to undo it and thus restore France's own continental primacy. France had allied with despotic Russia, a superpower in the making, with an insatiable if patient appetite for expansion. And the "encircled" Germans also saw themselves fighting to protect their burgeoning industry and commerce from the jealousy of the British, who feared the loss of their own global economic predominance to Germany's more vigorous forms of capitalism. Of course, the Imperial Germans clearly did have hegemonic ambitions in Europe. Among their leaders, many looked forward to defeating France once more—this time for good—and many dreamed of acquiring a vast Slavic hinterland. Germany would occupy Mitteleuropa—Central and Southeastern Europe—at Russia's expense. But according to the Germans, even their hegemonic ambitions were defensive. They were seeking a "global" balance of power in place of a merely European one. If Europe remained disunited, Russia and America would eventually partition control of the world between themselves. Germans also saw a divided Europe as vulnerable to a reawakening Asia. As Europe's natural leader, Imperial Germany's only course, its geopoliticians urged, was to break the constraints of Europe's traditional balance of power. By subordinating Europe to German leadership, Germany—and through Germany, Europe—would become a "world power," like Britain, the United States, or Russia. Since German rulers were unable to find a coopera-

---

[2] For an influential British analysis that viewed German ambition as insatiable even before World War I, see Sir Eyre Crowe's Foreign Office memorandum of 1907. Crowe (1864–1925) became Permanent Undersecretary of State for Foreign Affairs from 1920 to 1925. According to his 1907 memorandum, the German Empire was the heir of ambitious and aggressive Prussia. Consequently, "graceful British concessions" would "most certainly not lead to any improvement of relations with . . . Germany." Crowe's *Memorandum on the Present State of British Relations with France and Germany* may be found in George P. Gooch and Harold W. Temperley, eds., *British Documents on the Origins of the War, 1898–1914* (London: His Majesty's Stationery Office, 1927), vol. 3, p. 3.

tive way to unite and lead Europe, Germany ended up in mortal conflict with Britain, France, Italy, Russia, and the United States. In such
a conflict, Germany could not prevail militarily. Both Germany and its
neighbors paid a terrible price for Europe's collective failure to reconcile the diverging interests of its nation states.

Germany and Britain

Imperial Germany's geopoliticians did have a conciliatory diplomatic
strategy of sorts: Germany would support Britain's global empire
against the Americans if Britain would support Germany's hegemony
on the continent against France and Russia. The strategy was not entirely far-fetched. The British had long been sensitive to the threat to
their empire from the rising superpowers. At the start of the twentieth
century, Joseph Chamberlain, a powerful and visionary radical leader,
promoted an imperial tariff that he hoped would convert the white
parts of the empire into a federal entity with economic and political
potential comparable to the United States. Part of Chamberlain's vision was a bargain to accommodate the Germans by confirming their
preeminence on the continent. But Chamberlain failed to reorient
British policy. To begin with, most British commercial and financial
interests preferred the immediate advantages of free trade and of investing wherever they pleased over any putative long-term advantages
of building an integrated imperial bloc.[3] At the same time, the British

---

[3] The formation of an integrated imperial bloc was hampered by the contrasting patterns of British trade and investment in the later nineteenth century. Profitable investment opportunities were to be had in the empire, although the imperial share of
investment declined from a peak of 67 percent in 1885 to 25 percent during the
1890s. But British trade with the colonies remained relatively stationary at the same
time as trade with Russia, the United States, and France increased. Moreover, the
colonies tended to develop commercial links of their own with foreign countries—
reducing their trade with Britain. The proposition that expanding and consolidating
the empire would bring greater trade to Britain was difficult to sustain in the face of
the statistics: Britain's annual trade declined from £305 million in 1883 to £277
million in 1893—despite the expansion of the empire during that period to include
Egypt, the Sudan, Nigeria, Somaliland, Bechuanaland, Zululand, East and Central
Africa, Rhodesia, and Upper Burma, to mention only the most important. Chamberlain's ideas for an imperial economic bloc were therefore a nonstarter among many of

chose to go on sustaining the traditional European balance of power, despite the changing global balance. Not surprisingly, they therefore saw Germany as a threat rather than as an ally. Their choice had far-reaching geopolitical implications. Unable to convert the Commonwealth into a durable source of national power, Britain grew progressively overstretched in its pretensions and commitments. Diplomatically, instead of finding an accord with Germany to counter the Americans, Britain appeased the United States around the world and, in Europe, allied with France and Russia against Germany. As the Germans saw it, the British preferred to confront the new world of the twentieth century with traditional eighteenth-century formulas.

When war finally came in 1914, Britain found that the old European balance-of-power game had grown disastrously expensive. The cost of preventing Germany from dominating the continent severely undermined Britain's global financial predominance. In the end, defeating Germany required importing an external hegemon, the United States. By World War II, keeping America in Europe had developed into Britain's basic geopolitical strategy, the logical counterpart to refusing an accommodation with Germany.[4] World War II confirmed the

---

the most influential figures in the City. See William L. Strauss, *Joseph Chamberlain and the Theory of Imperialism* (Washington, DC: American Council on Public Affairs, 1942), esp. ch. 6, and also Keith Robbins, *The Eclipse of a Great Power: Modern Britain 1870–1992* (London: Longman, 1994), pp. 55–56.

[4] The prospect of a grand Anglo-German deal did, however, have considerable appeal in Britain during the interwar period. The former prime minister, David Lloyd George, tried to promote close cooperation with Weimar Germany, as did the economist John Maynard Keynes. Joseph Chamberlain's son Neville, British prime minister from 1937 to 1940, also tried to "appease" Nazi Germany's desire to expand, at least to neighboring territories with a Germanic population. A new European war, Chamberlain reckoned, would force Britain to sacrifice its empire and solvency for problematic American support. Among other costs would be a war with Japan, which would end Britain's lucrative commercial position in China. But not even Chamberlain could achieve an Anglo-German accommodation—not surprising given the unpromising character of a Germany dominated by the Nazis. In the end, Chamberlain saw no alternative to an Atlantic strategy, despite his considerable mistrust of America and his pessimistic—and accurate—assessment of the strategy's consequences for postwar Britain's global position. Arguably, Britain's unhappy postwar history—eclipsed by America and alienated from Europe—flows from this basic geopolitical

British in their Atlantic strategy. They were among the earliest and most ardent Cold Warriors and tried to make the Cold War the catalyst for perpetuating and consolidating an Atlantic community. The same strategy inclined Britain to resist joining wholeheartedly in the postwar schemes for European integration. As the British saw it, any European Community should be less a self-contained union of its own than a component part of an Atlantic community that included the Americans. Britain, with its special Anglo-Saxon relationship, was to be the pivot between Europe and the United States.

Germany and France

France, like Britain, blamed the world wars on German aggression. It was France, after being defeated by Germany in 1870, that had slowly put together the coalition that ultimately defeated the Germans in World War I. But revenge was not sweet. In the orgy of European self-destruction that accompanied Germany's defeat, France itself was greatly weakened. Like the British, the French felt constrained to rely on the Americans to keep down the Germans in the future. After Versailles, however, the United States welched on its promise to guarantee French security with a treaty.[5] Disillusioned, the French began to explore collaborating with Germany around a common European project: a confederacy built around a special relationship between

---

conundrum, which Britain has not yet been able to resolve. Britain has seen an Atlantic community become a reality but, as Neville Chamberlain feared, has not thereby been able to save its own global position. See Paul Kennedy, *The Realities behind Diplomacy: Background Influences on German External Policy, 1865–1980* (London: Allen & Unwin, 1981). For an acute study of Britain's unhappy struggle with its postwar dilemmas, see Hugo Young, *This Blessed Plot* (London: Macmillan, 1998).

[5] At Versailles, the American president, Woodrow Wilson, joined the British to fend off French efforts to dismember Germany and saddle it with heavier reparations and restrictions. The quid pro quo was to have been a treaty whereby the United States guaranteed French security. Wilson wanted the League of Nations to be the guarantor, and when the League failed in the U.S. Senate, he let the bilateral U.S.-French treaty die as well, although opponents of the league, like Henry Cabot Lodge, favored it. For a study of Wilson's foreign policy, concentrating on the crucial period 1917–1919, see N. Gordon Levin, *Woodrow Wilson and World Politics* (New York: Oxford University Press, 1968), especially pp. 171–172 and 253–260.

France and Germany. The goal found expression in the visionary scheme for *Paneuropa* that began to be promoted soon after World War I.[6] Europe was to form a confederacy, led by France and Germany, that would make internal European wars impossible and would also vigorously promote Europe's collective interests in the global system. In effect, Paneuropa accepted Imperial Germany's project of European unity in the interests of a global balance but sought to achieve that unity by Franco-German collaboration rather than German conquest. For a moment, Paneuropa became France's geopolitical substitute for the American alliance that failed to materialize after World War I. Between the wars, official Franco-German cooperation reached its high point with the Locarno Pact of 1925, engineered by the German foreign minister, Gustav Stresemann, and the French foreign minister, Aristide Briand, together with their British counterpart, Austen Chamberlain, son of Joseph and half brother to Neville. The collaboration seemed promising initially but was waning by 1927. Stresemann died in 1929 and Briand in 1932. When France and Germany could not resolve their differences over Eastern Europe, their European project stalled, and it could not survive the economic crisis that brought Hitler to power in 1933. But it was resurrected after World War II, with American blessing, when it became a major inspiration for the European Community.

Meanwhile, the European system had endured another terrible bloodbath. Germany's second bid for hegemony was a monstrous par-

---

[6] *Paneuropa* sprang from the fertile mind of Count Richard Coudenhove-Kalergi, a former Hungarian diplomat whose federalist movement gained considerable popularity shortly after World War I. His ideas prefigure the Gaullist response to American hegemony after World War II. The main aim was a European economic and political coalition as a third force between Russia and America, constituted along the lines of the "Europe of the States" made famous by General de Gaulle. Coudenhove was wary of U.S. domination and of a U.S.-Russian condominium. Only by uniting, he thought, could Europeans play a constructive world role and be an American ally rather than protectorate. Paneuropa was to be the center of a triple alliance (the United States, Europe, and Russia) to secure world order. Coudenhove's ideas fostered the Franco-German rapprochement discussed below. See Count Richard Coudenhove-Kalergi, *Paneuropa, 1922 bis 1966* (Vienna: Herold Druck-und Verlag, 1966). For the postwar influence of Coudenhove's ideas, see Bernard Voyenne, *Histoire de l'idée européene* (Paris: Payot, 1964).

ody of its first. Hitler embraced the same geopolitical rationale as the Imperial Germans: the need to acquire Mitteleuropa for Germany and to dominate the rest of Europe in order to create a global balance. But his lunatic racism, excluding most other Europeans, mocked any collaborative pan-European vision.[7] Germany's second defeat left Europe even more wretched than its first.[8] Russia, hideously devastated at home, kept its victorious armies in Central Europe to form an imperial glacis. The Americans, prodded by the British and the French, responded with a military protectorate for the continent's western half. Thus, Europe, whose major states had once carved up the world, was itself divided between two peripheral "superpowers." Germany itself was in ruins, deprived of much of its traditional territory and partitioned and occupied by its conquerors. Of the two new German

---

[7] Hitler's totalitarian corporatist model did, by itself, have some external appeal. Albert Speer, Hitler's minister for armaments and war production, tried to emphasize the technocratic side of Nazism and downplay its dark, racist side, which he disliked, not least because it undermined the efficiency and appeal of Nazi technocracy. See Albert Speer, *Inside the Third Reich*, trans. Richard and Clara Winston (New York: Macmillan, 1970). Conservative technocrats, notably in Vichy France, were sometimes attracted to the vision of a centrally managed and rationally integrated European economy. See, for instance, Robert O. Paxton's works, most notably *Vichy France: Old Guard and New Order* (New York: Knopf, 1972); updated French edition published as *La France de Vichy 1940–44* (Paris: Editions de Seuil, 1997). A substantial part of the population of the Soviet Union, particularly in the Ukraine, initially welcomed the Germans as deliverers from the Bolsheviks. Indeed, a Russian army, commanded by General Andrey Vlasov, fought with the Germans against the Soviet Union. See Stephen C. Nedell, *Collaboration or Liberation: Andrey Andreyevich Vlasov and the Russian Liberation Movement* (Oswego: State University of New York, 1995).

[8] Upwards of thirty million people died in World War II in Europe, approximately the population of modern-day Argentina. The French lost 620,000 and Britain 260,000. Poland lost a fifth of its people. Germany lost about five million. No one is sure how many the Soviet Union lost, but conservative estimates are around twenty-five million. In 1946, European agricultural production was at only 63 percent of its 1938 level, and for the first quarter of 1946, European industrial production was only 68 percent of its 1938 level, despite war mobilization. The German figure was 22 percent. See R. Ernest Dupuy and Trevor N. Dupuy, *The Encyclopedia of Military History: From 3500 B.C. to the Present* (New York: Harper & Row, 1986), pp. 1198ff., and Walter Laqueur, *Europe in Our Time: A History 1945–1992* (New York: Penguin, 1992), pp. 3–12.

states that emerged from the rubble, one was a Russian satellite and the other an American military dependency. The racist horrors of the Nazi regime, once exposed, left the postwar Germans with a disabling burden of guilt whose effects last to the present day. The supposedly victorious European powers did not seem much better off. Britain, which had lost much of its wealth during the war, rapidly gave up most of its empire afterward. France, which had been defeated, occupied, exploited, and fought over, was deeply divided politically and soon caught up in exhausting and futile colonial wars.

Despite these unpromising origins, the postwar order proved surprisingly stable and, for Western Europe at least, highly prosperous. That order reflected a series of grand projects promoted by the leading powers: the global Pax Americana, the Soviet Marxist bloc, the Atlantic Alliance, and West European transformation and integration. The first two projects sprang from the imaginations of the superpowers, as the chapters in part II spell out. The Americans, bemused by a liberal and hegemonic view of history, had been nurturing the vision of a global Pax Americana since the late nineteenth century. Woodrow Wilson had tried to proclaim it after World War I. Franklin Delano Roosevelt was determined to succeed where Wilson had failed. The Soviet project, an insulated Communist bloc in Eurasia with global pretensions, found its rationale in Marx's predictions about the instability and implacable hostility of capitalism. By contrast, the latter two projects, the Atlantic Alliance and rejuvenated Europe's integration, were, in many respects, European rather than American initiatives. At the start of the Cold War, it was the British and the French who prodded the Americans into the Atlantic Alliance, as a military response to Stalin's bloc. Both saw the alliance as a way to contain Germany as well as the Soviet Union. In effect, NATO, institutionalizing an external hegemon, was the realization of Britain's long-term strategy for dealing with the instability of the European state system. In due course, Europe's confederal alternative also appeared. Paneuropa waxed as France, repeating its experience after World War I, grew progressively disillusioned with the "Anglo-Saxons" and rediscovered the virtues of collaborating with the Germans to build a new European order.

Basically, what separated the Anglo-Saxon Atlantic project from the Franco-German European project was a different prescription for remedying the historic instability of Europe's state system, the instability manifested so tragically in both world wars. The Atlantic Alliance assumed Europe to be intrinsically unstable and therefore to require an external balancing power. The European Union assumed that Europe was not irremediably unstable; Europeans in general, and French and Germans in particular, were capable of reconciling their national interests and of harmonizing them into a collective interest within a common institution.

Arguably, a tacit French conversion to elements of the German rationale for World War I has been the essential intellectual foundation for the postwar Franco-German partnership—the driving force behind the European Union. In effect, the French have accepted the old German argument that Europe needs to unite if it is to flourish in a new global environment otherwise dominated by outsiders. This conversion, moreover, has fundamentally separated the postwar French from their allies of the first half of the century, the British, who have continued to rely on importing an external hegemon. This disjuncture of historical imagination and sympathy between the British and the French runs through postwar European politics and continues to bedevil the future of the whole European project.

It is difficult to imagine either the Atlantic or the confederal solution's coming into being without the Cold War. America's new role as Europe's external hegemon had to be welcomed by the Europeans and agreed to by the Americans themselves. For this to happen, the Europeans had to be exceptionally weak and the Americans exceptionally strong. And both had to share a sufficiently grave threat. All these conditions were supplied by Hitler's defeat and Stalin's victory in World War II. Europe's confederacy was also greatly helped by the Cold War, which divided Germany, removed Eastern Europe as an object of Western contention, especially between France and Germany, and left sensitive military matters to NATO. The Cold War also ensured American support for European unity.

As later chapters discuss at length, the subsequent postwar order in Europe was not so much bipolar as "tripolar." Within the West, transatlantic tensions grew increasingly manifest as the postwar era unfolded. Strategic problems grew more acute and expensive to resolve.

27

The United States and the European Community were major commercial rivals in an increasingly competitive world economy and began to disagree sharply over global economic structures and policies. Nevertheless, Cold War pressures kept things together through the 1980s. Ultimately, it was the Soviet Union that was not up to its postwar role. This was not surprising. Aside from its own notorious internal shortcomings, it was facing an opposing alliance of the two most advanced regions of the world—the United States and Western Europe—plus Japan and much of the rest of Asia, eventually including China.

The end of the Cold War, reopening Europe's old questions, has also posed new questions for the United States, as the chapters in part III explain. America must decide how seriously it wishes to pursue the role of unique superpower in a "unipolar world" and, for that matter, on what terms it wishes to continue its military role in Europe. Whatever is decided, new American relationships must be developed with Europe, Russia, and China.

The states of Europe face complementary challenges. They must decide how long and on what terms they still want their American hegemon. This depends, above all, on whether their own postwar confederacy can be made an adequate substitute. But Europe's confederal prospects cannot be determined by diplomatic and geopolitical needs alone. Ultimately, they depend on the inner character of Europe's nation states, including their intimate and uneasy relationship with capitalism. These states remain the confederacy's principal actors. Many postwar analysts have wondered, of course, why Europe needs to go on having its traditional nation states at all. The next two chapters explore why they are not easily dispensed with.

SELECTED SOURCES

Interpreting the Great Wars

For my own extended attempt to analyze the complexities of the German question, see David P. Calleo, *The German Problem Reconsidered* (Cambridge: Cambridge University Press, 1978). Among the numerous writers on whose insights I have drawn are Luigi Albertini,

The Origins of the War of 1914 (Oxford: Oxford University Press, 1952); Ludwig Dehio, *The Precarious Balance: Four Centuries of the European Power Struggle*, trans. Charles Fullman (New York: Knopf, 1962); Erich Eyck, *Bismarck and the German Empire* (New York: Norton, 1964); Sidney D. Fay, *The Origins of the World War*, 2nd edition (New York, Macmillan, 1930); Fritz Fischer, *Germany's Aims in the First World War* (New York: Norton, 1967); Konrad Jarausch, *The Enigmatic Chancellor: Bethmann Hollweg and the Hubris of Imperial Germany* (New Haven: Yale University Press, 1967); Henry Kissinger, *Diplomacy* (New York: Simon & Schuster, 1994), ch. 5; Eckart Kehr, *Battleship Building and Party Politics in Germany 1894–1901* (Chicago: University of Chicago Press, 1973); H. W. Koch, *The Origins of the First World War: Great Power Rivalry and German War Aims* (New York: Taplinger, 1972). Hitler's geopolitical apology is given in *The Testament of Adolf Hitler*, ed. François Genoud (London: Cassel, 1961).

For Joseph Chamberlain, see Peter T. Marsh, *Joseph Chamberlain: Entrepreneur in Politics* (New Haven: Yale University Press, 1994). Chamberlain's dilemmas were representative of a wider strand of British geopolitical soul-searching at the turn of the century. See Lawrence James, *The Rise and Fall of the British Empire* (London: Little, Brown, 1994), ch. 10. A major theme for Chamberlain, and for those around him, was the need to rethink traditional assumptions about British isolation. At the turn of the century, many among the British elites—often, but not exclusively, Conservative and Liberal Unionist—were alarmed about Britain's world position. Their concern, however, did not necessarily lead to any particular prescription for British foreign policy. Perhaps their most common salient characteristic was their diffidence about an alliance either with Germany or with the United States. See Paul Kennedy, *The Realities behind Diplomacy: Background Influences on British External Policy, 1865–1980* (London: George Allen & Unwin, 1981), pp. 110–117. For a sympathetic presentation of Joseph Chamberlain's vision of an Anglo-German rapprochement, see Julian Amery, *Life of Joseph Chamberlain* (London: Macmillan, 1969), vol. 5, p. 17. Chamberlain's views on relations with Germany are placed in context by Raymond Sontag, *Germany and England; Background of Conflict, 1848–1894* (New

York: Norton, 1969). For the arguments of one of Chamberlain's leading opponents, see Robert James, *Rosebery* (New York: Macmillan, 1963), or E. T. Raymond, "The Man of Promise: Lord Rosebery," in *Portraits of the Nineties* (London: T. F. Unwin, 1921). For the politics and economics of Britain's commitment to free trade, see Bernard Semmel, *The Rise of Free Trade Imperialism* (Cambridge: Cambridge University Press, 1970).

Britain's gradual evolution from splendid isolationism to Atlanticism is placed in a general framework in David Thomson, *England in the Twentieth Century* (Baltimore: Penguin, 1965). A. J. P. Taylor, *The Struggle for Mastery in Europe: 1848–1914* (Oxford: Clarendon, 1954), especially ch. 18, places Britain's dilemmas in their European context. See also George Monger, *The End of Isolation* (New York: T. Nelson, 1963). For a detailed study of Anglo-American relations at the turn of the century, see A. E. Campbell, *Great Britain and the United States, 1895–1903* (Westport, CT: Greenwood Press, 1960), and Bradford Perkins, *The Great Rapprochement: England and the United States 1895–1914* (London: Victor Gollancz, 1969).

British conciliation of the United States before World War I went hand in hand with determined alliance-building attempts across Europe. See R. W. Seton-Watson, *Britain in Europe, 1789–1914* (Cambridge: Cambridge University Press, 1938). For France's construction of the anti-German alliance with Russia, see George F. Kennan, *The Fateful Alliance: France, Russia and the Coming of the First World War* (New York: Pantheon Books, 1984).

For a powerful advocate of Atlanticism at the time of World War II, see Clarence Streit, *Union Now* (New York: Harper, 1939). For an earlier and influential social Darwinist view of Atlantic unity, based on the cultural superiority of "Anglo-Saxon" civilization, see J. R. Seeley, *The Expansion of England* (London: University of Chicago Press, 1898). For my own views on the origins and development of the idea of the "Atlantic community," see David P. Calleo and Benjamin M. Rowland, *America in the World Political Economy* (Bloomington: Indiana University Press, 1973), pp. 57–62.

For further discussions of Neville Chamberlain's appeasement, see Keith Middlemas, *The Strategy of Appeasement* (Chicago: Quadrangle Books, 1972); William R. Rock, *British Appeasement in the*

1930s (New York: Norton, 1977); and Simon K. Newman, *March 1939: The British Guarantee to Poland: A Study in the Continuity of British Foreign Policy* (Oxford: Clarendon Press, 1976). Chamberlain's views on appeasement were also shaped in part by the urgency with which the British chiefs of staff stressed that they were incapable of defending the empire across the globe from simultaneous attack by Germany, Italy, and Japan. By the time of Munich, Japanese threats to the status quo in Asia were only adding to the isolationist pressures coming from within the empire itself. See Paul Kennedy, *The Realities behind Diplomacy,* op. cit., ch. 5.

For studies of Britain in the immediate postwar world, see Herbert Nicholas, *Britain and the United States* (Baltimore: Johns Hopkins University Press, 1963), and F. S. Northedge, *British Foreign Policy: The Process of Adjustment* (London: Praeger, 1962). For early postwar Anglo-American tensions in Asia, see also Lanxin Xiang, *Recasting the Imperial Far East: Britain and America in China, 1945–1950* (Armonk, NY: M. E. Sharpe, 1995). For my own early assessment of postwar Britain's options and predispositions, see David P. Calleo, *Britain's Future* (New York: Horizon Press, 1968), esp. pp. 42–47. Hugo Young, in *This Blessed Plot* (London: Macmillan, 1998), stresses the continuing difficulties that Britain has had in coming to terms with its changed circumstances, and with the new Europe.

France and Germany

For further discussion of Paneuropa, see David P. Calleo and Benjamin M. Rowland, *America and the World Political Economy* (Bloomington: Indiana University Press, 1973), pp. 78–80. For Briand's "Plan for European Union," heavily influenced by Coudenhove's idea, see *Survey of International Affairs 1931* (London, 1932), and F. G. Stambrook, "The German-Austrian Customs Union Project of 1931: A Study of German Methods and Motives," in Hans W. Gatzke, ed., *European Diplomacy between Two Wars* (Chicago: Quadrangle Books, 1972). For a study of the Locarno process and the eventual estrangement between Briand and Stresemann, see Jon Jacobson, *Locarno Diplomacy: Germany and the West, 1925–1929* (Princeton: Princeton University Press, 1972). For the breakdown, see

Arnold Wolfers, *Britain and France between Two Wars* (Hamden, CT: Archon Books, 1963), pp. 61ff.

The Franco-German rapprochement after World War II is discussed by F. Roy Willis, *France, Germany and the New Europe, 1945–1967* (Stanford: Stanford University Press, 1968), and Patrick McCarthy, ed., *France-Germany, 1983–1993: The Struggle to Cooperate* (New York: St. Martin's Press, 1993), as well as below in ch. 8. French enthusiasm for NATO and subsequent disillusionment with the "Anglo-Saxons" is analyzed by Michael M. Harrison in his magisterial survey, *The Reluctant Ally: France and Atlantic Security* (Baltimore: Johns Hopkins University Press, 1981). De Gaulle's memoirs feature sharply the contrast between his own hopes for Europe and Churchill's commitment to America. See their conversation during Churchill's triumphant visit to Paris starting on November 10, 1944, in Charles de Gaulle, *Memoirs*, collected ed. (New York: Simon & Schuster, 1964), vol. 3, *Salvation*, pp. 58ff. Churchill's war memoirs make no specific reference to this conversation but show generally his reserve toward recognizing de Gaulle's government in August 1944, as well as his warming support, publicly voiced in the Commons on October 27, 1944. Churchill, impressed by de Gaulle's popular backing and the élan of troops in the new French army, grew more inclined to see France playing a key role in the near future and pressed Roosevelt and Stalin to give France greater recognition. See Winston S. Churchill, *Triumph and Tragedy* (Cambridge, MA: Houghton Mifflin, 1953), ch. 16. Recently released British documents show Roosevelt and Churchill apparently plotting together to eliminate de Gaulle in 1943. See Warren Hoge, "Churchill and Roosevelt Wanted de Gaulle Out, Britain Discloses," *New York Times*, January 6, 2000, p. 13; also, Claude Patrice, "Churchill voulait éliminer de Gaulle, ce méchant chicaneur," *Le Monde*, January 7, 2000, p. 1.

Europe's States and State System

INTERDEPENDENT SOVEREIGNTY

FOR DECADES, knowledgeable analysts have been urging and predicting the demise of Europe's nation states. The arguments are familiar. The essential character of these states supposedly impels them to preserve their self-determination in as unhindered a condition as possible. But in Europe's closely crowded state system, unilateral assertions of national self-interest and sovereignty easily become self-defeating, indeed self-destructive. The military realm illustrates the point vividly. Neighboring states, vigorously and separately pursuing their own security, together create a climate of universal insecurity. After two world wars, it seems obvious to most Europeans that they can no longer afford the kind of assertive national independence that led to those wars. Only by limiting itself—by pooling with other sovereignties—can a European nation state effectively pursue the most fundamental aim of any national sovereignty, self-preservation. Advanced public opinion has come to a similar conclusion in the economic sphere. To remain in the front ranks of advanced nations, European states must pool their national economies into a regional economy and make their national economic policies together, or in close consultation with each other. In effect, practical sovereignty in Europe is quite different from theoretical sovereignty. Sovereignty cannot be effective without cooperation. Interdependence may not condemn European states to disappear, but it does compel them to cooperate.

Particularly since World War II, however, many analysts have believed that the complications of sovereignty are so disabling for cooperation that Europeans would be better off abandoning their traditional system of nation states for some form of genuine federal system. There are, of course, several schools of federalism. Some prescribe a sort of neomedieval Europe—where the sovereign power of nation states is fragmented—part going to rejuvenated regions and part to a federal center that keeps the peace and handles the continent's common business. Others would like to see Europe imitate the United States and become a huge continental federation with relatively weak "states" and a strong central or "federal" government. Neither the prescriptions nor the analyses behind them are new. The United States, with its well-articulated federalist theories, was already in existence by the late eighteenth century. More than five centuries earlier, Dante advocated unifying Europe under its Holy Roman Emperor. Napoleon's empire, with its Code Napoléon, conjured up the prospect of a united Europe ruled by a centralized technocracy, a vision Napoleon himself is said to have sought to promote from St. Helena.

As Napoleon's example should remind us, however, Europe's failure to unify over the centuries has not been from lack of trying. The repeated efforts to end Europe's system of independent states form the familiar narrative of the continent's modern history. Until now, at least, these efforts have all failed. Why has the traditional system of sovereign states proved so durable? It is, after all, only a modern phenomenon. In ancient times, much of the continent was united under the Roman Empire—with its universal law, administration, and language. Rome's disintegration led western Europe into its "Dark Ages." But already by the start of the ninth century, Charlemagne was reconstituting the western Roman Empire, although in a decentralized, pluralistic, and Christian form.[1] That medieval form of continental unity disintegrated with the Renaissance and the Reformation—to be succeeded, in due course, by the system of "sovereign" and secular

---

[1] The Eastern Roman Empire lasted, of course, until 1453 but embodied its own distinct form of Christianity and Byzantine political culture. Thereafter, the separation of Eastern Christendom from the West was reinforced by alien conquests. Much of the old Eastern Empire was conquered by the Ottoman Turks, and much of Russia, another large part of Orthodox Europe, was ruled by the Mongols from the mid-thirteenth to the late fifteenth centuries. The division between Byzantine and Latin Europe, Orthodox and Roman Catholicism, and so on, persists to the present day and, in some respects, bedevils attempts to create a post-Soviet pan-European system. For a discussion of the legacy of the division, see Timothy Garton Ash, "The Puzzle of Central Europe," *New York Review of Books*, March 18, 1999.

states that has persisted to the present day, even if now significantly modified by a "European union."

In their early modern versions, most European states tended to be "absolute," with the unconditional sovereignty of the state embodied in the absolute sovereignty of its ruler. According to the seventeenth-century English philosopher Thomas Hobbes, this was the only arrangement capable of taming society's natural anarchy, its "war of every man against every man."[2] This was a view widely shared in the midst of the ruinous civil wars of religion endemic in many regions after the Reformation. Nevertheless, assertions of absolute royal power inside Europe's states regularly clashed with the more balanced "constitutional" views surviving from the Middle Ages, where power was checked by rights, reciprocal obligations, and overlapping institutions and jurisdictions. Much of the domestic history of Europe's states has been taken up with the struggle to reconcile the more modern idea of sovereignty with a medieval legacy of constitutional checks and balances and protected regional liberties. That medieval heritage endures not only in federalist writings that advocate fragmenting and dispersing the sovereignty of Europe's states but also in the proclivity inside many of those states for constitutional systems that divide power and leave wide space for civil society and regional autonomy.

This same constitutionalist tradition also found expression in proposals to accept the legitimacy of Europe's sovereign states but to organize their relations within "confederal" or interstate structures that would provide machinery to settle disputes and make wars unprofitable. The Duc de Sully (1560–1614), close adviser to the popular and talented French king Henri IV (1555–1610), proposed a "grand design" to link all Christian nations.[3] Jean-Jacques Rousseau (1712–1778), proud citizen of Geneva, floated a confederal scheme

[2] Thomas Hobbes, *Leviathan, or The Matter, Forme and Power of a Commonwealth Ecclesiasticall and Civil* (1651), ed. and with an introduction by Michael Oakeshott (Oxford, UK: Blackwell, 1957), p. 82.

[3] See Maximilien de Béthune, duc de Sully, *Sully's Grand Design of Henry IV: From the Memoirs of Maximilien de Béthune, duc de Sully,* ed. with an introduction by David Ogg (London: Sweet & Maxwell, 1921).

modeled after the ideas of the Abbé de Saint-Pierre.[4] Napoleon's conquerors instituted a confederal Concert of Europe to keep Europe's great powers in regular collaboration for peace keeping. Although the concert system functioned formally for only a decade and a half, it persisted in many ways until the middle of the nineteenth century.[5] After World War I, the victorious allies, prodded by Woodrow Wilson, instituted the League of Nations, a grandiose global concert of powers. During World War II, it was reborn as the United Nations. Meanwhile, in the 1920s, European visionaries had begun promoting a confederal Paneuropa, an ideal that helped to inspire the postwar European Union.

As chapters 8 and 13 discuss in detail, today's European Union is a hybrid of confederal and federal features and has been a remarkable success. So far, however, the EU has not so much attenuated Europe's states as rejuvenated them. Despite everything, Europe's states have left the twentieth century alive and well.

Managing a Europe of States: Classic Theories

Not surprisingly, how to manage a contentious system of sovereign but interdependent states has been a favorite topic among Europe's political philosophers, particularly during the Enlightenment. By the eighteenth century, various broad schools were well established and persist to our own time. For our purposes, it seems useful to distinguish three: hegemonic, balance-of-power, and liberal.[6]

---

[4] Jean-Jacques Rousseau, "Abstract and Judgement of Saint-Pierre's Project for Perpetual Peace (1756)," in Stanley Hoffman and David P. Fidler, eds., *Rousseau on International Relations* (Oxford, UK: Clarendon Press, 1991), pp. 53–100. Rousseau's confederal schemes are particularly interesting given his insistence in the *Social Contract* on both the need for a free state to be animated by a sovereign "general will" and his pessimism about a diverse society's capacity to sustain such a will.

[5] The concert broke down formally in 1829, although the Great Powers continued to meet fairly regularly to resolve tensions until the Crimean War. Thereafter, occasional grand conferences featured on the diplomatic scene until the beginning of World War I, but the mechanism for regular consultation was gone. See Henry Kissinger, *Diplomacy* (New York: Simon & Schuster, 1994), pp. 78–103.

[6] Obviously, there are other ways of classifying theories of interstate or international

The hegemonic school projects Thomas Hobbes's domestic prescriptions into interstate relations. Just as a "war of all against all" is inevitable within the commonwealth unless a single sovereign power imposes order, peace among neighboring states requires that one be clearly predominant. This interstate hegemony may be organized through an empire, a federation, a confederation, or a simple alliance,

---

relations. Contemporary theorists are generally but awkwardly divided into realists (and neorealists) and liberals. Realists are traced to Machiavelli and Hobbes, liberals to Smith and Kant. Realists and neorealists focus on state power as the ultimate determinant of state interaction, while contemporary liberals, assuming a national harmony in markets and democratic polities, focus on a diversity of factors, including the international economy and the global flow of ideas and information. Liberalism connotes cooperation and integration among states, while realism connotes more narrow calculations of state interest. This same broad differentiation is reflected in the popular but misleading distinction between "idealism" and "realism."

My tripartite classification—hegemonic, balance-of-power, and liberal—seems best for the book's expository and heuristic purposes. In effect, I divide "realism" into two schools: hegemonic and balance-of-power or pluralist. This makes it easier, for example, to contrast the mindsets of advocates of American hegemony, global and regional, against the assumptions of advocates of European integration, who look forward not only to a stronger Europe but to a more balanced international system. Both the hegemonists and the Europeanists are "realists" but have quite different views and preferences for the interstate system.

Over time, of course, schools combine elements of each other. Liberalism, for example, has evolved a certain affinity with hegemonic imperialism, on the grounds that a liberal system requires one superior power to keep order and rescue markets from their periodic "failures." See, for example, Charles P. Kindleberger, *The World in Depression* (Los Angeles: University of California Press, 1973), or Eugene V. Rostow, *Law and the Pursuit of Peace* (Lincoln: University of Nebraska Press, 1968). Pluralist liberals, by contrast, tend to favor a rule-based system reinforced by an effective balance of power to prevent any one country from aspiring to exempt itself from the rules that apply to others. See, for example, Jacques Rueff, *The Monetary Sin of the West* (New York: Macmillan, 1971). For various analyses focusing on these issues in the world political economy, see Benjamin M. Rowland, ed., *Balance of Power or Hegemony: The Interwar Monetary System* (New York: Lehrman Institute/ New York University Press, 1976), in particular, Robert J. A. Skidelsky, "Retreat from Leadership: The Evolution of British Economic Foreign Policy, 1870–1939"; Judith L. Kooker, "French Financial Diplomacy: The Interwar Years"; Harold van Buren Cleveland, "The International Monetary System in the Interwar Period"; and my own essay, "The Historiography of the Interwar Period: A Reconsideration." For liberalism contrasted with mercantilism, see below, note 11.

so long as a single dominant power is the practical result.[7] Hobbes's prescription has often been pursued among Europe's states but never reliably fulfilled—at least until the second half of the twentieth century, when the hegemon was external. Over the centuries, a variety of indigenous candidates have presented themselves for the hegemonic role in Europe. Spanish and Austrian Habsburgs were succeeded by Bourbon and Napoleonic French, followed in turn by Imperial and Nazi Germans. Bids for hegemony involved many elements of power—economic, social, and cultural as well as military—and required an idealistic vision to galvanize supporters and resources. The Habsburgs, for example, animated their cause with the Counter-Reformation, while Napoleon fused elements of the French Revolution and Enlightenment technocracy. Opponents of would-be unifiers countered with ideals of their own: traditional feudal liberties, Protestantism, raison d'état, nationalism. As each of the great bids for hegemony exhausted itself, Europe reaffirmed its plural system of independent states. Hence, the Westphalian settlement imposed on the exhausted Habsburgs in 1648, or the congress of great powers designed to keep the peace after Napoleon's defeat. In each instance, Europe's rulers recognized collectively the legal and moral legitimacy of a system of independent states and affirmed a structure of diplomatic rules to govern their interdependent coexistence.

Behind this resilient pluralist state system lay a self-conscious theory of statecraft designed to nip any swelling hegemony in the bud. This balance-of-power or pluralist school reflects an ancient perspective, succinctly captured by Lord Acton in the nineteenth century: "Power tends to corrupt and absolute power corrupts absolutely."[8] In other words, domination leads to exploitation. The pluralist school therefore resists fiercely the interstate hegemony that the Hobbesian

---

[7] The idea that the international society, like a society of humans in nature, is "anarchic" is a primary assumption of neorealist analysis, formulated most clearly in Kenneth N. Waltz, *Theory of World Politics* (Reading, MA: Addison Wesley, 1979). Theories of hegemonic stability are one of the solutions for this state of anarchy. Balance-of-power theories are, of course, another.

[8] Letter to Bishop Mandell Creighton, April 3, 1887. Quoted in Louise von Glehn Creighton, *Life and Letters of Mandell Creighton D.D. Oxon. and Cam., Sometime Bishop of London* (London: Longmans, 1904), vol. 1, p. 372.

school proposes. Instead, it prescribes a balancing of power, sustained by a wary policy of shifting alliances, to prevent any one state or group of states from growing predominant. Where interstate relations are closely interdependent, pluralist theorists often favor confederal structures, within which member states, still sovereign and still acting out of national self-interest, can nevertheless focus on common interests, set bounds to their antagonisms, and manage their disputes peacefully. In this confederal form, the balance-of-power approach to international relations, like the constitutionalist approach within a single state, aims to limit and harmonize distinct and contentious powers within an overarching cooperative structure.

The balance-of-power school is, of course, as concerned with power and anarchy as the hegemonic school. Both schools are "realist" in this respect. But the pluralist cure for anarchy is a self-conscious balancing among several independent states, rather than a surrendering of power by all to one. Neither school, however, believes that peace among states can be achieved without constant exertion. Neither maintains that human nature or human society is perfectible. For both, self-destructive conflict is part of human nature and can be kept at bay only by continued effort. As a guide to those efforts, theorists often invoke some variety of natural law; a concordance of power, wisdom, and virtue is meant to infuse rulers with an inherent sense of justice and self-restraint. For hegemonists, natural law enlightens and tempers the absolute ruler at home or the ruler of the predominant superpower in Europe. For pluralists, respect for natural law is meant to infuse all parties with the underlying self-restraint needed to sustain constitutional checks and balances in the domestic state, or to animate a concert of partner states in a European confederacy. In neither hegemonic nor balance-of-power school does natural law guarantee a rational order, but it can be a guide to those struggling to maintain one. Neither is natural law a logically necessary element for either school. Hegemonists can simply believe in the natural right of the strongest to rule. As Spinoza once observed, big fish eat little fish by natural right.[9] The balance-of-power school has per-

---

[9] "For instance, fishes are naturally conditioned for swimming, and the greater for devouring the less; therefore fishes enjoy the water, and the greater devour the lesser

haps greater need for the guidance of an innate moral equilibrium. But presumably, pluralists can also simply believe in the right of the clever weak to hobble the stupid strong. Being a pluralist or a hegemonist is, from this perspective, a function of being the weaker or stronger party. Talleyrand once counseled his compatriots that, since France was intrinsically Europe's most powerful state, its welfare was best preserved by abstaining from behavior that would unite the rest of Europe against it—in other words, by strictly respecting the independence of others.[10] In short, both Realist schools can be inspired either by Machiavelli's *Prince* or by his *Discourses*, by Nietzsche as well as by Aristotle or the Stoics.

In contrast to the hegemonic and balance-of-power schools, the "liberal" school is a more modern product, nurtured in the Enlightenment of the seventeenth and eighteenth centuries. It sees the universe as not only rational but also naturally harmonious. Liberals see the diplomatic cosmos as Newton saw the physical—as a system of separate but similar units, moving in harmony, with universal rules easily accessible to human reason. This liberal vision can be fitted to hegemonic or balance-of-power prescriptions.[11] But its natural affinity is with democracy, national self-determination, and the free market. Peace and harmony are natural in the liberal worldview. War and oppression, therefore, have to be considered the results of unnatural institutions and irrational practices. Eliminate these, liberals believe, and natural harmony will prevail. Thus, Thomas Paine (1773–1809), pamphleteer of the American Revolution, preached that abolishing kings, nobles, and privileged classes of all sorts, as well as obscur-

---

by sovereign natural right." Benedict de Spinoza, *Tractatus Theologico-Political, Writings on Political Philosophy*, ed. A. G. A. Balz (New York: Appleton-Century-Crofts, 1937), p. 27.

[10] Charles Maurice de Talleyrand-Périgord, Prince de Benevent, *The Correspondence of Prince Talleyrand and King Louis XVIII during the Congress of Vienna*, ed. Georges Pallain (New York: Da Capo, 1973), "Letter 100," pp. 516ff. and notes.

[11] François Marie Arouet de Voltaire (1694–1778), for example, author of *Essai sur l'histoire générale et sur les moeurs et l'ésprit des nations depuis Charlemagne jusqu'à nos jours* (1756), *Siècle de Louis XIV* (1751), and *Candide* (1759), was a fitful admirer of government by enlightened despots and was also a sometime friend and guest of the "enlightened" Prussian king, Frederick II.

antist churches, would open the way not only to harmonious democracy within states but also to perpetual peace among them.

In the eighteenth century, liberal ideas played a critical role in launching America's grand experiment in continental federalism. One of the most important theorists of the American experiment was James Madison (1751–1836), third president of the United States, principal author of the *Federalist Papers*, and "father" of the American Constitution. The basic problem of politics, as Madison saw it, was how to prevent "factions"—special interests—from seizing control of government and exploiting public power for private gain. Madison saw political factions as would-be monopolists in a political marketplace. To prevent any one of them from succeeding, it was best to keep a great many of them competing. His federal remedy was to enlarge the "orbit" of the state to create such diversity that no single faction, or amalgam of factions, would be strong enough to form a stable majority, and thus to appropriate public power for private purposes. He assumed, in other words, that the political marketplace should work like the ideal liberal economy. Competition should lead to decisions that favor the general interest, unless colluding special interests form a monopoly power (majority) that distorts the market's decisions. Enlarging the political marketplace was, of course, a prescription that favored a large American federation. American federal ideas ran in a quite contrary direction to the nationalist theories developing in Europe, where nation state theories, often inspired by Rousseau, emphasized not only the importance of achieving a democratic consensus, but also the limits to the extent of such a consensus, a topic taken up presently.

Mercantilism and Liberalism

Considering liberalism reminds us that how Europe's states developed was naturally much affected by their economies. Capitalist enterprise of one sort or another was already well implanted in the early modern period, and European states were generally much involved in its workings. Budding capitalist industry and commerce frequently depended heavily on state regulation and support. For productive enterprise to flourish, states had to maintain general law and order and establish and defend a reliable system of property rights, taxation, and commercial regulation. Close involvement of government seemed only natural, since the success of a state depended heavily on the strength and prosperity of its economy. Just as early states tended to be absolute in their governance, the traditional early relationship between states and economies tended to be "mercantilist." Mercantilism was a political and economic doctrine that subordinated the economy to the state. Enterprise was to be promoted and trade regulated by subsidies, protectionist duties, and quotas—all in the interest of the state. Since the absolute state was frequently at war with its neighbors, it was preoccupied with accumulating the precious metals needed to finance its wars. The state's interest thus required building productive power and commerce that would result in a trade surplus, which meant—in turn—an accumulation of precious metals. In other words, classic mercantilism, serving the absolutist state, naturally focused on sustaining a balance-of-payments surplus.

Mercantilism encouraged imperialism—as the means to control more trade and thus gather more resources. Increasingly, Europe's mercantilist states fought their wars not only at home but all around the world. As early as the fifteenth century, Europe's states, through conquest, migration, piracy, and trade, began imposing themselves elsewhere. Europe's own regional balance, as well as its economic progress, was intimately connected to these external developments. The Habsburg dynasty's bid for European hegemony, for example, rested not only on its overwhelming amalgamation of territory on the European continent, but on Spain's vast empire in the New World and the riches extracted from it. Classic mercantilism was thus intimately connected with imperialism as well as absolutism.

Mercantilism fitted well enough with hegemonic and balance-of-power theories of international relations, but not with liberal theories, whose view of harmonious domestic and international systems was increasingly bound up with the economic doctrine of free trade. For liberals, free trade in the economic sphere became the counterpart to democracy in the political sphere. Seventeenth-century liberals, like John Locke (1632–1704), defended private property rights, including the right to trade freely, as a barrier against the political pretensions of absolute states. By the eighteenth century, the economic dimension of liberalism was taking on a life of its own. Adam Smith (1723–1790), a Scot as well as the most famous of the eighteenth-century British liberal economists, saw English mercantilism and English imperialism as two sides of the same absolutist coin. He preached free markets at home and free trade abroad not only because he believed these prescriptions would secure domestic political and economic liberty and international peace, but also because free markets would lead toward an optimum of economic efficiency and general prosperity. In the Smithian tradition, free competition naturally results in optimal gains shared by all. Freeing trade thus removes the pretext for empires. Similarly, Smith's friend and fellow Scot, David Hume (1711–1796), championed the gold standard—because he believed sound money and firm restraints on government debt would limit absolutism and protect private property as well as stop states from wasting the society's resources on senseless imperial warfare. In effect, both Smith and Hume proposed the liberal ideal of economic efficiency in place of classic mercantilism's emphasis on power and empire. For them, the free market, if allowed to follow its own natural laws, was the intrinsic order that would limit governments at home and prevent them from warring against each other abroad.

Imperialism, Free Trade and the Global Economy

Initially, Western imperialism did not so much unify the world as project Europe's own divisions on it. By the late eighteenth century, however, even as Smith was writing his *Wealth of Nations*, a more integrated "global" system had begun to form. This was less the product of liberal ideas than of the Seven Years' War (1756–1763), when mercantilist Britain decisively defeated mercantilist France in North America and India. Half a century later, Napoleon's defeat at Waterloo confirmed not only the old pluralist state system in Europe, but also Britain's nascent hegemony in the rest of the world. Ironically, Smith's liberal doctrines, conceived in opposition to the English imperialism of the eighteenth century, became the official ideology of the triumphant British Empire of the nineteenth century, as well as of the Pax Americana of the twentieth. This reconciliation of liberalism with hegemonic imperialism went hand in hand with the evolution of an increasingly integrated global economy and diplomatic system. As the world's supreme naval power, Britain not only covered much of the globe with its colonies, protectorates, and dominions but also traded and invested heavily elsewhere—notably in the United States and in Latin America. In effect, Britain built a global capitalist economy around itself, with London as its preeminent commercial and financial center. As hegemon of this global system, Britain saw Europe as its major global enemy. Britain's national aim was not to unite and rule the Continent, but to keep it divided. England's culture had always been profoundly linked to the rest of Europe, but the nineteenth-century British grew inclined to visualize themselves in "splendid isolation" from the Continent, and indeed to define themselves as a superior nation in opposition to Europe.

Since Britain was still securely the world's "first industrial nation," British manufacturers were highly competitive and had little to fear from free trade, a doctrine that Britain naturally embraced and promoted throughout the global economy that it dominated. But by the mid-nineteenth century, this "free-trade imperialism" of the British was beginning to arouse powerful opposing reactions among the rest of Europe's states. These arose, in part, for traditional mercantilist reasons: Continental states were themselves aspiring to catch up with Britain's economic prowess and growing covetous of Britain's global position. But the reactions also reflected Europe's flowering nationalism, whose emphasis on "community" was gradually transforming traditional absolute states into consensual and increasingly democratic nation states. In so doing, nationalism transformed not only Europe's states but their state system as well. The next chapter considers these changes, and chapter 5 considers the implications for European capitalism.

SELECTED SOURCES

Interdependent Sovereignty

For Dante's imperial plan for Europe, see Dante Alighieri, *De Monarchia* (Indianapolis: Bobbs-Merrill Educational, 1978). For the visions of European unity ascribed to Napoleon at St. Helena, see his *Memoirs*, ed. Somerset de Chair (London: Faber & Faber, 1948), and those of the people around him at St. Helena, in particular, Emmanuel-Auguste-Dieudonné, Comte de Las Cases, *Memorial de Ste-*

Hélène (1822). For a discussion of the authenticity of ascribing these visions to Napoleon, see Vincent Cronin, *Napoleon Bonaparte* (New York: Morrow, 1972), appendix A, p. 448. For the persistence of medieval constitutionalism in the West, see Frederick M. Watkins, *The Political Tradition of the West* (Cambridge: Harvard University Press, 1942).

For broad studies of European struggles for hegemony, see Ludwig Dehio, *The Precarious Balance* (New York: Knopf, 1948), and Paul Kennedy, *The Rise and Fall of the Great Powers* (New York: Random House, 1987). For a theoretical exposition of why states seek hegemony, see Robert Gilpin, *War and Change in World Politics* (New York: Cambridge University Press, 1981).

Managing a Europe of States: Classic Theories

For early international relations theorizing, see Paul A. Rahe, *Republics Ancient and Modern: Classical Republicanism and the American Revolution* (Chapel Hill: University of North Carolina Press, 1992). For a classic study of the state and state system as they developed in Renaissance Italy, one that emphasizes the self-conscious and aesthetic character of the early states, see Jacob Burckhardt, *The Civilization of the Renaissance in Italy,* trans. Samuel Middlemore (London: Sonnenschein, 1890). For the Renaissance theorists, see J. G. A. Pocock, *The Machiavellian Moment: Florentine Political Thought and the Atlantic Republican Tradition* (Princeton: Princeton University Press, 1975).

For a classic exposition of the balance of power, see David Hume, "Of the Balance of Power" and "Of the Balance of Trade," in *Essays Moral, Political and Literary* (Indianapolis: Liberty Classics, 1987). For a contemporary analysis of balance-of-power as a principle in statecraft, see Henry Kissinger, *Diplomacy* (New York: Simon & Schuster, 1994). For the Peace of Westphalia and Cardinal Richelieu's ideas about giving each kingdom its proper sphere of influence, see Carl J. Burckhardt, *Richelieu and His Age*, 3 vols. (New York: Harcourt Brace, 1970). For the self-conscious reconstruction of the balance of power after the Napoleonic Wars, see Guglielmo Ferrero, *The Reconstruction of Europe*, trans. Theodore Jaeckel (New York: Putnam, 1941), and also Harold Nicholson, *The Congress of Vienna* (New York: Harcourt Brace, 1946). For a further elaboration of Talleyrand's ideas, see Charles Maurice de Talleyrand-Périgord, Prince de Benevent, *The Correspondence of Prince Talleyrand and King Louis XVIII during the Congress of Vienna*, ed. M. G. Pallain (New York: Da Capo, 1973). For a biography, see J. F. Bernard, *Talleyrand: A Biography* (New York: Putnam, 1973).

For a study of Madison and Madison's federalism, see Stanley M. Elkins, *The Age of Federalism* (New York: Oxford University Press, 1995). For a comprehensive recent biography, see Ralph Louis Ketchum, *James Madison* (Charlottesville: University of Virginia Press, 1990). For the European influences on America's constitutional founding fathers, see Carl Becker, *The Declaration of Independence: A Study in the History of Political Ideas* (New York: Knopf, 1942). These influences were continental as well as British. Franklin and Jefferson, for example, were very much at home in the world of Parisian intellectuals.

Mercantilism and Liberalism

For a discussion of the workings of early capitalism and its effects outside Europe, see Fernand Braudel, *Civilization and Capitalism, 15th–18th Century* (London: Fontana Press, 1979), and also Immanuel Wallerstein, *Geopolitics and Geoculture: Essays on the Changing World-System* (Cambridge and New York, Paris: Cambridge University Press and Maison des Sciences de l'Homme, 1991).

The most notable practitioner of classic mercantilism was Jean-Baptiste Colbert (1619–1683), Louis XIV's chief minister. His admirable reforms for developing the domestic economy and foreign trade were undermined by the Court's extravagance and the extensive series of wars in the later years of Louis's reign. An intelligent illustration of evolving mercantilist thought in England is Thomas Mun (1571–1641), *Discourse on England's Treasure by Forraign Trade* (1664). For general surveys of mercantilism, see J. W. Horrocks, *A Short History of Mercantilism* (London: Methuen, 1925), or E. F. Heckscher, *Mercantilism* (London: Allen & Unwin, 1935). For a discussion of Mun's work, see Christopher Chivvis, "Thomas Mun and England's Balance of Payments" (Manuscript, SAIS European Studies, 1999).

It should be noted that Adam Smith railed against big government and its debts, among other things, because he disliked English imperialism. Likewise, David Hume championed the gold standard to prevent London from creating credit to finance its wars. See Adam Smith, *An Inquiry into the Nature and Causes of the Wealth of Nations* (1776), ed. R. H. Campbell, A. S. Skinner, and W. B. Todd, 2 vols. (Indianapolis: Liberty Classics, 1981), book 4, and David Hume, *Principles of Economics and Taxation* (1821), ed. E. C. K. Gonner (London: G. Bell, 1927).

Imperialism, Free Trade, and the Global Economy

For the ideology of free trade within the British Empire, see Bernard Semmel, *The Rise of Free Trade Imperialism: Classical Political Economy, the Empire of Free Trade and Imperialism, 1750–1850* (Cambridge: Cambridge University Press, 1970); also his *The Liberal Ideal and the Demons of Empire: Theories of Imperialism from Adam Smith to Lenin* (Baltimore: Johns Hopkins University Press, 1993). See also Lawrence James, *The Rise and Fall of the British Empire* (New York: St. Martin's Press, 1994). Richard Cobden (1804–1865) was a tireless and effective promoter of free trade in the *Pax Britannica*. See his essays "The Balance of Power" and "Protection of Commerce," reprinted in *Political Writings* (New York: Kraus Reprint, 1969). The concept of Britain as the "first industrial nation" is elaborated by Peter Mathias in *The First Industrial Nation: An Economic History of Britain, 1700–1914*, 2nd ed. (New York: Methuen, 1983). For "splendid isolation" from Europe and an "Anglo-Saxon" global community instead, see J. R. Seeley, *The Expansion of England* (London: University of Chicago Press, 1898). For an early collaborative effort to link and analyze the free trade rationale for the Pax Britannica with that of the Pax Americana, see David P. Calleo and Benjamin M. Rowland, *America in the World Political Economy* (Bloomington: Indiana University Press, 1973), ch. 3.

From States to Nation States

Communitarian Nationalism

ADAM SMITH wrote his liberal critique of mercantilism in the eighteenth century, when the great technological and social transformations of modern life were still relatively modest, at least by comparison with what would follow. By the nineteenth century, change was accelerating rapidly, thanks not only to the effects of capitalist enterprise and Enlightenment ideals and technology, but also to the rise of the radically different worldview of Romanticism, vigorously in revolt against the Enlightenment. While capitalism and technology were dramatically altering daily life, Romantic visions about how life should be lived and communities organized were colliding with the Enlightenment ideals that had flourished in the eighteenth century. In the new politics that resulted, the traditional state of the ancien régime began turning into the nation state, a metamorphosis that reflected a new Romantic view of the political community. This new view profoundly affected the social and economic functions of Europe's states, reorienting them toward the modern world of mass societies, welfare systems, and global capitalism. A new kind of state naturally changed the character of the interstate system and, in due course, of the global system as well.

Since Europe's nation state is a political formula that is still very much alive in Europe and, indeed, has spread throughout the world, it is worth considering the philosophical ideas that lie behind its appeal. As a political formula, it marries the ancient Greek Idealist view of the state, associated with Plato and Aristotle, with the modern Romantic concept of culture, associated with Herder.

In the Idealist approach of the ancient Greeks, the state is defined as a self-conscious community of consenting and cooperating citizens, aspiring to pursue a balanced good life together and thus to approximate the ideal of a good society, a view that makes the education of the citizenry the key to politics—good or bad. Citizens linked together in this common pursuit share thereby a collective political self, in addition to their more distinct identities as individuals or members of a family or social class. In the successful community, this shared public identity and interest that goes with citizenship is pervasive enough to permit a working reconciliation of the antagonisms that naturally arise from the more distinctive identities that divide the citizenry.

In the Middle Ages, by contrast, Christian political theory denied the state and citizenship so comprehensive a moral scope. Instead, it saw the church as a parallel institution to the state, each possessing authority in its own proper sphere, and each with distinct ideals, identities, and values. Such a view of politics left the Christian citizen with divided loyalties in a plural society, held together by a common faith. The shattering of Christian unity and the subsequent wars of religion provoked a return to the unitary state—not only the absolute Roman state of the ancien régime, where order was imposed by a sovereign, but also, in due course, the old Greek ideal of a participatory political community held together by an overriding single shared identity. Jean-Jacques Rousseau forcefully represented that Greek formula in his *Social Contract* (1762). In his ideal state, vigorously participating citizens are animated by a shared "general will" to virtue. Only in such a community is authority legitimate and are people truly free. Like Plato and Aristotle, Rousseau was much concerned with spelling out the conditions that might permit such a common identity to develop and persist. Citizens had to share a political culture, together with institutions that encouraged a shared ardor for the common good. Otherwise, Rousseau feared, the natural conflicts of interest in society would preclude consensus based on the common good, and the state would become an apparatus of oppression rather than a community of virtue. The French Revolution was the catalyst for spreading such ideas throughout Europe. A state's legitimacy, the French Revolution taught, could no longer base itself merely on past conquest, historical habit, or utilitarian convenience. It required free and actively consenting citizens.

This Idealist view differed in critical respects from the absolutist perspective of the ancien régime, which tended to see the state as a band of governors—a governing apparatus ruling and performing services for a passive population of apolitical individuals. It also differed from the traditional liberal view found, for example, in John Locke's *Second Treatise on Government* (1689), where the concept of a "people" is an abstraction to be summoned in exceptional cases to get rid of an oppressive government. In contrast to Rousseau, in Locke what creates a "people" and how its consensus is sustained remain relatively underdeveloped. Rousseau's Idealist approach is also very different from that of the federalist James Madison, who emphasized diversity rather than consensus as the cure for factionalism.

Seeing the state as a moral partnership of consenting citizens naturally calls for a theory of community. Whereas liberals tended to assume the harmonious consentient community as a given, Idealists believed the consensus needed for a united and free community was difficult to reach and even more difficult to sustain. Nor did they believe it could be extended very far. The ancient Greek Idealist philosophers, Plato and Aristotle, could not imagine their ideal polity stretched beyond the confines of a single city state. Rousseau fitted his *Social Contract* to his native Geneva rather than to Europe's major states. But Rousseau also knew that modern states had to be larger to survive. Thus, a state seeking not only legitimacy but survival had to stretch its Idealist consensus over a unit large enough to endure militarily and economically—a problem the Greek city state was ultimately unable to resolve.[1]

The concept of the cultural nation, favored and developed by Romantic philosophers, seemed to provide a ready solution. As a practical matter, citizens of an Idealist state had to be able to communicate in order to cooperate. Hence, they presumably required a common language and a shared universe of cultural symbols, monuments, and myths. Their sense of mutual political identity needed to be reinforced by a common history—real and imagined. These are all qualities that characterize the Romantic conception of a nation. Romantic thinkers,

---

[1] For Rousseau's principal attempt to apply the *Social Contract* to a putative nation state, see Jean-Jacques Rousseau, *The Government of Poland* (1762), in Frederick Watkins, ed. and trans., Rousseau, *Political Writings* (New York: Nelson, 1953).

moreover, developed psychological concepts of the self that made room for notions of collective identity. Those who shared a culture shared some part of a collective self, which reinforced their sense of common citizenship. But of course, real national cultures are not monolithic. Instead, as products of a long history, they tend to be internally diverse. Thus, a political community that shared a common national culture would be both unified and diverse at the same time. Through the nation state, freedom, unity, and diversity could somehow be reconciled. As these concepts became widely accepted, it grew to seem natural that a state, to sustain the consensus that made its sovereignty legitimate, had to be congruent with a cultural nation. Historical events speeded the linkage. Nationalism, initially spread by the French Revolution, became a powerful ideal to rally opposition to Napoleonic hegemony across Europe. Thus, both the Revolution and its Napoleonic aftermath helped to fuse the idea of the nation with the idea of the state.

As nineteenth-century capitalism created societies that were increasingly industrial and urbanized, the nation state proved a better formula for governing than the typical dynastic and authoritarian state of the Enlightenment. Nationalism helped to assuage class conflict and to give governments the legitimacy and patience to manage the long transformation from absolutism to constitutional democracy. Nationalist philosophers undoubtedly brought to state theory a more organic view of communities than their Enlightenment predecessors, along with a more adequate psychology of individual and group identity and a more developmental view of history.[2] And in the end, it was

---

[2] By "nationalist" theorists of the state, I mean not only revolutionaries who were trying to create a nation state (e.g., Giuseppe Mazzini, or the two great operatic composers who were hugely influential in creating their respective nations—Giuseppe Verdi and Richard Wagner) but also politicians and theorists, often conservative constitutionalists, who were trying to transform existing states into communities that embraced the whole population, as a means for coming to terms with change and democracy. In Germany, Fichte and Hegel are obvious illustrations. In Britain, there is the rich tradition of Edmund Burke, Samuel Taylor Coleridge, and Benjamin Disraeli that culminated in a flowering of "neo-Hegelian" British political philosophers in the late nineteenth and early twentieth centuries. Bernard Bosanquet, *The Philo-*

the states that successfully became nation states that survived. The happiest results occurred in well-established countries, like Britain, where nationalism flowed through strong constitutional and liberal structures that permitted an efficacious balance between individual rights, regional and ethnic identities, and collective solidarity. The United States itself grew into a nation state, with nationality ostensibly defined by political and constitutional ideals, powerfully reinforced by shared historical myths and cultural norms.

Nationalism, of course, has its dark side—as was already abundantly clear in the French Revolution. In states with fragile political consensus, nationalism can grow "integral" or "totalitarian," rejecting cultural pluralism and creating consensus through xenophobic terror. To define its own identity, the would-be nation may feel compelled to go to war with its neighbors. Nationality, moreover, seldom provides precise criteria for citizenship or state boundaries. People belong to a political "nation" if they wish to and others accept them. In regions of uncertain nationality or mixed cultures, making nationality the foundation for political consensus and legitimacy can become, in itself, a major source of conflict. Even the most established nations, like France, have numerous ethnic and cultural subdivisions, some of them suppressed and resentful. In would-be nation states—like early-nineteenth-century Italy or Germany—either governed by imperial foreign rulers or broken up into an aggregate of smaller authoritarian states, nationalism provided the agenda for revolutionary changes of regimes as well as radical redrawings of state boundaries. In the Habsburg, Russian, and Ottoman Empires, nationalism was a perennial incitement to insurrection and repression.

In relations among Europe's states, nationalism powerfully rein-

---

sophical Theory of the State (London: Macmillan, 1920), is a particularly powerful and comprehensive statement of this tradition. Theodore Dwight Wolsey is an interesting and distinguished American version; see his *Political Science; or, The State Theoretically and Practically Considered* (New York: Scribner's, 1877). Every European country has parallels. Arguably, the tradition flowered later in France, at least politically, where it informed the political philosophy of General de Gaulle, himself much influenced by the "Romantic" epistemology of Henri Bergson. See Charles de Gaulle, *Le Fil de l'epée* (1932), translated as *The Edge of the Sword*, trans. Gerard Hopkins (Westport, CT: Greenwood Press, 1975). See also below, note 5.

forced the ideal of a Europe of states as opposed to a unified Europe. Arguably, nationalism also added to the difficulties of managing so interdependent a state system. By creating a more intense political community that gave greater legitimacy to governments, nationalism allowed warring states to mobilize huge resources. Rejuvenating the state by turning it into a community of participating citizens meant that wars between states automatically became wars between peoples and cultures. Taming the anarchy and limiting the violence of interstate relations became all the more difficult. Among nationalism's principal liabilities, therefore, was its tendency to exacerbate Europe's problems of interstate order.

Nationalist Coexistence: Herder's Garden of Nations

Logically, the problems of managing interdependence among nation states could be treated within the old prenationalist interstate theories. Nation states could simply be substituted for traditional states. Nationalist theorists could easily adopt a balance-of-power approach to international order, wherein weaker nation states carefully guarded their independence by allying against stronger neighbors. Nationalists of this pluralist school could also favor a confederacy, where nation states acknowledged mutual rights to independence and collaborated to preserve them. Of course, nationalist theorists, especially from big states, could also favor a hegemonic interstate system, particularly when their nationalism was combined with Social Darwinism and racism, as it frequently was among later-nineteenth-century writers. Most early nationalists, however, took a liberal view of the interstate system. In other words, they thought cooperation among states would be the norm once certain political and economic preconditions were met, in particular once multinational empires were broken up and their constituent nations were set free. Nevertheless, liberalism and Idealist nationalism had quite different philosophical roots. In the end, the tensions between the two schools were difficult to reconcile.

To grasp the liberal nationalist worldview and its inner tensions, it is useful to consider the ideas of one of its earliest and most celebrated theorists, Johann Gottfried von Herder (1744–1803), a German

Protestant clergyman, famous as a philologist and literary critic, who formulated the modern Romantic concept of the nation. His writings illuminate the rich cultural, aesthetic, and psychological foundations of the nation state formula and thereby help to explain its enduring appeal. As a liberal as well as a nationalist, Herder also laid the groundwork for a liberal nationalist theory of international relations, an approach that remains influential to the present day.

The roots of Herder's nationalism lay in his resentment of French cultural hegemony over Germany. As a German and a Romantic, Herder found it unbearable that the neoclassical culture of the French Enlightenment should dominate Germany's princely courts, where the manners of Versailles were the model and French was often the spoken language. He was outraged at the way French critics and their German followers set universal rules of taste and dismissed other cultures as uncouth, including that of the Germans themselves. German culture was being abused, he thought, because Germans lacked a unified state.

In his reactions against the artistic rules of French neoclassicism, Herder reflected the Sturm und Drang phase of Romanticism, with which he was closely associated. Like other early Romantics, he found the eighteenth-century Enlightenment's views on art, personality, and freedom to be mechanical, monotonous, and sterile. Romantics like Herder demanded freedom for individuality, in particular for the individuality of the artistic genius, which they were inclined to believe required expression in hot emotion rather than cold reason. But Herder grew uneasy at the solipsistic and amoral tendencies in Sturm und Drang's enthusiasm for unfettered individuality. That every artist was free to create his own private moral and aesthetic universe was for Herder a troubling prospect.

Herder's nationalist concepts of *Volk* and *Kultur* were his way of reconciling the free artist with those communal rules needed for collective social and cultural order. Herder believed that everyone shared a common humanity, but that history had divided mankind into separate peoples. Each people (Volk) developed its distinct national culture (Kultur)—a bundle of linked ideas, memories, and sentiments that was its reaction over time to a particular environment and a collective historical experience. These distinct cultures were the natural subdivisions of humankind. Each elaborated its own insight into human potential, and each had to be understood on its own terms. The national culture also gave individual artists their "rules"—the aesthetic and moral framework within which they could work out their own individual visions. Individualism had thus to be defined collectively as well as personally.

Herder was himself a prodigiously learned and gifted scholar of the literature of several nations. His deep insight into and respect and love for many cultures, past and present, were manifest: "No nationality has been totally designated by God as the chosen people of the earth; above all we must seek the truth and cultivate the garden of the common good."[3] Nevertheless, Herder's psychology of identity and creativity limited his cosmopolitanism. For Herder, even the greatest individual genius was always partly communal, the product of the particular culture that nurtured it. Individuals, by absorbing the insights of other cultures, could greatly enrich their own personal vision and perhaps broaden the horizons of their own national culture as well. But they could not, at the same time, renounce their national identity without destroying their own cultural integrity and vitality, and becoming as deracinated and sterile as eighteenth-century Germany's Francophone aristocrats. As Herder saw it, "The inundated heart of the idle cosmopolite is a home for no one."[4]

By making individualism national, Herder merely transferred the problem of rules from the personal to the interstate level. If history had given every culture its own standards, what values applied to humanity as a whole? Were there no standards across all cultures that provided the moral framework for the coexistence of nations? What standards, for instance, should apply across Europe's own interstate system?

Herder's answer was a grand Romantic theory of history that anticipated Hegel. Throughout nature, Herder felt the presence of God, and throughout human history, he felt the workings of this same divine energy, or *Kraft*, exploring and unfolding humanity's potential. Na-

[3] Bernard Suphan, ed., *Herder's Sämtliche Werke*, 33 vols. (Berlin, 1877–1913), vol. 17, p. 212.
[4] Ibid., vol. 13, p. 339.

tional cultures were the chapters of the human story, each to be understood and appreciated on its own terms. History was a garden where each national flower possessed its own particular beauty, not to be crowded out by its neighbors or uprooted by imperial gardeners. The diversity of cultures was the key to general human progress, and to Europe's own particular vitality.[5]

NATIONALISM AND LIBERALISM

In our own time, the inadequacy of Herder's Romantic vision of peaceful national coexistence seems self-evident. We know that nationalism can grow fanatically intolerant, and that its communitarian ideal can mutate into totalitarian tyranny and compulsive aggression. Nevertheless, Herder's vision of peaceful national coexistence has continued to have great appeal. Perhaps the most important reason lies in its easy affinity with the traditional liberal school of international order. Herder's free nations, coexisting harmoniously while perfecting their respective cultures, seem an obvious parallel to liberal economies in the Smithian tradition, trading peacefully in world markets to optimize their respective advantages. Moreover, the national self-determination preached by Herder's nationalists seemed a natural complement to Smith's crusade against imperialist mercantilism.

---

[5] The same elements infused a rich philosophical movement in Germany, with powerful reverberations throughout the rest of Europe and America. Among numerous distinguished philosophers, Georg Wilhelm Friedrich Hegel (1770–1831) is the most famous and influential. Herder's immediate political successor in Germany was Johann Gottlieb Fichte, whose *Addresses to the German Nation* (1808) politicized Romantic and Idealist notions found in Herder's thought. Herder's liberal nationalism soon found explicit political expression among foreign writers as well. See, for example, the theorist of Italian nationalism, Giuseppe Mazzini, *The Duties of Man*, trans. E. A. Venturi (London: Chapman & Hall, 1862). Woodrow Wilson's formula for national self-determination, which also emphasized the liberal free market, may be seen as another Herderian offshoot. See Alfred Cobban, *The Nation State and National Self-Determination* (New York: Thomas Crowell, 1969), pp. 62–66. For Wilson's ideas, see Arthur Link, *Woodrow Wilson: Revolution, War and Peace* (Arlington Heights: Horlan Davidson, 1979), or August Heckscher, *Woodrow Wilson: A Biography* (New York: Scribner's, 1991).

Smith's nineteenth-century disciple, Richard Cobden, for example, was not only a fervent opponent of imperialism but also an avid promoter of national self-determination.[6] So, of course, was Britain's great nineteenth-century Liberal prime minister, William Gladstone. Free trade among independent and democratic nation states would bring peace and prosperity to all, Cobden taught and Gladstone believed, and would thereby make empires obsolete, together with hegemonic and balance-of-power politics.

As I noted at the end of the last chapter, continental nationalists were quick to observe how free trade and even national self-determination were doctrines particularly well suited to Britain's own national interest. Free trade was a rational policy for the world's most advanced economy, so competitive that it no longer needed its superior military and naval power to prevail in free markets around the world. National self-determination was a useful lever for breaking up rival imperial systems, seeking to protect themselves from Britain's commercial supremacy. A Latin America of weak "national" states was more easily penetrated than a Spanish empire. A free and united Italy was expected to be a more accessible market than a series of Habsburg-dominated provinces. In time, as other European countries saw economic development as the way to modernize and solidify national solidarity and power, Britain's "free trade imperialism" began to arouse fierce nationalist opposition. European nationalism revolted against Cobden's liberal globalism. Imperial Germany sought to convert this nationalist revolt into its rationale for World War I. Unless united under Germany, its leading state, Europe would become a subordinate part of the Anglo-Saxon global hegemony. After World War II, as the global Pax Americana replaced the moribund Pax Britannica, fusing free trade and global hegemony became an American specialty and aroused similar opposition from Europe's rejuvenated nation states.[7]

---

[6] Cobden's arguments are cogently summarized in two essays "Balance of Trade" and "Protection of Commerce," reprinted in *Political Writings* (London: Routledge/Thoemmes Press, 1995).

[7] De Gaulle saw Roosevelt's visions—the "Big Four" cooperating to uphold world order globally or national self-determination for Europe's overseas empires after

In summary, despite their mutual attraction, Romantic nationalism and economic liberalism were bound to be uneasy bedfellows. Not only was there a clash of national interests between the most advanced industrial state and those racing to catch up, but nationalists and liberals tend to have fundamentally different views about states and markets. Politically, nationalists are followers of Rousseau rather than of Madison. And while enlightened nationalists may be champions of a European confederacy, their Rousseauist concern about an active popular consensus makes them unsympathetic to centralized federalism, whether political or technocratic. Nationalists may want a united and cooperative European system, but within it, they still expect nation states to be the organizers of popular consent and repositories of political legitimacy. Economically, communitarian nationalists are more concerned about national solidarity than about the free market. Nationalist proclivities for interfering with markets in the name of communitarian values has, in due course, provoked a powerful neoliberal reaction, as the next chapter will discuss.

Before going on to chapter 5, the reader may find it helpful to consult the appendix that follows this chapter, a "Glossary of Terms and Arguments."

APPENDIX: GLOSSARY OF TERMS AND ARGUMENTS

Terms and Methodology

The book uses certain terms—Idealist, nationalist, liberal, communitarian, corporatist, and mercantilist. Not everyone uses these terms in the same way, and some further explanation may be helpful. Obviously, these terms raise many issues of method that cannot be resolved by a brief appendix (or a long one either). Nevertheless, explaining them further should help to reveal the basic approach that informs judgments in the book as a whole. This section may thus serve

---

World War II—as America's "will to power cloaked in idealism." Charles De Gaulle, *The Complete War Memoirs of Charles de Gaulle, 1940–6* (New York: Simon & Schuster, 1964), p. 573. See also chapter 6, note 1.

both as a glossary of terms and as a shorthand summary of some of the main historical arguments.

The idea of the nation state is relatively modern, but behind it lies something much older—the idealized *polis* of the ancient Greeks. Philosophical Idealism is the root that they share. As I note in chapter 4, Rousseau is the link between Idealist ancients and Idealist moderns, an insight greatly developed in the late-nineteenth century by the British neo-Hegelian philosopher Bernard Bosanquet (1848–1923), from whom I have learned a great deal.[8]

Idealism may be defined as a basic philosophical approach that sees human perceptions, or the reality that human beings perceive, as a reflection or embodiment of preexisting ideas, meaning ideal forms. There are, of course, many schools of Idealism—ancient and modern. For the classic Greek Idealists, these forms either exist independently in a sphere of their own and impress themselves imperfectly on the world (Plato), or are inherent in the world as genetic codes giving direction to the life and death of individuals according to their species (Aristotle). Ethically, Idealism postulates a model form for the human soul and its development—a good life. According to Plato and Aristotle, this model soul reflects a just balance of its constituent powers: the intuitive capacity for grasping the truth, beauty, and reason that form a good life; the willpower, courage, and organizational capacity to pursue that life with success; and the physical vigor needed to sustain it. Every individual needs to find his own proper balance of these elements—contemplative, executive, and physical—according to his own gifts and station in the community.

Communitarianism

Both Plato and Aristotle also believed that individuals, in order to achieve a good life for themselves, need to be part of a political community, a polis or city-state, whose citizens are bound together in harmonious pursuit of the ideal good. Education—the proper development of ideal citizens—was the raison d'être of their polis. And like their ideal citizen, their ideal state needs to find a just balance of

---

[8] Bernard Bosanquet, *The Philosophical Theory of the State* (London: Macmillan, 1889, 1923).

the same elements. In this sense, the state is the individual citizen writ large, just as the individual citizen is the state writ small. In our terminology, this presumption of identity between the good state and the good citizen makes Plato and Aristotle communitarians. In their Idealist republics, citizens obey freely; they share a general will based on a proper ethical vision of a good life—for the individual as for the community.

Modern Idealist nationalists—Herder, Burke, Coleridge, Hegel, Mazzini, Bosanquet, or a philosophically minded statesman like de Gaulle—followed Rousseau in reviving and appropriating the Greek Idealist view of the state. Like the Greeks, they believed a proper state was a community of balanced constitutional elements held together by a shared identity among citizens. The ideal nation state, like the ideal polis, required a strongly rooted consensus about how to constitute the community in order to pursue the good life collectively. Nationalists stressed that political consensus was the product of a national culture of shared values and identities evolved over time, a concept developed at length by Herder. Herder believed that all national cultures shared a common *Humanität*—or basic human nature—but that the potential of that basic humanity was so copious that each national culture was a unique expression of it. National cultures did share a common moral ground but expressed it in distinct ways.

Probably the major philosophical difference between the Greek Idealists, like Plato and Aristotle, and modern nationalist Idealists, like Herder and Hegel, lies in their differing views of time and history. The classical Idealism of Plato and Aristotle is essentially static. The actual embodiment of ideals may vary according to the circumstances in which they are nurtured. But, the ideal forms behind these embodiments do not change. By contrast, modern nationalists, deeply influenced by Romanticism, add a dynamic evolutionary element to their Idealism. Individuals live out their lives within their genetic possibilities, but species also evolve, perhaps through great men who break and recast the human mold. Political forms, themselves following a dialectic logic, also evolve through history. For the Romantic Idealists, in other words, history is the critical dimension for the realization of ideas. Herder sees divine energy in history—*Kraft*—realizing itself through time, discarding old forms or transforming them into new ones in a dialectical process spread out over the centuries.

Hegel sees history as an arena for competing ideas seeking to complete themselves. New ideas generate new ideas in reaction. In due course, clashing opposites unite in a synthesis that is a new beginning, itself a new thesis that generates new opposites. Coleridge's "Idea" of the British Constitution postulates a set of balances within the British polity, evolving dialectically over the centuries. In Hegel's grand vision of Europe's history, political life had evolved dialectically through ancient empires, city states, barbarian feudal kingdoms, and absolute states into constitutional nation states.

The State's Economic Dimension: Mercantilism versus Liberalism

Political theory and economic theory inevitably cover a good deal of common ground. The prescriptions of the one need to be harmonized with those of the other. Plato and Aristotle, for example, spell out the economic conditions conducive to realizing their political ideals. Naturally, they believed that the organization of labor and the economy should be subordinated to the moral and aesthetic ends of the community. The typical European state of the early modern era, however, was not Idealist in the Greek sense or communitarian in any sense. It was typically constructed around a ruler or government and defined by its claim to sovereignty—a monopoly of coercive power over a defined population of subjects. The absolute state's existential preoccupation was sustaining this sovereignty, a goal that required not only irresistible power over its own subjects but adequate power to protect itself against rival states. Such a state was conceived as a remedy to the savage warfare of "all against all," characteristic of later Renaissance Europe as Christian unity disintegrated into merciless sectarian conflict. Subordinating the economy to the needs of the absolute state meant not only keeping the regime adequately armed but the population well fed and happily occupied. Mercantilism was the economic school that grew up to serve these twin needs of the absolute state. Mercantilists counseled rulers to foster industrial and agricultural improvements and to use the state's power to promote a favorable trade balance—the latter to generate the silver and gold needed to hire soldiers. Protected trade was thus a major weapon in the mercantilist armory. Mercantilist preoccupations often led Europe's absolute states into empire building in order to accumulate more resources and control more trade. Mercantilist states were thus often at war, or getting ready for war.

61

The classic theories of international relations spelled out in chapter 3—hegemonic, balance of power, and liberal—were attempts to rationalize or transform the competition among these power-seeking sovereign states. Liberal theory was the most radical. Liberals assumed that conflict among states was unnatural and proposed to end it. Liberal theories were a sort of moral Newtonianism, products of the worldview of the seventeenth- and eighteenth-century Enlightenment. In the liberal universe, political liberty and free economic competition—at home and abroad—were expected to lead to an automatic harmony of interests that maximized welfare and brought universal peace.

Like the later Idealist nationalists, liberals conceived of the state as not merely a band of rulers but as a community of citizens sharing an inclusive consensus. But whereas nationalists, like the Greek Idealists before them, were preoccupied with the difficulty of sustaining consensus—of reconciling freedom with order—liberals tended to take consensus for granted.[9] Their focus was on individual liberty and initiative rather than on communitarian solidarity. Thus, as chapter 4 observes, liberals and nationalists were uneasy bedfellows. Nationalists soon began to accuse liberals of trying to base society on egoism and greed. The free market, nationalists noted, is designed to produce losers as well as winners, at least in the short run. Whereas liberals celebrated competition, communitarian nationalists noted the inegalitarian and socially divisive consequences of unfettered capitalism.

Communitarian Economics

The communitarian nation state naturally called for a similarly communitarian form of economy. Chapter 5 discusses the various communitarian prescriptions for the shortcomings of the free market. These

---

[9] See, for example, John Locke's *Second Treatise on Government* (1689). Locke was intimately involved in the struggles leading up to the Glorious Revolution of 1688 and for urgently practical reasons was concerned with justifying the right of a "people" to dismiss their government when it became unbearably tyrannical. Like Richard Hooker (1554?–1600) before him or Rousseau afterward, Locke used the social contract as the metaphor to justify a government's dismissal. But, unlike Rousseau, Locke was not concerned with the possibility that the "people" themselves might be tyrannical, mistaken, or fragmented.

stretch from Marxism, rejecting both capitalism and the nation state itself, to various socialist, social democratic, or fascist theories that rely on the state to compensate for the market's shortcomings. Assigning the state such an active economic role required something more than classic liberal economics. Communitarian nationalism thus began to socialize liberalism and also to bring about a certain practical revival of mercantilism. This "neomercantilism," like the old mercantilism, sought to structure and manipulate markets for the benefit of the state. But the communitarian nation state had different aims from the absolute state. Moreover, by the nineteenth century, the most successful European nation states—Britain, France, the Low Countries, Switzerland, or the nascent Germany—all had deeply implanted liberal elements that were themselves an integral part of the national consensus. Accordingly, nationalist theorists began to scramble liberal and mercantilist ideas into a variety of mixed formulas. Similarly, liberal economists began to recast the classic doctrines in a more communitarian spirit.[10]

Over the decades, a rich panorama of practical experiments has resulted. Among these is corporatism, a political-economic system that formally organizes certain key groups—employers, workers, and professionals—into corporations or syndicates. Economic decision making is left to regular bargaining among these groups, with the governments participating in varying degrees. Nowadays, many contemporary West European countries manage their economies in a corporatist fashion. Austria, Germany, and Holland are good examples of this "Rhenish capitalism." In the interwar years, Fascists and Nazis also favored corporatist structures, although these generally masked highly authoritarian or totalitarian states, the latter a pathology of nationalism: Idealist political consensus without Idealist political ethics. In the postwar years, Keynesian capitalism provided a liberal model for modifying markets to serve broad communitarian goals; French

---

[10] As discussed in chapter 5, Friedrich List, *The National System of Political Economy* (1840), is a classic German-American blend of neomercantilism and liberalism. In the British tradition, John Stuart Mill, *Principles of Political Economy* (1848) is a major illustration of liberalism modified for communitarian purposes. In many respects, Mill anticipates Keynes.

indicative planning pioneered by Jean Monnet, provided another.[11] In effect, these models reflect differing fusions of liberalism and mercantilism. Both streams of ideas, it seems, still flow strongly and mix together in countless ways.

If there is so much convergence and confusion between modern liberalism and modern mercantilism, why use the term "mercantilist" or "neomercantilist" at all, since, for liberals, it invariably implies a dysfunctional atavism long since exploded by enlightened economics? Why not simply admit—as liberal economists do—that in a fallen world, policymakers are inevitably forced to consider externalities— national defense and power, personal security and stability, or a healthier or more pristine environment? To satisfy liberal economic sensibilities, these noneconomic values merely have to be redefined as market choices with a price—the consumption or efficiency foregone to pursue them. Wherever possible, liberals counsel, these choices should be left to the individual rather than imposed by the government.

I find it philosophically and ethically unsound to describe economic concerns based on communitarian values as externalities. Moreover, I see no reason not to admit that communitarianism implies a certain revival of mercantilism to serve it. The self-conscious use of the term mercantilism seems to me justifiable on simple historical grounds. Using it points up important elements of continuity in Western political thought and practice. Its juxtaposition with liberalism gives a richer and truer picture of our own intellectual and cultural roots—a picture that makes us less likely to fall heedlessly into too uncritical an embrace of either liberal or communitarian values. No doubt, intelligent communitarians are usually somewhat liberal as well as somewhat mercantilist. Nevertheless, there is a not insignificant distinction between a tradition that gives priority to the community and one that gives priority to the market. Each has its own characteristic dangers. These are better controlled if both traditions are out in the open and studied seriously.

---

[11] For a survey of early postwar political-economic models in the West, see, Andrew Shonfield, *Modern Capitalism: The Changing Balance of Public and Private Power* (London: Oxford, 1965). For a more recent influential study, see Michel Albert, *Capitalisme contre capitalisme* (Paris: Seuil, 1991).

SELECTED SOURCES

Romanticism, Nationalism, and the State

For Jean-Jacques Rousseau and his concept of the general will, see Frederick Watkins, ed. and trans., *Political Writings* (New York: Nelson, 1953). See also Stanley Hoffman and David Fidler, eds., *Rousseau on International Relations* (Oxford: Clarendon Press, 1991), book 2. For contrasts, see John Locke, *Second Treatise of Government* (New York: Dutton, 1943), ch. 13, and Alexander Hamilton, John Jay, and James Madison, *The Federalist Papers* (New York: Modern Library, 1937). For Madison's ideas in particular, see especially Paper Number Ten.

For my own early attempts to grasp the links between Romanticism, Idealism, and nationalist theories of the state and of interstate relations, see David P. Calleo, *Coleridge and the Idea of the Modern State* (New Haven: Yale University Press, 1966); for a general discussion of the Romantic worldview in politics, see its ch. 3. For a more recent discussion, see also my essay "Reflections on the Idea of the Nation State," in Charles Kupchan, ed., *Nationalism and Nationalities in the New Europe* (Ithaca: Cornell University Press, 1995). For a discussion of Romanticism as a reaction to and alternative of the Enlightenment, see Paul Johnson, *The Birth of the Modern World Society 1815–1830* (New York: HarperCollins, 1991). For an exploration of the Romantic worldview through the life of one of the leading Romantic artists, see Jacques Barzun, *Berlioz and the Romantic Century* (Boston: Little Brown, 1950). See also his *Classic, Romantic and Modern* (London: Secker & Warburg, 1961). For a fine example of the British neo-Hegelians, in the tradition of Burke and Coleridge, see Bernard Bosanquet, *The Philosophical Theory of the State* (London: Macmillan, 1920). For a discussion of General de Gaulle's philosophical roots, see Paul Marie de la Gorce, *De Gaulle entre deux mondes* (Paris: Fayard, 1964), and David P. Calleo, *Europe's Future*, op. cit., ch. 4; *Britain's Future* (New York: Horizon Press, 1968), and *The Atlantic Fantasy* (Baltimore: Johns Hopkins University Press, 1970).

For a sampling of the wide range of modern writings on the cultural roots of nationalism, see Benedict Anderson, *Imagined Communities* (London: Verso, 1991); Ernest Gellner, *Nationalism* (London:

Weidenfeld & Nicolson, 1997); and Eric Hobsbawm, *Nations and Nationalism since 1780: Programme, Myth, Reality* (Cambridge: Cambridge University Press, 1990). For two classic studies of the roots of the idea of a nation, see Hans Kohn, *The Idea of Nationalism: A Study in Its Origins and Background* (New York: Macmillan, 1944), and Ernest Renan, "Qu'est que c'est une nation?" reprinted in *Qu'est-ce que c'est une nation? et autres écrits politiques* (Paris: Imprimerie Nationale, 1996).

The hegemonic version of nationalist thought, tied up with Social Darwinism, is discussed, for the Anglo-Saxon case, by Richard Hofstadter, *Social Darwinism in American Thought* (Boston: Beacon Press, 1944), ch. 10. For a noted German nationalist historian with Social Darwinist tendencies, see Heinrich von Treitschke (1834–1896), *History of Germany in the 19th Century*, trans. Eden and Cedar Paul (London: Jarrold, 1915).

Liberal Nationalism: Herder's Garden of Nations

For a discussion of Herder and his philosophy, see Robert R. Ergang, *Herder and the Foundations of German Nationalism* (New York: Columbia University Press, 1931); Isaiah Berlin, *Vico and Herder: Two Studies in the History of Ideas* (New York: Viking Press, 1976); and also David P. Calleo, "Reflections on the Idea of the Nation State" in Charles Kupchan, ed., *Nationalism and Nationalities in the New Europe*, op. cit.

For reactions against "free trade imperialism," see the writings of Bernard Semmel, in particular *The Rise of Free Trade Imperialism* (Cambridge: Cambridge University Press, 1970) and *The Liberal Ideal and the Demons of Empire: Theories of Imperialism from Adam Smith to Lenin* (Baltimore: Johns Hopkins University Press, 1993).

The Nation State and Capitalism

FOR THE NATIONALIST communitarian, a free society requires not only liberty but also a nurturing community. Liberty alone provides only a mockery of individual freedom unless coupled with economic opportunity and a humane standard of living. Unregulated capitalism is by nature inclined toward inequality and cyclical instability. The capitalist free market, without political oversight, cannot be counted on to provide the economic needs of the Idealist nation state. Idealist nationalism thus provided new grounds for state interference in the economy. One result was a new kind of liberalism, trying to incorporate communitarian values. Another was a reconstituted mercantilism—broad and not oriented toward the absolute state's need to accumulate gold to finance wars, but toward the nation state's communitarian political, social and economic agenda.[1]

DESTABILIZING CAPITALISM

The view that capitalist market economies grow progressively unstable and accelerate class conflict was already commonplace by the early nineteenth century, and not only among communitarian nationalists. No one expressed it more directly than capitalism's own great analyst and apologist of the time, David Ricardo (1772–1823). Ricardo, turning liberal economics into the "gloomy science," concluded that capitalism was bound by an "iron law of wages" and would ultimately fall into stagnation, punctuated by frequent crises. Single-minded pursuit of economic efficiency, including free trade, was Ricardo's only remedy, but one that would, he thought, only postpone capitalism's unhappy dénouement. State interference was bound to make matters worse. Not surprisingly, nationalist communitarians

[1] For a more extended definition of these terms, see the appendix at the end of chapter 4.

67

often objected strongly to Ricardo's analysis and almost always to his prescriptions of laissez-faire. Ricardo's contemporary, the English Romantic poet and conservative political philosopher Samuel Taylor Coleridge (1772–1834), fiercely objected to perceiving all social, economic, and political questions through "the medium of the market." Free enterprise was essential to liberty and social "progression," Coleridge agreed, but was not sufficient for a good society. For that, the "Spirit of Commerce" had to be balanced by the "Spirit of the State." The economic problems of modern society, according to Coleridge, were not the result of scarcity, as Ricardo taught, but of greed—a greed enshrined and sanctified in liberal ideology. For Coleridge, economic, social, and cultural balance were all closely entwined. Like Plato and Aristotle, Coleridge saw the ideal state as a partnership of citizens pursuing a good life. To be a man required being a citizen, and his good state was meant to be the ideal environment, given the time and place, for rearing good men. A few decades later, the Italian nationalist Giuseppe Mazzini (1805–1872), otherwise faithfully mirroring Herder's vision of peaceful national coexistence, was also preoccupied with the dangers to national solidarity of the irresponsible and disruptive "egoism" of laissez-faire. Nationalist sentiments like these, from left or right, are at the root of the modern welfare state.

This tension between the values of nationalist communitarianism and capitalist efficiency continues to preoccupy modern European politics, no less today than in former times. Undoubtedly, capitalism has created the wealth that makes contemporary Europe's welfare states possible. But it is also true that capitalism's restless economic dynamism periodically threatens to undermine the social, cultural, and political ties that modern states also require. The logic of capitalism implies free trade and the global mobility of factors of production. The logic of nation states implies protecting national self-determination and social solidarity. Partisans of one logic naturally consider the other obsolescent and dysfunctional. Enthusiasts of global capitalism, highly conscious of today's enlarged possibilities for efficiencies of production and marketing, see less and less reason to tolerate political goals that obstruct those possibilities—goals like preserving job security or traditional communities. Communitarian nationalists, giving their priority to national solidarity or perhaps power, see no need to endure the social inequalities and disruptions of raw capitalism, given today's greatly increased wealth and technocratic capacity. Nor are nationalists disposed to forgo their own nation's technological development merely because others have a head start and advanced products can be purchased more cheaply abroad. The conflicting sentiments ebb and flow with circumstances. When capitalism is booming, efforts to curb its wayward vitality are widely resented. When it enters one of its periodic crises, giant firms, no less than ordinary citizens, seek refuge in their nation states. Similarly, when capitalism is robust, nationalists are eager to channel its benefits. But when it is weak, the state is undermined and nationalists grow eager to foster enterprise and entrepreneurship.

POSTWAR EUROPEAN SOLUTIONS

Modern European theorists have made the links between nation states and their economies a rich field for speculation, and their ideas have helped to generate a series of diverse national experiments. For our purposes, the visions of four theorists seem particularly appropriate: Friedrich List and Karl Marx from the nineteenth century and John Maynard Keynes and Friedrich von Hayek from the twentieth. Each of the four confronted the relationship between the modern nation state and the modern market economy head on. Each developed a distinct resolution that became an archetype for policymaking after World War II.

FRIEDRICH LIST: NATIONALIST CAPITALISM

Friedrich List (1789–1846) was a German liberal nationalist, deeply imbued with the Idealist view of reality that returned to fashion with Romanticism. In his active and varied career, he was a newspaper editor, a propagandist for customs unions, an entrepreneur who developed a coal mine, and a visionary railroad promoter. Some of his formative years were spent in the United States, where he supported the protectionist demands of the Pennsylvania manufacturers and was much influenced by Hamiltonian ideas of national development.[2] List is famous, above all, for his nationalist critique of Adam Smith's celebrated concept of the "division of labor." It is not merely the division of labor that makes the modern economy possible, List taught, but the "union of labor"—the "confederation or union of various energies, intelligences, and powers on behalf of a common production."[3] An efficient union of labor depends on being situated in a cultural community conducive to it, in other words, in a nation with broadly shared cultural and moral values that foster cooperation. Linked to these values are many of a society's nonmaterial elements: culture, morality, communication, and fellowship, together with human rights, laws, politics, and national security. To grasp the influence of such immaterial elements as liberty of thought and conscience on the productive force of nations, List suggested reading "the history of England and then that of Spain."[4] A rich civic culture had made England durably prosperous, while the lack of such a culture had left Spain poor, despite the huge wealth that had passed through Spanish hands. List sharply criticized Smith and his followers for their "materialism"—for depicting mental forces as mere by-products of material circumstances. Accordingly, List defended spending for education, the arts, justice, or defense not only for aesthetic, moral, or military reasons but also for the sake of the economy's efficiency. Such expenditures were "consumption of present values" to nourish "future productive powers." He ridiculed the view of economic development that led Smith to count such expenditures as subtractions from economic values. The causes of idleness and wealth among men could not be explained merely by a study of their limbs and other body parts, while one ignored "the spirit which animates the individuals, the social

[2] Alexander Hamilton (1755–1804), Secretary of the Treasury in Washington's cabinet. His proposals for national development are laid out most clearly in his *Report on Manufactures*, submitted to the House of Representatives on December 5, 1791. Reprinted by the U.S. Department of the Treasury as *Report of the Secretary of the Treasury on the Subject of Manufactures* (Elmsford, NY: Maxwell Reprint, 1970).

[3] Friedrich List, *The National System of Political Economy* (New York: Augustus M. Kelley, 1966; originally published 1841), pp. 149–150.

[4] Ibid., p. 139.

order which renders their energy fruitful, and the powers of nature which they are in a position to make use of."[5]

List used his Idealist, communitarian analysis of production to defend selective forms of protectionism—as the means to nurture national productive powers not yet ready to compete in an open market. List conceded that free trade was more efficient in the short run, the best way to maximize "exchangeable values" for present consumption. But long-term economic growth required a diverse and balanced economy—including manufacturing. Such an economy was essential for the nation's continuing cultural, social, and political development, which was essential, in turn, for its continuing economic development. Where a nation was not yet adequately developed, free trade could impede balanced and symbiotic political and economic growth. In his own time, List opposed free trade as a policy for Germany or the United States on such neomercantilist grounds. Neither country, he believed, was ready to compete openly with Britain. Under such circumstances, List thought, free trade would ensure permanent British commercial domination and was being promoted by the British for that reason.

List, however, was also keenly aware of the interdependence of nation states, and ardently in favor of international cooperation. A state, he thought, should respect the right of its neighbors to achieve the same balanced development that it should be seeking for itself. And once a nation's economy had developed, it should adopt free trade—as a discipline to maintain its economic prowess as well as to keep its national society open and liberal. In effect, List tried to modify liberal free trade into a sort of balance-of-power theory—a pluralist doctrine of fair play, both among equally developed nation states and between developed and developing states.

List sensed that international political economic competition would be highly dynamic in the future. Ultimately, Europe's nation states, drawn together around a unified Germany, Holland, Belgium, and Switzerland, would form a confederal customs union to balance Britain's global hegemony. He believed the nascent American economy

---

[5] Ibid., p. 136.

would derive many advantages from its large-scale economic, political, and cultural integration. To balance the United States, Britain would be forced to join Europe.

In both world wars, German apologists used the Listian notion of a global balance as a rationale for their geopolitical showdown with Britain and the rest of Europe. Uniting Europe under their hegemony, they argued, was necessary to create a counterbalance in the world to Britain and the United States. Today's European Union, led by France and Germany together, embodies the project in a more authentically Listian form.

MARX AND LENIN: SELF-DESTRUCTIVE CAPITALISM

List died in 1846—two years before Karl Marx (1818–1883) and Friedrich Engels (1820–1895) issued their *Communist Manifesto*. Few writings have ever expressed as vividly the communitarian critique of unregulated global capitalism:

> [The bourgeoisie] has left no other bond between man and man than naked self-interest, than callous "cash-payment." It has drowned the most heavenly excesses of religious fervor, of chivalrous enthusiasm, of philistine sentimentalism, in its icy water of egotistical calculation. It has resolved personal worth into exchange value, and in place of the numberless indefeasible chartered freedoms, has set up that single, unconscionable freedom—Free Trade. In one word, for exploitation, veiled by religious and political illusions, it has substituted naked, shameless, direct, brutal exploitation.[6]

Marx's materialist philosophy, like that of Smith and Ricardo, subordinated politics to economics and thereby denied List his nationalist remedy—that the nation state, by asserting the countervailing values of national fellowship and solidarity, could reform the faults of capitalism. So long as capitalism remained the prevailing economic form, Marx argued, national politics and culture would only reflect bourgeois dominance. Since the state was merely the "executive commit-

[6] Karl Marx and Friedrich Engels, *The Manifesto of the Communist Party* (New York: International Publishers, 1937; originally published 1848), p. 11.

tee" of the bourgeoisie, no genuine national community was possible. Only after a revolution had abolished private property and social classes could the general interest of the community emerge. The traditional state would then "wither away," and war among states would come to an end.[7] Capitalism's own fall was inevitable, Marx argued, because as a system it was not only unjust but unstable—so unstable and crisis-prone that it would ultimately self-destruct. By amassing too much capital in too few hands, it stunted demand and atrophied profits. Disaffected have-nots grew progressively more numerous, while the shrinking number of capitalists, drowning in surplus capital and therefore condemned to low returns from normal enterprise, entrapped themselves in desperate speculation.[8]

Lenin (1870–1924), Marx's avowed disciple and founder of the Soviet Union, was inspired by World War I to provide Marxists with a more elaborate theory of international relations.[9] In an economy where monopoly capitalism was dominant, a shrinking capitalist minority accumulated excessive capital and thereby inhibited the growth of domestic demand. Reasonable profits could no longer be earned from investments at home. Investors turned inexorably to speculative schemes in relatively underdeveloped parts of the world. High profits from exploiting labor abroad, moreover, could be used to buy off significant parts of the society and workforce at home. National states, captive to their cliques of capitalist monopolists, competed viciously

[7] "In proportion as the exploitation of one individual by another is put an end to, the exploitation of one nation by another will also be put an end to. In proportion as the antagonism between classes within the nation vanishes, the hostility of one nation to another will come to an end." Karl Marx and Friedrich Engels, ibid., p. 45.

[8] In various writings, Marx also stresses capitalism's "transformation problem" as an explanation for its declining profits and instability. The use of labor-saving machinery, while it augments the "reserve army of the unemployed" and thus keeps down wages, also, by reducing the use of labor, simultaneously reduces the entrepreneur's capacity to garner "surplus value" (what labor produces over its own cost)—which Marx believed is the only real source of capitalist profit. See Karl Marx, *Capital: A Critical Analysis of Capitalist Production*, ed. Friedrich Engels, trans. Samuel Moore and Edward Aveling (New York: International Publishers, 1967; vol. 1 originally published 1867 and vol. 2 originally published 1885–1894), ch. 25.

[9] V. I. Lenin, *Imperialism, The Highest Stage of Capitalism* (New York: International Publishers, 1939; originally published 1917).

for imperial territory. As Lenin read the history of the times, mature capitalist states that had already acquired empires, like Britain, clashed with late-developing capitalist states that now needed empires, like Germany. That was how Lenin explained World War I. The only cure, Lenin believed, was to get rid of capitalism. With luck, war would catalyze the revolutions that would do so.

After World War II, Marxist ideas were powerfully influential far beyond the Soviet Union and China, where they ostensibly formed the official state ideology. Indeed, they enjoyed an almost hegemonic ascendancy over large segments of the intellectual establishments of the West. The Soviet Union's ignominious decay in the later twentieth century has collapsed Marx's popular appeal for a time but may well strengthen it in the longer term. The Soviet Union, after all, was an odious caricature of Marxist principles. In many ways, its very existence shielded postwar Western capitalism. Now that the terrible Soviet experiment is gone, it is easier to appreciate why Marxism exercised so powerful an appeal in the past and to reflect more soberly on its possible relevance for the future. Marx's basic idea that capitalism is unstable by its very nature has had wide currency over several generations. In today's circumstances, it does not yet seem ready for the museum of history.

KEYNES: TECHNOCRATIC NATIONALISM

John Maynard Keynes (1883–1946), probably the most influential of twentieth-century economists, agreed with List and Marx that markets might reach results that were undesirable for the national community as a whole, or indeed for the economy itself. According to Keynes, Britain's high unemployment of the 1920s reflected just such a dysfunctional market equilibrium, as did the Great Depression of the 1930s. The national economy had stabilized at a low point because people wanted to save more than entrepreneurs wanted to invest. Left to itself, Keynes decided, the market would not find its way back to full employment. Profits were too anemic to lure entrepreneurs into investing and were unlikely to improve, among other reasons, because labor costs were too high for the existing level of productivity. The root causes were a combination of political, economic, and social factors. Wages, held up by unions and the dole, could not fall low enough to restore profits. High unemployment meant that consumption, despite the dole, was too low. Meanwhile, interest rates, already low, could fall no further because savers would refuse to risk their capital. The dismal deflationary round could continue indefinitely. Only government could break the vicious circle—by directly boosting demand and investment, preferably through spending on public works. In short, the market required enlightened government intervention to work properly.[10]

In his fashion, Keynes was wrestling with the three interdependent paradoxes with which this series of chapters began. His primary concern was with the self-destructive instability of capitalism, which he believed appropriate national macroeconomic manipulation could resolve. But his state-based solution eventually confronted him with our other paradoxes: the tension between national solidarity and global capitalism, as well as between national sovereignty and international interdependence. In his later years particularly, Keynes grew preoccupied with how his interventionist national prescriptions for full employment could be combined with a liberal international order—in other words, how a communitarian national economy could be reconciled with an open and liberal global economy. Like the European "functionalists" after World War II, Keynes looked to international institutions to resolve the tensions between national and global imperatives. As World War II drew to a conclusion, triumphant Americans were insisting on a global economy based on free trade and easily convertible currencies. Keynes struggled with them to create a monetary regime with enough leeway for the national demand management that he prescribed. He imagined a world central bank under technocratic direction—the "Clearing Union" that was his goal for the Bretton Woods Conference in 1944, where he was head of the British delegation. But Keynes had lost his battle before the conference began. The "Bretton Woods system" that emerged did include the International Monetary Fund (IMF) but otherwise fell far short of

[10] See John Maynard Keynes, *The General Theory of Employment Interest and Money* (New York: Harcourt Brace, 1936), in particular ch. 24.

Keynes's hopes. In any event, implementing the Bretton Woods system was delayed until 1958, when it was revived under rather different circumstances, only to collapse and disappear by the early 1970s. As later chapters discuss in detail, the Bretton Woods conundrum—national economic management in a global economy—has continued to bedevil European and American governments throughout the postwar era.

FRIEDRICH VON HAYEK: NATIONALIST PATHOLOGIES AND LIBERAL CURES

Friedrich von Hayek (1899–1992) was an Austrian economist who came westward as a refugee from the shipwreck of the Habsburg empire. He arrived at the London School of Economics in 1930 and at the University of Chicago in 1950. By the end of his life, he was revered as the sage of "neoconservatism" in America and of "Thatcherism" in Britain. Hayek's teachings represent a rejuvenated liberalism, formed in reaction to various pathological varieties of communitarianism. For Hayek, these included not only the Nazi and Soviet totalitarianism that engulfed his old homeland but also postwar inflationary "neo-Keynesianism," along with social democratic welfarism in general. While not equating the West's postwar evils with fascism, Hayek saw them nevertheless linked by a common tendency to endow states and their governments with inflated moral and technocratic pretensions. Inevitably, these led to abuses that threatened not only economic efficiency but political and individual freedom. As a practical matter, Hayek argued, combining communitarian democracy with communitarian welfare inevitably meant spiraling government debt. Given the populist character of Western democracies, politicians could be expected to compete for popular favor by offering more benefits, but without raising the revenue to pay for them, since high taxes were unpopular and, ultimately, self-defeating. Financing the rapidly mounting fiscal deficits almost inevitably meant monetizing them. This led to an accelerating inflation that threatened private capital. Trying to manage that inflation meant heavier and heavier state controls over the economy. Governmental power, mobilized in a corrupted political marketplace, confiscated capital at the same time that it destroyed liberty and economic efficiency.

Hayek's solution, however, was not laissez-faire capitalism. In this respect, he was more a continental than an Anglo-Saxon liberal. Unless there is a strong state to provide a proper legal framework, Hayek taught, neither a free market nor a free society can endure. The principal function of states, according to Hayek, is to enact and enforce clear, efficacious, predictable, and equal rules to govern the market. Hayek also believed it is the state's duty to care for the indigent. At times, Hayek also believed, the state has special responsibility for a stable money supply—the "loose joint" of the market economy.[11] In each of these tasks, however, Hayek set strict limits on the legitimate use of state power. That power had to be rigorously disciplined by respect for individual liberty and property. The state's monetary role, for example, must be exercised in as measured and predictable a fashion as circumstances will allow. And it is critical that the state not stray from enforcing impartial justice, or caring for the helpless, into pursuing "distributive justice," in other words, into reallocating wealth according to socialist ideals. In short, where Marx and Keynes emphasized the destabilizing tendencies of market freedom, Hayek emphasized the dangers of unlimited state power, draped in good intentions and driven by technocratic arrogance.

By the end of the postwar era, Hayek's critique was influential not only among neoliberals, who adopted it wholesale, but also among many communitarian statists, who adopted it selectively. Hayek's prescriptions became the medicine not only for transforming post-Soviet economies but also for treating "Eurosclerosis"—the symptom of West European communitarianism out of control. His teachings were embodied in the European Union's drive to achieve monetary union

---

[11] Friedrich von Hayek, *Constitution of Liberty* (Chicago: University of Chicago Press, 1960), pp. 324ff. In other works, however, Hayek espoused other monetary arrangements—from the gold standard in *Good Money* (London: Institute of Economic Affairs, 1976; revised in 1978) to "competitive money," in *Choice in Currency: A Way to Stop Inflation* (London: Institute of Economic Affairs, 1976).

around the strict fiscal and monetary regime imposed by the Maastricht criteria and the subsequent Stability and Growth Pact.[12] In effect, Hayek was appropriated by continental communitarians—not to abolish the postwar welfare state but to rejuvenate it with a diet.

NEW CHALLENGES FOR OLD IDEAS

In their own ways, List, Marx, Keynes, and Hayek were all major inspirations for the world that developed after World War II. List, Marx, and Keynes were preoccupied with the self-destructive tendencies of capitalism. Marx believed that these tendencies were incurable because the nation state was inevitably the servant of capitalist interests that were ultimately self-destructive. Arguably, Marx's practical contribution to the postwar order was the Soviet Union. Perhaps it is not altogether fanciful also to credit him with the Atlantic Alliance that was formed in reaction. Ironically, the very existence of the Soviet Union helped to rejuvenate Western Europe's nation states and their capitalist economies. It took the Soviet demise for Marx's predictions of capitalist self-destruction to begin regaining some measure of long-term plausibility.[13]

Meanwhile, the spirits of List and Keynes presided over capitalism's postwar nationalist rejuvenation. Both writers could be called neomercantilists. They believed that the functioning of the market should serve the broader purposes of the national community. And they taught that capitalism's failings could be corrected through governmental oversight and national collaboration. List believed in a selective use of commercial protection; Keynes preferred indirect manipulation of the macroeconomy. Both approaches were widely employed in postwar Europe. Each called for strong states, served by skillful and faithful technocrats, imbued with a strong sense of na-

[12] Chapter 11 discusses in detail Maastricht and EMU. Many of the prescriptions embodied in EMU can also be traced to another famous libertarian monetarist of the twentieth century, Milton Friedman. See Milton Friedman, *Capitalism and Freedom* (Chicago: University of Chicago Press, 1962).

[13] See David P. Calleo, "Restarting the Marxist Clock: The Economic Fragility of the West," *World Policy Journal*, vol. 13, no. 2 (Summer 1996).

tional solidarity. Both List and Keynes were internationalists as well as nationalists. Both thought the neomercantilist states they prescribed should be reinforced and harmonized by imaginative new structures for interstate cooperation. A century after his death, List's ideas helped inspire the European Community. Keynes, near the end of his life, negotiated the International Monetary Fund. Hayek's time came later, as the West's communitarian democracies finally began suffering the inflationary blight he had long predicted for them. He provided a diagnosis and what became a popular cure for saving the welfare state from its own worst instincts.

The fusion of communitarian nation states, stabilized welfare capitalism, and a European confederacy has been postwar Europe's great collective achievement. Drawing on ideas and principles we have been discussing in these past four chapters, the postwar order saw benign and highly creative solutions to Europe's traditional problems. These solutions, often embodying quite different lessons from the past, had numerous contradictory tendencies that gradually undermined their efficacy. But their longevity and coexistence was favored by rather special conditions—above all, the common Soviet enemy. Following the collapse of the Soviet Union in 1991, the contradictory pressures within Europe's postwar formulas grew more intense. The next group of chapters explores the rise, disintegration, and continuing dynamism of this postwar order.

SUMMARY: RIVAL LESSONS AND PRESCRIPTIONS

This group of chapters on the living past began by noting three paradoxes that run through modern European history:

- Sovereign nation states are closely interdependent.
- Capitalism grows self-destructive as it develops.
- Nation states and capitalism are both symbiotic and fundamentally antagonistic.

The first half of the twentieth century indicates what happens when these paradoxes cannot be managed successfully. Europe did much better in the century's second half, with a felicitous amalgamation of historic lessons and prescriptions, whose simultaneous application was largely made possible by the Cold War. These lessons and prescriptions applied in the postwar era fall into three sets. The first set deals with Europe's constituent unit, the nation state:

The nation state formula has prevailed almost everywhere in Europe— and spread throughout the world—because it has proved the most successful framework for holding together a pluralistic modern society. According to this nationalist formula, a shared cultural and historical consciousness is needed to sustain a working political consensus. A strong overarching sense of national identity permits a wide degree of individual liberty and social diversity without threatening political and social peace. Democratic states do not flourish when extended beyond such a nationalist consensus.

The second set deals with Europe's nation state system:

Since Europe's state system is inherently and dangerously unstable, some kind of regional superstructure is needed to sustain peace. Since no one European state can maintain a durable hegemony over the others, the superstructure must be provided by a confederacy, perhaps led by a special partnership among Europe's great powers. Otherwise, order must be imported from an external hegemon, in effect, from the United States.

There is a further global corollary to American hegemony in Europe:

American hegemony in Europe implies American hegemony in the world. A confederal Europe with indigenous leadership implies a more balanced global system.

A third set deals with the nation state and capitalism. Here there are two sharply antithetical prescriptive lessons—Marxist and neomercantilist:

The Marxist perspective

Capitalism and nation states are fundamentally antithetical. Capitalism is individualistic and global by nature. Its economic efficiency is hindered by all forms of collectivism—communitarian nationalism as well as Marxist communism. If allowed free rein, global capitalism will eventually render the European nation state obsolete. As capitalism undermines the state, it will grow progressively unstable and self-destructive.

The neomercantilist perspective

The nation state and capitalism are symbiotic. National solidarity requires the growth, prosperity, and opportunity that only capitalism has been able to provide. Capitalism needs the legal, regulatory, macroeconomic, and political framework that only a strong, well-ordered state can provide. Capitalism and the nation state each have excesses that the other is needed to correct. Capitalism's market freedom is a necessary bulwark against the characteristic abuses of state power. Capitalism's intrinsic and ultimately self-destructive instability requires a "neomercantilist" economic role for the state that stabilizes and regulates growth to provide a tolerable degree of economic security and opportunity for all citizens.

The Cold War saw these lessons and their prescriptions embodied in the east and west of Europe, and indeed all around the world. The next group of chapters explores how the rival prescriptions were able to coexist in the Cold War and the legacies that the Cold War has left behind.

SELECTED SOURCES

A number of terms are used at the chapter's beginning that are defined more closely in the appendix to chapter 4. For my analyses of various writers, I have drawn from one or two of their major works.

Destabilizing Capitalism

For David Ricardo, see his *Principles of Political Economy and Taxation* (Amherst, NY: Prometheus Books, 1996; originally published 1819). For Samuel Taylor Coleridge, see *The Collected Works of Samuel Taylor Coleridge, No. 6, Lay Sermons* (1817), ed. R. J. White (Princeton: Princeton University Press, 1972) and No. 10, ed. John Colmer, *On the Constitution of the Church and State According to the Idea of Each* (1829), op. cit., 1976. David P. Calleo, *Coleridge and the Idea of the Modern State* (New Haven: Yale University Press, 1966). For Giuseppe Mazzini, see *The Duties of Man*, trans. E. A. Venturi (London: Chapman & Hall, 1862).

List

For Friedrich List, see *Das nationale System der politischen Oekonomie* (1841), published in English as *The National System of Political Economy* (New York: Augustus M. Kelley, 1966). For List's life, see Margaret E. Hirst, *Life of Friedrich List* (1909) (New York: Augustus M. Kelley, 1965), and William Otto Henderson, *Friedrich List, Economist and Visionary, 1789–1846* (London: F. Cass, 1983).

Marx and Lenin

See Karl Marx and Friedrich Engels, *The Communist Manifesto* (1848) (New York: International Publishers, 1937), and Karl Marx, *Das Kapital: Kritik der politischen Ökonomie* (1867, 1885, 1895), ed. trans. (1887) Samuel Moore and Edward Aveling; ed. Friedrich Engels (Moscow: Progress, 1978).

A lapidary exposition and analysis of Marx's ideas is to be found in Robert L. Heilbroner, *Marxism, For and Against* (New York: Norton, 1980).

V. I. Lenin, *Imperialism, The Highest Stage of Capitalism* (1917) (New York: International Publishers, 1939).

For the idea that the Soviet demise might rejuvenate Marxism, see David P. Calleo, "Restarting the Marxist Clock: The Economic Fragility of the West," *World Policy Journal*, vol. 13, no. 2 (Summer 1996).

Keynes

For Keynes's ideas, see John Maynard Keynes, *Essays in Persuasion* (London: Macmillan, 1931), *A Treatise on Money* (London: Macmillan, 1930), and *The General Theory of Employment, Interest and Money* (London: Macmillan, 1936). I have also drawn heavily on the volumes of Robert J. A. Skidelsky's *John Maynard Keynes: A Biog-*

raphy, in particular volume 2, *The Economist as Savior, 1920–1937* (London: Macmillan, 1992) and volume 3, *Fighting for Britain, 1937–1946* (London: Macmillan, 2000), the latter for Keynes's efforts in the months prior to Bretton Woods to build a world regime able to reconcile global capitalism and discretionary national macroeconomic management. For more on Keynes and Bretton Woods, see Sir Roy Forbes Harrod, *The Life of John Maynard Keynes* (New York: Harcourt, Brace, 1951); Richard Gardner, *Sterling Dollar Diplomacy in Current Perspective: The Origins and Prospects of Our International Economic Order* (New York: Columbia University Press, 1980); and David P. Calleo and Benjamin M. Rowland, *America and the World Political Economy* (Bloomington: Indiana University Press, 1973).

Hayek

My exposition of Hayek's ideas is based on *The Constitution of Liberty* (Chicago: University of Chicago Press, 1960), arguably the most comprehensive and definitive of his major writings. Throughout his long life, his particular views changed on one topic or another. As I note, his prescriptions on monetary matters ranged from reinstating the gold standard to "competitive money." See his *Choice in Currency: A Way to Stop Inflation* (London: Institute of Economic Affairs, 1976) or *Good Money* (London: Institute of Economic Affairs, 1976, 1978). For a comprehensive discussion of Hayek's life and views, see Stephen F. Frowen, ed., *Hayek: Economist and Social Philosopher: A Critical Retrospect* (New York: St. Martin's Press, 1997).

Legacies of the Cold War

To WHAT EXTENT did the postwar era bring fundamental and durable improvements to Europe's state system? To answer requires exploring the basic character and dynamics of Cold War Europe. How was it structured, internally and in its global relations? How did its once highly conflictual parts settle into peaceful and stable cohabitation? And what elements and dynamic forces have survived from that postwar experience?

To get a handle on such questions, theorists of international relations regularly use the concept of a "system." To speak of a system among a group of countries implies a distinct pattern of persistent and coherent relationships, with rules of the game, different roles, and a rough pecking order.[1] Alongside governments, numerous other actors may participate significantly: international organizations, nongovernmental organizations, business firms, labor unions, churches, foundations, universities, the media, political parties, national and international bureaucracies, professional associations, pressure groups of all sorts, networks of friends, and families. Rendering these relationships into a system is a work of the imagination—a paradigm framed by the analyst's eye and constructed in the analyst's mind. The aim is to select, and thus to simplify, in order to find some broad pattern to international relationships, often to facilitate practical policymaking.

To simplify is often to falsify. Any single paradigm is likely to be incomplete and therefore to provide a misleading picture of any real historical situation.[2] Europe's military arrangements during the Cold War, for example, can certainly be described as a "bipolar system."

[1] For a careful theoretical definition of a "system," see Kenneth N. Waltz, *Theory of International Politics* (Reading, MA: Addison-Wesley, 1979), pp. 38–59.

[2] Robert K. Jervis makes this point with considerable force. See his "Complexity and the Analysis of Political and Social Life," *Political Science Quarterly*, vol. 112, no. 4 (1997).

Most European states fell into one of two military alliances confronting each other across the middle of Germany. Each was headed by an external "superpower" that gave "reassurance" by extending nuclear "deterrence" to protect its bloc. Nevertheless, bipolarity does not adequately capture postwar Western Europe's own inner political relationships, its place in the world economy, its overall relations with the United States, or even its relations with the Soviet bloc. In other words, bipolarity is insufficient to describe Europe's broader postwar political and economic networks.[3] But if bipolarity is inadequate, so is any other single systemic paradigm.

The practical solution is to present postwar Europe through a number of overlapping but differentiated paradigms. To proceed in this way is merely to admit the complexity of history and the limitations of our ability to grasp it. Except perhaps in the mind of God, the real world is inevitably an unruly crowd of distinct systems, with only a limping coherence among them. The same observation, of course, may be made about the human mind itself.

---

[3] The Western bloc was certainly not as unified as bipolar imagery sometimes suggests. Even in the military realm, postwar relations among the Western states had strong pluralist characteristics, as evidenced by the independent French and British nuclear deterrents. General de Gaulle was the most outspoken Western leader to challenge bipolarity, in particular by taking France out of NATO, a decision that the United States felt constrained to accommodate. See below, chapter 7. To a much more limited extent, the same broad point about internal challenges to bipolarity can doubtless be made about relations in the Warsaw Pact. See Christopher Jones, *The Military-Political Mechanisms of the Warsaw Pact* (Washington, DC: National Council for Soviet and East European Research, 1980).

The Three Postwar Systems: An Overview

IT SUITS OUR purposes here to see postwar Western Europe living not in one system but in three. The Atlantic Alliance with its American protector formed one—the western half of bipolar Europe. Western Europe's own inner network of relationships organized around the Common Market formed another. And the global economy—a Pax Americana organized initially by the United States but with an increasing role for Western Europe and for Asia—formed a third. To these three, a fourth might be added—a nascent pan-European system developing across the Iron Curtain.

Each system sprang from a different set of political and economic ideals and national aspirations. Liberal Americans, like Franklin Delano Roosevelt, were determined to create a global political economy after World War II. Bipolarity arose as the Soviets brutally extended and insulated their communist system and the West reacted with the Atlantic Alliance. West Europeans created their own system as they transformed their national economies and sought to create some sort of European union.

The link between these postwar projects and the various historical theories, lessons, and national projects discussed in the last group of chapters seems broadly obvious. The Pax Americana resurrected the American fusion of liberal and hegemonic principles embodied in Woodrow Wilson's aborted grand design for global order after World War I. Stalin was inspired by the Marxist-Leninist picture of capitalism as unstable, imperialist, and implacably hostile. The American response to Stalin satisfied the need for a benign hegemon, not only to exclude the Soviets but also to contain the Germans. The ambitions of European states for economic rejuvenation reflected national communitarian lessons refined from interwar and wartime experience. The drive for West European integration reflected not only federalist ideas, some imported from America, but in particular the interwar themes of Franco-German collaboration in Paneuropa, including the notion of a new European place in a global balance of power. Each system embodied a distinct worldview, drawing different lessons from history and a different vision of the future. Each had its own inner logic, dynamism, and evolutionary path. But each also grew up in close company with the others, in criss-crossed relationships, sometimes antagonistic but frequently reinforcing. As a result, it is impossible to tell the story of one without regularly referring to the others.

AMERICA'S GLOBAL SYSTEM

The global system was the first to take institutional form. During World War II, President Roosevelt avoided committing himself to a postwar Atlantic Alliance that would make the United States responsible for managing Europe's security. America's national interest lay, he believed, in building a world system, global rather than transatlantic and liberal rather than anticommunist, a world order to incarnate the Wilsonian lessons. Only this project could restore the world to peace and prosperity, Roosevelt believed, and only the United States could undertake to lead it.[1] Like Wilson, Roosevelt saw American leader-

---

[1] See note 12 below. Roosevelt was too graceful and canny to commit himself to detailed grand designs, in the didactic manner of his secretary of state, Cordell Hull. As a result, many people underestimated Roosevelt's seriousness and determination, not least because of the quicksilver quality of his imagination and conversation. His secretary of the interior, Harold Ickes, once told him: "You are one of the most difficult men to work with that I have ever known." "Because I get too hard at times?" the President asked. "No," Ickes answered, "because you won't talk frankly even with people who are loyal to you. You keep cards close up against your belly. You never put them on the table." Cited in Robert Dallek, *Franklin D. Roosevelt and American Foreign Policy, 1932–1945* (Oxford: Oxford University, 1995), p. vii. In his international views, Roosevelt was influenced not only by Wilson, in whose wartime cabinet he had served, but also by the tough-minded geopolitical school formed around his presidential cousin, Theodore, and his circle of friends (e.g., Admiral Mahan, Henry and Brooks Adams, and Henry Cabot Lodge). De Gaulle, it seems, had no illusions about Roosevelt's ambitions and tough-mindedness. At their meeting in 1944, de Gaulle writes, Roosevelt sketched a "four-power directory—America, Soviet Russia, China and Great Britain [that would] settle the world's problems. I listened to Roosevelt describe his plans to me. As was only human, his will to power cloaked itself in idealism. The President, moreover, did not explain matters as a

ship being exercised through cooperative multilateral institutions. Mindful of Wilson's failure after World War I, Roosevelt cemented the foundations of his global system while World War II was still going on. Well before the war ended, he had the foundations of the United Nations in place—with its Security Council to organize collective security, an International Monetary Fund to manage an integrated monetary system, and a World Bank to promote and coordinate worldwide reconstruction and development. In due course, the General Agreement on Tariffs and Trade (GATT) followed to promote and regulate free trade.

Today, when the fashion is to doubt whether governments can achieve any purposeful end, it is well to recall how much the postwar Pax Americana was the product of deliberate policymaking. Power and ideas blended to produce results on a grand scale. American elites, reflecting on the lessons of the century, concluded that a peaceful and liberal global system was impossible without American leadership, since Europe had grown incapable of managing the world or itself. The time had come for the "American Century."[2] These Wilso-

---

professor setting down principles, nor as a politician who flatters passions and interests. It was by light touches that he sketched in his notions, and so skillfully that it was difficult to contradict this artist, this seducer, in any categorical way. I answered him, nevertheless, that in my opinion his plans risked endangering the Western world." Charles de Gaulle, *The Complete War Memoirs of Charles de Gaulle, 1940–6* (New York: Simon & Schuster, 1964), vol. 2, pp. 269–270. For poignant documentation of how tough Roosevelt could be with Churchill, dependent as Britain was on American help, see Harold D. Langley and Manfred Jonas, eds., *Roosevelt and Churchill: Their Secret Wartime Correspondence* (New York: Saturday Review Press, 1975). Among many excellent studies of Roosevelt, two that I have found particularly useful in capturing his elusive character are John Lamberton Harper, *American Visions of Europe* (Cambridge: Cambridge University Press, 1994), in particular ch. 2, and Ted Morgan, *FDR: A Biography* (New York: Simon & Schuster, 1985). For a moving study of Britain's predicament in the immediate postwar years, see Robert J. A. Skidelsky, *John Maynard Keynes: A Biography*, vol. 3, *Fighting for Britain, 1937–1946* (London: Macmillan, 2000). For my own earlier attempt to spell out the various strands of American globalism, see David P. Calleo and Benjamin M. Rowland, *America and the World Political Economy* (Bloomington: Indiana University Press, 1973), ch. 2.

[2] The title of Henry R. Luce's famous editorial, in *Life*, vol. 10, February 17, 1941, pp. 61–65.

nian ideas were doubtless simplistic, which perhaps was a reason for their efficacy. The postwar world economy is their monument.

EUROPE'S REJUVENATED NATIONS

Europeans emerged from World War II with lessons and visions of their own. They were determined to escape from their vicious inter-war cycle of economic stagnation, misery, social conflict, and repressive politics. They therefore sought a radical upgrading of their national economies and societies. Their ambition was not merely to "recover"—to return to the 1930s—but to transform their economies and political systems to entirely new levels of performance, security, and concord. The key to success, they believed, lay in promoting rapid growth—American-style—while constructing a safety net of welfare for the whole population. Growth would provide prosperity and opportunity for advancement, while welfare would sustain solidarity. Europeans were ready, in short, to apply communitarian and interventionist principles rooted in their nationalist past and reinforced by the lessons of their interwar and wartime experience. Not all these postwar European approaches could be called Keynesian in any strict sense, but all were neomercantilist, as I have defined the term. Most policymakers took for granted that their goals would require substantial state intervention, including tariffs, subsidies, and exchange controls, as well as general macroeconomic policies favorable to growth. Their determination and ultimate success rejuvenated Europe's traditional nation states with fresh legitimacy and power.

World War II also gave rise to a strong European movement, drawing both hegemonic and pluralist lessons from the past. "Good Europeans" differed over whether the new European state system should be "supranational," thereby taking sovereignty away from nation states, or confederal, thereby enhancing the old states and reinforcing their sovereignty. But Europeans on all sides of these issues believed that their states should never again go to war with each other, should cooperate actively to achieve their common economic welfare, and should concert their positions toward the rest of the world. The practical consequence was a new European state system organized around the European Community. The process began formally in 1951, when six continental nation states, with France and Germany at the core, established an ambitious "supranational" European Coal and Steel Community (ECSC), with American support. The next project—to create a European Defense Community—failed in 1954 despite, or perhaps because of, ardent American blessing. In 1958, however, the six states of the ECSC established Euratom and, most important, the European Economic Community (EEC), whose elaborate confederal structure henceforth provided powerful institutional support for a dynamic European system. Under Cold War conditions, the EEC naturally developed its competence primarily in the economic sphere. It nevertheless always had broader political goals that were never forgotten.[3] By the 1960s, the West European system was consolidating rapidly and had begun to recast the global economic system in a more plural form.

CONFLICTING AMERICAN AND EUROPEAN ASPIRATIONS

In the years immediately following World War II, American and European goals seemed in fundamental conflict. Both were haunted by memories of the prewar Depression but drew different lessons from their experiences. American policymakers were determined to reconstitute an open world economy, an essential outlet, they believed, for their country's enormously expanded productive capacity. European leaders were determined to avoid falling back into the domestic stagnation and social conflict of the interwar years. Since the war had amply demonstrated how nation states could mobilize societies for large collective purposes, European leaders expected to use that national political authority to rebuild their economies.

State intervention of the sort Europeans thought necessary for eco-

---

[3] The Schuman Plan, blueprint for the European Coal and Steel Community, for example, was designed to avoid further war between France and Germany by creating a joint authority of France, Germany, Belgium, Italy, Luxembourg, and the Netherlands to control their coal and steel production—a vital component for war-making. See Richard Mayne, *The Recovery of Europe: From Devastation to Unity* (London: Weidenfeld & Nicholson, 1970).

nomic transformation was not easily compatible with the classic free-trade and monetary convertibility being insisted on by the United States. Europeans were fearful that American globalist plans for liberal trade and capital movements would hobble their own national policies for postwar transformation. In effect, Europeans turned toward a Listian view. They saw American globalism as the natural ideology for the top country, trying to deny others the national tools needed to develop into rivals. Fear of America's overwhelming economic prowess also encouraged the Europeans to cooperate with each other—to build a confederal economy to shelter and enhance their resurgent national economies. A bloc, they hoped, might provide collectively the physical scale and cultural space for the big firms, advanced technology, and scientific research needed to allow Europe's nation states to be significant players in world competition with the Americans.

The early postwar American government, its international policies dominated by liberal ideologues, was initially unsympathetic. The 1944 Bretton Woods Conference, set up to determine the future world monetary system, had reflected an early confrontation. As noted in chapter 5, the British delegation, led by Keynes himself, struggled with the Americans to establish a liberal international monetary and commercial regime compatible with the requirements of Europe's transformation. Europeans expected heavy balance-of-payments deficits with the United States, the principal source of the capital goods needed to refashion their ruined economies. If trade deficits forced them to deflate, Europeans feared they would never achieve the rapid growth and full employment to which they aspired. The British felt they would be thrust back into the demoralizing patterns of the 1920s, when deflation to restore the pound had stunted their growth and saddled them with chronic high unemployment. Keynes had proposed a new international monetary system for Bretton Woods, oriented toward growth and full employment. Countries with large export surpluses would have been fined and constrained to expand their own domestic demand. Countries with external deficits would have been financed generously, with credit allocated by a staff of growth-minded technocrats, installed in the newly proposed International Monetary Fund. Keynes's rationale was to permit deficit countries to become more competitive through higher productivity, in other words, to achieve equilibrium through the fruits of investment and growth rather than through deflation and unemployment. In the lengthy negotiations leading up to Bretton Woods, Keynes failed to convince the Americans. A difficult period followed for U.S.-European relations. In 1945, Keynes once more undertook arduous and acrimonious negotiations with the Americans, this time to secure Britain a desperately needed loan. Though he got the loan, its conditions—requiring a convertible pound—greatly undermined its usefulness. Worn out from his efforts, Keynes died shortly thereafter.[4]

Cold War Solutions

By 1947, with the Cold War on the horizon, an inspired transatlantic accommodation was reached through the Marshall Plan. The Americans provided European governments with abundant financing to continue their economic transformation. The United States accepted that Europeans, in the interests of rapid development and regional cooperation, might temporarily discriminate against American currency and goods and in favor of each other. Despite earlier fears of a European "bloc," Americans became staunch promoters of European integration, which they convinced themselves would remain "outward looking." An integrated Europe, as it grew more competitive, should grow more disposed to global free trade. Meanwhile, it would be an easier target for American investment. In the longer term, integration should make Western Europe an indigenous political and perhaps military counterweight to Soviet power, a consideration of increasing importance to those Americans worried about their own geostrategic overextension. In short, Americans came to see a European bloc as an

[4] Churchill's famous Iron Curtain speech, given in Missouri on March 5, 1946, coincided with Britain's urgent loan application, a linkage that elicited considerable sardonic comment at the time. See Richard Gardner, *Sterling Dollar Diplomacy in Current Perspective: The Origins and Prospects of Our International Economic Order* (New York: Columbia University Press, 1980), pp. 237–254. For sources on Keynes's final years, see the references to R. J. A. Skidelsky's biography in the bibliography to chapter 5.

integral step in forming a global Pax Americana, rather than as a rival to it. The collegial habits cultivated in administering the Marshall Plan would, it was hoped, be the model for future relations.

The idea that free trade required a preliminary protectionist phase aimed at producing roughly equal partners was, of course, what Friedrich List had taught in the 1840s, along with his proposal for a European economic confederacy to balance the Americans. In effect, the Marshall Plan introduced a Listian corollary to the classic liberal doctrines of the Pax Americana. It thereby reconciled postwar European and American ambitions and permitted Roosevelt's global grand design to go forward. Americans, in pursuit of their global vision, supported Europeans in pursuit of their national and regional visions. Europeans, in turn, accepted the liberal global system in principle, so long as they were able to approach it in stages, and in a bloc together. The result was a felicitous synergy of enlightened American and European policies. Listian reasoning modified American policy not only for Europe, but toward Japan and "developing" countries as well. The American aim was not, of course, a mercantilist world economy of blocs but a liberal world economy of healthy trading partners. American sensitivity to a weak Europe's needs and aspirations would, it was hoped, lay the foundation for cooperative relations later, when Europe was strong.

Not only was the global system able to move forward thanks to the success of the European system, but the reverse was also true. Participating in the global as well as the bipolar system brought America's European allies many national advantages, among them access to the American market, heavy American investment, and a secure and ample supply of cheap raw materials, including oil. The resulting prosperity and rapid growth made it easier to build a European regional system, while the need to compete with the Americans globally, imposed by membership in the Atlantic system, also provided Europeans with a strong incentive to cooperate among themselves.

The counterpart to America's successful appeasement of its allies was its containment of the Soviet Union. While in 1944 Keynes had failed to secure a system that would provide adequate American credit for Europe's rebuilding, in 1947 the Americans themselves put forward the Marshall Plan. The Cold War had intervened to catalyze American support for Europe's rejuvenation. Thereafter, huge American official and private investment was available to finance Europe's economic transformations. Without the Marshall Plan's dollars and incentives to invest, Europe's postwar recovery was almost certain to be held up by a shortage of dollars. These were needed not only to buy American capital goods, but also to compensate for the collapse in Europeans' export trade, which, exacerbating the weakness of their currencies, crippled their ability to import raw materials.

After the Marshall Plan, the Cold War helped to sustain Western prosperity for the next half century. Arguably, it was the Cold War that eliminated interwar capitalism's fundamental flaw: its tendency to consume too little. Underconsumption was at the heart of Marx's nineteenth-century critique of capitalism, and Keynes's analysis of the interwar Depression had given it fresh credibility. Heavy government spending on arms, welfare, and investment cured capitalism's interwar tendency to absorb less than it could have produced. Instead, production was hard put to keep up with demand. Without the Cold War's political and military competition, the Keynesian remedies would probably never have been adequately applied.[5] When World War II ended, and massive government spending with it, demand was expected to fall sharply and a renewed depression was widely feared. Instead, the ambitious growth and welfare polices of postwar govern-

---

[5] Although Keynes grew increasingly venerated among British and American economists in the 1930s, his prescription to end the Depression—large fiscal deficits to jump-start consumption—was never adequately applied in Britain or the United States until World War II. Nazi Germany was probably the only large country that actually did employ "Keynesian" remedies in the 1930s. Once World War II had started, however, government borrowing quickly absorbed savings in both Britain and the United States, and government spending provided a massive boost to demand. Unemployment vanished and remarkable growth followed, particularly in the United States. Nevertheless, the first impulse in the United States after World War II was to balance the budget. For John Kenneth Galbraith's analysis of the Keynesian policies undertaken by Hitler and Speer, see J. K. Galbraith, *Economics, Peace and Laughter* (Boston: Houghton Mifflin, 1971), ch. 5. For Roosevelt's fiscal policies, see Herbert Stein, *The Fiscal Revolution in America: Policy in Pursuit of Reality* (Washington, DC: AEI Press, 1996), ch. 3.

ments helped to keep up demand and boost investment. And within a few years, the Cold War brought fresh military spending from the United States, with beneficent fallout in Europe and Japan. By the 1950s, Western economies, driven by the demand for both guns and butter, were firmly set on an expansive path.[6] For the most part, capitalist underconsumption became a thing of the past. Ironically, it was the Cold War that guarded capitalism from its Marxist fate; it was the bogus Marxist regime of the Soviet Union that came to the rescue of Western capitalism.

With demand management pumping up national economies to full employment and rapid growth, the liberal global economy of American postwar dreams grew feasible. In 1958, with European economies returning to healthy surplus, the Bretton Woods monetary rules could finally be applied and Europeans made their currencies convertible into dollars.[7] Meanwhile, the GATT had been whittling away at tariffs.[8] Western countries seemed increasingly caught up in the virtuous circle of the old liberal economic models. World trade was accelerating faster even than the rapidly growing economies of Europe. National economies began to meld into a genuinely global economy.[9]

---

[6] The West German economy grew at an average rate of 7.9 percent annually between 1950 and 1960; France at 4.5 percent; Italy at 5.6 percent; the United States at 3.2 percent; and the United Kingdom at 2.8 percent. *Yearbook of National Accounts Statistics 1965* (New York: UN Department of Economic and Social Affairs, 1966), p. 469.

[7] In 1950, Western Europe's collective current account deficit stood at $2.5 billion; by 1965, the same countries enjoyed a collective surplus of $2.5 billion. See Derek H. Aldcroft, *The European Economy 1914–1990* (London: Routledge, 1993), pp. 148–151.

[8] The General Agreement on Tariffs and Trade was established in 1948, and its first major tariff reduction was the Kennedy Round, which began officially in May 1964 and concluded in 1967. It was preceded by six lesser rounds, including the Dillon Round of 1960. See Ernest H. Preeg, *Traders and Diplomats* (Washington, DC: Brookings Institution, 1970), pp. 1–25.

[9] All Western European countries except the UK achieved rates of export growth in excess of 5 percent per annum throughout the 1950s and 1960s, and in the case of Germany and Italy, the rates reached double figures. Trade grew faster than output for the first time, something that had not been the case previously except in the 1930s, and then for quite different reasons. The bulk of the new postwar trade was intra-European, aided by the reduction in trade barriers between the states of Western

"Globalization" was still more dramatic in the monetary field. International investment was already heavy throughout the 1950s; the 1960s saw the start of a giant Eurodollar market, a global capital market free from direct government control. By the 1970s, everyday financial flows in the Eurodollar market dwarfed the currency reserves of all the major countries combined.[10] With capital markets internationalized, big corporations were able to gain new freedom and power in relation to nation states. The global system was also expanding geographically. Japan became a major economic power by the 1960s, its rapid growth ignited by American spending in the Korean War.[11] Fear of communism made the United States solicitous of Japan's domestic prosperity and thus tolerant of Japan's highly successful mercantilist trade practices. In the 1970s, other Asian economies began to grow rapidly through trade. Asia's miracles, like Europe's, benefited from the Cold War. In Asia as in Europe, the Cold War proved the catalyst for those accommodations that reconciled the global Pax Americana with the national aspirations of America's capitalist partners.

STALIN AND THE BIPOLAR SYSTEM

The Cold War also helped global capitalism to sustain its own internal discipline. The increasingly plural distribution of economic power

---

Europe. At the same time, the GATT process helped ensure that trade creation as well as trade diversion took place (i.e., not all the gains in manufactured trade within Europe were at the expense of third parties). Aldcroft, op. cit., p. 151.

[10] See below, chapter 9, note 3, for the Eurodollar market.

[11] The Japanese economy grew at an annual rate of 9.1 percent between 1953 and 1960, compared to a U.S. growth rate of 3.2 percent. However, Japanese per capita GDP did not exceed that of the United States until 1987. *Yearbook of National Accounts Statistics 1965* (New York: UN Department of Economic and Social Affairs, 1966), p. 46, and *National Accounts Statistics: Analysis of Main Aggregates 1988–9* (New York: UN Department of Economic and Social Affairs, 1991), pp. 6–7. For further analysis of early postwar Japanese growth, see Herman Kahn, *The Emerging Japanese Superstate* (Englewood Cliffs, NJ: Prentice Hall, 1970) and David P. Calleo and Benjamin M. Rowland, *America & the World Political Economy* (Bloomington: Indiana University Press, 1973), ch. 8.

naturally threatened to undermine American hegemony and provoke quarreling among the capitalist partners. But thanks to the Soviets, neither Europeans, Americans, nor Japanese could afford to quarrel over economic issues to a point that seriously threatened their military alliance. The need for security restrained not only diplomacy but domestic politics as well. Anticommunist centrists, committed to market capitalism and international free trade, tended to be predominant everywhere. But to avoid social conflict, they favored the welfare and countercyclical policies that kept capitalism popular as well as successful.

The Cold War was so beneficial to West Europeans and Americans alike that it is tempting to suggest that they invented it together. In reality, however, it was Stalin who took the initiative—by occupying several Central European countries to form a broad glacis, ostensibly to protect Russia from yet another Western invasion. Russian military presence in Europe was hardly a novel phenomenon. Russia had been making military excursions westward since the early eighteenth century. Between 1772 and 1795, Russia joined three times with Prussia and twice with Austria to partition Poland. Russia was itself frequently invaded by Western powers, massively on three occasions and significantly on two more, including an Allied incursion from 1918 to 1920. After Napoleon's invasion of 1812 and his subsequent defeat, Russia joined a concert of conservative regimes prepared to intervene throughout Europe to squash new revolutions. As late as 1849, Russian troops were invited into Hungary to suppress popular uprisings. But once their mission was accomplished, the troops withdrew.

Russia's incursion into Central Europe after World War II had a more permanent and menacing character. Nearly everywhere it went, the Red Army remained to establish brutal "satellite" regimes, despite wartime agreements that guaranteed independence and free elections to countries liberated from the Nazis. Within two to three years after Germany's defeat, the Soviet Union had consolidated direct military and political power over the Baltic states, Poland, Czechoslovakia, an Eastern rump of Germany, and much of the Balkans. One variety of totalitarian occupation, the Nazi, had been followed by another, the Soviet.

Many in the West refused to acknowledge Stalin's appropriations.

And many also refused to believe that the Soviets had exhausted their appetite for conquest. The communist coup in Czechoslovakia and the Berlin blockade of 1948 finally prompted the North Atlantic Treaty of 1949. The Korean War in 1950 completed the establishment of an American military protectorate over most of Western Europe, as well as Greece and Turkey. America's desire to reassure Europe was, of course, a key element in its prompt defense of South Korea. In 1955, the Soviets got around to formalizing their own sphere as the Warsaw Pact. By that time, Europe's bipolar system was well established.

Stalin's militant hostility after the war came as a rude shock to American aspirations. It tore away a huge Eurasian chunk from the anticipated liberal world economy. The "loss" of China in 1949 was a further heavy blow for Americans and British alike. Ultimately, the communists also prevailed in Indochina and were powerful in several other Asian nations. In a number of Western countries, most critically in France and Italy, large and indigenous Communist Parties, receiving Soviet support and susceptible to Soviet direction, waged an ideological battle from within. The Messianic and totalitarian character of the Soviet regime encouraged the view that the Cold War was a bipolar global struggle between "capitalism" and "communism"—two ideologically based models for modern political, economic, social, and cultural life.

Over the postwar decades, a great deal of intellectual energy has gone into arguing about the origins of the Cold War. Was the Soviet seizure of Eastern Europe merely a defensive reaction? Did aggressive American economic policies provoke it? Did the Americans welcome the Cold War in order to justify establishing their own hegemony over Western Europe? Something can be said on behalf of each argument. They enrich our understanding of the motives involved, but they do not provide much basis for either justifying the Soviets or blaming the Americans.

After two ferocious German invasions in less than three decades, not to mention the Allied intervention from 1918 to 1920, any Russian regime, paranoid or not, might have been expected to see the advantages of interposing a belt of subservient states. Such a glacis, while highly unpleasant for the countries walled up within it, did not in itself imply a Soviet ambition to occupy Western Europe. Nevertheless, Stalin's glacis was, in itself, a radical westward extension of Russian power. The West could hardly be blamed for reacting strongly against it, nor for arming itself against any further extension. Stalin's defensive strategy might well have been satisfied with a weak, nonaligned Western Europe, its subservience guaranteed by powerful indigenous Communist Parties. But if most West Europeans found such a prospect unappealing, it is difficult to blame them.

Undoubtedly, postwar American ambitions did threaten Stalin's regime. As George Kennan argued at the time, enlisting the Soviets into an open world economy, the Pax Americana of American dreams, was a goal utterly incompatible with the closed, totalitarian nature of the Soviet Union.[12] But while totalitarian aversion to contact with free societies may explain Stalin's behavior, it hardly legitimizes it.

Did the Americans welcome the Cold War as a pretext for making Western Europe a military protectorate? Roosevelt did have great geopolitical ambitions for postwar America, but they were for an indirect global hegemony rather than a direct leading role in Europe. As Roosevelt told Stalin at Yalta, he planned to return American soldiers home from Europe as quickly as possible. Truman's rapid postwar withdrawal and disarmament of American forces followed Roosevelt's long-standing intentions, as well as the basic urges of the American public. To be sure, a few years later, significant elements in America were prompt to embrace the new hegemonic role in Europe, once the Cold War gave it legitimacy. With NATO, the very large political-military establishment created in World War II found a new raison d'être. Numerous scholars, journalists, scientists, clergy, union leaders, and all-purpose intellectuals found a career in the struggle to

---

[12] See George F. Kennan's "Long Telegram" from Moscow and "Mr. X" article, that is, U.S. Department of State, "The Chargé in the Soviet Union to the Secretary of State," February 22, 1946, *Foreign Relations of the United States 1946* (Washington, DC: U.S. Government Printing Office, 1969), vol. 6, pp. 696–709, and Mr. X, "The Sources of Soviet Conduct," *Foreign Affairs*, vol. 25, no. 4 (July 1947), pp. 556–582. For later insights, see George F. Kennan, *Memoirs 1925–50* (Boston: Little, Brown, 1972), esp. ch. 11. For a discussion of Kennan's views, see John Lewis Gaddis, *Strategies of Containment: A Critical Appraisal of Postwar National Security Policy* (New York: Oxford University Press, 1982), and John Lamberton Harper, *American Visions of Europe* (Cambridge: Cambridge University Press, 1994), ch. 3.

defeat West European Communists and their sympathizers. Big economic interests were also involved. Forces for the NATO commitment formed a large chunk of the American defense budget. And the U.S. military migration to Europe doubtless encouraged American firms to follow.

Early American enthusiasm for NATO was tepid, however, by comparison with that of the West Europeans. NATO fitted Britain's long-standing policy of conjuring up the New World "to redress the balance of the Old."[13] NATO seemed the ideal arrangement for keeping "the Americans in, the Germans down and the Russians out."[14] It thus served British interests to fan early Cold War fears in the United States. In NATO, moreover, Britain's military elite occupied a very favorable position. In the 1950s and 1960s, for example, of NATO's fourteen major commands, the Americans held seven, the British six, and the French one.[15] But Britain's longer-range strategic expectations were perennially disappointed. Britain became a nuclear power in 1952, but NATO did not free enough resources to allow Britain to continue playing a major global role. And as the Suez fiasco made clear, the United States could not be counted on to sustain the imperial ambitions of others. Still, the British could see no alternative to their Atlantic strategy, and they redoubled their efforts to be America's most faithful ally.

Surprisingly, given later postwar history, the French were initially as ardent for NATO as the British. The reasons were similar. The French were trying to hang onto their colonial empire. They could not also take major responsibilities for continental defense. Like the Brit-

---

[13] "I have called the New World into existence to redress the balance of the Old," as the then British foreign secretary George Canning said on December 12, 1826, regarding Britain's decision to recognize the former Spanish colonies in Latin America. Needless to say, Canning had something different in mind from American hegemony in Europe. Quoted in Ludwig Dehio, *The Precarious Balance* (New York: Knopf, 1948), p. 174.

[14] Lord Ismay's sardonic view of NATO, quoted in David S. Yost, *NATO Transformed: The Alliance's New Roles in International Security* (Washington, DC: U.S. Institute of Peace Press, 1998), p. 52.

[15] *The Military Balance 1963* (London: International Institute for Strategic Studies, 1962), p. 13.

ish, they also welcomed the bipolar solution to the German problem, although they made much better use of it. But the French drew different lessons from the Suez fiasco. They began not only to develop nuclear weapons of their own, but also to take their distance from the Americans in general, and to intensify their efforts for European integration. Suez also, of course, confirmed all their prejudices about British unreliability.

The Cold War and West European Integration

Aside from its contributions to postwar European economic success, the Cold War also supplied an excellent environment for Western Europe to develop a regional system of its own. A divided and occupied Germany greatly eased and encouraged Franco-German cooperation, while the Soviet appropriation of so much of Central and Eastern Europe removed a traditional source of Franco-German contention. Being able to leave security to NATO under American leadership also allowed Europeans to avoid the dangerous issue of military primacy among themselves.

For France and Italy, the bipolar system also had important domestic consequences. Both countries had large Communist Parties that had resisted the Nazi occupation. Since large segments of the Right had cooperated enthusiastically with the Germans, a radical Leftist ascendancy, led by the Communists and backed by Soviet pressure, seemed a distinct possibility. The Cold War blocked that possibility. The divide between Communists and anti-Communists split the Left, while anti-Communism gave a new unity and respectability to the Right. It also proved an open sesame for abundant American aid to Rightist parties. The consequences were particularly vivid in Italy, where the large Communist Party (PCI) struggled unsuccessfully for decades to shed its pro-Soviet image and the Socialist Party (PSIUP) split in two. With the Left in such disarray, the centrist Christian Democrats remained the major party in every postwar government until the 1990s. In France, where the Gaullist party helped to restore the Right, the Left was divided and out of power from the 1950s until

François Mitterrand's election to the presidency in 1981. By then, the Communists (PCF) had shrunk to a very junior partner.

PAN-EUROPEAN STIRRINGS

By the 1960s, many Western analysts began to think the bipolar division of Europe would last indefinitely, a prospect many endorsed with equanimity. The Berlin Wall, put up in 1961, appeared to stabilize Germany's division. After the Cuban Missile Crisis of 1962, a general tendency toward superpower detente seemed to stabilize nuclear deterrence. As the European Community began intensifying Western integration, attention tended to shift away from breaking down the Iron Curtain. Nevertheless, many far-sighted statesmen—George Kennan, Charles de Gaulle, Konrad Adenauer, and Kurt Schumacher are good examples—had always been skeptical that Europe's bipolar division could last. All thought it unlikely that the German nation would remain split forever, or that a European Community could build itself durably on the presupposition that Germany would remain divided. As de Gaulle saw it, Germany's reunification would be the product of Europe's general reunification, as the two superpower blocs eventually disintegrated. He gave voice to this logic with his attacks on the wartime Yalta Agreement, which he described as a deal negotiated by the superpowers and Britain in the absence of the Europeans.

By the mid-1960s, de Gaulle had decided that it was time to begin developing a pan-European system, and he began pressing his elusive vision of "Europe from the Atlantic to the Urals." Following de Gaulle, however, few French leaders seemed in any hurry to press for pan-European aspirations. But West Germans did begin exploring more intimate relations with their Eastern European neighbors. The initial West German policy, set down by the great postwar chancellor, Konrad Adenauer, declared Germany's division illegitimate, refused to recognize the German Democratic Republic, and tried to prevent other Western states from doing so as well. Given the realities of Soviet military power, Adenauer's position seemed, in practice, to favor the status quo. But German leaders after Adenauer were more conciliatory and therefore more adventurous. By the late 1960s, progress toward superpower detente began to provide cover also for a pan-European detente. Germany's first postwar Social Democratic chancellor, Willy Brandt, launched a new *Ostpolitik* to open up the Eastern countries to Western economic and cultural influence. By the early 1970s, German diplomacy had consummated a round of treaties with Eastern neighbors, including an agreement with the German Democratic Republic.[16] Brandt disavowed any intent to force changes in the bipolar status quo. His actual strategy was to alter the status quo by accepting it formally. Once communication and trade were reopened, he thought time could be expected to do the rest. Trade, heavily financed by West German loans, developed rapidly, and a nascent pan-European political and economic system started to take form.

Both superpowers were drawn into this process for their own ambivalent reasons. The Soviets hoped that access to Western technology would prove a shortcut for their own lagging development. They also hoped concessionary Western trade would help to stabilize the regimes of their East European dependencies, as well as sow dissension among the Western powers. The Americans were eager to stabilize the status quo by improving the diplomatic atmosphere and reducing the arms race. Measures to build mutual confidence would, they hoped, lower the risk of military confrontations. The Nixon administration also hoped the Soviets might help to make America's retreat from Vietnam less humiliating. Americans and Europeans both were eager to promote human rights in the Soviet bloc. East-West economic and political ties proliferated in the 1970s, and the nascent pan-European system developed its own institutions. The "Helsinki Process," with its recurring convocations of the Conference on Security and Cooperation in Europe (CSCE), promoted arms control and trade agreements as well as norms for human rights.

Detente, of course, had its competitive aspects within the West, as

---

[16] By 1972, treaties recognizing the postwar borders and promising nonaggression and cooperation had been signed and ratified with the USSR, Czechoslovakia, Poland, and East Germany. For details, see Keesing's Research Report, *Germany and Eastern Europe since 1945: From the Potsdam Agreement to Chancellor Brandt's "Ostpolitik"* (New York: Scribner's, 1973).

the Soviets were well aware. De Gaulle's initiatives for a "Europe from the Atlantic to the Urals" presupposed not only a disintegrating of the Soviets but also a marginalization of the Americans. The latter were wary of allowing detente to become a pretext for downgrading the Atlantic Alliance. The French, meanwhile, were concerned that Brandt's Ostpolitik might signal a rebirth of German Middle European imperialism. Accordingly, they were determined to cultivate their own special relationship with the Soviets and others.

On balance, although the pan-European system remained relatively undeveloped, it was nevertheless a highly useful complement to the bipolar and European systems. It ameliorated their worst features, but in a fashion that appeared unthreatening to their stability. Pan-European detente helped to normalize relations between the superpowers, allowed West European states more freedom to maneuver, and gave Warsaw Pact countries relief from the terrible claustrophobia that otherwise engulfed them. It protected NATO and the European Community by channeling German ardor for reunification in a peaceful and productive direction. By the mid-1970s, moreover, the limits to any pan-European system grew apparent. Thus, on balance, detente reinforced German allegiance to the West.

In summary, postwar Europe lived in three distinct systems: bipolar, European, and global. Despite the obvious tensions, the three systems were mutually reinforcing in many respects. Their collective equilibrium, however delicate intellectually, was sturdy and resilient in practice. Detente seemed to strengthen rather than undermine that equilibrium.

THE SOVIET COLLAPSE AND THE POSTWAR SYSTEMS

The disintegration of the Soviet Union by 1991 threw Europe's cozy systemic relationships into confusion. Nevertheless, there was more continuity with the past after the Cold War than might have been expected. The global system continued its rapid and troubled evolution, and the West European system reacted vigorously to its new challenges. And while the bipolar system disappeared in its old form, the United States and Russia still weighed heavily on the European scene. Each system has continued to struggle, as before, to impose its perspectives and patterns on the future. Each continues to have its own evolutionary path, inner logic, and dynamic tensions. The new "post–Cold War order" thus seems likely to be more a redefinition and rebalancing of these old systems than a fresh creation. To get some sense of how this rebalancing is likely to proceed requires a deeper look into the postwar evolution of each—the task of the next three chapters.

SELECTED SOURCES

Europe's Rejuvenated Nations

For the various means by which Europe was reconstructed following the war, see Alan S. Milward, *The Reconstruction of Western Europe 1945–51* (Berkeley: University of California Press, 1984). See also his *European Rescue of the Nation State* (Berkeley: University of California Press, 1992). The economic lessons applied by European states are explored in Andrew Shonfield, *Modern Capitalism: The Changing Balance of Private and Public Power* (Oxford: Oxford University Press, 1965). Shonfield emphasizes the differing national approaches. For further studies, see, for example, J. C. R. Dow, *The Management of the British Economy 1945–1960* (Cambridge: Cambridge University Press, 1964); William James Adams, *Restructuring the French Economy* (Washington, DC: Brookings Institution, 1986); and John Lamberton Harper, *America and the Reconstruction of Italy, 1945–1948* (Cambridge: Cambridge University Press, 1986). Europe's postwar recovery was held up by a shortage of dollars with which to buy American goods, especially capital goods, and a collapse in Europeans' export trade, which exacerbated the weakness of their currencies and thus crippled their ability to import raw materials. The Marshall Plan helped by providing dollars and investments, and the Pax Americana favored cheap raw materials. See Derek H. Aldcroft, *The European Economy 1914–1990* (London: Routledge, 1993), pp. 108–121, and also W. W. Rostow, *The World Economy, History and Prospect* (London: University of Texas Press, 1978), pp. 236–238.

For discussion of early European integration, see Richard Mayne, *The Recovery of Europe: From Devastation to Unity* (London: Weidenfeld & Nicholson, 1970). F. Roy Willis analyzed the roots of postwar Franco-German cooperation in *France, Germany and the New Europe, 1945–1967* (Stanford: Stanford University Press, 1968), while François Duchêne explored the role of the architect of the European Coal & Steel Community (ECSC) in *Jean Monnet: The First Statesman of Interdependence* (New York: Norton, 1994). For my own analysis of the different strands of the European movement, see David P. Calleo, *Europe's Future: The Grand Alternatives* (New York: Horizon Press, 1965). On the Schuman plan as an economic model, see Louis Lister, *Europe's Coal and Steel Community* (New York: Twentieth Century Fund, 1960), and William Diebold, Jr., *The Schuman Plan: A Study in Economic Cooperation* (New York: Praeger, Council on Foreign Relations, 1959). For American support and British opposition—based on differing reactions to the political motives behind the plan—see Dean Acheson, *Present at the Creation* (New York: Norton, 1969), pp. 382–389, and Hugo Young, *This Blessed Plot* (London: Macmillan, 1998), pp. 44–70.

Conflicting American and European Aspirations

For the clash of American and European visions of their postwar futures, see Harold van Buren Cleveland, *The Atlantic Idea and Its European Rivals* (New York: McGraw-Hill, 1966). For American desires to retrench after World War II, see Herbert Stein, *Presidential Economics: The Making of Economic Policy in America from Roosevelt to Reagan and Beyond* (Washington, DC: American Enterprise Institute, 1988).

For the formation of postwar global financial institutions, see Richard Gardner, *Sterling Dollar Diplomacy in Current Perspective: The Origins and Prospects of Our International Economic Order* (New York: Columbia University Press, 1980), ch. 12, and Susan Strange, "International Monetary Relations," in Andrew Shonfield, ed., *International Economic Relations of the Western World 1959–1971* (Oxford: Oxford University Press, 1976), vol. 1. For my own analysis, see David P. Calleo and Benjamin M. Rowland, *America and the World Political Economy* (Bloomington: Indiana University Press, 1973), pp. 88–89.

For Keynes's postwar views and negotiations, see Sir Roy Harrod, *The Life of John Maynard Keynes* (New York: St. Martin's Press, 1963), pp. 621–693; Richard Gardner, *Sterling Dollar Diplomacy in Current Perspective: The Origins and Prospects of Our International Economic Order* (New York: Columbia University Press, 1980) and especially Robert J. A. Skidelsky, *John Maynard Keynes*, vol. 3, *Fighting for Britain, 1937–1946* (London: Macmillan, 2000), which provides a definitive picture of Keynes's role in his last years and of Anglo-American economic relations in that period. For Skidelsky's earlier studies of Keynes and the failure to apply Keynesian views before the war, see Robert J. A. Skidelsky, *John Maynard Keynes*, vol. 1, *Hopes Betrayed 1883–1920* (London: Macmillan, 1983), and *John Maynard Keynes*, vol. 2, *The Economist as Savior 1920–1937* (London: Macmillan, 1992); also see *Politicians and the Slump: The Labour Government of 1921–1931* (London: Macmillan, 1967).

Cold War Solutions

For Listian views in American policy toward Japan, see David P. Calleo and Benjamin M. Rowland, *America in the World Political Economy* (Bloomington: Indiana University Press, 1973), ch. 8. Studies of the resultant Japanese and Asian growth abound. For a start, see The World Bank, *The East Asian Miracle* (New York: Oxford University Press, 1993), which stresses the role of the public sector in guiding the growth of Asian tigers.

Stalin and the Bipolar System

For histories of the Cold War, see, for example, Martin Walker, *The Cold War: A History* (New York: Holt, 1995), and John Lewis Gaddis, *The Long Peace: Inquiries into the History of the Cold War* (New York: Oxford University Press, 1987). For the start of Cold War, see John Lewis Gaddis, *We Now Know* (Oxford: Oxford University Press, 1997); Louis Halle, *The Cold War as History* (New York:

Harper & Row, 1967); and Vojtech Mastny, *The Cold War and Soviet Insecurity: The Stalin Years* (Oxford: Oxford University Press, 1996). For Stalin's motives, see Milovan Djilas, *Conversations with Stalin* (New York: Harcourt, Brace, 1967). For Russian interventions in eastern Europe in the nineteenth century, see Edward C. Thaden, *Russia's Western Borderlands, 1710–1870* (Princeton: Princeton University Press, 1984).

For Britain's continuing enthusiasm for NATO, see Nicholas Henderson, *The Birth of NATO* (Boulder, CO: Westview Press, 1983). For Ernest Bevin's role, see Allan Bullock, *Ernest Bevin: Foreign Secretary 1945–1951* (London: Heinemann, 1983). For general studies of postwar British foreign policy, including reactions to the Suez crisis, the event that finally marked Britain's passing as a global great power, see F. S. Northedge, *British Foreign Policy: The Process of Adjustment* (London: Praeger, 1962), and Herbert Nicholas, *Britain and the United States* (Baltimore: Johns Hopkins University Press, 1963). For my own analysis of Britain's changing fortunes, see David P. Calleo, *Britain's Future* (New York: Horizon Press, 1968).

For early French enthusiasm for NATO and subsequent disappointment, particularly after Suez, see Michael M. Harrison, *The Reluctant Ally: France and Atlantic Security* (Baltimore: Johns Hopkins University Press, 1981).

For early German attitudes toward NATO, see Wolfram Hanrieder, *Germany, America, Europe: Forty Years of German Foreign Policy* (New Haven: Yale University Press, 1989).

For an authoritative Italian view of NATO, see Sergio Romano, "Italy and the New Europe," in David P. Calleo and Philip H. Gordon, eds., *From the Atlantic to the Urals: National Perspectives on the New Europe* (Arlington, VA: Seven Locks Press, 1992).

The Cold War and West European Integration

For the domestic tensions engendered by the Cold War in France and Italy, see H. Machin, ed., *National Communism in Western Europe* (London: Methuen, 1983). For the later history of American fears of the Left in Europe, see Dana Allin, *Cold War Illusions* (London: Macmillan, 1995), ch. 5.

Pan-European Stirrings

George Kennan's views on the future of Europe are best expressed in his Reith Lectures, to be found in his *Memoirs* (Boston: Little, Brown, 1972), vol. 2, ch. 10. De Gaulle's attacks on Yalta and his formulation of the concept of "Europe from the Atlantic to the Urals" can be traced in his speeches and his memoirs and are summarized in volume 3 of his *War Memoirs* (New York: Simon & Schuster, 1960). The rationale behind Willy Brandt's Ostpolitik can be found in his *My Life in Politics* (New York: Viking, 1992) and is discussed by Wolfram Hanrieder in his *Germany, Europe, America: Forty Years of German Foreign Policy* (New Haven: Yale University Press, 1989). See also Walter F. Hahn, "West Germany's Ostpolitik: The Grand Design of Egon Bahr," *Orbis*, vol. 16, no. 4 (Winter, 1973), pp. 859–881. I have provided my own analysis, along with a bibliographical essay, in David P. Calleo, *The German Problem Reconsidered* (Cambridge: Cambridge University Press, 1978), ch. 8.

For the American reaction to such pan-European stirrings in the Johnson administration, see, in particular, Under Secretary Eugene V. Rostow's speeches given on November 24, 1966, to the Ministerial Council of the Organization for Economic Cooperation and Development in Paris, *Department of State Bulletin*, vol. 56, no. 1436 (January 2, 1967), p. 24 and on September 11, 1967, to the Atlantic Treaty Association in Luxembourg, Department of State Bulletin, vol. 57, no. 1475 (October 2, 1967). For the skeptical position adopted toward *Ostpolitik* in the Nixon administration, see Henry Kissinger, *The White House Years* (Boston: Little, Brown, 1979), pp. 408–412, 529–530. The logical conclusion of these pan-European stirrings was the development of a more structured system of negotiations within Europe and between the superpowers. For a discussion of the Conference on Security and Cooperation in Europe (CSCE) process, see Jonathan Dean, *Watershed in Europe: Dismantling the East-West Military Confrontation* (Lexington, MA: Lexington Books, 1987). For the Strategic Arms Limitation Treaty (SALT) process, see John Newhouse, *Cold Dawn: The Story of SALT* (New York: Holt Rinehart & Winston, 1973).

Bipolar Europe

IF ANY SINGLE system appeared to characterize the postwar era, it was the Cold War's bipolar system. It defined strategic relations in Europe and globally, and it also set the framework for Western Europe's political-economic integration. As we shall see, it has left a troubling legacy—an America that is too strong, a Russia that is too weak, and a Europe that is too dependent.

The bipolar system was initially a Russian creation. The Soviet Union's victory in World War II began it, and the Soviet Union's collapse in 1991 ended it. For both the Russians and the Americans, the bipolar system embodied a great expansion of their traditional geopolitical roles. Both showed signs of overextension during the Cold War. When the weaker Soviet pole did finally disintegrate, it seemed a great victory for the West. But it was also a great shock, above all for Western Europe, whose geopolitical situation grew more complex.

This paradox was not altogether unanticipated. The last chapter noted how comfortable Western governments were with many aspects of the bipolar status quo. Even in the heyday of the Cold War, distinguished analysts used to argue that few in power really wanted things to change. It seemed easy enough to discount the official rhetoric to the contrary. In the early 1950s, for example, President Eisenhower's Secretary of State, John Foster Dulles, talked boldly of "rolling back" the Soviet tide from Eastern Europe. But when the opportunity seemingly presented itself with the Hungarian uprising in 1956, the administration appeared more interested in consolidating the Western bloc than in breaking up its Eastern rival. Similarly, General de Gaulle seldom lost an opportunity to rail against the Yalta Agreement—the occasion when, as he saw it, Europe's division had been agreed to by the superpowers, with Britain acquiescing and France excluded. To defy the bipolar hegemonies that had resulted, de Gaulle built an independent nuclear deterrent, left NATO, criticized American policies around the globe, and institutionalized a Franco-German partnership that implied a challenge to American primacy in Western Europe. Nevertheless, many analysts found it hard to take de Gaulle's revisionist intentions seriously, since the bipolar system gave France the closest thing to complete and automatic security ever enjoyed in its long history as a nation state. De Gaulle was widely thought merely to be maneuvering to improve France's position within the Atlantic Alliance, rather than intending to pull down a structure so very favorable to French interests.

In the 1970s, Germany's Ostpolitik under Willy Brandt seemed a more genuine assault on bipolarity. The Germans, divided and occupied, had plausible reasons for serious dissatisfaction. Their new Ostpolitik caused considerable unease in other Western capitals, but most analysts remained confident that the Soviet Union was powerful and brutal enough to sustain Germany's division indefinitely. And however Machiavellian the German strategy may have been in its revisionist intentions, it could be rationalized as, de facto, an acceptance of the status quo. Brandt's policies, improving the diplomatic atmosphere and mitigating the effects of Soviet tyranny, seemed merely to make the bipolar system safer and more stable.

AMERICAN REVISIONISM: NATO's STRATEGIC PARADIGM

Perhaps the most significant Western revisionism toward the bipolar order originated within the United States itself. American dissatisfaction stemmed less from impatience to roll back the Soviets than from the dilemmas of extending nuclear deterrence to Western Europe. The strategic problems, it seemed, could be resolved only by greatly augmenting the financial costs. As it was widely assumed that the Soviets enjoyed a clear superiority in conventional forces, America's deterrent strategy relied, sooner or later, on a "first use" of nuclear weapons. So long as the United States held a monopoly of such weapons, or at least of the capacity to deliver them effectively, a first-use strategy was credible. But as the Soviets developed a nuclear force capable of retaliating directly against the continental United States, American strategic planners grew more and more anxious, and their strategy began to lose credibility, above all among themselves. The less credible the deterrent, they reasoned, the greater the risk that it would be challenged, particularly if the stakes appeared to be limited to some incremental Soviet gain, seized with only conventional forces. The anomalous Western position in Berlin was an obvious example. What would the United States do if the Soviets began to take the city with conventional forces? Was it credible, planners asked themselves, that the United States would respond by initiating a nuclear war that would threaten the survival of America's own major cities? The American solution was to give its policy more options—by building up conventional forces and deploying "battlefield" and "theater" nuclear weapons, while also tightening American control over "escalation," meaning the choice of options.

The American search for military options made West European governments apprehensive and restive. European planners thought their best deterrent strategy was to guarantee that any war starting in Europe would escalate quickly to intercontinental nuclear exchanges. Britain and France developed nuclear forces of their own and claimed they would use them to trigger escalation whether the Americans wished it or not. The more certain the escalation, they reasoned, the less the danger of a war's actually starting. For American planners, however, the more certain the escalation, the greater the risk to the United States. It was in America's vital interest that any war starting in Europe should remain there. It was therefore intolerable to leave the United States with no choice between surrender to Soviet conventional forces and an intercontinental nuclear war.

This basic conflict of interest between the United States and its European allies lay behind most of NATO's recurring strategic debates. The outcome was a series of elaborate transatlantic compromises. The British and French, with differing degrees of reluctant U.S. help, achieved their own nuclear forces and went on justifying them as "triggers" to ensure that any European war would rapidly become intercontinental. But NATO's "flexible response" doctrine, proposed in the early 1960s and adopted in 1967, called for substantial conventional forces as well as tactical and regional nuclear forces, with escalation controlled by a centralized and U.S.-dominated command structure. In other words, NATO's arrangements reflected

America's vital interest in confining escalation to Europe. The utility of the strategy presumably depended on the credibility of the conventional options. That credibility depended on whether the forces were available to carry these options out. The United States accordingly posted some 300,000–400,000 of its own soldiers in Europe throughout the Cold War and began insisting by the early 1950s that Germany be rearmed. Nevertheless, NATO's conventional defense continued to have numerous glaring deficiencies. Europeans had little interest in providing enough additional manpower to encourage NATO to rely on conventional deterrence. De Gaulle, of course, opposed flexible response from the start, and NATO could not formally adopt it until France had withdrawn from the integrated military structures in 1966. Ironically, France's defection, by depriving NATO of the secure use of French forces and space, in itself made any serious Western conventional defense problematic. Paradoxically, the large number of American troops stationed in Europe, intended to provide NATO with options for conventional deterrence, reassured Europeans about the reliability of American nuclear deterrence. The United States, Europeans thought, could not allow its several hundred thousand "hostages" to perish without resorting to nuclear defense.

Whatever the military efficacy of flexible response, its economic price was very high—particularly for the United States, which was constrained to keep a large standing army in Europe. Successive American administrations fretted over the high cost. Americans regularly complained about European "free riding" and demanded more "burden sharing." When the Americans abolished the draft and went over to a professional army in 1973, the costs of conventional forces escalated further. By the 1980s, the Pentagon was declaring the NATO commitment responsible for roughly half the defense budget.[1]

---

[1] Throughout the 1980s, NATO costs regularly constituted 40 percent to 60 percent of the U.S. defense budget. In 1981, for instance, the U.S. Defense Department estimated that the cost of forces formally committed to NATO, in Europe or elsewhere, stood at approximately $81.1 billion, or around 51 percent of the total defense budget for 1981. See Department of Defense Administration, *Department of Defense Estimates* (1981). For an overview of U.S. spending on NATO, see Department of Defense Administration, *Department of Defense Estimates* (1990), p. 165. For a more general analysis of defense expenditures by country, see World Development Indicators, *Defense Expenditures and Trade in Arms*, 1992, p. 45.

TABLE 7.1
U.S. Defense Expenditures and Overall Budget Deficits
(in billions of 1982 U.S. dollars)

Year	1980	1985
Defense expenditures	164.0	230.0
Budget deficit	− 87.3	− 190.6

Source: Historic Tables Budget of the United States Government Fiscal Year 1990
(Washington, DC: United States Government Printing Office, 1989), pp. 128, 129, 20.

Americans were growing preoccupied with budget deficits and debating the linkages between imperial "overstretch" and economic decline. NATO seemed a major illustration of America's inability to maintain a rational balance between strategic commitments, military needs, and fiscal means.

Eventually, these accumulating strategic problems, with their heavy financial consequences, might have provoked a disintegrating crisis in NATO. Certainly the strategic differences over extended deterrence were not any closer to being resolved in the 1980s than in the 1950s or 1960s. Indeed, the Cold War's final decade saw intense interallied disputes over "Euromissiles" and the Reagan administration's Strategic Defense Initiative. Paced by escalating defense spending, American fiscal deficits exploded (see table 7.1). Arguably, the tensions could not have been endured indefinitely, particularly as public opinion grew increasingly alarmed at the outsized and growing budget deficits. Nevertheless, most political and military analysts imagined that nuclear fears, hegemonic pleasures and European quarrels would ensure America's NATO role indefinitely, whatever the fiscal consequences. In any event, Soviet problems, much worse, ended the Cold War before the West's own difficulties grew unmanageable.

THE SOVIET IMPLOSION

As one of the major events of the twentieth century, the collapse of the Soviet Union provides a rich subject for controversy among historians, economists, ideologists, and philosophers of the human condition. The Soviet demise was not the result of any direct foreign intervention but was an internal implosion of the Soviet political and economic system itself. One basic issue is whether that inner collapse was coincidental or systemic, in other words, whether it was the product of a serendipitous convergence of personalities and situations or came from deep inner flaws that undermined the Soviet Union from the start. The obvious answer is both. By the 1980s, many analysts saw the Soviet system suffering from a deep rot, more deadly than the chronic ailments of the West, and likely, sooner or later, to bring abrupt disruptions and discontinuities. Certainly, the disaffection of the "satellites" in Eastern Europe was obvious. Resistance was growing increasingly courageous and costly to suppress—above all, in the largest Soviet "satellite," Poland, which, thanks to its embattled history and fervent Catholicism, had a special moral and institutional relationship with the West. At the same time, the accident of Gorbachev, and arguably also of Reagan and Kohl, helped to precipitate matters. A further question is whether the weakness of the USSR was endemic to the Soviet system itself or arose primarily from the competitive burdens that the Soviets assumed with their bipolar role in the Cold War. Certainly, in any balance of basic economic resources, the Soviets were outweighed by the United States and, indeed, by the West Europeans as well.[2]

My aim here is not to attempt a comprehensive analysis of the Soviet implosion, an enormous subject of its own, but rather to explore the likely consequences for Europe. But the two tasks are not easily separated. Many of those features of political and economic culture that led to the Soviet breakdown are widely seen as still blocking reform in the successor states. Failed national reform, in turn, stands in the way of progress toward any new pan-European system. Analysts have focused on three fundamental Soviet internal weaknesses: the dysfunctional character of the Soviet economic apparatus, the corruption and demoralization of Soviet elites, and the growing centrifugal pressure from the USSR's non-Russian minorities.

---

[2] 1989 GDP (using purchasing power parities) in billions of dollars: United States $4,989.5; Soviet Union $4,122.4; and EEC $4,322.9. OECD, *National Accounts of OECD Countries* (Paris, 1992), p. 241. Measurements of the Soviet GDP were inevitably problematic and during the Cold War were exaggerated high.

THE DYSFUNCTIONAL ECONOMY

Descriptions of the Soviet economy in its late stages are usually so derogatory that it becomes difficult to visualize the superpower that once defeated Nazi Germany, defied America, and overawed Europe. Such studies generally focus on the breakdown of the Soviet system's control mechanism—the planning institutions of its "command economy." These grew progressively incapable of perceiving the country's economic needs or providing for them. The deterioration has several explanations. One is the changing nature of the modern economy. In the heyday of heavy industry, the age of steel, the Soviet command system was able to bring together the massive resources needed to build the mills and produce the tanks and tractors that the times demanded. As industrial technology evolved and products grew more diverse, the volume, speed, and complexity of the information needed began to overwhelm the Soviet planning system. While Soviet science and engineering were often of very high quality, the old command mechanism was ill adapted to promote the dynamic application of new technology to production, except perhaps in limited, high-priority areas like space exploration, or in the military sphere generally. The system stifled the process of spontaneous technological diffusion, so significant for development in Western economies, where consumer industries are so important. Consumer goods were the Soviet system's great failure. By its very nature, "socialist accounting" was ill adapted to such industries. Without a market, there was no reliable way of measuring demand or even costs, and it was difficult to sustain quality. The system mostly went on grinding out old products in old ways. Of course, the Soviet economy, formed in the midst of revolution, totalitarian terror, and war, was never designed to meet the civilian needs of a prosperous consumer class. But as the Cold War faded and Soviet society evolved, the economy's dysfunctional control mechanism grew more and more disabling for the system as a whole.

The Soviet command economy, so absurd from Western consumerist perspectives, did suit the Soviet ruling class in certain fundamental respects. It did serve to perpetuate the power of the industrial, military, and party elites that ran the control system, whereas producing

117

and distributing consumer goods efficiently would have meant displacing centralized planners with a market. The existing system, moreover, seemed well suited to military production. Given a reasonable level of technological and professional competence, which the Soviet economy certainly possessed, successful military production required no market mechanism. Central planners made the decisions. Whether their decisions were correct could be tested only in military conflict. Happily, the evolution of bipolar strategies for nuclear deterrence, combined with the stable and clearly demarcated boundaries between the superpower blocs in Europe, meant that Soviet military power was never really tested—except to suppress unruly civilian populations within the Soviet sphere itself. For a long time, Soviet autocracy was sufficiently confident and brutal to meet this challenge with ease. The Soviet economic system was thus well adapted to its function: to keep the elites in power by preparing for a war that was never likely to occur. What it could not do was to produce consumer goods. Elites could indulge themselves by special access to foreign imports, but this was not a sustainable solution for the population as a whole.

The West, of course, had its own military-industrial system, which occupied a significant part of many Western economies, notably the American. Arguably, the mechanisms of command for these military segments of the American economy were not so very different from those of the Soviets. Whatever market mechanism existed for military products was constrained by the government's interest in preserving the productive and innovative capacity of the major firms. But in the West, military economies coexisted with much larger civilian economies that were run mostly on market principles. The relative size of the military sector was ultimately controlled by a budgetary process that was, in effect, a democratic political market, where military claims on the government's budget had to compete with civilian claims that could not be ignored. Western governments were ultimately subject to voters, consumers of private as well as of public goods. Whereas the Soviet formula could produce guns but not butter, the Western formula was constrained to produce both. While the West's double imperatives led to overspending and inflation, the more single-minded Soviet formula led eventually to the regime's demoralization and collapse.

DEMORALIZATION OF SOVIET ELITES

Ironically, the teachings of Marx and Lenin provide an instructive theoretical framework for analyzing the degeneration of the Soviet Union. Marx described capitalism as a system wherein a cohesive political-economic ruling class dominated and exploited both state and economy in order to perpetuate its own power. In reality, the Soviet political economy came much closer than anything in the capitalist West to approximating that Marxist paradigm. But whereas Marx imagined capitalists using their ascendancy to accumulate capital for investment, the Soviet ruling class used its domination to sustain military power for war and repression. As a military-industrial complex, the Soviet system worked all too well. The problem lay with its further pretensions.

Every society has what might be called its constitutional myth—the ideal that rulers are meant to be serving and that gives them their legitimacy and authority. The Soviet state claimed Marx as its prophet and lawgiver. Marx condemned capitalism because he believed it was inherently exploitative. A communist system was supposed to represent the real interests of ordinary citizens and was ultimately supposed to produce a more abundant and just society than capitalism. Accordingly, Soviet rulers regularly promised to "overtake" the capitalist West.[3] Communism would eventually provide its citizens with a

---

[3] Nikita Khrushchev, First Secretary of the Communist Party from 1953 to 1964, was particularly notable for making such promises. At a U.S. embassy reception in Moscow in 1956, for example, he told the capitalist states, "Whether you like it or not, history is on our side. We will bury you." Although this statement was often misinterpreted as a military threat, he was predicting the Soviet Union's inevitable victory in peaceful economic competition. Khrushchev unveiled an ambitious Seven Year Plan for 1959–1965 at the January 1959 Extraordinary Twenty-first Congress of the Communist Party of the Soviet Union. The Soviet Union was to overtake the United States in per capita industrial and agricultural production by 1970, he boasted. In

better civilian economy than the capitalist West, and with benefits more equitably distributed. For obvious reasons, this was a goal the monopolistic Soviet war machine could never meet. Soviet reality therefore presented an increasingly clear and demoralizing gap between Marxist ideals and Soviet practices.

Marx, of course, did suggest that an iron dictatorship would be needed to guide the transition from capitalism to communism. He thus provided a moral cover for several decades of terrible Soviet oppression.[4] But it is hard to believe that Marx built his splendid cathedral of utopian ideas in order to perpetuate a barbarous war machine, sustained by a permanent apparatus of domestic terror. There were numerous visionaries in the nineteenth century who were obsessed with national power and war. But Marx was not one of them. He was not a Clausewitz, Spencer, Treitschke, or Tirpitz. On the contrary, despite his pretensions to dispassionate scientific objectivity, his writing was genuinely infused with burning indignation over capitalism's systematic exploitation of ordinary people by those in power. He dreamt of a society where exploitation could no longer take place.[5]

1961, he also predicted that the Soviet Union would overtake the United States in wealth per head of population within twenty-five years. At the time, his promises seemed plausible since between 1950 and 1960, the annual growth rate in the Soviet Union was thought, erroneously, to be around 7 percent per annum. In the 1970s, however, growth in the Soviet Union stalled and never recovered its earlier momentum. See Robert J. A. Skidelsky, *The Road from Serfdom* (New York: Penguin, 1995), pp. 1–16, and William J. Tompson, *Khrushchev: A Political Life* (New York: St. Martin's Press, 1995), pp. 171–172, 200–201.

[4] The necessity for a "dictatorship of the proletariat" is noted in the *Communist Manifesto*: "Of course, in the beginning, this [proletarian revolution] cannot be effected except by means of despotic inroads on the rights of, and on the conditions of bourgeois production: by means of measures, therefore, which appear economically insufficient and untenable, but which, in the course of the movement, outstrip themselves, necessitate further inroads upon the old social order, and are unavoidable as a means of entirely revolutionizing the mode of production." Karl Marx and Friedrich Engels, *Selected Works*, vol. 1 (Moscow: Foreign Languages Publishing House, 1950), p. 50. See also Robert L. Heilbroner, *Marxism For and Against* (New York: Norton, 1980), and Richard Pipes, *The Russian Revolution* (New York: Knopf, 1990).

[5] Again, according to the *Communist Manifesto*, it was capitalism's "bourgeois private property" that facilitated the systematic exploitation of the masses: "Modern bourgeois private property is the final and most complete expression of the system of

The Soviet Union was clearly not the society of his dreams. To read Marx, as fledgling Soviet elites presumably were constrained to do, was to raise awkward questions about the legitimacy of the Soviet system. As the system matured, its contradiction of Marxism grew more glaring. It was Lenin himself who taught that revolutions succeed only when the old ruling classes have grown demoralized and no longer feel able to carry on in the old way. The causes of their demoralization are generally moral and cultural. The old elites no longer believe in what they are doing. They therefore cease to believe in their own legitimacy.[6]

Arguably, the gap between Marxist ideals and Soviet realities was a good deal worse under Stalin than under Gorbachev. Yet, the Soviet regime showed amazing strength and resilience under Stalin. It defeated the Germans in World War II and faced down the West in the early Cold War. What had happened to the party elites by Gorbachev's time? From the start of the Soviet experiment, the only way to reconcile Marx's egalitarian ideals with Soviet reality was to invoke the capitalist enemy. A period of resolute dictatorship was needed, Marx himself had said, to protect the nascent communist society from the inevitable hatred of its capitalist enemies, at home and abroad. For a long time, Soviet experience matched Marx's fears and therefore continued to justify his dictatorial remedy. The Western allies did send forces to Russia during and after World War I. And in World War II, the Germans subjected Russia to a massive assault of pitiless ferocity. It was the German invasion, of course, that turned the Soviet Union into a military colossus and set its fateful postwar pattern. Previously, the Soviet Union had not been an impressive military power. The revolution had destroyed what was left of the old imperial

---

producing and appropriating products, that is based on class antagonism, on the exploitation of the many by the few." Only eliminating private property could lead to a society without exploitation. Op. cit., p. 45.

[6] According to Lenin, a "revolutionary situation" presupposes "the impossibility of the ruling classes to preserve their domination in unaltered form. For a revolution to come about it is normally insufficient that 'those down below did not desire' to go on in the old way; it is also requisite that 'those up above were unable' to go on in the old way." See "The Symptoms of a Revolutionary Situation," *The Lenin Anthology*, ed. Robert Tucker (New York: W. W. Norton, 1975), p. 275.

army. And while Trotsky had created a Red Army to replace it, Stalin had purged that army of its officer corps in the 1930s. Hitler's invasion provoked a military response that amazed everyone—Stalin not least. The Russians showed themselves a great nation, despite their execrable regime. In a series of tremendous battles, they halted and broke the Germans. Victory made them a military superpower and brought them into the middle of Europe. Understandably, Russians took immense pride in their victory. The memory of it sustained the older generations of communist elites for the next four decades. And thanks to the Cold War, the West could still be painted as an implacable enemy, legitimating postwar Russia's dictatorial military state. Thus, so long as Marx's fears continued to be ratified by the capitalist West, the Soviet model could go on combining Marxist ideals with an exploitative totalitarian dictatorship.

By the 1980s, the combination was breaking down. Four decades is a long time to live off past military glory. Succeeding generations grew bored with reminiscences and impatient to inherit. The Soviet system had already begun unraveling soon after Stalin's death. Stalin had used recurring bouts of terror to control the system's elites. Economic development was producing a more technocratic sort of elite, not so amenable to sustained totalitarian discipline. Under Stalin's successors, the elites managed to contain the state's terror, or at least to insulate themselves from it. Terror gave way to corruption. In a system whose ideals remained remote from its reality, and where power was arbitrary and unaccountable, corruption was natural, once iron discipline was relaxed.

DETENTE AND THE SOVIET DEMISE

Detente with the West hastened the demoralizing process in several ways. Thanks to extensive arms control negotiations and wide contacts among political and military experts, detente gradually permitted significant parts of the Soviet elites, the younger generation particularly, to gain considerable familiarity with the West.[7] The acquain-

---

[7] For a vivid description of how the Soviet Union "discovered" America, see Georgy Arbatov, *The System* (New York: Times Books, 1992), pp. 295–329.

tance had disturbing effects. Recurring negotiations made clear that the West was not bent on destroying the Soviet Union and thereby undermined the principal rationale for the Soviet dictatorship. Wider exposure to the West made obvious to Soviet elites how backward their system was in providing a decent standard of living for common people. Embarrassment grew as the West's detente diplomacy repeatedly confronted the Soviets over their barbaric trampling of human and national rights, at home and among their tributaries.

Opening up nations like Poland, with deep Western roots and courageous and rebellious populations, encouraged more and more open resistance to Soviet tyranny. Detente also set Americans and West Europeans to competing and thus undermined the view of the West as a united capitalist bloc. De Gaulle's ideas and maneuvers made it possible to think once more of West European states that might be Russia's natural partners. Brandt's Ostpolitik, by discrediting the ritual demonization of Germany, removed a major psychological obstacle to a new Soviet diplomacy. In short, detente encouraged the Soviet imagination to roam beyond its Stalinist perimeter.

Detente also addicted the Russians to closer economic relations with the West. Elites wanted the West's consumer goods. The regime wanted Western technology—to find shortcuts for developing their civilian economy as well as for updating military technology. Western Europe was eager to trade, even if the United States was not. As time went on, the Soviets, and especially their East European allies, grew lopsidedly dependent on Western Europe (see table 7.2).

TABLE 7.2

Trade Balances ($ million) of Central and Eastern European Countries (1999)

	Export	Import	Balance
Bulgaria	0.80	4.23	−3.43
Hungary	4.50	5.66	−1.16
Poland	6.13	8.18	−2.06
Romania	3.87	6.23	−2.64
Russian Federation	25.79	30.84	−5.15

Source: OECD Economic Outlook (Paris: OECD, December 1990), pp. 54–55.

WESTERN HARD-LINERS AND THE SOVIET COLLAPSE

Ironically, just as detente was leading the Soviets into a new perspective, it was being hotly disputed in the United States. Even in the early 1970s, Henry Kissinger, promoting his own "superpower detente" to cover American weakness after Vietnam, criticized Brandt's Ostpolitik and complained regularly of Europe's tendencies toward "self-Finlandization." By the end of the 1970s, American strategic experts, galvanized by the Committee on the Present Danger, urgently warned against a new missile gap or "window of vulnerability." President Carter, shocked by the Soviet invasion of Afghanistan in 1979, reacted with a major military buildup, with economic sanctions and a general ideological offensive. The Reagan administration, taking office in 1981, pursued Carter's policies with a vengeance. U.S. military spending jumped 50 percent in real terms from 1979 to 1985.[8]

Was American suspicion of detente justified? And did the Carter-Reagan military buildup hasten the Soviet collapse? The answer to both questions is yes, but perhaps for reasons different from those sometimes advanced. Trends within the Soviet system, as within the West, were often contradictory. While a significant part of Soviet elite opinion, heavily influenced by detente and typified by Gorbachev, was evolving away from Stalin's confrontational stance, a countertrend was also visible, particularly among the military. In the mid-1970s, as American enthusiasm for detente was reaching its apogee under the Nixon and Ford administrations, the Soviet military's estimate of its own relative prowess was also reaching a new high. The Americans had abandoned Vietnam, and their willingness to fight anywhere seemed questionable. Congress was cutting military budgets, the draft was abolished, and American armed forces were in considerable disarray. The Soviets, having finally learned how to equip their warheads with multiple independently targeted reentry vehicles (MIRVs), could, for the first time, achieve genuine strategic parity with the Americans. Hence, the window of vulnerability that so bemused Western strategic analysts. Optimism about their military position encouraged a more

---

[8] With 1992 as base (100), defense expenditure stood at 55.81 in 1979 and 83.51 in 1985. See *Economic Report of the President* (Washington, DC: U.S. Government Printing Office, 1999), p. 337.

adventurous and aggressive mood among the Soviet military. Soviet forces began probing relatively peripheral regions like Angola and the Horn of Africa. At the end of the 1970s, they invaded Afghanistan to shore up a tottering client regime. That proved a major mistake—a Soviet Vietnam that, in addition, triggered a fresh military buildup in the United States.

Reagan's inflated arms spending in the 1980s may have been grotesque, with unhappy long-term consequences for the American and world economies, but it did have healthy effects on the Soviet elites. A particularly flamboyant part of the American buildup was the Strategic Defense Initiative, a diffuse and exotic antimissile program with an almost unlimited potential for future spending. SDI may have made little sense for American strategic deterrence at the time, but it discouraged Soviet expectations of ever achieving decisive technological military superiority. In short, Reagan's spending, along with their own defeat in Afghanistan, punctured the inflated expectations of the Soviet military.

The European missile crisis of the late 1970s and 1980s demonstrated a similar pattern of aggressive Soviet military initiatives with self-defeating consequences, thanks to firm Western responses. In the late 1970s, the Soviets deployed their new and highly accurate SS20 missiles, ostentatiously targeted on Western Europe. The deployment was taken as a sign not only of the Soviet military's new technological confidence but of its determination to "Finlandize" all of Europe. Arguing over how to respond caused a great deal of political turmoil within the Western alliance. But in the end, Germany and several other West European countries agreed to deploy new and highly accurate American Pershing II intermediate range missiles, a development that significantly degraded the Soviet Union's strategic position. The new Soviet belligerence also brought an unprecedented reconciliation between French and American policies within NATO, as France's president, François Mitterrand, appeared dramatically before the Bundestag to urge the Germans to deploy the Pershing missiles. Meanwhile, Britain and France, with strong American backing, proceeded with a major upgrading of their own nuclear deterrents.

The West, meanwhile, had adopted a two-track approach to missile deployment: Firm resistance to pressure was combined with willingness to negotiate general arms reduction across Europe. This balanced policy, inaugurated during the Carter administration, was skillfully conducted to success under the Reagan administration. Given his earlier firmness, Reagan's unexpectedly warm reaction to Gorbachev's arms control proposals at their Reykjavik meeting in 1986 greatly encouraged Gorbachev to proceed with a new European policy.

GORBACHEV'S REVOLUTION

Gorbachev's new foreign policy represented a radical shift in Soviet perceptions. Stalin's whole postwar strategy had begun to seem increasingly self-defeating. His enormous forward deployment of military power had provoked a countering alliance that locked the West European states and the United States together. The competitive military buildup that followed was one the West could afford much better than the Soviets. In short, Stalin's defensive glacis had united the West and trapped the Soviet Union in an arms race it could not win. Detente offered the prospect of a Soviet escape from disadvantageous bipolarity into a new pan-European system. Gorbachev's vision of a "common European house" was his enlightened response. The rewards for the West were much greater than hardly anyone expected, and much more than many desired. Between 1989 and 1991, Germany was reunited, and the Soviets were gone from Eastern Europe. Gorbachev's Soviet regime was nevertheless unable to play the ambitious pan-European role he had envisaged for it. Instead, the Soviet Union itself disintegrated. Improving relations with the West had deprived the Soviet dictatorship of its principal rationale and implied radical domestic reform. Gorbachev was unable to manage that reform.

Gorbachev's major domestic initiatives were embodied in *perestroika* and *glasnost*—economic restructuring and free discussion. He hoped to introduce both without renouncing the Communist Party's hegemony over the economy and political system. But he was unable to create a convincing new Marxist model to justify continuing the old hegemony. Meanwhile, his foreign policy undermined his power at home. As reformist and nationalist revolts swept Eastern Europe, Gorbachev's failure to save the Soviet-imposed regimes sent revolutionary shock waves back to the Soviet Union, where centrifugal nationalist forces were ready to break loose. Gorbachev's position had so deteriorated by 1991 that an abortive coup of protesting Communist hard-liners led to his downfall. Power passed to Boris Yeltsin, elected leader of the emerging Russian Federation, who crushed the Communist coup and shoved Gorbachev aside. Yeltsin abandoned the effort to reform communism within Russia and pressed ahead with a radical program to create a market-based democracy. In effect, Yeltsin hoped to save reform by turning Russia into a Western nation state. Meanwhile, the other Soviet republics, imitating Russia, seized their independence. Soon, most of Soviet Eurasia was pursuing "transformation"—from an imperial command economy and dictatorship to national market-based democracies. All that remained of the old Soviet Union was a loosely organized Commonwealth of Independent States.

Unsurprisingly, Russia's would-be market economy soon encountered intractable economic, social, and political obstacles. Fabulous wealth was quickly appropriated by a few, often those old Soviet elites in a position to make off with state assets. Meanwhile, general industrial production collapsed. A large part of the civilian population experienced a profound drop in living standards. State revenue evaporated to the point where essential services could not be provided in many regions and the military was unable to feed, house, or clothe its own men. All in all, Russia's breakdown in the early 1990s was one of the great economic catastrophes of modern history. Thereafter, the search for a viable new socioeconomic model proved elusive. After a period of ostensibly trying to adopt Western liberal reforms wholesale, with discouraging results, Russia sought its own national version of a mixed economy. But many of the ingredients were unpromising. The old Soviet model was discredited, but nothing viable—liberal or mercantilist—came quickly to replace it. Instead, widespread criminality mocked liberal and mercantilist ideals alike.

LEGACIES OF BIPOLAR EUROPE

In Stalin's time, a totalitarian, isolated, and autarkic Russia was able to defy the world. By abandoning the Soviet Union, Yeltsin's Russia deliberately made itself less autonomous and self-determining. The new Russia soon grew very weak. Having ceased to be an autocratic empire, it was underdeveloped as a nation state. Its political and administrative functionaries were plagued with corruption and incompetence, and its civil society was only half formed. These internal insufficiencies remained the principal barriers to Russia's entering into intimate relationships with the states, societies, and economies of the European Union, or to Russia's assuming a European or world role worthy of its potential. Nevertheless, this new and distracted Russia continued to weigh heavily on Europe and Asia. The collapse of the Soviets left a vacuum that the other participants in the old bipolar system felt impelled to fill. The Americans were challenged to make the global system "unipolar," and the West Europeans to make their European system pan-European. Pursuing such ambitions, however, did not necessarily fit the inner logic either of the global system, which had been growing increasingly plural, or of the European Union, whose corporatist institutions were not easily adaptable to broad eastward expansion. As a result, the decade that followed the Soviet collapse saw growing disorder and unease in the world. In Europe itself, the decade ended with a new Balkan war.

In effect, once the Soviet threat was overthrown, it grew easier to appreciate the former advantages of Soviet strength. At the start of the Cold War, it had been Soviet strength that pressured the Americans and Europeans toward mutual accommodation. And it had been Soviet strength that suspended the German problem and made possible a Franco-German partnership. Soviet strength kept order over regions of Europe with a demonstrated capacity for dragging the rest of the continent into their quarrels. And Soviet strength kept some lid on the fermenting violence and criminality of Central Asia. In the Far East, Soviet strength worked to contain adventurism from Mao's China. For the most part, these contributions to world order did not depend on the peculiar nature of the Soviet regime. A strong democratic Russia should have been able to play the same useful role. But throughout the 1990s, a strong Russia did not exist, and many of Europe's security problems derived from its sudden absence.

A weak and volatile Russia must thus be counted as one principal legacy of the bipolar system. An overarmed and overambitious United States is another. American strategic perspectives nourished during the bipolar era are difficult to fit within the different sort of world order in prospect for the twenty-first century. Bipolarity has left enduring legacies to Europe as well. Britain and France are independent nuclear powers, while Germany lacks many normal attributes of military sovereignty—a reality that seriously affects the prospects for European military collaboration. Above all, European states share a collective legacy of military dependency despite increasing political-economic power. In summary, the bipolar system gave Europe a half century of peace but left a troubling legacy of lopsided and incomplete development. The 1990s were spent struggling with the consequences.

SELECTED SOURCES

American Revisionism: NATO's Strategic Paradigm

Among the most convincing and influential analysts arguing for the durability of the bipolar status quo was Anton De Porte, *Europe between the Superpowers* (New Haven: Yale University Press, 1979).

For General de Gaulle's challenge to the Atlanticist paradigm over the years, the ideal starting point is his own writing, *The Wartime Memoirs of Charles de Gaulle*, collected edition (New York: Simon & Schuster, 1968), especially vol. 2, *Unity*, pp. 268ff, and vol. 3, *Salvation*, ch. 5. See also the postwar *Memoirs of Hope: Renewal and Endeavor* (New York: Simon & Schuster, 1971), especially the chapters "Europe" and "The World." For various views of Gaullist grand strategy, see John Newhouse, *De Gaulle and the Anglo Saxons* (New York: Viking Press, 1970), and Edward A. Kolodziej, *French International Policy under de Gaulle and Pompidou: The Politics of Grandeur* (Ithaca: Cornell University Press, 1974). For the persistence of Gaullist ideas in France, see Philip H. Gordon, *A Certain Idea of France* (Princeton: Princeton University Press, 1993). For good general studies of de Gaulle, see Paul-Marie de La Gorce, *De Gaulle entre deux mondes: Une vie et une époque* (Paris: Fayard, 1964); Stanley Hoffman, *De Gaulle, artiste de la politique* (Paris: Editions du Seuil, 1973); Jean Lacouture, *Charles de Gaulle* (Paris: Seuil, 1984–1986); and Don Cook, *Charles de Gaulle: A Biography* (New

York: Putnam, 1983). For an exceptionally detailed and balanced discussion of French postwar policy, see Michael M. Harrison, *The Reluctant Ally: France and Atlantic Security* (Baltimore: Johns Hopkins University Press, 1981). For my own analysis of Gaullist policy, see David P. Calleo, *Europe's Future: The Grand Alternatives* (New York: Horizon Press, 1965), ch. 4, and *The Atlantic Fantasy* (Baltimore: Johns Hopkins University Press, 1970), pp. 57–74.

For French disillusionment with NATO, see General André Beaufre, *NATO and Europe* (New York: Knopf, 1966). For the debate over flexible response, see Lawrence Freedman, *The Evolution of Nuclear Strategy* (London: Macmillan/International Institute for Strategic Studies, 1981), and John Lewis Gaddis, *Strategies of Containment: A Critical Appraisal of Postwar American National Security Policy* (New York: Oxford University Press, 1982). I discuss the evolution of NATO strategy in considerable detail in David P. Calleo, *Beyond American Hegemony: The Future of the Western Alliance* (A Twentieth Century Fund Book; New York: Basic Books, 1987), especially chs. 3–5. For the strategic rationale of the French independent deterrent, see General Pierre Gallois, in particular his *Stratégie de l'age nucléaire* (Paris: Calmann-Levy, 1961), translated as *The Balance of Terror: Strategy for the Nuclear Age* (Boston: Houghton Mifflin, 1961). For a refined version of "multilateral deterrence," see General André Beaufre, *Dissuasion et stratégie* (Paris: Armand Colin, 1964), translated as *Deterrence and Strategy* (New York: Praeger, 1965). Putative American aid for France's deterrent and its rejection is discussed in Michael M. Harrison, *The Reluctant Ally*, op. cit., pp. 80–81. For later clandestine U.S. aid, see Richard Ullman, *Securing Europe* (A Twentieth Century Fund Book; Princeton: Princeton University Press, 1991). For the British nuclear deterrent and its rationale, see Lawrence Freedman, *Britain and Nuclear Weapons* (London: Macmillan, 1980).

For American insistence on German rearmament, see Richard Mayne, *Postwar: The Dawn of Today's Europe* (New York: Schocken Books, 1983), pp. 311–316; Frank A. Ninkovich, *Germany and the US: The Transformation of the German Question since 1945* (New York: Twayne, 1995); and John L. Harper, *American Visions of Europe: Franklin D. Roosevelt, George F. Kennan, and Dean G.*

Acheson (Cambridge and New York: Cambridge University Press, 1994). For Germany's NATO role in general, see Catherine McArdle Kelleher, "Germany and NATO: The Enduring Bargain," in Wolfram Hanrieder, ed., *West German Foreign Policy: 1949–1979* (Boulder, CO: Westview Press, 1980).

I analyzed the growing cost of U.S. military spending and its economic consequences in David P. Calleo, *The Imperious Economy* (Cambridge: Harvard University Press, 1982), especially ch. 9, and also in *The Bankrupting of America* (New York: William Morrow, 1992), in particular ch. 5. For the concept of overstretch in a long-term historical framework, see Paul Kennedy, *The Rise and Fall of the Great Powers* (New York: Random House, 1987), especially pp. 114ff.

For various views on the SDI debate, see Robert W. Tucker, George Liska, Robert E. Osgood, and David P. Calleo, *SDI and U.S. Foreign Policy* (Boulder, CO: Westview Press/The Johns Hopkins Foreign Policy Institute, 1987). For SDI spending and its impact, see Harry Waldman, *The Dictionary of SDI* (Wilmington, DE: Scholarly Resources, 1988), and Paul H. Nitze, *The Impact of SDI on U.S.-Soviet Relations* (Washington, DC: U.S. Department of State, 1986).

The Soviet Implosion

The literature on the Soviet collapse is enormous. For an introduction and overview, see John Lewis Gaddis, *Russia, the Soviet Union and the United States: An Interpretative History* (New York: McGraw-Hill, 1990); Helène Carrère d'Encausse, *Stalin's Successors: Leadership, Stability, and Change in the Soviet Union* (Cambridge and New York: Cambridge University Press, 1980); Seweryn Bialer, *The Global Rivals* (New York: Knopf, 1988); George F. Kennan, *At a Century's Ending: Reflections 1982–1995* (New York: Norton, 1996); or Zbigniew Brzezinski, *The Grand Failure: The Birth and the Death of Communism in the Twentieth Century* (New York: Scribner, 1989). Many analysts in the 1980s noted elements of internal Soviet decay, but it was widely argued that no one realized how imminent and complete the Soviet implosion would be. For the reasons, see John Lewis Gaddis, op. cit., and Robert English, "Sources, Methods, and Competing Perspectives on the End of the Cold War," *Diplomatic History*, vol. 2, no. 2 (1997). The role of Pope John Paul II and of Polish Catholicism in bringing down the Soviet Empire is discussed by Edward Stourton, *Absolute Truth* (London: Viking, 1998), chs. 6–7, and also, from a Catholic perspective, by George Weigel, *The Final Revolution: The Resistance Church and the Collapse of Communism* (Oxford: Oxford University Press, 1992).

The Dysfunctional Economy

For an analysis stressing the inherent contradictions of the Soviet economy and its mechanisms, see Janos Kornai, *The Socialist System* (Princeton: Princeton University Press, 1992). For the failure to produce consumer goods and the rise of black market economies, see Valery Kontorovich and Michael Ellman, *The Disintegration of the Soviet Economic System* (London: Routledge, 1992), and Seweryn Bialer, *The Soviet Paradox* (New York: Knopf, 1986).

For a comparison of the military-industrial complexes in the West and in the Soviet Union, which reveals some striking similarities, see Michael Brzoska, *Arms and Warfare: Escalation, De-escalation and Negotiation* (Columbia: University of Southern Carolina, 1994), and Stephen C. Cimbala, *US Military Strategy and the Cold War Endgame* (Ilford, Essex: Frank Class, 1995).

Demoralization of Soviet Elites

For a sociological analysis of Soviet decline, stressing the progressive demoralization of elites and citizens, see M. Voslensky, *Nomenklatura: The Soviet Ruling Class* (Garden City, NY: Doubleday, 1984); also Boris Yeltsin, *Against the Grain* (New York: Summit Books, 1990), and Alexander Dallin and Gail Lapidus, eds., *The Soviet System: From Crisis to Collapse* (Boulder, CO: Westview Press, 1995). For the broader implications for Europe, see Robert J. A. Skidelsky, *The Road from Serfdom* (New York: Penguin, 1995).

For the view that Marxism leads inevitably to a totalitarian system, see Martin Malia, *The Soviet Tragedy: A History of Socialism in Russia, 1917–1991* (Princeton: Princeton University Press, 1944), and

Richard Pipes, *A Concise History of the Russian Revolution* (New York: Knopf, 1995).

For the increasing gap between Marxist ideals and Soviet realities, see Konstantin Simis, *USSR, the Corrupt Society: The Secret World of Soviet Communism* (New York: Simon & Schuster, 1982). For the effects of Stalin's purges on the Soviet army and its recovery in the war, see Dmitri Fedetoff White, *The Growth of the Red Army* (Princeton: Princeton University Press, 1944).

For a study of the corruption endemic in the Soviet system from the time of Leonid Brezhnev onward, see William A. Clark, *Crime and Punishment in Soviet Officialdom: Combating Corruption in the Political Elite 1965–1990* (New York: M. E. Sharp, 1993). The passing of the generations played an increasing role in undermining the legitimacy of the Soviet System, a subject explored by Seweryn Bialer, *The Domestic Context of Soviet Foreign Policy* (Boulder, CO: Westview Press, 1989). For an analysis of the transformation of the Soviet elite after the collapse of the Soviet Union, see Olga Kryshtanovskaya and Stephen White, "From Soviet Nomenklatura to Russian Elite," *Europe-Asia Studies,* vol. 98, no. 5 (1996).

Detente and the Soviet Demise

For human rights in the detente process, symbolized by Basket 3 of the Helsinki Accords, see Cathal J. Nolan, *Principled Democracy: Security and Rights in US Foreign Policy* (Westport, CT: Greenwood Press, 1993). For the embarrassment of Soviet elites and a sense of the effects of detente on them, see Georgi Arbatov, *The System: An Insider's Life in Soviet Politics* (New York: Times Books, 1992), and Mikhail Gorbachev, *Memoirs* (New York: Doubleday, 1996). For Margaret Thatcher's personal assessment of Gorbachev, see *The Downing Street Years* (London: HarperCollins, 1993), pp. 461–463. For the increasing Soviet dependency on Western trade, see Angela Stent, *From Embargo to Ostpolitik: The Political Economy of West German-Soviet Relations: 1955–1980* (Cambridge: Cambridge University Press, 1981). For the pipeline dispute and tensions over "Eurocommunism," see Dana Allin, *Cold War Illusions* (New York: St. Martin's Press, 1995). For Kissinger's critique of Ostpolitik as "self-

Finlandization," see Henry Kissinger, *The White House Years* (Boston: Little, Brown, 1979), pp. 408–412, 529–530.

Western Firmness and the Soviet Collapse

For a comprehensive history of detente, including the increased assertiveness demonstrated by Soviet forces in the mid-1970s, see Raymond Garthoff, *Detente and Confrontation: American-Soviet Relations from Nixon to Reagan* (Washington, DC: Brookings Institution, 1985). See also Fred Halliday, *Soviet Policy in the Arc of Crisis* (Washington, DC: Institute for Policy Studies, 1981). For the American strategic reaction, see Dana Allin, *Cold War Illusions*, op. cit. For a favorable view of the Reagan buildup and its effects on the Soviets, see Daniel Wirls, *Buildup: The Politics of Defense in the Reagan Era* (Ithaca: Cornell University Press, 1992). For the Pershing II missile dispute, see Lawrence Freedman, *Arms Control: Management or Reform?* (London: Routledge, 1986), as well as Allin, op. cit. For Mitterrand's speech before the Bundestag urging the Germans to deploy American missiles, see *20 Jahre Deutsche-Französiche Zusammenarbeit/20 Années de coopération Franco-Allemande,* Reihe Berichte und Dokumentation (Bonn: Presse und Informationamt der Bundesregierung, 1983).

Gorbachev's Revolution

For Gorbachev's policies, see Mikhail Gorbachev, *Memoirs*, op. cit. For a good account of his internal reforms, see Donald R. Kelley and Shannon G. Davis, *The Songs of Sergei: Khrushchev and Gorbachev as Reformers* (New York: Praeger, 1992). David Remnick captures well the drama of the Soviet collapse in *Lenin's Tomb: The Last Days of the Soviet Empire* (New York: Random House, 1993). See also John Dunlop, *The Rise of Russia and the Fall of the Soviet Empire* (Princeton: Princeton University Press, 1993). Boris Yeltsin, the major beneficiary of the collapse of the Soviet Union, gives his own account in *The Struggle for Russia* (New York: Times Books, 1994). For the parlous state of post-Gorbachev Russia, see Stephen White and Alex Pravda, eds., *Developments in Russia and Post-Soviet Politics* (Durham, NC: Duke University Press, 1994).

Confederal Europe: From Rome to Maastricht

EUROPE'S HYBRID COMMUNITY

OF THE THREE postwar systems, the most indisputably "European" was formed around the European Community (EC), organized by the West European states behind their NATO shield. When the Soviet Union collapsed, that European Community was widely expected to be the primary beneficiary. By the end of 1991, the EC's member states, led by France and Germany, had already negotiated the Treaty of Maastricht, renamed themselves the European Union and declared their intention both to "deepen" their integration and to "widen" to the east. Achieving Maastricht's goals, however, seemed to call for basic changes in the European Community's already complex constitutional character. That character had evolved in a very particular way over the Cold War and was not easy to change quickly.

Students of Europe from my generation have been trying to analyze the character of the European Community since its early days. As a young professor at Yale, I went to Paris and wrote a book, *Europe's Future: The Grand Alternatives*, published in 1965.[1] As I saw it then, four basic models were competing to shape Europe's future: America's Atlantic Europe, Jean Monnet's federal Europe, de Gaulle's confederal Europe of States, and an anarchic Europe of States—"Nobody's Europe," as I called it. Each model implied a distinct combination of members, ambitions, and internal machinery. And behind each model were different interests, values, and ideals—different ways of looking at the world and of viewing history and the future. By the end of the Cold War, all four models—Atlantic, federal, confederal, and anarchic—had proved not so much antagonistic as complementary. They seemed not only to have survived and flourished but entwined. The European Union of the 1990s was the hybrid offspring

[1] David P. Calleo, *Europe's Future: The Grand Alternatives* (New York: Horizon Press, 1965).

of all four models, hence its polymorphous character, dynamism, and limitations.

THE MODELS: ATLANTIC EUROPE

In the vision of an Atlantic Europe, Europe is America's economic partner, together with Japan, managing an integrated world economy held together by free trade, convertible money, and internationalized business firms. Culturally, Europe and North America are close branches of a common civilization, the "West." This Atlantic vision makes it natural for the United States to be an active European power and gives Europe and America a broad common interest in building a world shaped in their own common image—a commercialized global village of easy mass communication and cosmopolitan sensibility.

Within Europe, Atlanticism's most ardent votaries have usually come from the British, Dutch, and Scandinavians, or the Protestant wing of the Christian Democratic Party in Germany. Atlanticists have played an ambivalent role in the European movement itself. Characteristically, they shrink from the "Carolingian" and "Catholic" vision common among many of the principal French, German, Belgian, and Italian architects of the postwar European system. Keeping the European project "outward looking" toward the United States and the global economy in general has been the Atlanticists' constant refrain. The United States has rallied European Atlanticists to defend NATO, and sometimes to resist particular European initiatives regarded as harmful to American interests, like the Common Market's agricultural policy. But successive U.S. administrations have never turned resolutely hostile to European integration, and therefore have nearly always disappointed integration's European opponents. Indeed, American backing was often an important element in the European Community's early success. In general, moreover, the American presence made it easier for Europeans to integrate. NATO provided collective security without requiring Europeans to resolve highly divisive military issues among themselves. And the very existence of an Atlantic Alliance helped to calm those Europeans whose natural inclination was to fear continental integration.

136

BRUSSELS FEDERALISM

Federalism in the early postwar era took a number of significant forms. Some of its leading theorists—the Italian Altiero Spinelli, for example—proposed a federal superstate to supplant the national states. Others, like Henri Brugmans, visualized a neomedieval or "personalist" Europe of autonomous regions, local communities, and corporatist associations. While these diverse federalist visions continue to inform European politics to the present day, they have long since been eclipsed by federalism's great "functionalist" experiment in Brussels. Its early institutions—the European Coal and Steel Community, Euratom, and the European Economic Community—came into existence in the 1950s as the initiatives of statesmen like Robert Schuman and Paul-Henri Spaak and were backed solidly by major national leaders like Konrad Adenauer and Alcide de Gasperi. The ideas underlying them were brilliantly promoted among European and American elites and public opinion through the discourses and tireless lobbying of Jean Monnet and the able people around him, and by the European Commission's first president, the German Christian Democrat Walter Hallstein. Numerous academic apologists joined in, many of them Americans inspired by the political scientist Ernst B. Haas.

Functionalist ideas were beguilingly simple and optimistic and were decorated with behaviorist concepts fashionable among social scientists. Integration in one economic sector was expected to "spill over" to others, with proliferating and accelerating consequences. As member states opened and integrated their economies, their disputes would gravitate to Brussels for settlement. Interest groups and politics would refocus on the European level, and ultimately, sovereignty itself would migrate to that level. The Community's nascent governing structure would gradually evolve into a European federal government. That structure consisted of four main institutions: the Council of Ministers, the Commission, the Parliament, and the Court of Justice.

The Council of Ministers was set up as the deliberative body wherein ministers, representing the governments of the member states, were to negotiate the Community's basic policies. The Commission was the Community's administration, each member state naming two Commissioners, with intensive bargaining in the Council determining the allocation of portfolios among them. Commissioners and their staffs formed a collegial body of civil servants, drawn, in many instances, from the cream of national politicians and bureaucrats. As civil servants of the Community, they were expected to be unbeholden to national instructions or interests. The Commission also had a key policymaking role, since it alone had the formal power to initiate proposals before the Council. Functionalist theorists expected that power of initiative to be exploited vigorously, since the Commission could credibly claim to be acting in the interest of the whole, rather than pushing particular national interests. With its disinterested technocratic expertise, the Commission was expected to head off conflicts among member states with timely solutions in the common interest. Brussels federalists expected the Commission, thus empowered, to become Europe's executive branch as well as its bureaucracy.

The Brussels federalists also expected the European Parliament eventually to play a major role. Initially, deputies were members of delegations sent by national parliaments. Their functions were mostly decorative, since the real decision making went on between the Council and the Commission. But Brussels federalists expected that, as the Commission's powers increased, pressure would grow to make it responsible to the Parliament. They also anticipated that deputies would eventually be elected directly, a step taken in 1979. Federalists expected the Parliament, fortified with a popular mandate, to gain the power to choose the Commission's president and other members, and to overturn its directives. The Commission would become like a national cabinet in a parliamentary system. It could continue in office only so long as it commanded a working majority in the Parliament. In short, the European Parliament was ultimately to play the same role in the European Community as national parliaments play in most European states. Most of this new power—for both the Commission and the Parliament—was expected to be gained at the expense of the Council of Ministers. Brussels federalists imagined that the Council, lacking the critical power of legislative initiative, would eventually atrophy into a chamber analogous to the German Bundesrat or the British House of Lords, able to delay and refine policies but not to initiate them. Meanwhile, the European Court of Justice would progressively enforce decisions from Brussels and iron out national anomalies in laws, rights, and regulations.

Behind these expectations was a distinct view of politics. Early Brussels federalists tended to be benevolent technocrats who disliked the mass democracy of the modern nation state. They deplored its complications for rational policymaking and feared the opportunities it offered for evil manipulation. These were reactions understandable from a generation traumatized by Hitler. To its critics, however, Brussels federalism was naively elitist and apolitical, skilled in bureaucratic politics but with little philosophical or practical understanding of how popular democracy actually works in a modern nation state.

THE EUROPE OF STATES

Within the early Community the rival model to the Brussels federalism of Monnet and Hallstein was the confederal Europe of States, for which General de Gaulle was the principal animator and apologist. De Gaulle never doubted that Europe's nation states would and should remain the continent's centers of democratic legitimacy. His reasoning followed the traditional rationale for Europe's nation state formula and the state system that followed from it: The bonds that held a people together were forged in history. Once formed, they could not be dissolved without violent struggles and terrible losses. Democracy depended on such bonds. Governments not sanctioned by such deeply rooted national legitimacy were inevitably arbitrary and fragile. New bonds could not be ordered at will. No *areopagus* of apolitical civil servants, like the European Commission, could, by itself, successfully substitute for Europe's national governments. Attempting such a substitution, would enfeeble Europe's nation states in the process and leave Europe's peoples without the means for collective political will, vulnerable to internal strife and tyranny, and to external domination.

De Gaulle's approach to the interdependence of Europe's nation states, however, was less traditionally nationalist. He was very much aware of the force of technological change and the rising pressures for international economic integration. And given these pressures, he believed Europe's nation states needed to open their economies to each other and harmonize their practices and policies. He was also keenly sensitive to the overwhelming political and military presence of the two superpowers—in Europe and throughout the world. Given the superpowers, European states needed to concert their interests and efforts. Doing so required a confederal "Europe of States"—to provide the locus and machinery for continuous consultation and bargaining among Europe's national systems.[2] Even though every state would retain a veto on matters of vital national interest, de Gaulle insisted, the institutions and spirit of the confederacy would nevertheless exert a salutary pressure to harmonize those interests and arrive at joint policies. Doing so would give member states more practical control over their external—and indeed internal—environments than they could otherwise expect. In effect, de Gaulle saw the Community as a way to enrich rather than diminish the real sovereignty of its member states.

[2] De Gaulle's European vision is still frequently described as *l'Europe des patries*. On occasion, however, he explicitly preferred the term *Europe of States*: "I have never personally, in any of my statements, spoken of a 'Europe of nations,' although it is always being claimed that I have done so. It is not, of course, that I am repudiating my own; quite the contrary, I am more attached to France than ever and I do not believe that Europe can have any living reality if it does not include France and her Frenchmen, Germany and its Germans, Italy and its Italians, and so forth. Dante, Goethe, Chateaubriand belonged to all Europe to the very extent that they were respectively and eminently Italian, German and French. They would not have served Europe very well if they had been stateless, or if they had written in some kind of integrated Esperanto or Volapük. But it is true that the nation is a human and a sentimental element, whereas Europe can be built on the basis of active, authoritative and responsible elements. What elements? The states, of course; for, in this respect, it is only the states that are valid, legitimate and capable of achievement. I have already said, and I repeat, that at the present time there cannot be any other Europe than a Europe of States, apart, of course, from myths, stories and parades." See his press conference of May 15, 1962, in *Major Addresses, Statements and Press Conferences of General Charles de Gaulle, May 19, 1958–January 31, 1964* (New York: French Embassy, Press and Information Division, 1964), pp. 175–176. For more discussion, see David P. Calleo, *Europe's Future*, op. cit., p. 128, and Philip H. Gordon, "Between the Past and the Present: French National Security Policy and the Gaullist Legacy" (Washington, DC: Johns Hopkins University School of Advanced International Studies, unpublished Ph.D. thesis, 1991).

The notion that integration can enhance sovereignty has perhaps not been well understood. It is worth considering carefully, since it is critical to explaining the practical success of the Community throughout the postwar era, despite its failure to become a federation. Broadly speaking, Gaullist confederalism represents, in my view, a major advance in ideas about the nation state and the European state system, as discussed in chapters 3 and 4.

In theory, of course, any binding engagement one state makes with another can be considered a "loss" of sovereignty.[3] In practice, however, every state finds its sphere of successful free agency sharply limited by the reactions of its neighbors, particularly in a crowded and closely interdependent region like Europe. Under such circumstances, if a confederacy increases a state's ability to anticipate and influence the behavior of its neighbors, that state's sovereignty is enhanced rather than reduced. In such a perspective, a state's sovereignty needs to be considered not merely as a legal concept, but also in its practical, moral, and existential dimensions. In practice, national sovereignty is always limited by objective conditions, including the reactions of neighbors. Under the circumstances, national sovereignty means, first of all, a legitimate government with the formal power to choose among the options available, as opposed to having to follow choices directly dictated by a foreign power. In other words, for a nation state, as for an individual in society, practical freedom means being an actor rather than merely an object. For a state caught up in a closely interdependent system, practical sovereignty lies in being treated as a player—in being listened to by neighboring states, in bargaining actively with them, and in having its own national interests taken into account by them. Like free will, however, practical sovereignty also implies having desirable choices to make. A state is not free insofar as, like a galley slave under the lash, coercive, external conditions severely limit its real choices. But the nation state that limits its theoretical sovereignty to enter a consensual confederacy, and that consequently enlarges its possibilities and advances its pros-

---

[3] A point made clearly by Maurice Couve de Murville, the French foreign minister for much of de Gaulle's tenure. See Couve's *Une Politique Etrangère* (Paris: Plon, 1971), ch. 9, pp. 347–384.

pects, is thereby enhancing its effectiveness and, hence, its real freedom. In actual practice, this has been the postwar experience of Europe's states with their Community, which explains its success and durability.

Philosophically, this way of looking at national sovereignty and freedom within a confederation is, in some critical respects, analogous to Rousseau's view of the individual's freedom within a state governed by a legitimate general will. The individual is free insofar as a general will prevails that corresponds to his own "real" will as a national member of a collective self. According to the old formula of the nation state, it is national identity that helps to create a community or convergence of interests that may give concrete substance to that collective self. Whether a national identity can, without dissolving, also take on a confederal identity and thereby create a community of converging interests among several distinct nation states determines whether a confederacy can succeed and how far it can be extended.

NOBODY'S EUROPE

The fourth model in *Europe's Future*—"Nobody's Europe"—began in my mind as a residual category, an anarchic as opposed to a confederal Europe of States, a paradigm where European states turn away from the cooperative institutions being proposed by de Gaulle and the Brussels federalists and revert to the comparative anarchy of the first half of the twentieth century. When I was writing, in the mid-1960s, Germany and France had fallen out within the EEC, Britain was being excluded, and the United States and France were also at loggerheads in NATO. Reversion to Nobody's Europe did not seem an impossible scenario. Indeed, it still is not. As I reflected further, however, I began to see this anarchic paradigm less as merely a failure of the other models than as an essential dimension of any of them. Each of the other models for postwar Europe—confederal, Atlantic, and even federal—was meant to be a voluntary union of free states. To hold together, each would require an underlying balance of power to prevent excessive exploitation of the weak or the strong. Such a balance seemed the indispensable foundation for any voluntary union of free states. European cooperation has not meant the end of Europe's national states or their rivalries. Rivalries and power struggles have continued to describe a good part of the relations among member states throughout the history of the European Community. And competition and power balancing are normal politics within the European nation states themselves, indeed within all states that are constitutional and plural. Constitutional democracies achieve their internal unity not by eliminating all their contentious political forces, but by providing a rational framework for competition among them—one that sets rules that check the strong, protect the weak, promote shared perspectives and effective common actions. Similarly, the nascent European Economic Community could not expect to eliminate struggles among its member states. But it could hope to provide them with a moral and institutional framework to protect individual national rights and accentuate common national interests.

But so long as Europe's community remains voluntary, a condition unlikely to change without some major crisis, it will endure only insofar as it does not rob the member nation states of their sense of freedom and dignity or excessively harm their interests. In this respect, the potential to revert to Nobody's Europe within the European Community has been like the right of revolution in any single nation state or federation. The threat to revolt and withdraw is the ultimate defense against tyranny. From this perspective, the often-expressed fear of a "renationalization" of policy in Europe is misplaced. The policy of a nation state is and should be national. To be a good European is not to lack a sense of national interest, but to define that national interest in a fashion that takes reasonable account of the national interests and collective welfare of Europe's other states. It means habitually formulating national interests in constant dialogue with others. Such habits have been the essence of Europe's postwar political miracle. But underlying this miracle has been a complex set of balances among and within the member states themselves, balances sustained by numerous formal and informal constitutional habits. The rough equality between postwar France and Germany has encouraged this evolution by preventing the emergence of any one overwhelmingly dominant power.

POLYMORPHOUS EUROPE

It seems obvious that today's European Union does not correspond entirely to any one of my four models of the 1960s but is the hybrid offspring of them all. Each model has made its own indispensable contribution. America's Atlantic Europe has helped to protect, stabilize, and provoke a European Union; to keep it reasonably "outward looking"; and to provide a favorable global setting. Nobody's Europe, the old balance-of-power system just beneath the surface, has helped to preserve the mutual restraints needed to keep Europe's confederacy together. Brussels federalism has provided the administrative machinery and ambitious élan that have made a Union possible, while confederal Europe has provided legitimacy and political direction to the whole.

Since the European Union's member states are themselves pluralist democracies with market economies, the postwar European system has developed not merely as a community of national governments and cosmopolitan technocrats; it encompasses and is greatly affected by all sorts of nonstate actors and institutions, including markets that often defy state direction. While most of these have a national base, some are more European than national, and not a few are extra-European. In such a European system, questions of identity, loyalty, and authority are inevitably complex. Thus, the balance and distinctions between federal and confederal models remain forever subtle and dynamic.

THE FRANCO-GERMAN ENGINE

Making Europe's union progress over the past half century has, of course, required more than a well-balanced structure or a talented and dedicated bureaucracy. Special leadership has been needed from among the member states themselves—leadership generous enough to give convincing definitions of collective interest and weighty enough to induce the others to follow. While every country has made its contribution, France and Germany have undoubtedly been the two leading states. By often collaborating closely, they have together provided the direction and drive needed to sustain and advance the great European project. As the confederacy's membership has grown larger and more diverse, their leadership has grown all the more essential.

The relationship between this Franco-German "couple" has necessarily been complicated. Both governments have believed that returning to their former unmitigated rivalry would be self-defeating and probably catastrophic—for themselves and for Europe as a whole. As a result, both have sought common ground in broader "European" solutions. In cultivating this habit over several decades, they have, in effect, usurped the leadership that Brussels federalists expected the Commission to monopolize. Naturally, France and Germany have their own historic interests and cultural ties with other states; each has often led its own particular bloc within the union. French and German dealings have thus often had a broader representative quality. At the same time, smaller states have grown skilled in lobbying their interests within the national political systems of the two leaders. The French and Germans, moreover, have generally sought to reinsure their positions vis-à-vis each other by cultivating outside connections—with the United States, Russia, Britain, Italy, and smaller European countries. Germany, for all sorts of reasons, has been inhibited from trying to lead Europe by itself. France, intrinsically the weaker partner, has generally been the more ambitious and determined. Neither one has wanted to affront the interests of smaller European states to the point where they become seriously uncooperative. Again, the threat of a regression to Nobody's Europe has had a healthy effect.

In short, France and Germany have together created a hybrid hegemony to go with a hybrid Europe. The hybrid hegemony has some special advantages. Collectively, it tends to be more sensitive to the rest of the union. When France and Germany do settle on a policy together, it usually has more appeal and legitimacy for the rest than a policy backed by only one or the other. There are also obvious disadvantages, which grow apparent whenever quick decisions are needed and the couple have differences that take time to resolve. Not surprisingly, the European Union has been more successful in the economic sphere than in the diplomatic or military spheres, both of which often require rapid and decisive action to be effective. With the advent of the European Monetary Union at the turn of the century, however, the need for rapid "crisis management" may well extend to the economic sphere as well.

ISSUES OF ENLARGEMENT

From the start, Europe's postwar community has derived its particular character, and probably also its practical success, not only from its clever organization, but also from the special constraints that limited its membership and scope. Because of the Cold War, the initial membership was effectively restricted to Western Europe. As Britain initially chose to remain outside, the original six members were continental and preponderantly Catholic states, with mostly Christian Democratic leaders.[4] Franco-German predominance was glaringly obvious. In 1958, after the two had struck a basic deal, the EEC went forward. A general customs union was to benefit German industry and a Common Agricultural Policy was to benefit French agriculture.

The membership question in the early years was whether the Community might extend to northern European countries led by Britain, countries traditionally Atlanticist in orientation and generally suspicious of the Catholic and mercantilist continent. After having tried to throttle the European Economic Community at its birth in 1958, Britain applied to join it in 1961. Domestic opposition in Britain was strong, and the negotiations were tortuous. Finally, Britain, Denmark, and Ireland were admitted in 1972, together with Norway, which soon, however, took its leave. In the 1980s, the Community expanded to poorer parts of southern Europe—by admitting Greece in 1981, after it had ejected its government of colonels, followed by Portugal and Spain in 1986, after Salazar and Franco had passed from the scene. In 1995, membership expanded to "neutral" Austria, Finland, and Sweden—prosperous Western countries previously marginalized by the Cold War.

[4] In 1958, the founding members were Belgium, France, the Federal Republic of Germany, Italy, Luxembourg, and the Netherlands. All had governments headed by Christian Democrats, except for France, where General de Gaulle had just come to power.

Each enlargement brought its own problems. British and Scandinavian membership raised the issue of whether the Community's cohesion and drive would be diluted by countries diffident toward the more ambitious agricultural, industrial, and political goals of the earlier members. Admitting Britain, a major European state with strong anti-European groups throughout its political spectrum, greatly complicated the Community's governance. But it did not necessarily weaken the drive toward more integration. Instead, British opposition was often the catalyst for galvanizing Franco-German cooperation to deepen the Community's institutional structure. Arguably, British skepticism and obstructionism helped to give continental members greater consciousness of their own deeper common interest in the European project.

The Mediterranean expansion of the 1980s brought forward the issue of how a network of Community policies and regulations, developed among relatively advanced and prosperous countries, could be adapted for poorer countries and how expansion's costs might be allocated. The Community resolved the issue by "leveling up" rather than "leveling down." The newcomers were constrained to accept, over a long transition period, the full *acquis communautaire*—the existing common regime of regulations and costs. This was a strategy that deprived poor countries of the cheap costs and less exacting regulations that were their natural advantage. In turn, they were compensated by generous Community transfers and capital investment. These were expected to provide the infrastructure and educational facilities needed to make poorer new members competitive, and to subsidize them in the interim. Among the primary beneficiaries, of course, were producers and workforces in the richer countries, particularly those in industries vulnerable to lower-priced competition.

Enlargement in the mid-1990s—to Austria, Finland, and Sweden—raised different issues. All three were rich but traditionally neutral. Admitting them had particular implications for the European Union's aspirations to have common diplomatic, security, and defense policies. These aspirations grew increasingly significant as the twentieth century drew to a close. After 1989, however, all previous issues of enlargement paled against the pan-European challenge posed by the collapse of the Soviet Empire in Eastern and Central Europe.

Enlargement and Constitutional Overload

The Community's original six member states were, in their various ways, strongly committed to their collective project. Over the years, moreover, a high degree of economic convergence gradually developed among them. Later additions increased the Community's diversity and discord and thus challenged its hybrid institutional structure. Institutions appropriate for six relatively homogeneous countries began to seem unwieldy with fifteen more diverse and often less committed members. Brussels federalists, of course, brought forward their traditional solutions: Community institutions should grow more supranational. An enlarged Council of Ministers should restrict the veto power of single states. Many more of its decisions should be reached by weighted majority voting. A larger and more diverse membership also called for a more powerful and streamlined Commission. To give that Commission democratic legitimacy, it should be chosen by a more representative and better-organized European Parliament and held responsible to it.

Throughout the postwar decades, however, progress along these federalist lines was extremely slow. European states were willing gradually to extend the scope of their cooperation, but not to relinquish their "sovereign" control of it. It was within these framing restrictions that Franco-German initiatives kept the European project moving forward, impelled not least by the fear that a stalling of momentum would unleash centrifugal forces of disintegration. Characteristically, each new cycle of enlargement was followed by a new cycle of integration. The conditions of the Cold War, however, ensured that those initiatives would be largely in the economic sphere.

Cold War Boundaries

The Cold War limited not only the Community's membership but also its scope. Since an American military protectorate seemed the most satisfactory security arrangement for West Europeans, European security cooperation ran through NATO rather than the European Community. In effect, a basic transatlantic compromise conceded military matters to NATO and gave America's blessing to European political and economic integration. Transatlantic military cooperation had, of course, its own tensions; basic strategic differences occasionally boiled over into public quarrels. And clashing American and European diplomatic and economic interests—as during the demise of Bretton Woods, the Middle Eastern oil crisis, or the disputes over trade with the Soviet bloc—sporadically renewed interest in endowing the European Community with a collective diplomatic and even military arm of its own. By the 1970s, political cooperation among the member states had rooted itself in regular semiannual European summits and numerous ministerial meetings. But further progress in this direction was leisurely. So long as the Cold War lasted, none of the major powers in the Community seriously wanted to change the political and military status quo. West Germany and Italy depended on the Americans for nuclear defense and saw no alternative. Britain automatically opposed collective European capabilities that might serve to make the American protectorate seem redundant. France was in no position to replace the Americans as Europe's nuclear defender. And the Americans, despite their perennial complaints about inadequate burden sharing, saw no desirable alternative to their protector's role.

Meanwhile, the economic sphere continued to offer ample scope and incentive for further European integration. The 1980s ended on a particularly successful note. Continental Europe's national economies were booming and converging, as the Single European Act of 1987 was rapidly fusing their markets and a European Monetary System (EMS) was helping to keep their exchange rates stable. Converging macroeconomic policies among the leading countries were making monetary union with a common currency seem a realistic goal for the 1990s.[5] Even in the military sphere, the West European Union (WEU) had been revived, and Europeans were already experimenting with mixed military forces in the Franco-German Brigade and the Euro-

---

[5] In 1988, German, French, Italian, and British growth rates were all between 3.7 and 5.0 percent. In 1989, however, the Italian rate dropped to just below 3 and the British rate to just over 2 percent.

149

corps. In other words, in the years just before the end of the Cold War, Europe's hybrid system seemed remarkably successful. It provided a framework that accommodated Europe's nation states, with all their tenacious cultural diversity and fierce political energy, but biased their relations toward cooperation. West European states seemed finally to have found an ideal way to govern their diverse continental system. Meanwhile, Gorbachev's reforms were opening the prospect of a rapprochement with Eastern Europe and a controlled easing of bipolarity. A gradual reintegration of the continental system seemed feasible, one that could stabilize the Cold War's peace, improve the lot of those caught up in the Soviet empire, and, at the same time, preserve the gains of West European integration.

THE SOVIET SHOCK

The Soviet collapse radically altered Western Europe's sheltered postwar setting and promised a much more volatile internal and external environment. In place of a single stabilizing threat came a diversity of security problems, some reminiscent of an unhappy past. A big Germany once more made its neighbors apprehensive and began to seem problematic internally. Central and Eastern European states were weak and open. One of the largest of these states, Yugoslavia, was breaking up in vicious ethnic warfare. The Soviet Union itself was disintegrating, and its principal successor state, Russia, was weak and unstable. Since European and American security interests were no longer yoked together by an obvious common enemy, the United States could not necessarily be counted on to look after Europe's security problems. In any event, these were not a nuclear threat from a rival superpower but a horde of local conflicts and police problems that seemed not so amenable to American direction. At the same time, a severe and stubborn recession, starting in the early 1990s, underscored Western Europe's vulnerability in a less friendly world economy. Faced with such conditions, the community's hybrid system, with its leisurely bargaining and generous trade-offs, threatened to grow paralyzed and dysfunctional.

The Maastricht Treaty, signed in December 1991, was Europe's ambitious response. Major leaps forward in Western integration were to reorder the old Community so that it could effectively control the new situation. The goals were the familiar aspirations of West European integration: the single-market, monetary union and a common foreign and security policy, together with institutional and constitutional streamlining. Maastricht threw in harmonized norms for justice, immigration, and social policy. Few seemed to appreciate just how much the Community's new challenges of the 1990s would complicate pursuing this Western path of the 1980s. At Maastricht, rather than reconsider or delay their old goals, Europe's leaders reaffirmed them and advanced the timetable. They did so, however, without securing a consensus on the constitutional reforms that might make such goals realistic, above all for a pan-European membership. It is too early to tell whether they made a major historic error. Part III explores the issue further, but assessing Europe's further prospects first requires a closer look at Europe's evolving relations with the global economy. Globalization, threatening Europe's prosperity, has also generated powerful new incentives for its integration.

SELECTED SOURCES

The Models: Atlantic Europe

For my own discussion of the roots of Atlanticism, see David P. Calleo and Benjamin M. Rowland, *America and the World Political Economy* (Bloomington: Indiana University Press, 1973), pp. 16–84. For an influential Atlantic view before World War II, see Clarence K. Streit, *Union Now* (New York: Harper, 1939). For a powerful illustration of the Wilsonian strand in American policy, see Cordell Hull, *Memoirs* (New York: Macmillan, 1948). For how Atlanticism meshed with postwar European visions, see Harold van Buren Cleveland, *The Atlantic Idea and Its European Rivals* (New York: McGraw-Hill, 1966). For a later postwar version, see Eugene V. Rostow, *Law, Power and the Pursuit of Peace* (Lincoln: University of Nebraska Press, 1968). For a current Atlanticist vision, see Francis Fukuyama, *The End of History and the Last Man* (New York: Free Press, 1992).

Brussels Federalism

For diverse federalist visions in the early postwar years, see Altiero Spinelli, *The Eurocrats: Conflict and Crisis in the European Community,* trans. C. Grove Haines (Baltimore: Johns Hopkins University Press, 1966); Henri Brugmans, *L'Idée européenne, 1918–1965* (Brussels: Elsevier, 1965) and *Panorama de la pensée fédéraliste* (Paris: La Colombe, 1956); and Emmanuel Mounier, *Liberté sous conditions* (Paris: Editions de Seuil, 1946). For Walter Hallstein promoting the federalist idea, see his Clayton Lecture, "United Europe—Challenge and Opportunity," delivered at the Fletcher School of Diplomacy on April 16, 1962 (2738/PP/62-En). The academic school of functionalist federalist thought is best approached through Ernst B. Haas, "International Integration: The European and the Universal Process," in *International Organization,* vol. 15 (1961), and *The Uniting of Europe: Political, Social, and Economic Forces, 1950–1957* (Stanford: Stanford University Press, 1958). For histories of Jean Monnet's ideas and heroic labors, see Richard Mayne, *The Recovery of Europe: From Devastation to Unity* (New York: Harper & Row, 1970); Francois Duchêne, *Jean Monnet: The First Statesman of Interdependence* (New York: Norton, 1994); and Jean Monnet, *Memoirs* (Garden City, NY: Doubleday, 1978).

The Europe of States

For de Gaulle's Europe of States, see the chapter "Europe" in Charles de Gaulle, *Memoirs of Hope: Renewal and Endeavor,* trans. Terence Kilmartin (New York: Simon & Schuster, 1971). For my earlier analyses, see *Europe's Future: The Grand Alternatives* (New York: Horizon Press, 1965), ch. 4, and also David P. Calleo, *The Atlantic Fantasy* (Baltimore: Johns Hopkins University Press, 1970), ch. 5. For de Gaulle's views on technological change and national independence, see his *Vers l'armée de métier* (Paris: Berger-Levrault, 1944; originally published 1934), especially pp. 87ff. For Gaullist ideas on sovereignty, see also Maurice Couve de Murville, *Une Politique étrangère, 1958–1969* (Paris: Plon, 1971), in particular pp. 285–430.

For more discussion, see David P. Calleo, *Europe's Future*, op. cit., p. 128.

The Franco-German Engine

For the evolution of postwar cooperation, see F. Roy Willis, *France, Germany and the New Europe, 1945–1967* (Stanford: Stanford University Press, 1968), and Julius W. Friend, *The Linchpin: French-German Relations 1950–1990* (New York: Praeger, 1991). For later years, see Patrick McCarthy, ed., *France-Germany, 1983–1993: The Struggle to Cooperate* (New York: St. Martin's Press, 1993), and also David P. Calleo and Eric Staal, eds., *Europe's Franco-German Engine* (SAIS European Series, Washington, DC: Brookings Institution, 1997). For Europe's political cooperation in the 1970s, see Anthony Forster and William Wallace, "Common Foreign and Security Policy," in Helen Wallace and William Wallace, eds., *Policy-Making in the European Union* 3rd ed. (Oxford: Oxford University Press, 1996), pp. 411–435.

Expanding the Community

For how new members were leveled up to meet the acquis of the old members, see Richard Baldwin, Pertti Haaparanta, and Jaakko Kiander, eds., *Expanding Membership of the European Union* (New York: Cambridge University Press, 1995); Gerald Schneider and Patricia A. Weitzman, eds., *Towards a New Europe: Stops and Starts in Regional Integration* (Westport, CT: Praeger, 1995); and Pierre Laurent and Marc Maresceau, eds., *Deepening and Widening* (Boulder, CO: Lynne Rienner, 1998).

The Soviet Shock

For further discussion of enlargement after the Soviet Union's collapse, see chapter 13. For the economic consequences of the Soviet collapse for European integration, see chapters 9 and 11; for the security consequences, see chapter 14.

Europe in the Global Economy

EVEN BY THE early 1950s, much of the postwar world, the unhappy Soviet bloc excepted, had begun to fulfill Roosevelt's dreams for a Pax Americana. Within America's benign geopolitical shelter a global political economy began reconstituting itself. Resurrected Europe and Japan became once again major centers of world commerce and finance. Many nations in Asia and Latin America availed themselves of the system's abundant capital and open markets and took off toward the ranks of advanced industrial economies. But like every political-economic system, the postwar Pax Americana contained inner tensions that, unless controlled, pointed toward decay and collapse. In the early postwar years, a great deal of friction existed between Europe and the United States. Americans and Europeans had quite different ideas about how the world economy should be organized. American statecraft was pressing hard to impose its liberal Wilsonian model. Europeans were determined to transform their national economies and leery of schemes that would hobble national policy with international rules and obligations. More and more, they also wanted to form a bloc of their own. American globalism and European nationalism seemed set on a collision course.

The Cold War helped greatly to inspire a highly productive compromise, as chapter 6 discusses. Not only did the presence of an overweening common enemy impose political accommodation among the transatlantic allies, it also cured interwar capitalism's near-fatal syndrome: the combination of deflation, underconsumption, and unemployment. The cure was what Keynes had prescribed: government spending. The Cold War provided the necessary justification: for arms to hold off the Soviet hordes and for investment and welfare to smother Marxist class conflict. Meanwhile, the fashionable "neo-Keynesian" economists of the day assured their receptive governments that fiscal deficits and easy money, by anticipating growth, were thereby securing it. Expansive policies, initially designed to stimulate crippled economies in the interwar Depression, were successfully applied to robust economies in the postwar boom.

In due course, the new prosperity led to new problems. In the decade before World War II, the prevailing economic climate had been chronic deflation. Two decades after the war, it was becoming chronic inflation.[1] Postwar governments were pressed to fulfill simultaneous demands for more arms and welfare and for more public and private investment and consumption. They began to cover these demands with fiscal deficits and easy money. Systemic inflation was the result. The particular character of this inflationary syndrome, and how it was dealt with, naturally differed from one Western country to another, and significantly between the United States and the Europeans. By the 1960s, these differences were feeding a new transatlantic conflict of interest.

U.S. INFLATION AND THE END OF BRETTON WOODS

During most of the 1950s, the Eisenhower administration struggled with the inflationary tendencies generated by the huge jumps in U.S. military outlays initiated by the Korean War.[2] The administration tried to limit both military and civilian spending, even in the face of two recessions within its eight-year term. The Democratic opposition charged that the United States was lagging behind the Soviets militarily and behind both Europe and the Soviets economically. The

[1] From 1945 to 1965, the U.S. consumer price index (CPI) rose on average 1.5 percent annually; from 1965 to 1972, on average 4.1 percent annually; and from 1972 to 1974, on average 8.6 percent annually. Other industrial countries showed similar acceleration in the early 1970s. In Germany, for instance, consumer price inflation averaged 3.4 percent between 1968 and 1971 and 6.5 percent between 1972 and 1974. Comparable figures for France were 5.4 percent and 9.1 percent. International Monetary Fund, *International Financial Statistics Yearbook 1998* (Washington, DC: International Monetary Fund, 1998), p. 124; *OECD Economic Outlook: December 1987* (Paris: OECD, 1987), p. 180.

[2] U.S. defense expenditures were 6 percent of GDP in fiscal year 1950 and 10.2 percent in 1952. U.S. Office of Management and Budget, *Budget of the U.S. Government, Fiscal Year 2000* (Washington, DC: Executive Office of the President, Office of Management and Budget, 1999), p. 266.

succeeding Kennedy administration was determined to reverse what it saw as American decline. It pursued a military buildup, an upgrading of the welfare system, and a growth-oriented macroeconomic policy. The Johnson administration that followed accelerated the Kennedy initiatives. Intervention in Vietnam escalated and spending for the "Great Society" gathered momentum, while monetary policy remained easy, despite rapid growth. Neo-Keynesian fiscal doctrines, popularized to rationalize a tax cut in 1964, could be summoned to justify federal deficits under almost any circumstances. Inflation was a natural consequence; it first became manifest in a worsening balance of payments. As the Vietnam War continued, fiscal conditions also deteriorated and domestic price inflation rose rapidly. By early 1968, the administration was having great difficulty maintaining the exchange rate of the dollar.

Inflation in the United States soon began to erode the global economic arrangements of the Pax Americana, in particular the Bretton Woods monetary system. Bretton Woods called for convertible currencies and fixed exchange rates. Parities were to be changed only according to rules and by agreement. The dollar, the system's anchor, was convertible into gold at a fixed rate. The provisions of Bretton Woods did not really come into effect until 1958, when a recovered, prosperous, and integrating Europe finally felt confident enough to make its currencies convertible with the dollar. Within little more than a decade, the Bretton Woods system was moribund.

The United States, thanks to its foreign aid and investment, had been running a substantial balance of payments deficit throughout the 1950s. Contrary to what was expected, making European currencies convertible in 1958 did not reverse this imbalance. Instead, the glut of dollars on world markets continued to grow. The flood of expatriate dollars was, of course, welcome in the late 1940s and 1950s, when Europe's growth and prosperity depended heavily on American credit. But by the 1960s, the dollar glut was more and more resented among America's transatlantic creditors, not least because American deficits were thought to stoke inflation in Europe itself. In 1965, a serious public quarrel began between the United States and France over the international role of the dollar. It was widely believed in Europe that the dollar glut came from an overly expansive American monetary policy. Because Bretton Woods made the dollar the indispensable reserve currency, Americans could print their money at will, and the rest of the world was supposed to go on accepting it for international settlements. Not only did the French regard the situation as unfair economically and abusive politically, but they also saw it as an insidious mechanism whereby the United States could "export inflation" to Europe. By 1965, General de Gaulle was predicting that declining confidence in the stability of the dollar's value would eventually undermine the whole fixed-rate system. Within a few years, his prediction had been realized.

By the late 1960s, the surplus dollars accumulating abroad had gathered into a huge offshore capital market—the "Eurodollar Market." This market's abundant credit, free from government regulation, helped to fuel prosperity overseas, including the hectic growth of multinational enterprise in Europe—the *défi américain* that so agitated the French. In due course, the size of the Eurodollar Market dwarfed the foreign exchange reserves of all the Western countries, the United States included.[3] With so vast a pool of uncontrolled credit available for speculation, maintaining a fixed-rate system became increasingly problematic.

By the late 1960s, the United States itself had grown dissatisfied with fixed exchange rates. By mid-1968, defending the dollar, given high military spending for the Vietnam War and high civilian spending for Johnson's Great Society programs, required the administration to impose controls on foreign investment, Congress to raise taxes, and the Fed to push up interest rates.[4] These conditions persisted into the Nixon administration and were unwelcome politically, among other

---

[3] In 1970, the size of the Eurodollar market was $57 billion, compared with total gold reserves in the United States of $11 billion and total gold reserves of all countries of $37 billion. The foreign exchange reserves of all countries then totaled $93.24 billion and those of the United States $14.49 billion. Bank for International Settlements, *Annual Report*, no. 41 (Basel: Bank for International Settlements, 1971), pp. 127, 157; *International Financial Statistics Yearbook 1998* (Washington, DC: International Monetary Fund, 1998), p. 46.

[4] Various capital controls had been imposed progressively throughout the 1960s. See U.S. President, *The Economic Report of the President, February 1999* (Washington, DC: U.S. Government Printing Office, 1999), pp. 329, 407, 413, 419.

things, because they helped to provoke a sharp economic slowdown. In addition, American producers began to complain that the dollar was "overvalued" and was causing the United States to lose its competitiveness. By 1971, the United States was running its first trade deficit since the nineteenth century.[5] Bretton Woods, which made the dollar convertible into gold at a fixed parity, supposedly made it technically impossible for the dollar to devalue. But many American economists argued that, since the Europeans unreasonably refused to revalue, the United States should assume an attitude of "benign neglect" toward defending its currency.

On August 15, 1971, President Nixon, confronted with a huge run on the dollar, announced his "New Economic Policy." Its centerpiece was an indefinite suspension of dollar convertibility, coupled with domestic wage and price controls.[6] Alarmed Europeans hoped the result would be a once-for-all devaluation. But given inflationary pressures in the United States, including the continued monetization of large fiscal deficits, Nixon's new economic formula emerged as expansionary macroeconomic policies, with chronic inflationary tendencies complemented by frequent depreciations of the dollar. When wage and price controls were lifted at the start of 1973, after Nixon's election in November 1972, American price inflation exploded.[7]

EUROPEAN INFLATION

By 1973, however, Europe's troubles with inflation could no longer be blamed exclusively on the Americans. By the late 1960s, Europeans were generating their own currency shocks—with the British pound and French franc devaluing and the German mark rising. These perturbations reflected not only the unstable dollar but also the increasing inflationary pressure being generated within the European economies themselves. In 1968, a powerful wave of strikes and gen-

[5] Ibid., p. 444.
[6] The provisions of Nixon's New Economic Policy are included in *The Economic Report of the President* (Washington, DC: U.S. Government Printing Office, 1972).
[7] U.S. consumer price inflation reached 3.4 percent in 1972 and 12.3 percent in 1974. Wages, by contrast, were only 6.4 percent higher in nominal terms by 1974.

eral public unrest broke out in Paris and spread all over Europe. To calm the riotous popular fevers, many governments and employers had granted generous social benefits and wage increases and then relied on inflation and currency depreciation to lower the real costs and restore industrial profits. As a result, by the early 1970s, several European states, notably France (but not Germany), had adopted an inflationary course parallel to that of the United States.

There were, however, important transatlantic differences. American inflation could be blamed on too much defense spending, particularly as the Vietnam War dragged on. It was thus linked to geopolitical "overstretch"—excessive military costs leading a hegemonic power into "decline." In Europe, where military spending was much lower, thanks to the American protectorate, too much social spending was the obvious culprit.[8] Europe's inflation thus reflected "Eurosclerosis," an excess of welfare spending and protective regulation. As their distinct but complementary ailments progressed, Europeans and Americans cultivated different but reciprocal grievances. Americans saw Europeans as prosperous "free riders," living off American military power and refusing equitable "burden sharing." Europeans saw the United States as an undisciplined "hegemon in decline," using political and military power to gain economic advantage.

With both Europe and America following expansive monetary courses, it was not surprising that a paroxysm of inflation swept the world economy in 1973, including an explosion of food prices, followed by a quadrupling of oil prices in 1974.[9] With economies reeling, central banks, including the U.S. Federal Reserve, sharply and abruptly restricted money supplies. A severe economic downturn was

---

[8] In 1970, the United States spent 7.9 percent of its GNP on defense. France spent 4.2 percent, and Germany 3.3 percent. Social security spending was 7.9 percent of GDP in the United States, compared to 15.2 percent in France and 11.3 percent in Germany. U.S. Arms Control and Disarmament Agency, *World Military Expenditures and Arms Transfers* (Washington, DC: U.S. Government Printing Office, 1975, 1982, 1990); OECD, *National Accounts* (Paris: OECD, 1999).

[9] Between 1970 and 1975, the world consumer price index rose by 64 percent, while the price of oil rose fivefold, and the price of wheat more than doubled. *International Financial Statistics Yearbook 1998* (Washington, DC: International Monetary Fund, 1998), pp. 124, 172.

only natural. In 1974, the United States experienced the worst recession since the 1930s.[10]

Thereafter, American and European macroeconomic policies began to diverge sharply. The recession prompted the United States to resume the expansive Nixon formula in 1975. Further monetary expansion was encouraged by the huge demand for liquidity throughout the international banking system after the oil shock, as countries borrowed heavily to cover their oil bills. The practice was actively encouraged by neo-Keynesian economists, who feared that the real effect of the oil price increase would be a massive deflation. As a result, the United States proceeded to inflate its way out of the oil shock. As inflation pushed up the general price level, oil's price fell relatively. For a variety of reasons, including the enhanced U.S. position in the Middle East after the 1973 war, oil producers did not raise their prices correspondingly, at least not until the Iranian revolution in 1979.[11]

Europeans, lacking America's dollar franchise and relatively autarkic economy, felt unable to follow the Americans in inflating their way out of the oil crisis. Europe's national economies felt more vulnerable to accelerating prices and wages and to rapidly accumulating government debt. Mostly without oil of their own, European governments felt driven to make real rather than merely financial adjustments to the oil shocks. This adjustment meant curbing consumption and increasing investment—to improve productivity in order to import less and be able to export more. For such policies, inflation was anathema.

FROM THE NIXON FORMULA TO THE REAGAN-VOLCKER FORMULA

These different courses led to sharp transatlantic conflict. The Carter administration, taking office in 1977, continued the expansionist

[10] U.S. gross national product shrank by 0.5 percent in 1974 and by 1.3 percent in 1975. In Europe, the picture was mixed: the UK economy contracted by 1.8 percent in 1974 and a further 1.1 percent in 1975, while in Germany output was stagnant in 1974 and fell by 1.3 percent in 1975. In France, it rose in both years. *OECD Economic Outlook: December 1987* (Paris: OECD, 1987), p. 174.

[11] For a further discussion, see David P. Calleo, *The Imperious Economy* (Cambridge: Harvard University Press, 1982), pp. 129ff.

Nixon formula and pressured Europeans to join the United States to form a neo-Keynesian "locomotive" of rich countries, expanding their economies to pull the rest of the world out of its slump. European governments resisted. The Germans finally sought to appease the Americans by stimulating their economy in 1978, but the second oil shock of 1979, catching them in an expansive phase, soon made them regret doing so. By 1979, the Americans themselves were forced to abandon the Nixon formula. Price inflation was again rampant in the United States. The dollar began falling rapidly, with dramatic rises in interest rates and in the prices of gold and oil.[12]

In the United States, as in Europe, large sections of the public began to grow alarmed at inflation and to associate it with national decline. Carter, eventually catching the change of mood, named a strong-minded chairman to the Federal Reserve, Paul Volcker, whose abrupt monetary check to galloping inflation stopped the dollar's fall and closed out the 1970s with another severe recession. Carter's conversion to austerity should have put the United States and the Europeans on a parallel course. But when the Reagan administration took power in 1981, Volcker's monetary rigor was soon complemented by a large increase in military spending, accompanied by a "supply-side" tax cut. Huge fiscal deficits resulted.[13] Since Volcker's Fed nevertheless continued its tight monetary policy, and American domestic saving remained at its habitual low level, financing the fiscal deficit

---

[12] Between 1978 and 1981, the interest rate on treasury bills almost doubled from 7.2 percent to 14.1 percent. The oil price jumped from $14.3 to $36.7 per barrel over the same period, and the price of gold shot up from $178.1 per ounce in the first quarter of 1978 to $648.0 per ounce in the third quarter of 1980. *IMF International Financial Statistics Yearbook 1992* (Washington, DC: International Monetary Fund, 1992), p. 97; *IMF International Financial Statistics Yearbook 1998* (Washington, DC: International Monetary Fund, 1998), p. 172; *IMF International Financial Statistics, Supplement on Price Statistics* (Washington, DC: International Monetary Fund, 1986), pp. 160–161.

[13] Reagan's "supply-side" tax cut was a right-wing variant of the neo-Keynesian logic of Johnson's 1964 tax cut. See David P. Calleo, *The Bankrupting of America: How the Federal Deficit Impoverishes the Nation* (New York: William Morrow, 1992), pp. 35–36, 116–120. Between 1981 and 1986, the federal deficit widened from $79 billion to $221.2 billion, while the debt stock more than doubled from $994.8 billion to $2,120.6 billion. *Economic Report of the President* (Washington, DC: U.S. Government Printing Office, 1999), pp. 419–420.

obliged the Treasury to borrow most of the rest of the world's free capital. Very high American interest rates attracted foreign money in abundance and also sent the floating dollar's exchange rate to unprecedented heights.[14] In effect, a new "Reagan-Volcker formula" of the 1980s—sucking in foreign capital and pushing up the dollar—replaced the "Nixon formula" of the 1970s—exporting capital and depreciating the dollar. Not surprisingly, under the Reagan-Volcker formula, America's trade and current account balances deteriorated sharply. By 1983, the United States was running not only a massive fiscal deficit but a massive external deficit as well. The fiscal deficit thus became the "twin deficit."[15]

U.S. Deficits and Global Stability

Reagan did not, of course, invent either of the twin deficits of the 1980s, although his policies exacerbated them hugely. Strictly speaking, the federal budget was in balance for only one fiscal year between 1960 and 1998.[16] America's external deficit was more venerable still. In one form or another, the United States was in deficit with the world economy throughout most of the postwar era. The nature of the external deficit varied. In the 1950s and 1960s, the United States often had what was then called a *basic deficit* and also a *liquidity deficit.*[17]

---

[14] Between 1981 and 1985, the dollar appreciated by 7.5 percent against the Japanese yen, and by 23.1 percent against the German mark. *Economic Report of the President* (Washington, DC: U.S. Government Printing Office, 1999), p. 452.

[15] Following small surpluses in 1980 and 1981, the U.S. current account balance recorded a deficit of $11.4 billion in 1982 and $44.0 billion in 1983. By 1985, it had expanded to $115.3 billion. *Economic Report of the President* (Washington, DC: U.S. Government Printing Office, 1999), p. 444.

[16] In 1969, the federal government recorded a small surplus of $3.2 billion, equivalent to 0.3 percent of gross domestic product. *Economic Report of the President* (Washington, DC: U.S. Government Printing Office, 1999), pp. 419–420.

[17] The "basic" balance was defined as the balance on current account plus the balance on long-term capital account and government grants. The "liquidity" balance also included short-term nonbank capital flows. *Economic Report of the President* (Washington, DC: U.S. Government Printing Office, 1972), p. 154. For further discussion, see David P. Calleo, *The Bankrupting of America: How the Federal Deficit Impoverishes the Nation* (New York: William Morrow, 1992), ch. 6.

The first meant, in effect, that the American real economy was dispensing more abroad—including military aid and private investment—than it was earning from abroad, despite a significant trade and current account surplus. The liquidity deficit meant that there was, in addition, a substantial leakage of American "hot money" into the world economy. By the 1970s, the United States also had a regular trade deficit, despite the weak dollar. By the early 1980s, with the advent of Reagan's strong dollar, the habitual trade deficit had turned into a habitual current account deficit—a category that includes "services" and hence the repatriated earnings from American investments abroad. The big current account deficit has, of course, survived both the Reagan administration and the Cold War. In the 1990s, after a brief improvement, it began setting new records.[18]

It is difficult to imagine any other country sustaining deficits of this kind with the world economy for half a century. America has owed its privileged position to two special characteristics. The dollar's role as the world's indispensable reserve and transactions currency has meant that the United States could either print or borrow money as it wished. And America's huge and relatively autarkic national economy has meant that prices of exports and imports have had relatively little effect on the general level of domestic prices in the United States.

The deficits themselves have reflected America's dual nature as global hegemon and democratic nation state. One role calls for guns, the other for butter. Unable to renounce either choice sufficiently to bring its world accounts into balance, the United States has used its huge size and hegemonic monetary power to induce the rest of the world to finance its deficits. From an American perspective, it has seemed very much in the world's interest to do so. Certainly, during the Cold War, it was in the interest of those rich European countries whose defense formed so large a part of America's hegemonic military burden. From this perspective, the various American formulas for financing deficits by manipulating the dollar were the mechanisms for

---

[18] The U.S. current account deficit widened from $4.4 billion in 1991 to $338.9 billion in 1999, a new record in absolute terms, if not in relation to GDP. *OECD Economic Outlook, December 1998* (Paris: OECD, 1998), pp. 241–242; *OECD Main Economic Indicators, April 2000* (Paris: OECD, 2000), p. 52.

the indirect imperial taxation needed to sustain the Atlantic Alliance and the Pax Americana.[19]

During the Cold War, America's deficits became an integral part of the way the global system functioned. Following Europe's recovery, America's heavy export of investment capital and growing appetite for imports of goods became critical ingredients for Asia's mushrooming growth. Since the 1970s, America's bilateral trade deficits have been primarily with Asian countries—first with Japan and then, additionally, with the "little tigers" like Korea, Taiwan, Thailand, and Hong Kong. By the 1990s, the United States was also running a large and rapidly growing trade deficit with China. By the end of the century, Asian growth and American indebtedness had grown disturbingly interdependent. Europe also traded heavily with Asia, but its bilateral trade was roughly in balance.[20]

Another striking consequence of America's special global economic position is the huge pool of unregulated international capital

---

[19] I developed this argument in a series of books that document much of the analysis here. See David P. Calleo, *The Imperious Economy*, op. cit., especially chs. 5 and 7; *Beyond American Hegemony* (A Twentieth Century Fund Book; New York: Basic Books, 1987), ch. 7; and *The Bankrupting of America: How the Federal Deficit Impoverishes the Nation*, op. cit., especially ch. 6.

[20] The U.S. trade deficit with Asia almost doubled between 1990 and 1996 to $79.8 billion, largely as a result of a growing negative imbalance with China, which grew from $11.5 billion to $42.4 billion. The United States also ran sizable deficits with Japan and Taiwan throughout the 1990s, although its trade with Korea, Hong Kong, and Thailand was roughly in balance. The European Union's trade deficit with Asia was much smaller, amounting to $15.3 billion in 1996. It consistently ran deficits with Taiwan, China, and Japan, but these were partly offset by surpluses with Hong Kong and, to a lesser degree, with Singapore. By the 1990s, the U.S. current account deficits were financed in good part by foreign direct investment. This came mainly from the EU, which, for example, accounted for 57 percent of new investment in 1995, and from Japan, with 19 percent in the same year. Direct investments by the Association of Southeast Asian Nations (ASEAN) countries were negligible. Foreign direct investment inflows typically covered around half the U.S. current account deficit between 1992 and 1998. *Direction of Trade Statistics Yearbook 1997* (Washington, DC: International Monetary Fund, 1997), pp. 74, 453; *OECD International Direct Investment Statistics Yearbook, 1997* (Paris: OECD, 1997), pp. 340–341; *International Financial Statistics Yearbook, 1998* (Washington, DC: International Monetary Fund, 1998).

formed thanks to America's exported dollars. Undoubtedly, many of the effects have been beneficial. Easy credit has greatly augmented the growth not only of Western and Japanese multinational enterprise but also of industry and commerce in many developing countries. But so huge a pool of unregulated capital in the hands of private investors naturally encourages speculation and malinvestment throughout the world, including the hectic currency speculation that has helped to make exchange rates routinely and excessively unstable following the 1960s.[21] In effect, after the 1960s, the United States gave up trying to provide a stable international currency—a "public good" for the global economy and initially considered an essential hegemonic duty. Thereafter, thanks in good part to America's continuing outsized defense burdens, it has proved impossible to develop a stable international monetary system based on multilateral rules. In the absence of this public good, financial institutions and national economies have everywhere felt increasingly threatened by the volatility of international currency markets. Private actors have had to make their own provisions against risk. Profound changes began taking place in the nature of global capitalism. Enormous markets have developed for "hedging" in its multifarious forms. Firms active in the world economy began consolidating their resources against currency shocks that were becoming routine. Slowly, the international economy has grown more and more dominated by "multinational" firms—large enough to protect themselves in the erratic markets characteristic of a world with unstable exchange rates.[22] Giant financial institutions, with the capital to run the huge risks, have developed to service their needs. Arguably, European monetary union at the end of the century was itself a product of the same reaction against chronic monetary instability.

[21] Between 1973 and 1980, the dollar depreciated by 12.6 percent against its main trading partners. It then appreciated by 63.4 percent between 1980 and 1985, before depreciating again by a further 41.1 percent over the period from 1985 to 1995. *Economic Report of the President* (Washington, DC: U.S. Government Printing Office, 1999), p. 452.

[22] For a delineation of various types of multinationals, see Michael Veseth, *Selling Globalization: The Myth of the Global Economy* (Boulder, CO: Lynne Rienner, 1998), p. 34.

Eurosclerosis

Already by the 1970s, Europeans felt they had good reason to be nervous about their prospects in the global economy. The causes, however, were internal as well as global. Most European economies were struggling with bouts of Eurosclerosis, a sort of socioeconomic *crise de foie*, where government sectors expanded inexorably, fiscal conditions deteriorated, stagflation grew endemic, labor was too expensive and inflexible, and an excess of taxation and regulation stifled entrepreneurship. Eurosclerosis seemed the mirror image of American decline. America's problems could be attributed to domestic neglect and geopolitical overstretch, Europe's to domestic overindulgence and geopolitical atrophy.

Eurosclerosis—the combination of democracy, statism, welfarism, and inflation—had long been anticipated in the visions and warnings of continental neoliberal economists, like Friedrich von Hayek or the French monetarist Jacques Rueff. Their warnings seemed to be coming true following the eruption of discontented Parisian students and workers in May 1968. French unrest was quickly replicated in most other European countries. These troubles were widely interpreted as signaling a new postindustrial society, where the old capitalist culture of competitive hard work and saving was replaced by a new ethic of personal self-fulfillment, leisure, and fellowship—a cultural change made possible by the affluence generated in the 1950s and 1960s. While the revolutionary exhilaration of 1968 beguiled many analysts, classic liberals saw disturbing echoes of the fascist violence of the interwar years. De Gaulle saw it as the collective *chie en lit* of a people spoilt by prosperity.

A few years later, the oil shock of 1974 brought home to Europeans the precariousness of their economic situation. The explosion of wage and fuel costs sharply reduced the profitability of their firms, which could not easily be reestablished. If currencies were devalued, prices simply rose in tandem. As import prices were raised, wages tended to follow. Low profits meant falling investment, which diminished future productivity—a malignant spiral pointing toward economic decline and social unrest.[23] Given an urgent need to restrain wages and increase profits, European analysts found inspiration in classical liberal policies that promised to prompt investment by lowering the cost of capital. These prescribed limiting consumption—especially government-induced consumption—in order to increase the pool of savings. And they also prescribed strict monetary discipline—to purge capital markets of their inflationary expectations and thereby to lower interest rates further.

This had long been the preferred strategy of the German Bundesbank. By refusing to ratify inflationary budgets or wage settlements by creating more money, it had hoped to compel Germany's governments, business firms, and unions to make decisions based on a noninflationary reckoning of costs and income. Consequently, the German mark was often "overvalued" by comparison with the dollar or other European currencies. To remain competitive, German firms were forced to invest heavily to keep improving their productivity, and also to be careful of costs and attentive to quality. They naturally gravitated toward producing upscale products with high profits, the demand for which is often less sensitive to price changes. German workers, very well paid, were also highly skilled and efficient. With its strong currency, and with products whose prices could be raised without greatly affecting demand, the German economy did better during the first oil shock than the more inflationary French or Italian economies.

After the oil shocks of the early 1970s, many French economic strategists grew into ardent converts to the German model. Rising oil prices meant that devaluing the franc no longer seemed a useful tool for restoring profits and competitiveness. Sustaining high living stan-

[23] Over the period 1970–1980, investment grew by on average 1.9 percent a year in Europe, compared to 3.6 percent in the United States. Rates of return on capital in the business sector also tended to be lower in Europe, averaging 11.7 percent between 1975 and 1979, compared to 15.5 percent in the United States, while European labor costs also rose more rapidly, expanding by 11.4 percent a year between 1973 and 1979, compared to 8.2 percent in the United States. *OECD Economic Outlook: June 1998* (Paris: OECD, 1998), p. 174; *OECD Economic Outlook: June 1992* (Paris: OECD, 1992), pp. 133–134.

dards, the French decided, required specializing, like the Germans, in advanced industries with high profits. Promoting such industries would require stricter market discipline than in the past. Managers and unions should no longer rely on government subsidies and general inflation to bail out unsustainable wage and investment costs. Ending this inflationist mentality would eliminate the inflation premium on interest rates and wages. More investment would promote the higher productivity needed to remain advanced and competitive. In other words, France needed to enter the same virtuous circle that seemed to explain Germany's comparative strength. These ideas began to shape French policy during the presidency of Valéry Giscard d'Estaing (1974–1981), when the government of Prime Minister Raymond Barre (1976–1981) sought to impose a new anti-inflationary *rigueur* on the economy.

France's conversion to German virtue propelled a new advance in European integration. Giscard and Helmut Schmidt, the German chancellor from 1974 to 1982, shared similar and compatible views of their respective national interests. Together, they began building a European Monetary System (EMS) in the 1970s. Giscard hoped it would help him to stiffen monetary policy in France. In effect, Giscard used the EMS to borrow the German Bundesbank for disciplining the French economy, and in a fashion, that would also help to reinforce the Bundesbank's policy at home. Giscard and Schmidt deplored the expansionist macroeconomic policies of the Carter administration and feared the inflationary effects would spread to Europe. Both hoped the EMS would bring greater stability to currencies throughout the European Community as a whole and thus shelter Europe's internal exchange rates from the declining dollar. By the early 1980s, however, their experiment had faltered. As noted earlier, Schmidt, under heavy pressure from the Carter administration as well as his own socialist left wing, joined the American locomotive to reflate the world economy, only to have the second oil shock of 1979 hit the expanding German economy with particular severity. His government fell in 1982 and was replaced by Helmut Kohl's new coalition, which quickly restored Germany's habitual fiscal balance.

Meanwhile, rigueur proved unpopular with French voters. Giscard fell in the presidential election of 1981. François Mitterrand rose to power with a Socialist-Communist alliance, united around a program combining neo-Keynesian reflation with nationalization of faltering firms. Once elected, Mitterrand's alliance did nationalize and rejuvenate numerous firms and did try to reflate the French economy. But the franc, up against Reagan's superstrong dollar and the newly strong deutsche mark, was soon forced into a series of devaluations. The French economy proved highly vulnerable to the inflationary consequences. By March 1983, after three devaluations in eighteen months, Mitterrand realized France could not continue its expansive policies alone. To do so, he decided, would mean leaving the European Monetary System, a move that would gravely damage the whole postwar European construction, including the special relationship with Germany that had been a major French priority since the war. He reversed his economic course and pursued rigueur with fortitude for his remaining thirteen years as president. The belief that growth and prosperity required eliminating inflation and reducing government borrowing became the *pensée unique* among respectable French analysts and policymakers. Along with high real interest rates, Europe's problems were also ascribed to excessive labor costs that depressed profitability and investment.[24] United around this common theme, the Franco-German partnership entered a new phase of intensity.

By the mid-1980s, with France and Germany on the same economic course, the Bundesbank's neoclassic liberal analysis began to gain ascendancy in other European countries. Even Italy began to converge its macroeconomic policies on the German model, while Margaret Thatcher, Britain's prime minister since 1979, imposed her own austere monetary regime on Britain.[25] In several countries, record

---

[24] See Harold van Buren Cleveland, *Europe in the Economic Crisis of Our Time*, op. cit., especially pp. 185–189; and Jean-Pierre Landau, "The French Economy in the New Europe," in David P. Calleo and Alex T. Lau, eds., *France and the New European and World Order, SAIS Review (Special Issue)* Fall, 1993, pp. 79–87.

[25] For a concise account of the Thatcherite monetarist experiment, see Robert Skidelsky, *Mrs. Thatcher's Revolution* in David P. Calleo and Claudia Morgenstern, eds., *Recasting Europe's Economies: National Strategies in the 1980's* (Lantham, MD: University Press of America, 1990). For a skeptical account, see Peter Jenkins, *Mrs. Thatcher's Revolution* (Cambridge: Harvard University Press, 1988), especially pp. 281–283.

unemployment was an obvious consequence. But it was expected to diminish once inflationary expectations were dissipated. Real interest rates were then supposed to fall and thereby to power an investment-led boom. That was not, however, what happened. Instead, as fiscal discipline made capital more abundant in Europe, the Reagan administration's heavy borrowing and high interest rates drew it off to America.[26] Once more, it seemed, national economic policies in Europe were disrupted by the vagaries of global finance dominated by the Americans. Instead of a home-grown boom led by domestic investment, Europeans enjoyed an export-led boom induced by the high dollar. This left them vulnerable whenever Fed policy aimed to push down the dollar's exchange rate, which the Fed began to do in the mid-1980s. Frustrated Europeans, vulnerable to the dollar and more vulnerable still to volatile exchange rates among themselves, began planning a monetary union with a single currency.

Burgeoning plans for further integration gave Europe's economies an optimistic momentum of their own. By the end of the 1980s, European growth rates were surging. The European Community agreed on a single European market in 1987. In 1990, the French and Germans engineered agreement for a full European Monetary Union by the end of the century. The two great initiatives went hand in hand. A single market meant ending national barriers to trade and services. The ensuing deregulation throughout the EC made members all the more vulnerable to currency instability among themselves. The danger was increased by the volatile dollar, which fell by over 45 percent against the DM between 1985 and 1990![27] The European Monetary Union was the obvious solution. Either the EC would go forward to monetary integration or it would risk having to abandon trade integration.

By the late years of the 1980s, Europe, uniting around classic liberal norms, seemed to be making itself an oasis of stability. Neoliberal

---

[26] The bulk of the U.S. deficit was financed by capital from Japan and Germany. Flows of German portfolio investment abroad—most of it into the U.S. treasury bill market—rose from USD 2.7 billion in 1981 to USD 40.8 billion in 1988. *International Financial Statistics Yearbook, 1998* (Washington, DC: International Monetary Fund, 1998), pp. 434–435.

[27] *Economic Report of the President* (Washington, DC: U.S. Government Printing Office, 1999), p. 452.

rigueur seemed the cure for Europe's postwar ailments and the formula for its prosperous future. While the Americans struggled with financial instability in the late Reagan and Bush years and worried about decline, Eurosclerosis began to give way to Europhoria. But when the postwar era abruptly ended, bringing Soviet collapse and German unification, Europe's boom soon ended as well. Eurosclerosis seemed to return with a vengeance, and Europe's global position seemed more uncertain than perhaps at any time since the early postwar years. As the bipolar system collapsed, and world competition intensified, the resolve for unity among Europe's states was tested in a more demanding fashion than ever before.

SELECTED SOURCES

I first discussed many of the themes raised in this chapter, in particular the American role in the global economy, in David P. Calleo and Benjamin M. Rowland, *America and the World Political Economy* (Bloomington: Indiana University Press, 1973), and continued to develop the argument presented here in subsequent books: *The Imperious Economy* (Cambridge: Harvard University Press, 1982), *Beyond American Hegemony* (A Twentieth Century Fund Book; New York: Basic Books, 1987), and *The Bankrupting of America: How the Federal Deficit Impoverishes the Nation* (New York: William Morrow, 1992). Readers interested in pursuing these arguments further will find them documented and developed at length in these various books.

Inflation, American Style

For a long-cycle view of commodity prices and the general evolution of the world economy from the late nineteenth century to the 1970s, see Phillip Cagan, *Persistent Inflation: Historic and Political Essays* (New York: Columbia University Press, 1979). For discussions of the inflationary tendencies in postwar American history, see W. W. Rostow, *The World Economy: History and Prospect* (London: University of Texas Press, 1978).

U.S. Inflation and the End of Bretton Woods

For de Gaulle's criticism of Bretton Woods and of America's behavior within the international monetary system, a critique relying heavily on the analysis of his adviser Jacques Rueff, see the general's press conference of February 4, 1965, in *Major Addresses, Statements and Press Conferences* (New York: French Embassy and Information Division, 1967), vol. 2, pp. 179–181. See also David P. Calleo, "De Gaulle and the Monetary System: The Golden Rule," in Robert O. Paxton and Nicholas Wahl, eds., *De Gaulle and the United States* (Oxford: Berg, 1994), pp. 239–255. Jacques Rueff's arguments are most pungently expressed in *The Monetary Sin of the West* (New York: Macmillan, 1972). For a comprehensive view of his economic and social philosophy, see *The Collected Works of Jacques Rueff*, ed. W. H. Bruce Brittain and E. M. Claassen (New York: Lehrman Institute, 1982). For the rise of the Eurodollar market and collapse of the Bretton Woods system, see Susan Strange, "International Monetary Relations," in Andrew Shonfield ed., *International Monetary Relations of the Western World: 1959–71* (London: Oxford University Press, 1976), vol. 2, pp. 59–61, 179–194, and Carl H. Stem, John H. Makin, and Dennis E. Logue, eds., *Eurocurrencies and the International Monetary System* (Washington, DC: American Enterprise Institute, 1976). For a well-informed contemporary analysis of the end of the Bretton Woods system, see Harold van Buren Cleveland, "How the Dollar Standard Died," *Foreign Policy*, vol. 5 (Winter 1971–1972) pp. 41–51. For a good running account of American policy toward the international monetary system, see Robert Solomon, *The International Monetary System 1945–1981* (New York: Harper & Row, 1982). For a path-breaking study of the consequences of monetary inflation and the breakdown of stable exchange rates, see Susan Strange, *Casino Capitalism* (Oxford, UK: Blackwell, 1986). For her subsequent analysis of multinational corporations and governments in this new environment, see *States and Markets* (Oxford, UK: Blackwell, 1988). For a defense of "benign neglect," see Lawrence B. Krause, "A Passive Balance of Payments Strategy," *Brookings Papers on Economic Activity*, no. 3 (1970). Milton Friedman had previously made the case for floating exchange rates in *Dollars and Deficits* (Englewood Cliffs, NJ: Prentice-Hall, 1968), especially ch. 9.

European Inflation and the Oil Shocks

For a study of 1968 and its aftermath in Europe, see Raymond Aron, *The Elusive Revolution: Anatomy of a Student Revolution* (London: Pall Mall Press, 1970). For the explosion of inflation in 1973, see Harold van Buren Cleveland and W. H. Brittain, *The Great Inflation: A Monetarist View* (Washington, DC: National Planning Assocation, 1976). For a magisterial study of the oil shocks—their causes and consequences—see W. W. Rostow, op. cit., especially chs. 18 and 26. For the recession of 1974, see Otto Eckstein, *The Great Recession* (Amsterdam: North-Holland, 1978). For my own views, see David P. Calleo, *The Imperious Economy*, op. cit., pp. 105–117.

From the Nixon Formula to the Reagan-Volcker Formula

For a rationale for the locomotive theory, on the grounds that the oil shocks were deflationary in their ultimate effects, see Paul Mc-Cracken, ed., *Toward Full Employment and Price Stability* (Paris: OECD, 1977). For an American critique, see Geoffrey E. Wood and Nancy Ammon Jiankoplos, "Coordinated International Expansion: Are Convoys or Locomotives the Answer?" *Federal Reserve Bank of St. Louis Review*, vol. 60, no. 7 (July 1978), pp. 11–19. For the Downing Street economic summit of May 1977, where the locomotive featured strongly, see Robert D. Putnam and Nicholas Bayne, *Hanging Together: The Seven-Power Summits* (Cambridge: Harvard University Press, 1984), pp. 69–71. For the second oil shock and European states' expansionary policies, see Stanley W. Black, "Learning from Adversity: Policy Responses to Two Oil Shocks," in *Essays in International Finance*, no. 160 (Princeton: Princeton University Press, 1985), pp. 13–16.

For a critical analysis of the economic policies of the Reagan years, see Benjamin M. Friedman, *Day of Reckoning: The Consequences of American Economic Policy under Reagan and After* (New York: Random House, 1988). Paul Volcker's role is well chronicled but unfairly judged in William Greider, *Secrets of the Temple: How the Federal Reserve Runs the Country* (New York: Simon & Schuster, 1987). The supply-side "revolution" is dissected by Robert L. Heilbroner, "The Demand for the Supply-Side," *New York Review of Books* (June 11,

1981), pp. 37–41, and David Stockman, *The Triumph of Politics* (New York: Harper & Row, 1986). I have analyzed the domestic causes and international effects of Reagan's deficits in *The Bankrupting of America*, op. cit., especially chs. 4–6, and *Beyond American Hegemony*, op. cit., especially chs. 6 and 7.

Euroscelerosis

For warnings of the perils facing postwar Europe's economies, see Friedrich von Hayek, *Full Employment at Any Price?* Occasional Papers, no. 45 (London: Institute of Economic Affairs, 1975), and Jacques Rueff, *The Age of Inflation* (Chicago: Regnery, 1964). Euroscelerosis is discussed in Michael Emerson, ed., *Europe's Stagflation* (Oxford: Oxford University Press, 1984), and R. Z. Lawrence and C. L. Shultz, eds., *Barriers to European Growth: A Transatlantic View* (Washington, DC: Brookings Institution, 1987).

The various economic strategies pursued by the United States and major European states in the 1980s are analyzed in several essays contained in David P. Calleo and Claudia Morgenstern, eds., *Recasting Europe's Economies: National Strategies in the 1980s* (Lanham, MD: University Press of America/Washington Foundation for European Studies, 1990). For European and American responses placed in a global context, see Harold van Buren Cleveland's contribution, "Europe in the Economic Crisis of Our Time," pp. 157–199. For the French conversion to German virtue in the 1970s, as well as Mitterrand's own later conversion, see Patrick McCarthy's chapter, "France Faces Reality: *Rigueur* and the Germans," pp. 25–75. For British views, see Robert J. Skidelsky, "Mrs. Thatcher's Revolution," pp. 101–130. Thatcher's own views are to be found in her memoirs, *The Downing Street Years* (London: HarperCollins, 1993), especially chs. 4 and 5. For an insider's view of French attitudes, see Jean-Pierre Landau, "EMU and the Franco-German Relationship," in David P. Calleo and Eric R. Staal, eds., *Europe's Franco-German Engine* (Washington, DC: Brookings Institution, 1998), as well as Jean-Pierre Landau, "The French Economy and the New Europe," in David P. Calleo and Alex T. Lau, eds., *France in the New European and World Order, SAIS Review*, vol. 13 (Fall 1993, Special Issue). For more details about the tergiversations of Mitterrand's early economic policies, see Philippe Bauchard, *La Guerre des deux roses* (Paris: Grasset, 1986). For a close chronicle and analysis of French and German economic policy and convergence in the 1970s, see Juerg Boche, "National Strategies and Cooperation: Franco-German Economic Relations Since the First Oil Shock," unpublished dissertation, European Studies, Johns Hopkins Paul H. Nitze School of Advanced International Studies. For an interesting and critical analysis of the merits and weaknesses of official French policy, see J. Fitoussi, *Competitive Disinflation: The Mark and Budgetary Policy in Europe* (Oxford: Oxford University Press, 1993). For a further bibliography discussing the consequences of monetary instability, see below, chapters 11 and 12. For the origins of the European Monetary System, see Peter Ludlow, *The Making of the European Monetary System* (London: Butterworth Scientific, 1982).

Cold War Lessons, Old and New

FOR THE DURATION of the Cold War, Western Europe's three systemic arrangements—bipolar, regional, and global—coped successfully with the continent's perennial problems. These distinct but overlapping systems reflected various enlightened if sometimes conflicting prescriptions from Europe's "living past." A benevolent external hegemony coexisted with a powerful indigenous confederacy. Capitalism waxed as Cold War spending gave substance to economic theories emphasizing state action to spur growth and humanize the market with a safety net for all. European welfare states and European integration, transatlantic hegemony, and global capitalism all flourished together. Meanwhile, the Soviets created an "Eastern Europe," where Soviet tyranny sustained its own fearsome order and claustrophobic economic stability. Naturally, there were tensions among the diverse Western systems and prescriptions, but the Cold War kept them under control. The Soviet enemy was the linchpin that held things together. When that pin snapped, the three Western systems, disoriented, quickly began competing to shape the new European and global order.

This sudden disorientation reopened old questions. European states found themselves confronted with the familiar paradoxes of their history: sovereign states that must cooperate to preserve self-determination, as well as volatile global capitalism that multiplies the wealth needed for national prosperity but, at the same time, threatens national solidarity. Four decades of the Cold War generated their own further legacies and lessons. Europeans, Americans, and Russians emerged with radically different endowments and perspectives.

Of our three postwar systems, the "bipolar" was naturally the most immediately and radically changed by the Soviet collapse. Militarily, the United States was left as unique "superpower" in a "unipolar" world. America's large Cold War military, diplomatic, financial, industrial, and academic establishments naturally favored a new age of triumphant global hegemony. But the rest of the country was not necessarily for it. Diffidence toward foreign entanglements and fear of "overstretch" remained a powerful countervailing lesson in America's public consciousness. The political system as a whole began to shy away from hegemony's military burdens, economic costs, and constitutional discipline. Since nothing important seemed to threaten American security in the 1990s, the actual exercise of American leadership and power tended to be fitful and intermittent. As the presidency continued its constitutional decline, American foreign policy grew more and more "privatized" by special interests—bureaucratic, political, and economic.

For Western Europe, the bipolar system's legacy was collective military dependence on the United States, but with significant differences of degree. Britain and France were independent nuclear powers with reasonably well-rounded military forces capable of independent action; Germany and Italy were not. In general, the Cold War had demonstrated to Western Europe the advantages of an external military hegemon. But that hegemon had come along with a Soviet rival. Together, they made a geopolitical framework that justified the American protectorate—for Americans as well as for Europeans—and also limited it. That bipolar framework had also proved favorable to Western Europe's own confederal integration, which, in turn, constituted a useful political and economic counterbalance to American military hegemony within the West. In short, while the Cold War, provoked by the Soviet threat, had installed American hegemony, it had also balanced and limited it.

Without the Soviet threat, it has become more difficult to see Americans or Europeans continuing indefinitely to accept America's postwar role in Europe. The aggressive forward position of the Soviets had called for a countervailing forward American deployment. With Russia weak after the Cold War, the American position is more problematic. Nevertheless, Russia remains potentially powerful and is dangerous even when weak. Some American presence can be justified as insurance against the resumption of a powerful and hostile Russia, or of internecine quarrels among Europeans themselves. But without the urgent Soviet threat, continuing the American protectorate in its traditional form is more than likely to seem excessive and superfluous—to Americans and Europeans both.

A preferable outcome would be for a strong but friendly Russia to be integrated into a balanced pan-European system, together with a reduced American presence. Russia's ability to play a useful European role is made difficult, however, by the consequences of the abject failure of the old Soviet model. For Eastern Europe and Russia itself, that failure has left a bitter legacy of dysfunctional malinvestment and corruption. The East's perversely distorted economic, political, and social development now poses formidable difficulties for creating a broad and cooperative pan-European system. Diplomatically, moreover, Russia emerged from the Cold War with a superpower mentality that has made its subsequent weakness not only more bitter but also less productive. Russia prefers to fancy itself a retired superpower, or a convalescing superpower on vacation, rather than a partner to Western Europe in a pan-European system. Dealing with Europe directly, instead of over its head with the United States, seems to Russians a geopolitical demotion. Russia, of course, has little to offer the United States, but its lingering bipolar pose alienates the Europeans and helps to prolong the American hegemonic role.

In the long run, perhaps the system most likely to benefit from the Soviet collapse is the Western confederacy, newly embodied in the European Union. Over time, it seems the obvious successor to American hegemony. Nevertheless, the Soviet collapse has also left the confederacy vulnerable to new challenges and old centrifugal forces. The Treaty of Maastricht gave the newly styled European Union a powerful thrust toward more integration, including explicit engagements to create common foreign, security, and defense policies. But the EU has nevertheless retained the political and institutional character built up over several decades during the Cold War. By making Europe's nation states much more effective, and hence enhancing their practical sovereignty, integration has given them fresh legitimacy. The EU has thus developed as a hybrid. It has remained a confederacy of sovereign nation states, even though there have been strong "federal" elements of growing significance. The lesson of the EU's postwar history was, therefore, that integration succeeds when member states can compromise around broadly shared interests, particularly those shared by France and Germany. Cold War experience also suggested that European integration works best as a civilian project. Its difficulties mount in the realms of security, defense, and geopolitics. With the end of the Cold War, the great question has been the EU's role in any new pan-European system. Taking the leading role in organizing such a system has seemed to require expanding the Union's membership to Eastern Europe and developing capabilities for collective security and defense. The hybrid constitution has made it difficult to do either quickly.

The EU's impetus toward further integration has always depended heavily on what goes on in our third postwar system, the global political economy. Throughout the Cold War years, global economic pressures pushed European states toward making common cause. Opening their markets to world trade and finance made them particularly concerned with counterbalancing the Americans economically. United States commercial diplomacy was often aggressive toward European interests, and giant American firms seemed a threat to Europe's economic self-determination, or to its status as a competing source of advanced technology in the world. European governments and business firms derived various lessons from the situation. One was to look for transatlantic alliances and global niches. Another was to foster "national champions" and perhaps pool them to create Europe's own global giants. All in all, the experience throughout the Cold War years encouraged greater European solidarity. This was particularly true in the monetary field. Europe's national economies, engaged in a more and more genuine single market, were increasingly vulnerable to exchange rate changes among themselves. These changes were often triggered by abrupt shifts in U.S. monetary policies, reacting to America's troubled Cold War finances, and taking advantage of the dollar's hegemonic position. Already by the 1970s, these experiences had become a powerful incentive for advancing toward full European monetary union.

The demands of the global economy also raised old issues about the coexistence of capitalism and European nation states. Creating giant multinational firms in a single market increased pressure for more centralized forms of federal regulation than single nation states. Pressure for monetary union also pointed toward a more centralized federal control of national macroeconomic policies. The end of the bipolar system challenged Europe's communitarian nation states in

179

still another fashion. The Soviet collapse could be interpreted not only
as a vindication of market capitalism but also as a decisive defeat for
communitarian politics and economics of all kinds. This lesson, popular in post–Cold War Britain and the United States, was fiercely contested in the EU countries of continental Europe. Nevertheless, EU
states in later Cold War years were increasingly cognizant of what
might be called the Hayekian imperative: the need to trim back over-
developed welfare states. This meant restoring fiscal balance to permit
a macroeconomic climate favorable to investment. It also meant reducing costs for Europe's firms, so that they could compete with those
in the United States and Asia. More deregulation was required to
eliminate rigidities in labor markets and to loosen bureaucratic tram-
mels generally. European states increasingly used their community in
Brussels to strengthen themselves in global markets and to impose on
their own economies a more competitive trade-off between humane
welfare and economic efficiency. Confederal integration was thus,
more and more, a vital tool for successful national policies. Given this
experience over several decades, it was not surprising that strengthening their union was soon the common reaction of Europe's states to
the Soviet collapse.

POST–COLD WAR IDEOLOGIES

The end of the Cold War, brought about by the ignominious Soviet
collapse, naturally provoked an upsurge of Western triumphalism,
with votaries of various political economic ideals and formulas seeking to take the high ground in the struggle to dominate the post-Soviet
future. The Soviet implosion was widely claimed as a positive victory
for Western liberal capitalism. The inflationary shocks of the 1970s
had already shifted a significant part of elite opinion from neo-
Keynesian indulgence to Hayekian rigor.

For Hayek, the road to totalitarian serfdom is paved with communitarian good intentions. His writings make vivid the dangers implicit
in communitarian nationalism: Demagogic politics result in more and
more fiscal spending and borrowing. Inflation seems the easy way out
but provokes heavier and heavier state intrusion into the economy and

control over life in general. Hence, the bloated public sectors, creeping inflation, and "Eurosclerosis" of recent decades, not to mention the Fascist and Nazi dictatorships of the interwar years, or the monstrous Soviet system throughout its existence. Neoliberal writers like Hayek, by underscoring the dangers of runaway communitarianism, have helped to spark the countervailing measures needed to contain them. As a consequence, the European integration of the 1980s and 1990s was increasingly identified with a policy of greater macroeconomic rigor and liberal deregulation. By the end of the century, however, a communitarian counterattack was apparently gathering force.

The New Europe

THE DISINTEGRATION of the Soviet Union in the early 1990s, ending the postwar era, shook up the various postwar systems and set their institutions to competing for roles in the "new world order." The International Monetary Fund and World Bank grew deeply involved in trying to supervise the transformation of Russia and the other post-Soviet economies. Events soon put much of Asia under international tutelage as well. Meanwhile, NATO, anticipating a new "unipolar" security system, began transforming itself from a defensive regional alliance into a general peacekeeping force under American direction.

Among all the postwar Western institutions, the European Community had the most to gain or lose from the Soviet demise. The end of the Cold War thrust the West Europeans out of their comfortable postwar shelter and tested their confederacy—constitutionally, militarily, and economically. The Soviet dissolution invited the European Community to expand, to make itself pan-European. But absorbing so many new and diverse members threatened to make the hybrid constitution unworkable. The end of the Soviet empire also inevitably changed Europe's security requirements and relationship to America and thereby challenged European states to endow their community with an effective military capacity. But the explosion of violence in Yugoslavia came well before they were ready to do so. Meanwhile, changes in the global economy threatened Europe's competitiveness, along with its comfortable and expensive communitarian life style.

European states reacted with the Maastricht Treaty, signed in February 1992. It changed the European Community into the European Union and committed the members to ambitious plans for further economic, political, diplomatic, and military integration, and for an enlarged pan-European membership.

The 1990s also saw a sharp rise in public criticism of the EU for its inadequacies, as well as a very considerable erosion of public support.

To some extent, this rise in critical reactions reflected the success of the EU in transforming itself from a vision into a concrete institution whose actions were of real significance. As its significance grew, so did impatience with its traditional and continuing structural inadequacies. Old quarrels among federalists, Gaullists, and Atlanticists took on fresh life. And with so many radical changes in Europe and around the globe, it was only natural to question whether the West European visions of a half century earlier were adequate to the challenges of a very different new world. Pan-European critics objected that the EU was giving precedence to old projects for "deepening" in Western Europe over its real historical challenge, which was "widening" to Eastern Europe. And globalist critics found European integration an inappropriate and obsolescent response to a rapidly evolving world economy.

Maastricht's projects, together with the issues raised by its various critics, are obviously central to Europe's future and form the natural subjects for our concluding chapters. Chapter 11 considers the ambitious agenda laid out at Maastricht, in particular, the European Monetary Union and what it revealed about the motives driving Europe's leaders in the 1990s. Chapter 12 considers whether the advancing global economy generally favors a European bloc. Chapter 13 deals with extending the EU's scope and membership, and with adapting its traditional constitutional structure to suit. Chapter 14 raises issues of pan-European security, along with the EU's prospects for a common foreign and security policy. Chapter 15 considers three models for a future pan-European system. A final chapter considers Europe's place in the new world order that seems to be evolving and, in particular, Europe's increasingly uneasy relationship with America.

Europe after the Soviet Shock: Maastricht and the EMU

MAASTRICHT WAS the joint creation of three of postwar Europe's most formidable leaders—Jacques Delors, Helmut Kohl, and François Mitterrand. While its projects were boldly ambitious, they were not very original. In effect, they amounted to a triumphal reaffirmation of traditional aims. The European edifice was to have three "pillars." The first pillar was to be full economic and monetary union (EMU), for which the treaty set forth the requirements and a timetable. The second pillar, intergovernmental cooperation, was to expand from political cooperation to common foreign and security policy (CFSP). A third pillar was to be constructed around shared norms and procedures in legal and home affairs, including common rights for all European citizens, intensified police cooperation, and harmonized immigration policies, accompanied by a Social Chapter for labor, prescribing common rights for workers. Meanwhile, internal organizational reforms were to make the union's institutions more federal and repair their various democratic deficits. Aside from the EMU, details on the other goals were left to be worked out through a later intergovernmental conference (IGC) of member states. Its negotiations were to start in 1996 and a further treaty, the Treaty of Amsterdam, was to result in mid-1997. At Maastricht, Europe's leaders also committed themselves to "widening" the EU's membership. Negotiations for the first round of enlargement were set for 1998.[1]

---

[1] The formal legal provision for enlargement was set out in Article O of the Treaty of Union, which provided, without further clarification, that "any European State may apply to become a Member of the Union." The political and economic conditions attached to membership were subsequently sketched out by the European Council at Copenhagen in June 1993, and entailed, inter alia, a commitment to "democracy, the rule of law, human rights . . . the existence of a functioning market economy, as well as the capacity to cope with competitive pressures and market forces within the Union." The process was extended at the Amsterdam Intergovernmental Conference,

Maastricht's goals proved more difficult to reach than its architects had probably imagined. Progress over the rest of the decade was uneven and selective. The Treaty of Amsterdam was signed in mid-1997, as foreseen, but its concrete results were disappointing at the time. The EU's one indisputable major accomplishment in the 1990s was its Economic and Monetary Union, formed on schedule in 1998. With it, the West European states hazarded a giant step toward becoming a solidly integrated political-economic bloc. Continental governments pursued EMU with a degree of determination, tenacity, and political courage that surprised many observers and revealed a good deal about the perspectives and aspirations of Europe's leaders and political classes. After the Soviet collapse, Europe needed to reaffirm its geopolitical self-confidence with some resounding success that would catch the imaginations of people at home and abroad. Achieving EMU became the touchstone for the EU's ability to address its problems and, in particular, for the will and capacity of French and German governments to lead Europe together.

As EMU grew more imperative politically, however, it seemed to grow more difficult economically. Among other things, the geopolitical revolution of 1989 reversed the economic positions of the United States and Europe. The United States, overstretched during the Cold War, enjoyed a significant "peace dividend" after it. United States military spending was cut severely, and despite the Gulf War, major improvements followed in America's fiscal situation.[2] By contrast, the

---

concluded in June 1997, which opened membership negotiations with Poland, Hungary, Estonia, Slovenia, and the Czech Republic. See Graham Avery and Fraser Cameron, The *Enlargement of the European Union* (Sheffield, UK: Sheffield Academic Press, 1999), pp. 23ff.

[2] U.S. spending on national defense fell from a decade high of 6.2 percent of GDP in fiscal 1986 to an estimated 3.2 percent of GDP in fiscal 1998. The federal budget deficit fell from 5.1 percent of GDP to a surplus of 0.8 percent in the same period, despite increases in nondefense spending. See *Economic Report of the President 1999* (Washington, DC: U.S. Government Printing Office, 1999), p. 420. In constant 1992 dollars, national defense spending dropped from $325.2 billion in 1986 to $262.2 billion in 1994, before rising slightly to $272.4 billion in 1998, while the federal balance evolved from a $274.8 billion deficit in fiscal 1986 to a deficit of $107.4 billion in fiscal 1996 and a surplus of $60.8 billion in fiscal 1998. *Budget of the U.S. Government, Fiscal Year 2000, Historical Tables* (Washington, DC: U.S. Government Printing Office, 1999), pp. 23–24, 142–144.

end of the Cold War brought West Europeans new economic problems and did nothing to relieve them of their old Eurosclerosis. Europe's economic performance throughout most of the 1990s was very poor. In 1992, even economic integration seemed to be unraveling, as the European Monetary System collapsed and national macroeconomic policies began once again to diverge widely. Throughout the 1990s, real GDP growth in the European Union was roughly 20 percent lower than in the 1980s. In several member states, unemployment reached levels not seen since the Great Depression.[3]

This unhappy conjuncture made achieving EMU much more difficult. Maastricht set 1998 as the year for determining the initial group of member countries. In 1999, the euro was to become their common unit of account, and their exchange rates would be locked permanently. In 2002, their national currencies would disappear from circulation. The treaty suggested performance criteria that founding members should meet: Annual fiscal deficits were to be no greater than 3 percent of GDP, and accumulated government debt no greater than 60 percent of GDP. Inflation was to be no more than 1.5 percent higher than the average rate of the three least inflationary EU members, and long-term interest rates were to be no more than 2 percent higher. With the Treaty of Amsterdam, at the end of 1997, the EU states agreed to a further "Stability and Growth Pact," whereby EMU members were expected to sustain these initial criteria indefinitely.[4]

For most countries, achieving these criteria by 1998 became a much more heroic task than anyone had imagined. In the late 1980s, when the Maastricht Treaty was being planned and European macro-

---

[3] Overall EU growth dropped from an annual average of 2.4 percent per annum from 1981 to 1990 to an average of 1.9 percent per annum from 1991 to 1998. Comparable figures for the United States are 2.9 percent and 2.6 percent. Unemployment was far higher in the EU, averaging 10.6 percent over 1991–1998 compared to 6.0 percent in the United States. *OECD World Economic Outlook: December 1998* (Paris: OECD, 1998), pp. 191, 211.

[4] The "Stability and Growth Pact," as it was called, proposed fining members whose fiscal deficits exceeded 3 percent of GDP in any one year, unless there were exceptional circumstances. These included a fall in GDP of 2 or more percent in the previous year. For smaller contractions, the level of the fine—usually equivalent to 0.2 percent of GDP plus an additional 0.1 percent for each percentage point over the limit—was to be decided by the EU's Council of Finance Ministers (ECOFIN). *OECD Economic Outlook: December 1997* (Paris: OECD, 1997), pp. 21, 32.

economic policies were converging, the criteria seemed easily attainable for many member countries, certainly for France and Germany, although not for Italy.[5]

Why, thereafter, did these criteria become so difficult to meet? Why did Europe experience such sudden and prolonged hard times in the 1990s? There are three principal explanations: To begin with, the way the Germans handled the financing of their reunification led to a prolonged monetary crisis with abnormally high interest rates. Second, under such conditions, the drive to achieve the EMU criteria became, in itself, a further depressing factor. And finally, more fundamental changes in the world economy were working to make Europe less competitive.

THE GERMAN SHOCK

As soon as Germany was reunited, the Kohl government set out to transform the East German economy through a Blitzkrieg of huge state investments and abundant social benefits. The costs quickly and greatly surpassed all official estimates. Rather than raise taxes adequately, a move that Kohl apparently feared would alienate West Germans from the whole project of reunification, the federal government borrowed heavily. The Bundesbank, alarmed at the inflationary potential of the huge new spending, stuck fast to its traditional tight monetary policy.[6] The natural results were high interest rates and strong

---

[5] Of the five largest potential aspirants to EMU (France, Germany, Italy, Spain, and the United Kingdom), all except Italy would have met the debt and deficits criteria in 1989. However, only Germany would have met the inflation and interest rate criteria. By 1991, the situation was equally mixed. Only France and the UK were running fiscal deficits within the 3 percent limit. All except Italy would have met the debt criteria, but none but Germany would have satisfied both the inflation and the interest rate requirements. *OECD Economic Outlook: December 1998* (Paris: OECD, 1998), pp. 206, 220. By contrast, in 1997, no countries but Luxembourg and Finland met the criteria, although the United Kingdom met all except the interest and inflation rate requirements. See note 19.

[6] Fiscal transfers to the new eastern Länder—used to modernize infrastructure, create a more favorable investment climate, and bridge the income gap between west and

market pressure to appreciate the deutsche mark. Weaker European currencies were under corresponding pressure to depreciate against the mark.

The European Monetary System, Europe's partial monetary union of the 1980s, was soon in turmoil. In September 1992, the pound, the lira, and the peseta all left the system's European Exchange Rate Mechanism (ERM) and floated sharply downward against the mark.[7] Heavy market pressure to devalue then bore down on the French franc, despite the country's very low inflation. The French government, convinced that a strong franc was essential to the health of the national economy and determined to press forward to EMU in partnership with the Germans, defied "irrational" currency markets. By and large, the *franc fort* weathered the storm but saddled the French economy with abnormally high real interest rates over several years of stubborn recession and unprecedented unemployment. Financing the skyrocketing unemployment benefits led the French, in turn, to very high fiscal deficits.[8] Thanks to this perverse Franco-German con-

---

east—totaled DM 170 billion in 1991, or 5.5 percent of GNP. Despite tax increases—including a 7.5 percent levy on income tax liabilities and additional indirect taxes on oil and insurance—the general government balance went from a surplus of 0.1 percent of GDP in 1989 to a deficit of 3.3 percent in 1991. The Bundesbank responded by raising interest rates several times between late 1990 and mid-1992; the discount rate reached an all time high of 8.75 percent in July 1992—until the appreciation of the DM following the European Exchange Rate Mechanism (ERM) crisis in September allowed a slight relaxation. See *OECD Economic Outlook: December 1992* (Paris: OECD, 1992), pp. 70–75; *OECD Economic Surveys, Germany, 1992* (Paris: OECD, 1992), pp. 30–41.

[7] After leaving the ERM in September 1992, the pound depreciated by around 15 percent against the DM over the following two months, and the lira and the peseta by 11 percent each. *OECD Economic Outlook: December 1992* (Paris: OECD, 1992), pp. 82, 86, 114. On a daily-average trade-weighted basis, the pound weakened by 11 percent between 1992 and 1995, while the lira fell by 27 percent and the peseta by 18 percent. *OECD Economic Outlook: June 1996* (Paris: OECD, 1996), p. A41.

[8] The franc depreciated by approximately 3 percent against the DM in the first quarter of 1993, although it returned to the old parity by mid-June. Meanwhile, new rules permitting a deviation of 15 percent from the central parity helped to keep up appearances. The French Central Bank did what it could to stabilize the exchange rate: Three-month interbank rates peaked at slightly over 12 percent in the aftermath of the ERM crisis, though they returned to around 8 percent shortly afterward. Meanwhile,

juncture, the fruits of France's devotion to the EMU, and the franc fort were record interest rates, record unemployment, and record fiscal deficits. The situation appeared so untenable politically that the franc remained weak for years afterward and thereby prolonged the need for high real interest rates, despite France's very low inflation and growing trade surplus.[9] In effect, the Germans were using their monetary predominance to spread the costs of reunification, much as the Americans had earlier spread the costs of military hegemony through manipulating the dollar.[10] The French, who had thought they were embracing Hayek, instead found Reagan.

THE EMU SHOCK

The astonishingly high level of French unemployment—over 10 percent starting in 1992—put France's whole European strategy under great strain. For the first time since the early 1980s, strong voices began to be heard against European integration. In September 1992, the referendum called by Mitterrand to ratify the Maastricht Treaty barely succeeded in passing.[11] As French elites nevertheless hung on

---

unemployment rose from 9 percent of the labor force in 1990 to a peak of 12.3 percent in 1994, and the general government deficit widened from 2 percent of GDP in 1991 to 5.6 percent in 1993. *OECD Economic Outlook: June 1997* (Paris: OECD, 1997), pp. A25, A33; *OECD Economic Outlook: December 1993* (Paris: OECD, 1993), pp. 66–69.

[9] Between the first half of 1992 and the first half of 1995, short-term interest rates in France exceeded those in Germany by on average of 2.4 percent, and long-term rates by 1.9 percent, even though French inflation was on average a full percentage point lower and the franc appreciated by 8.2 percent on an effective basis over the same period. *OECD Country Survey: France, 1996* (Paris: OECD, 1996), p. 24.

[10] See Jean-Paul Fitoussi, *Le Debat interdit: Monnaie, Europe, pauvreté* (Paris: Arléa, 1995), pp. 100–108.

[11] On September 20, 1992, the French voted yes to the Maastricht Treaty by a margin of 51.04 percent to 48.95 percent. The Danes had previously rejected the treaty by 50.3 percent to 49.7 percent. *Keesing's Record of World Events*, vol. 38, no. 9 (September 1992). See also "France Votes Yes, but Only Just," *Financial Times*, September 21, 1992, p. 1, and Tom Redburn, "Few Accounts Are Settled by Referendum Outcome," *International Herald Tribune*, September 21, 1992. See also Chapter 1, note 4.

tightly to their European strategy, the French electorate grew moody and fitful—throwing out incumbents at every opportunity. Cohabitation became the norm rather than the exception. A Gaullist landslide in 1994 was succeeded by a Socialist landslide in 1997. Perhaps the most alarming sign of the electorate's ill humor was the growth of the far-right Front National—whose share of the first-round parliamentary vote jumped from 12.4 percent in 1994 to 14.9 percent in 1997.[12]

Europe's monetary problems were further complicated by the dollar, which began falling sharply and erratically against the deutsche mark in the later 1980s and did not start to recover firmly until 1997.[13] The concomitant flight from the dollar to the mark put still more pressure on the other European currencies. Those countries that broke with the common monetary discipline in 1992 and saw their currencies depreciate sharply, like Britain and Italy, enjoyed an export boom. By the middle of the decade, Britain also began to have substantially less unemployment than France or Germany.[14] Arguably, the EU could not sustain such a situation indefinitely. Either a monetary union would eliminate exchange rate instability and beggar-thy-neighbor devaluations or the single European market would break up. This was the position of the French, who pressed relentlessly to have EMU completed on time in 1999.

The official German position was more ambivalent. Given the pride of Germans in their mark, with all its historical and psychological baggage, Kohl faced a major political problem convincing his compatriots to give it up for Europe. The Bundesbank obviously did not relish relinquishing its power, and its potential opposition was a formi-

---

[12] The National Front was not the only minor party to increase its share of the vote in the first round. The PCF (Communist Party) share rose from 9.2 percent to 9.9 percent, and the Greens received 6.8 percent, compared to 4.0 percent in 1994. *Keesing's Record of World Events*, vol. 43, no. 6 (June 1997).

[13] Between 1985 and 1995, the exchange rate of the dollar fell roughly 51 percent in value against the DM. *OECD Economic Outlook: December 1997* (Paris: OECD, 1997), p. A40.

[14] In Britain and Italy, real exports of goods and services grew by 6.3 percent and 9.3 percent, respectively, between 1992 and 1995, compared to 4.2 percent for France and 2.2 percent for Germany. But unemployment remained high, averaging 9.8 percent in Britain and 10.7 percent in Italy. Comparable figures for France and Germany were 11.5 percent and 7.3 percent, respectively. *OECD Economic Outlook: December 1997* (Paris: OECD, 1997), pp. A12, A25.

dable threat. To preempt it, Kohl sought to reassure his countrymen that the new euro would be as hard a currency as the old mark. The German government was the prime mover behind the Stability Pact, whereby the Maastricht criteria for entering EMU were to be made perpetual.[15] It was transformed by the French into the Stability and Growth Pact and accepted by the member states with the Treaty of Amsterdam in 1997. The Bundesbank's strict interpretation of the criteria for entering EMU enjoyed strong popular support among the aging German population, concerned that a weak common currency would allow inflation to erode pensions and investments. After the initial boom from unification spending, however, Germany's own economic conditions also began to deteriorate. Soaring budget deficits finally forced new taxes, and with the Bundesbank still struggling to contain inflation, German unemployment reached record postwar levels.[16] From the perspective of Germany's industrialists and workers, the Bundesbank's diffidence about monetary union could be seen as an egregious misreading of the national interest. The Bundesbank, with its dogged opposition to EMU, began to seem a luxury that united Germany could no longer afford.[17] But whatever its inner thoughts, the Kohl government chose to play along with the Bundesbank and continued to champion a strict view of the convergence criteria.

By the later 1990s, it began to be recognized that Europe's economic malaise had more deep-seated causes than meeting the Maastricht criteria during a depressing conjuncture, or even than the financing of German reunification. Advances in technology were making

---

[15] The Stability and Growth Pact, as its name implied, bore the hallmark of a Franco-German compromise, satisfying French demands for job creation measures while allaying German fears over their cost. See Robert Graham and Wolfgang Munchau, "Stability Pact Language Is Ambiguous," *Financial Times*, May 4, 1998, p. 3, and Robert Peston, "Britain Helps Keep EMU on Track," *Financial Times*, June 17, 1997, p. 2.

[16] German unemployment reached a postwar high of 10.0 percent of the labor force in 1997 (standardized OECD definition). *OECD Economic Outlook: December 1998* (Paris: OECD, 1998), p. 212.

[17] For the implications of the fiscal cost of German unity, see U. Heilemann and Wolfgang Reinecke, *Welcome to Hard Times—The Fiscal Consequences of German Unity* (Washington, DC: Brookings Institution, 1995).

it easy to "downsize" expensive workforces in the West and, at the same time, to spread industrial production to the potentially huge workforces in the non-Western world. Western Europe's high costs—its strict regulations, generous benefits, and extensive workers' rights—threatened to make much of its labor noncompetitive. Major changes in Europe's postwar economic, social, and political cultures seemed called for. Many people welcomed the growing public awareness of such pressures. Globalist liberals saw technological change and the integrated world market as stern but benign taskmasters, pushing Europe toward a more efficient use of its resources and a more sustainable model of society. This view often translated into firm support for a strict adherence to Maastricht's eligibility criteria, and for extending them indefinitely through Amsterdam's Stability and Growth Pact.[18]

As Maastricht's deadlines approached, politics throughout Europe were increasingly oriented around EMU, and the game grew increasingly complex. By the summer of 1996, currency markets had apparently convinced themselves that EMU would happen, one way or another. But general economic conditions were still not cooperating. As late as 1997, only Luxembourg and Finland among the EU states actually met Maastricht's convergence criteria.[19] Continental Europe's leading governments responded with a decisive combination of Draconian cuts and creative accounting. By May 1998, when EMU was formally established, eleven EU members joined it: Austria, Belgium, Finland, France, Germany, Ireland, Italy, Luxembourg, the Netherlands, Portugal, and Spain. All, more or less, met the criteria. Three others, Britain, Denmark, and Sweden, met the criteria but declined to join. Only Greece was ineligible.[20]

Given the adverse economic conjuncture, forming the EMU on

---

[18] For the relationship between Europe's integration and economic growth, as seen by a social market liberal and top economic analyst for Deutsche Bank, see Norbert Walter, *The Evolving German Economy*, Special Issue, *SAIS Review* (Fall 1995), especially pp. 79–80.

[19] All the other potential candidates for EMU had levels of government debt in excess of the 60 percent limit, except for the United Kingdom, which did not meet the inflation and interest rate criteria. *OECD World Economic Outlook: December 1998* (Paris: OECD, 1998), p. 224.

[20] See Lionel Barber, "In the beginning . . . ," *Financial Times*, May 1, 1998, p. 21.

time was a remarkable exercise in sustained political will. In the matter of EMU, no one can rightly accuse leaders like Kohl, Mitterrand, Chirac, Juppé, Jospin, Prodi, or d'Alema of lacking political courage and resolve. Polls in Germany, for example, consistently showed a majority opposed to giving up the mark.[21] Kohl's support for EMU was nevertheless unflinching. By 1992, France was suffering from outrageously high unemployment that critics linked, not implausibly, to the inflexible determination with which successive governments had been sustaining the franc fort.[22] Nevertheless, the Gaullist government of Alain Juppé stuck resolutely to EMU and its deflationary criteria. And so did the socialist government of Lionel Jospin that took power after the election of 1997.[23] In Italy, the changes required

---

[21] While Kohl's CDU/CSU was the prime mover for EMU in Germany and Europe, conflicts existed within the coalition. In the summer of 1997, Finance Minister Theo Waigel suggested that a delay in the start date of EMU might not be tragic, and Bavarian prime minister Edmund Stoiber carried on a campaign against any "weakening" of the Maastricht criteria. Meanwhile, the German Social Democratic Party (SPD) remained unclear on its EMU stance, but chancellor candidate Gerhard Schroeder leaned increasingly away from commitment as the 1998 campaign went on. The former East German communist party, the Party of Democratic Socialism (PDS), grew stronger in its opposition to EMU, apparently as a way to broaden its largely regional appeal. See "PDS Woos West German Left," *Financial Times*, April 6, 1998, p. 2. Behind these calculations were polls showing half the Germans consistently disapproving giving up the DM, although resigned to its inevitability. Disapproval was particularly strong in the former East Germany, in part because of the prospect of a second currency change within a decade. See "Germany and EMU," *The Economist*, February 14, 1998, p. 51; "Ever Closer Union," *The Economist*, April 11, 1998, p. 21; and Charles Bremner, "Kohl Blunder Puts Euro Fudge on the Menu," *The Times*, May 30, 1997.

[22] See, for example, "'Competitive Disinflation': An Assessment of French Macroeconomic Policy since 1987," in J. Fitoussi et al., *Competitive Disinflation: The Mark and Budgetary Policy in Europe* (Oxford: Oxford University Press, 1993), pp. 17–30.

[23] Chirac, some say, called the June 1997 election to give Juppé a mandate to pursue the Maastricht criteria more rigorously. Polls showed roughly half of France in favor of the euro. After the election led to a socialist government, many analysts predicted that France would not meet the criteria. But the new premier, Lionel Jospin, promised "no pause, no retreat, no going back." Consequently, he was accused of going back on his election pledges, in which he had set himself against further budgetary tightening. But he made such pledges, it was sometimes explained, without really expecting to be elected, and the pledges were therefore inoperative. See "France Still Com-

to meet the EMU's fiscal profile constituted a budgetary revolution that threatened to alienate a considerable part of the electorate. Notwithstanding, the Center-Left government of Romano Prodi imposed the Draconian taxes and budgetary cuts needed to reduce Italy's customary huge fiscal deficit to Maastricht's 3 percent level.[24]

This extraordinary performance all around suggests an obvious question: Why did so many of Europe's leaders, of the Left as well as the Right, continue to see EMU as a long-term solution to their problems? Their faith seems all the more remarkable since many economists were themselves highly skeptical. The arguments that inspired the leaders went well beyond considerations of simple economic efficiency. The European Community has characteristically advanced by grand projects in one critical field, whose effects are then supposed to spill over into others. Support for a common European currency had been building for a long time. It was a project whose practical and symbolic consequences seemed on a scale worthy of the great challenges of the time. But the determination of Europe's leaders reflected more than dutiful devotion to continuing European integration. Leaders and elites shared a growing sense that European economies were entering a structural crisis in their relations with the global economy. EMU would, they thought, make their economies much stronger. Their reasoning reflected a potent if anomalous mixture of liberal, mercantilist, and protectionist perspectives.

---

mitted to EMU," *Financial Times*, June 20, 1997; "France Gambles on Softer EMU," *Financial Times*, June 30, 1997; and Charles Bremner, "Kohl Blunder Puts Euro Fudge on the Menu," *The Times*, May 30, 1997.

[24] In October of 1997, Prodi's government was nearly toppled when his unreconstructed Communist coalition partners opposed his pension reforms. Prodi had pushed for budget cuts of 25 trillion lire, which would have brought the deficit down to 2.8 percent of GDP in 1998 and were to include a controversial 5 trillion lire reduction in pension spending. Prodi eventually had to settle for an agreement which trimmed pensions by a third less than he had hoped. See Alan Friedman, "War and Peace in European Labor," *International Herald Tribune*, November 3, 1997, p. 1; Paul Betts, "Communists Offer Prodi One-Year Pact," *Financial Times*, October 6, 1997, p. 2; James Blitz, "Prodi Budget Unsettles Markets," *Financial Times*, September 30, 1997, p. 2; and James Blitz, "Italy's Unions Locked in Pension Talks," *Financial Times*, September 26, 1997, p. 2.

The Liberal Perspective on EMU

The standard liberal analysis of EMU cuts both ways. On the positive side, a common currency eliminates transaction and hedging costs. It makes prices more transparent and thus facilitates competition. It also encourages cross-border investment. Adding EMU's convergence criteria, strictly limiting inflation and fiscal deficits, was expected to force beneficial changes in Europe's self-indulgent macroeconomic policies.

Liberal skeptics often noted the formidable technical problems of making the transition to a single currency.[25] More fundamentally, they invoked the concept of an "optimal currency area." Whether a region is "optimal" for a single currency depends on the relative ease with which its prices and productive factors can adjust to the economic changes that come, sometimes brutally, from the world outside. In theory, if a putative currency area has sharp internal cultural, social, legal, or physical barriers that impede the flexibility of prices or the mobility of productive factors, that area will probably not benefit from having a common currency. Its distinctive parts will experience and react to external shocks differently and therefore will probably fare better with their own separate currencies. Changing exchange rates will be an easier way for these diverse parts to adjust to new competitive conditions than trying to change sticky prices and wages directly, or trying otherwise to force adjustments that meet strong social, cultural, or political resistance. In other words, trying to impose homogenous monetary conditions within too diverse an area can be expected to be more damaging than the extra costs of exchanging currencies or the costs that come from shifting exchange rates.[26]

---

[25] See, for example, John Nash, *Speech Delivered on April 7th 1998 at the Paul H. Nitze School of Advanced International Studies, The Johns Hopkins University, Washington D.C.*

[26] The Optimal Currency Area theory has generated a significant body of literature. For a good introduction, framed around the question of whether or not Europe forms one, see Paul de Grauwe, "Towards EMU without the EMS," *Economic Policy* (April 1994). For a cogent defense of EMU by one of the theory's inventors, see Robert Mundell, "Great Expectations for the Euro," *Wall Street Journal Europe*, March 24,

The United States offers a practical illustration for many of these arguments. It is a very large country, with distinct regions that differ significantly in productivity and competitiveness, and it has had a common currency for a long time. Less productive American regions usually have lower wages. Where wages do not adjust sufficiently, workers cannot find jobs and migrate to more prosperous areas. Since the United States is a country with relatively low population density and a single dominant language and culture, the adjustment process throughout the continent is relatively easy. As a relatively centralized federal state, moreover, the U.S. government provides significant budgetary transfers to disadvantaged regions.

The American case has a variety of lessons for Europe. In Europe's prosperous core—Benelux, France, West Germany, and Northern Italy—competitive conditions have been converging for a long time, and the problems of internal adjustment seem relatively manageable. Europe's less developed regions with relatively low productivity—the North of England, Northern Scotland, Northern Ireland, Southern Italy, Portugal, Greece, and East Germany—will presumably attract entrepreneurs and investors only by offering lower costs. If costs cannot be lowered by altering national exchange rates, disadvantaged regions will have to keep down wages, benefits, and taxes directly. Militant unions will have to be curbed. Alternatively, effective subsidies will have to be paid through transfers from rich regions. Insofar as regions remain uncompetitive, workers seeking decent employment will have to migrate.

Given Europe's prevailing welfare cultures, not to mention the habits of Eurosclerosis, adjustments of this kind will not be easy to achieve. Traditionally, subsidies to poorer regions have come largely from the budgets of their national states.[27] Members with significant

---

1998, p. 10; "Great Expectations for the Euro—Part II," *Wall Street Journal Europe*, March 25, 1998; and "Making the Euro Work," *Wall Street Journal Europe*, April 30, 1998. For an outspoken attack on EMU and its implications for U.S.-European relations, see Martin Feldstein, "The Euro and International Conflict," *Foreign Affairs* (November–December 1997), pp. 60–73.

[27] For the first phase of its history, from 1958 to 1975, the EEC and EC, as it then was styled, had no regional policy to speak of, despite substantial regional development outlays by national governments. The situation began to change in 1975 with the

depressed regions, like Italy and, or more recently, Germany, often have chronic fiscal deficits. Insofar as Maastricht's strict fiscal criteria are preserved, it will be difficult for national budgets to continue with such outsized regional subsidies. Mechanisms for transfers of funds to poorer regions will have to be developed further at the EU level. Developing such mechanisms will not be easy, given enduring national rivalries, the structural fiscal squeeze in most member states, and the high prospective expense of admitting several poor new countries to EU membership. As for regular large-scale migrations of workers from one region to another, these seem implausible, given Europe's linguistic and cultural differences.

Liberals fear that Europe's diversity will create such severe problems of adjustment that great pressure will be put on the EMU members to alter their commitment to a strict noninflationary monetary policy. Moderate inflation generally makes it easier to adjust real wages, prices, and taxes downward; nominal wages and taxes do not actually have to fall for real wages or taxes to decrease.[28] In the difficult period leading up to the EMU's formation in mid-1998, European governments firmly resisted inflationist arguments of this kind, despite record unemployment. Mainstream political leaders of the time remained faithful to the lesson that Europeans seem to have learned from the 1970s: that inflation is a dangerous and ultimately false remedy because it has a strong tendency to accelerate out of control. Certainly, this was the prevailing view in almost all West European governments—of Left or Right—as EMU was being formed. There-

---

creation of the European Regional Development Fund (ERDF) and was also helped by the reform of the Structural Funds in 1988. Until then, however, there was little evidence that money associated with ERDF assistance would not have been spent, in its absence, by national governments. See Loukas Tsoukalis, *The New European Economy* (Oxford and New York: Oxford University Press, 1993), pp. 232ff. On the magnitude of more recent transfers, see footnote 17 in chapter 13.

[28] For a classic essay on the temporary but hazardous use of "money illusion" to lower real wages and other prices, see Milton Friedman, "The Role of Monetary Policy," *American Economic Review* (March 1968), pp. 1–17. For an earlier version of money illusion, see David Hume, "Of Money," in Eugene Rotwein, ed., *David Hume, Writings on Economics* (Madison: University of Wisconsin Press, 1970), pp. 33ff.

after, Europe's conjunctural economic conditions began improving, but the recovery was delayed by worsening economic conditions elsewhere in the world, in particular the severe Asian financial crisis, which soon spread to Russia.[29] Liberals thus continued to fear that Maastricht's strict anti-inflationary policy, given the severity of the times, would prove difficult to sustain. And in fact, as the Left came to power in one major West European country after the other, the strictness and autonomy of monetary policy were more and more challenged.[30]

In summary, liberal analysis of EMU is ambivalent. An independent European Central Bank, with the Maastricht criteria enshrined in the Stability and Growth Pact, could prove the way to impose the rigorous policies of the old Bundesbank on a wider Europe; the result could be a major increase in Europe's economic efficiency and a more successful adaptation to global competition. In other words, a single European policy could prove more rigorous and effective than individual national policies. Alternatively, if global competition makes hard times habitual in Europe, as many fear, trying to sustain the same austere monetary and fiscal policies across so many diverse economies could easily result in major economic, social, and political confrontations. These might discredit the whole European project. From this perspective, it would be better to let each economy proceed toward rigor at its own speed, with occasional adjustments to exchange rates negotiated when needed. Competitive pressures from the global economy should be, in themselves, an adequate incentive for national reform. EMU would be merely a dangerous complication for Europe's collective adjustment.

---

[29] The international financial crisis caused growth in the OECD area to slow from over 3 percent in 1997 to around 2.2 percent in 1998, largely as a result of lower trade flows and a deterioration in business confidence. *OECD Economic Outlook: December 1998* (Paris: OECD, 1998), pp. 1–20.

[30] The challenge was particularly outspoken during the short-lived career of Oskar Lafontaine as Germany's finance minister in the Schroeder government that took office in October 1998. In certain respects, the positions espoused by Lafontaine grew more popular following his dismissal. See Haig Simonian, "Lafontaine Chooses Moment for Revenge," *Financial Times*, September 29, 1999, p. 1, and Haig Simonian, "Lafontaine Steps Up Feud," *Financial Times*, October 4, 1999, p. 3.

EMU: MERCANTILIST PERSPECTIVES

Even when presented by centrist liberals, arguments for EMU often had a strong mercantilist tinge. At the end of 1996, for example, former French President Valéry Giscard d'Estaing suggested that Europe's unemployment was closely linked to its overvalued currencies—in particular the mark and, by extension, the too-faithful franc.[31] Giscard argued that a common money could end the overvaluation of Europe's stronger currencies. In other words he hoped that the future euro would prove weaker than the old mark. Such arguments seemed framed with the Americans in mind. When its own home economy flags, the autarkic United States has been able to run an easier monetary policy, without caring very much about the domestic effects of a depreciating exchange rate. Because external trade is relatively small compared to the size of the national economy, domestic U.S. prices are not much affected. Thus, Americans can use an easier monetary policy when it seems called for, and appeared to be doing so very successfully throughout the early 1990s.[32] A periodically weak dollar does, moreover, help to sell American products in industries, like aircraft, where the United States and Europe compete closely. Since 1971, the United States has often made good use of its comparative advantage in beggar-thy-neighbor devaluations.

By comparison, the EU without a monetary union had several disadvantages. To begin with, as it became a genuine single market,

---

[31] Valéry Giscard d'Estaing, "Faut-il dévaluer le franc?" *L'Express*, November 21, 1996, pp. 28–38.

[32] Between 1992 and 1995, the U.S. economy expanded at an annual average rate of 2.6 percent; growth among Europe's four largest economies averaged 1.5 percent over the same period. *OECD Economic Outlook: December 1997* (Paris: OECD, 1997), p. A4. Although European short-term real interest rates fell considerably during the 1990s, they remained well above U.S. rates, averaging 5.8 percent in France and 3.4 percent in Germany between 1992 and 1995, compared to 1.7 percent in the United States. U.S. long-term real rates, on the other hand, were higher than German real rates and very similar to those in France. *OECD Economic Surveys: France 1995* (Paris: OECD, 1995), p. 24.

members were particularly sensitive to exchange rate changes among themselves. Those with strong currencies felt vulnerable to outsized devaluations by partners with a greater tolerance for inflation. When Britain and Italy dropped out of the EMS in 1992, their sharply depreciated currencies did benefit growth in their economies at the expense of the depressed French and German economies, in part because of the strong mark and faithful franc. German and French businessmen were outraged. Throughout the rest of the decade, French and German officials kept arguing vehemently that the single market was unlikely to survive unless completed by monetary union that would block such antisocial currency manipulation among the partners.[33]

A single market without monetary union also left Europeans feeling morbidly vulnerable to shifts in American monetary policy, since the gyrations of the ever volatile dollar put unequal pressure on different European currencies. As noted earlier, a weak dollar meant a very strong mark, which then caused trouble for the lira and the pound, and often for the franc as well. To sustain the exchange rate of the weaker currencies meant raising interest rates, an unpopular course given Europe's sluggish economies and high unemployment of the 1990s. As world currency markets grew increasingly erratic toward the end of the decade, EMU's case grew stronger, as the obvious way to end an integrating Europe's particular vulnerability to monetary disorder. A Europe firmly endowed with its own common money would assume a stronger, more comfortable, and less vulnerable place in the global economy.

Morbid sensitivity to exchange rate changes also denied Europe the possibility of imitating America's less rigidly restricted macroeconomic policies, the point stressed by Giscard d'Estaing in 1996, and of particular concern to Europe's communitarian Center-Left governments of the late 1990s. During the Clinton administration, the United States had skillfully used monetary policy to stimulate employment and growth, a modulated strategy whose success, together

---

[33] See, for example, Jean-Pierre Landau, "EMU and the Franco-German Relationship," in David P. Calleo and Eric R. Staal, eds., *Europe's Franco-German Engine* (Washington, DC: Brookings Institution, 1998), pp. 87–88.

with cuts in the defense budget, had even brought American fiscal policy into balance.[34] Individual EU members could not easily follow such a course because of their high mutual interdependence and vulnerability. But, collectively, with no exchange rates internally and a common exchange rate externally, the EU could become more like the United States. It could run an easier monetary policy without fearing acute internal dislocations and immediate large-scale inflationary pressures. Moreover, with a single currency, Europe could eventually demand that the Americans stabilize their exchange rate at a reasonable level. If the United States egregiously failed to do so, Europeans with a monetary union would be less vulnerable and probably in a better position to retaliate.

Mercantilist considerations like these indicate how wrong it is to explain EMU merely as a visionary federalist project. EMU had strong support from national leaders because they believed it favored national interests. The French, for example, committed themselves to EMU because they believed monetary rigor was, under existing global circumstances, the best way to bolster the competitiveness of their own national economy. To impose that rigor on their recalcitrant political system, French elites set out in the 1970s to borrow the Bundesbank. All along, the French saw EMU as a powerful instrument for ensuring a global monetary environment where the dice were not loaded against the big advanced economies of Europe, their own in particular.

Similar considerations affected the Germans. While many Germans

---

[34] The fall in defense spending was one major factor in America's return to fiscal balance (see note 2). From 1992 onward, it was combined with the effects of a sustained boom, adroitly nursed along by the generous monetary policy of the Federal Reserve under Alan Greenspan. The low interest rates that fueled the boom also helped control the deficit, since the cost of financing the federal debt fell greatly. Between FY 1992 and FY 1998, the costs of net interest (on budget) rose by only $66 billion in 1998 dollars—from $223 billion to $289 billion—despite an increase in gross fiscal debt in the same period of $1.541 trillion—from $4.002 trillion to $5.543 trillion. *Budget of the United States Government, Fiscal Year 1999, Historical Tables* (Washington, DC: U.S. Government Printing Office, 1998), pp. 48–49, 110–111. I have discussed Clinton's policies further in David P. Calleo, "A New Era of Overstretch?" *World Policy Journal*, vol. 15, no. 1 (Spring 1998), pp. 11–26.

lamented the donation of their peerless mark to Europe, the strong DM was, in fact, becoming a curse for significant elements in the economy. A very strong currency was admirably suited to the old Federal Republic, which for a long time came close to possessing a model economy. Reunification greatly altered Germany's situation. Fiscal debt rose rapidly, and the East German economy remained dysfunctional and expensive to maintain.[35] With the Bundesbank's habitual tight money pushing the currency upward, big firms increasingly escaped by diversifying their production internationally. Even many of Germany's smaller manufacturers—the famous Mittelstand, backbone of the economy and principal provider of its new employment—began moving segments of production to Eastern Europe.[36] Such trends hardly seemed promising for maintaining Germany's great postwar accomplishments, including well-paid industrial employment for its working population. And whereas EMU would help to relieve the German economy from its superstrong mark, if EMU were to fail, and France, Britain, and Italy were all to defect from the mark, the competitive position of German industry would be less than ideal.

Germans, like the French, also have seen EMU as a way to reshape the world's financial industry. With the euro eventually rivaling the dollar as a reserve and transaction currency, German bankers have anticipated great profits for the financial houses of Frankfurt.

For many economists, these are troubling arguments. They imply the intrusion of political power into markets and brandish the threat of protectionism. It seems naive, however, to assume that such argu-

---

[35] See notes 6 and 17.

[36] On the advantages to companies of shifting production abroad, see Peter Norman and Graham Bowley, "German Industry Is Learning Hard Lessons More Quickly than the Government in Bonn," *Financial Times*, May 29, 1997; also William Drozdiak, "New German Export: Jobs Head to Border; Eastern Neighbors See a Mini-Boom as Firms Flee High Costs at Home," *International Herald Tribune*, April 8, 1997, and Frederick Studemann, "Low Costs Lure Germans to East," *Financial Times*, October 2, 1996. For the domestic implications see Edmund L. Andrews, "Spin-Offs on Rise as German Industry Copes with Globalization," *International Herald Tribune*, November 19, 1998. The threat of moving production to Eastern Europe or elsewhere has also proved a potent bargaining tool for employers such as Volkswagen. See Anne Thompson, "How to Find Jobs for 4.4 Million Germans? Get Flexible," *Associated Press*, May 23, 1998.

ments have not weighed heavily on European decision makers. When all advanced countries have difficulty sustaining their living standards, it is idle to suppose that their political leaders can reckon otherwise. Nor is there any good reason why governments should not employ political power to sustain a macroeconomic and microeconomic environment favorable to their own national prosperity and competitiveness, so long as there are some mutually accepted rules and limits. In the long run, such rules are likely to be instituted and sustained insofar as there are both enlightened leadership in the principal states and an underlying balance of political and economic power among those states that limits excesses. In other words, economics and power politics are inextricably linked. In this respect, a mercantilist view of the world economy that is highly self-conscious about the balance of power is likely to be more realistic and productive—indeed, more liberal, if liberal means competition among equals—than a technical, market-oriented perspective that ignores the whole political dimension of competition.

Mercantilists, after all, have hold of a fundamental precept, one that has seemed true throughout most of modern history: Markets cannot function reliably without regulation by political power. Since the breakdown of Bretton Woods, the global system has proved incapable of sustaining the "public good" of stable international money. Private markets have compensated with the huge apparatus of hedging in all its forms. Financial firms, meanwhile, have undergone a series of gigantic mergers—needed to build the vast hoards of capital required to ride out the economic shocks that are commonplace. The resulting situation seemed to suit the United States well enough in the 1990s, given its huge and relatively autarkic economy. But it did not work so well for the states of Western Europe, whose interdependence makes them highly vulnerable to erratic exchange rates among themselves. Individual European states were not able to act effectively, since purely national measures to control capital movements risked destroying the single market needed to give European national economies the scale to remain in the prosperous front ranks of international competition. Unable to compensate for the lack of stable money on a national scale, European states undertook to do so on a confederal scale. They thereby gave themselves greater internal monetary stability and, perhaps a powerful tool for eventually negotiating a more stable world monetary system. In effect, they pooled their national sovereignty over money—trading national autonomies that had grown ineffective for a cooperative effort to raise themselves collectively to the power and scale of the United States.

EMU: Raising the Stakes

EMU greatly raised the stakes in the European game. With a common money, Europe's nation states committed themselves to a common fate as never before. The logic of EMU points Europe toward becoming an extremely powerful political and economic bloc. If it can fulfil that logic and bring itself to act as a coherent international force, no one else, other than the United States, will match its influence for a long time.

To proclaim a European Monetary Union is one thing; to run it successfully is another. As liberal critics of EMU note, finding a single monetary policy that is appropriate across so large and diverse a region as Europe cannot be easy, especially when that region is about to expand and diversify itself still further. But monetary politics are not easy in the United States either. It will take time for the EU to elaborate the necessary mechanisms and policies. For the EMU to function properly, adequate aid must be transferred to disadvantaged areas. No doubt, there will be occasional crises. But the EU does have ample experience in negotiating common policies among diverse partners. It has already absorbed several poorer new members, and it regularly subsidizes backward regions. In monetary matters at least, the two leading countries appear to share a rather robust consensus. Concerning money, the French are rather more "German" than is commonly thought, and the Germans rather more "French." Monetary fashions will doubtless change over the coming decades, but there is no reason to presume an unbridgeable cultural gap between the two major partners. Both probably have too much at stake to fail.

Success with EMU greatly strengthens the Western core and very probably reinforces the trends toward a union with wider scope. EMU will, in due course, make Europe a monetary superpower, the euro competing with the dollar for the world's savings and financial business. It will be difficult to be in such a position while remaining an American military protectorate.[37]

Very probably, a larger, more ambitious, and more diverse EU will have to grow more hegemonic and less corporatist in its internal arrangements. Dressing up increased central power in technocratic form is an old trick that has worked well enough in the past. To some considerable extent, that is what EMU does in the monetary field. But technocratic tutelage still has to be organized within the political structures of the EU's confederal form. Moreover, an EU extending its scope much further into strategic and military realms will not be so amenable to even the semblance of technocratic governance.

In effect, the EU's fundamental constitutional problem is the same as it has always been. Europe's confederacy is not built around a single state much more powerful than the rest. Rather it is a group of strong-minded medium and smaller states, each with distinct interests and traditions and a long history of warfare with the others. The practical problem has always been how to endow such a group of states not only with efficient coordinating structures but also with shared interests and coherent policies. Success depends not merely on collective goodwill and ability, but also on whether a coherent political economic bloc still seems the best strategy for resolving the basic challenges facing Europe's states after the Cold War. Before moving on to the practical issues of how such a bloc might be organized in the future, it seems wise to consider whether broad historical forces are still favoring it.

---

[37] See David P. Calleo, "The Strategic Implications of the Euro," *Survival*, vol. 41, no. 1 (Spring 1999), pp. 5–19.

Globalism and the Case for a European Bloc

THROUGHOUT THE postwar decades, European integration enjoyed wide popular support, at least in most continental countries. To European publics, integration seemed the enlightened and obvious response both to their continent's bloody past and to its present and future challenges. By the 1990s, however, public support had begun to waver, and expert analysts began wondering whether Europe's integration, at least in its postwar confederal form, was still an appropriate goal.[1] Triumphant global capitalism was challenging Europe's postwar welfare states, with their corporatist mentalities and self-indulgent communitarian bargains.[2] And the EU, with its cumbersome machinery and lavish handouts, seemed to rob Europe's states of the capacity either to adapt rapidly to competitive markets or even to protect their communitarian values. In effect, globalization was threatening to make Europeanization obsolescent.

GLOBALIZATION AND ITS CHALLENGES

Throughout most of the postwar era, Europe's external economic challenges had seemed to come mainly from the United States. In the 1980s, for example, European governments were still preoccupied with how their economies could avoid the shocks of America's volatile macroeconomic policies and how their firms could compete with giant American multinationals. By the 1990s, Europeans were growing increasingly conscious of a more general global challenge. Ad-

---

[1] See chapter 11, note 11.

[2] The term *communitarian* has come to refer broadly to those who emphasize the significance of fraternity or fellowship in societal, political, and economic arrangements, as opposed, for example, to competition. The term suits varieties of socialism, but also the welfare capitalism typical of postwar Europe. As I use the term in chapter 4, *communitarian economic policy* is a form of neomercantilism serving the ideals of the welfare state. See the appendix to chapter 4.

vances in technology were making it easy to downsize expensive workforces in the West and, at the same time, to spread industrial production to huge workforces in the non-Western world, tendencies accelerated by the demise of the Soviet Union and the opening up of China. Under these circumstances, Western Europe's high costs and sticky regulations threatened to make its home-based enterprises and labor uncompetitive. Compared to the booming United States, Europe in the 1990s seemed slow to deploy its resources to those new industries and services needed to sustain its high living standards. Home investment and growth began to decline. By the early 1990s, European unemployment had reached a scale unknown since the depression of the 1930s.[3] In effect, the globalization of economies seemed to have put Europe in an increasingly unfavorable position.

Globalization is meant to define a world economy whose actors have increasingly easy access to a common pool of resources—to global markets for capital, goods, labor, and services, and also to a common global pool of science, technology, and culture. This access changes the nature of competition by improving the prospects for efficiency. Footloose firms can sell their goods and services in wealthy economies, where workers are well paid, the community well endowed, and the environment protected, while producing those goods, and sometimes even services, in parts of the globe with cheap labor, low welfare costs, low taxes, and easy environmental regulation. Firms benefit competitively insofar as they can avoid the full costs of sustaining the rich markets where they sell. Thus, as many critics charge, globalization presents the prospect of widespread free riding. These criticisms notwithstanding, globalist prescriptions, variously elaborated, have been in high fashion among politicians, academics, and journalists throughout the West. At the turn of the century, globalization has become a modern mythology, a secular religion informed by neoliberal beliefs deeply implanted in Western cultures, and ardently promoted by the political, economic, intellectual, and cultural

---

[3] Investment in the EU fell in real terms by 0.3 percent in 1991, 0.3 percent in 1992, and 5.8 percent in 1993. Unemployment, meanwhile, rose from 8.0 percent to 10.6 percent. *OECD Economic Outlook: December 1999* (Paris: OECD, 2000), pp. 232, 215.

interests served by it.[4] In the new world of borderless competition, it is said, the world market provides a truly international culture, one that resists nationalist partition into distinct cultural camps.[5] Global corporations, run by managers responsible to shareholding investors, are the masters of this new world. Political control is eroded, as states either wither away or, already transformed from territorial to "trading states," seem likely to grow into virtual states—disembodied centers of knowledge and will, emancipated from their old nationalist "land fetish."[6] Global trends are said to presage a new class system, where old-style workers are less secure. Production workers, less mobile than capital, are trapped in a global competition for the cheapest and most docile labor. And workers who provide routine services are bound to the competitive fate of their localities. But globalization also creates a new elite of "symbolic analysts," those endowed with the knowledge to master the global web, and to combine and recombine globalized resources to create and serve globalized markets.[7] These cosmopolitan and footloose technocrats are liberated not only from states but from even the business organizations that require their services. They embody every consultant's fantasy.

Some of the globalist vision seems an obvious form of political-economic science fiction, with virtual states ready to relocate to outer space whenever the technology grows cost-effective. Why does this vision resonate so deeply in the contemporary imagination? There are a variety of reasons. As the perfectly free market, globalism embodies the dream world of every liberal economist. In recent years, this old-

---

[4] "Much of what is written about globalization turns out to be nonsense and is accepted mainly because . . . there are strong political and intellectual interests supporting it." Michael Veseth, *Selling Globalization: The Myth of the Global Economy* (Boulder, CO: Lynne Rienner, 1998), p. vii.

[5] See, for instance, Kenichi Ohmae, *The End of the Nation State: The Rise of Regional Economies* (London: HarperCollins, 1996), and Kenichi Ohmae, *The Borderless World: Power and Strategy in the Interlinked Economy* (London: HarperCollins, 1994).

[6] See Richard Rosecrance, *The Rise of the Virtual State: Wealth and Power in the Coming Century* (New York: Basic Books, 1999).

[7] See Robert B. Reich, *The Work of Nations: Preparing Ourselves for 21st Century Capitalism* (New York: Knopf, 1991), esp. pp. 177–180.

time religion of the economists has come to have wide appeal for others. The shocks of the 1970s greatly strengthened neoliberal sentiments and ideas. In Europe, as in the United States, Hayek was in and Keynes was out. It grew fashionable, particularly following the ignominious collapse of the Soviet Union, to doubt that politicians and bureaucrats could systematically alter the workings of markets in the general interest. Given rapid technological change, integrated world markets, reflecting "rational expectations," were seen as benign taskmasters, compelling a more efficient use of resources and a more sustainable model for society.[8] For many, fed up with the inflationary excesses of the welfare state, international corporations, driven to maximize profits, seemed better shapers of economic life than democratic nation states with communitarian pretensions. The latter were all too easily exploited by rent-seeking special interests manipulating ignorant populist enthusiasms. Globalization promised relief. An open global marketplace would limit the capacity of states to promote their inefficient clients and would strengthen firms against state interference. In this neoliberal optic, the world at the end of the twentieth century was finally reviving the promise of the late nineteenth century.[9]

In due course, the renewed ascendancy of neoliberalism began also

---

[8] Developed in the 1970s, rational expectations theory assumes that, in making decisions, individuals have access to all relevant information, including knowledge of the structure of the economic system, and that any errors in the analysis of that information are due to random forces. It has controversial implications for economic behavior. One of its most celebrated—and contested—predictions concerns the ineffectiveness of economic policy. According to the rational expectations approach, any systematic attempt to raise output above its natural level—as, for example, by increasing the money supply and raising prices above their expected level—will fail, as individuals adjust their expectations in line with the new policy. See Robert E. Lucas, Jr., "Econometric Policy Evaluation: A Critique," in Karl Brunner and Allan H. Meltzer, eds., *The Phillip's Curve and Labor Markets* (Amsterdam: North Holland, 1976), pp. 19–46.

[9] For a knowledgeable and spirited version of this argument, see Robert Skidelsky, *The Road from Serfdom: The Economic and Political Consequences of the End of Communism* (New York: Penguin, 1996). See also Janos Kornai, *Welfare after Communism* (London: Social Market Foundation, 1999).

to rejuvenate its traditional communitarian critics, who often resurrected arguments and sentiments prevalent among the communitarian nationalists and neomercantilists of the nineteenth century. To such critics, liberal zeal for market forces seems based on patently inadequate views of human nature and economic motivation, resulting in heroic Utopian assumptions about the quality of market decisions. Like Coleridge, List, and Mazzini, today's communitarian neomercantilists question not only the morality of market decisions but also their rationality. Among the most interesting contemporary critics of neoliberal globalization are those who, borrowing from research in physics, attribute to markets on a global scale not superior efficiency but a tendency toward chaos.[10] Mounting intellectual skepticism about the morality and rationality of markets encourages the rejuvenation of traditional antiliberal political and economic forces. Such forces, of course, never disappear. Neoprotectionists continue to argue for sheltering their economies from aspects of foreign competition likely to damage the national community. Neomercantilists, more inclined to embrace the world marketplace, nevertheless continue to press for using the state's power to improve competitiveness and to influence market outcomes in the national interest.[11]

[10] For a good summary, see Michael Veseth, *Selling Globalization: The Myth of the Global Economy*, op. cit., ch. 5.

[11] The U.S. debate over strategic trade illustrates many of these positions. In the 1970s, developments in the theory of industrial organization encouraged theoretical speculation about international trade in markets with less than perfect competition. A number of theories resulted indicating that, in monopolistic and oligopolistic markets, tariffs might be used to capture rents generated by imperfect competition and, moreover, that comparative advantage could be historically determined, a direct challenge to the Hecksher-Ohlin paradigm. Orthodox economists were aroused when President Clinton chose Laura Andrea Tyson, author of *Who's Bashing Whom: Strategic Trade in High Tech Industries* (Washington, DC: Institute for International Economics, 1992), as his first Chairman of the Council of Economic Advisers. See Paul Krugman, "Competitiveness: A Dangerous Obsession," *Foreign Affairs*, vol. 73, no. 2 (March 1994), pp. 28–44; also Ernest H. Preeg, "Who's Benefiting Whom? A Trade Agenda for High Technology Industries," *Washington Quarterly*, vol. 16, no. 4 (Fall 1993). For discussion of strategic trade theory, see Paul Krugman, *Rethinking International Trade* (Cambridge, MA: MIT Press, 1990); and Robert E. Baldwin, "Are

In summary, while economic globalization was in fashion at the end of the twentieth century, as at the beginning, state policies have continued to blend liberal, communitarian, mercantilist, and protectionist prescriptions. National mixes, moreover, have varied considerably. Individual European countries have reacted with quite different models. While the macroeconomic policies of the EU states have grown more convergent, national economic and political structures and cultures have continued to retain their distinctive characters. Arguably, with global pressures growing, the effects of such diversity may prove increasingly divisive among EU members. Conversely, global integration may provide a further incentive for European integration or change its character in a more federal direction. The issue is obviously critical for Europe's future but difficult to pursue in so abstract and general a form. It needs to be examined in the actual markets where globalization has seemed particularly significant. The rest of the chapter discusses Europe's general reaction to four such markets: for finance, for goods and services, for direct corporate investments, and for labor.

GLOBALIZED FINANCE: CHAOS?

The integration of world financial markets is probably the most important and convincing sign of a genuine global economy. In the past few decades, capital controls have been dismantled in most countries so that national equity and bond markets are often deeply affected by rapid flows of foreign money. In her vivid study of world finance, *Casino Capitalism*, Susan Strange writes about the people, mostly young, who operate the world's money markets. She pictures them peering into computer screens, successively active from one time zone to the next, and ceaselessly hurling hundreds and hundreds of billions of monetary assets around the globe. The system she describes seems very little controlled by governments, or even by its

---

Economists' Traditional Trade Policy Views Still Valid?" *Journal of Economic Literature*, vol. 30 (June 1992).

own corporate managers.[12] A particularly large and volatile pool of global money is in foreign exchange markets, whose daily financial flows were reckoned in 1998 at over $2 trillion, a sum that exceeded several times over the actual value of international trade in goods. There are, in addition, gigantic markets for other derivatives, in particular options to buy or sell stocks, bonds, or commodities. In other words, a huge mass of money in world capital markets is not being used primarily to purchase goods and services, or to make investments in the real economy, but to hedge such purchases and investments against the volatile value of money itself. In effect, the enormous monetary mass in these markets is a monster chasing its own tail.

So long as the monster remains preoccupied with itself, the effects on the real economies of the world are muted, although still of major significance. But when the monster turns outward and enters real economies directly, as, for example, it may do through currency speculation, the results can be highly destructive. Since substantial shifts in exchange rates have become commonplace, hedging has become an essential activity for international firms. So long as exchange rates are volatile, hedging is the only way global firms can attempt to orient their businesses toward real results rather than the gyrations of currency markets, over which they have little control. For these firms, hedging is part of the cost they must incur for operating in a global economy without stable exchange rates. In a world economy where national governments are collectively unable to provide stable money, private firms find their solution in the market and pay whatever price the traffic will bear.[13]

---

[12] Susan Strange, *Casino Capitalism* (Manchester, NY: Manchester University Press, 1997). For an inside view of one spectacular collapse, that of Barings Bank in February 1995, see Nick Leeson, *Rogue Trader* (London: Little Brown, 1996).

[13] Dr. Judith Paulus, a former student well acquainted with the practices of international firms, comments, "In a world where markets are the true arbiters of a company's performance, and technology allows instant transmission of results and trades, any surprises, especially in expected revenue and earnings, quickly lead to a market pummeling of the company's stock. That the market's expectation is met is more important than the actual numerical result. So companies hedge payables and receivables, interest rates, and obviously, currency rates. They do it, too, to keep local

The cost is considerable. A huge proportion of entrepreneurial energy and talent is absorbed. Of course, the benefits are clear. Hedging dilutes risk and allocates it to those most willing to accept it. Nevertheless, there are few, if any, perfect hedges, and safe results are far from assured. And given the wild swings commonplace among the world's major currencies, the stakes are often very high. Knowledgeable analysts are troubled by the potential for breakdown on a grand scale.[14] Ironically, in those financial markets where the globalization of economies is most complete, market rationality seems most uncertain. Worldwide currency and derivatives markets, linked by a vast electronic web, do sometimes seem better explained by chaos theory than by the customary models of market rationality.[15] The disturbing patterns of systemic disorder found in the huge currency markets are a far cry from the tranquil equilibrium of Newtonian physics. Wide and frequent gyrations in the values of currencies—random swings without rational patterns or predictable causes—seem difficult to rec-

---

management in other countries focused on the basics of growing a healthy business, in local currency terms, rather than worrying about exchange rate changes over which they have no control. Of course, speculation and lack of regulation have led parts of the derivative markets to spin vastly out of control, as we saw last year with Long Term Capital Management. And the sheer volume of international capital, and the rapidity with which it moves, can overwhelm small economies (the Thai experience) and confound even seasoned experts [as with] the predatory Soros assault on the pound sterling and the Bank of England." (Correspondence with the author, July 1999.)

[14] See for example, George Soros, *The Crisis of Global Capitalism: Open Society Endangered* (London: Little Brown, 1998).

[15] Before the collapse of Bretton Woods, the purchasing-power parity and Mundell-Fleming models were common ways of explaining how exchange rates were set. Thereafter, new models emerged, including Rudiger Dornbusch's theory of overshooting and William Branson's theory of portfolio balancing. Both emphasized macroeconomic conditions and investor rationality. Experience with the dollar in the 1980s, however, made clear that no one of these theories consistently explained the swings of major currencies. Some subsequent theories assert that the currency markets are entirely chaotic, while others admit some element of rationality, as in the near-rational-expectations model proposed by Paul De Grauwe. See Michael Veseth, *Selling Globalization: The Myth of the Global Economy*, op. cit., pp. 112–119; also Paul De Grauwe, *International Money: Postwar Trends and Theories* (Oxford and New York: Oxford University Press, 1996).

oncile with an efficient worldwide allocation of capital. Dynamic but unstable monetary values seem a major theoretical as well as practical limitation on the global integration neoliberals dream about.[16]

The political implications of a global market depend greatly on whether it can be seen to reflect rational reactions in the general interest. Global capital markets, for example, are said to have greatly reduced the power of nation states to shape their own economic environments. Even rich and powerful states are supposedly no longer able to sustain independent policies that defy the will of international money. Recent decades have seen impressive examples. Mitterrand's disastrous experiment with reflation in the early 1980s is one.[17] The breakdown of the European Monetary System in 1992, following German reunification, is another. A spectacular collapse of Asian currencies followed in the late 1990s, succeeded by the crash of Asian equity, bond, and property markets, resulting in a deep Asian recession. After the Asian debacle came the Russian and then the Brazilian.

Opinions on the rationality of these recent currency crises have varied sharply. In 1992, the reasons for the strength of the DM and the corresponding weakness of the lira and pound sterling seem clear enough. The weakness of the French franc in 1993 is more difficult to rationalize. Still more uncertain are the various Asian, Russian, and Latin American crises at the end of the 1990s. One view sees them as the natural outcome of irrational government policies that tried to sustain currencies without accepting the fiscal and monetary restraint needed to do so. From this perspective, the currency markets that forced these currencies to depreciate merely registered a higher economic rationality.[18]

---

[16] See Michael Veseth, *Selling Globalization: The Myth of the Global Economy*, op. cit., pp. 127–129.

[17] For an account of this episode, see Julius W. Friend, *France in the Mitterrand Years: The Long Presidency, 1981–1995* (Boulder, CO: Westview Press, 1998), pp. 31–46. See also above, chapter 11, for a further discussion of Mitterrand's monetary policies.

[18] Explanations of recent currency crises usually distinguish between those that stress the role of macroeconomic fundamentals and those that emphasize the role of speculative attacks and "contagion." The Russian, Asian, and Brazilian crises appear to have reflected a combination of the two: poor fundamentals—including low growth,

From another perspective, however, the unstable currency markets reflected primarily the malign influence of speculators, mobilizing huge sums from the world's bloated capital markets to trigger disproportionate speculative reactions for quick gains. Given the grotesque oversupply of speculative capital, currency markets do have a natural tendency to overshoot greatly. Their volatility adds all sorts of extraneous costs to doing business and, of course, creates the prospect of very large speculative profits as well as losses. Arguably, these conditions discourage rational long-term investment for growth. In addition, many analysts fear that the chaotic tendencies in these markets presage a sort of global financial meltdown. As it is, the thrashings of the currency markets have brought gigantic losses to many firms.[19] One obvious reaction in recent years has been a widespread amalgamation of financial firms, a pattern that reflects the high level of risk in today's enormous and volatile currency markets.[20] But such a

---

current account deficits, and excessive exchange rate appreciation—and adverse market sentiment. In the case of Asia, Paul Krugman has also drawn attention to the problem of moral hazard in the form of implicit government guarantees on bank liabilities, which induced banks to lend excessively to firms, creating an asset price bubble that subsequently burst. For an overview of recent currency crises, see *IMF World Economic Outlook, May 1999* (Washington, DC: International Monetary Fund, 1999), esp. pp. 66–87; for analyses of the Asian crisis, see Morris Goldstein, *The Asian Financial Crisis: Causes, Cures and Systemic Implications, Policy Analyses in International Economics 55* (Washington, DC: Institute for International Economics, 1998); Stephen Radelet and Jeffrey Sachs, *The East Asian Financial Crisis: Diagnosis, Remedies, Prospects*, Brookings Papers on Economic Activity (Washington, DC: Brookings Institution, 1998); and Martin Feldstein, "A Self-Help Guide for Emerging Markets," *Foreign Affairs* (March 1999). For Krugman's views, see, inter alia, Paul Krugman, "What Happened to Asia?" <http://web.mit.edu/krugman/www/DISINTER.html>.

[19] Such losses have been sustained not only by financial companies, but also by manufacturers. Often they have been compounded by the activities of unauthorized or "rogue" traders. Examples include Electrolux AB, Forexia AG, UBS, and, of course, the collapse of Barings Bank in February 1995. See Maria Kielmas, "Rogue Trader Costs Electrolux $29.1 Million," *Business Insurance*, vol. 34, no. 3 (January 2000); Clay Harris, "Investors Hit by Currency Trading Losses," *Financial Times*, September 20, 1999; and Philip Jeune and Clay Harris, "Forex Loss Leads to Jersey Charges," *Financial Times*, October 30, 1996. See also note 12.

[20] Examples include the recent mergers or attempted mergers between Deutsche Bank

pattern also raises doubts about how much real competition can be sustained with global financial markets increasingly dominated by a few large players. To the neomercantilist, the prescription is obvious. Political power is needed to set rules for firms and also to structure the markets themselves to keep their volatility within bounds. Logically, if financial markets are to remain global, this neomercantilist prescription calls for government action that is collective and multilateral as well as national. It implies not merely checks on rogue firms or wild capital flows, but also multilateral rules and surveillance to curb irrational national macroeconomic policies. In the present state of the world political economy, these prescriptions are obviously difficult to sustain, which doubtless greatly explains the persistent chaotic tendencies of global market. Our question here is whether chaotic global financial conditions encourage European integration. On balance, it seems that they do. The last chapter discussed how Europeans, as they moved toward a single market in the 1980s and 1990s, felt particularly vulnerable to volatility in currency markets. With the single market heightening interdependence, big swings in exchange rates among themselves threatened to destabilize domestic price and wage levels and aroused fierce resentments among competing firms and their states. Europeans hoped that EMU, with a stability pact added, would provide the fiscal as well as the strictly monetary framework needed to resolve this old problem among their integrating economies.

At the same time, Europeans continued to resent and fear the special monetary position occupied by the Americans. The United States, they noted, protects itself comparatively well from external shocks. Not only does it have a very large and relatively self-sufficient economy, but its monetary authorities control the supply of the world's major reserve and trading currency. For decades, as many Europeans see it, the United States has manipulated its money, also the world's,

---

and Dresdner Bank, Citicorp and Travellers Group, and UBS and Swiss Bank Corporation and the acquisition of Paribas by BNP. See, inter alia, "Deutsche's Big Gamble," *The Economist*, March 11, 2000; Andrew McCathie, "Consolidation Moves Gather Pace in European Banking Sector," *Deutsche Presse-Agentur*, September 10, 1999; and Gillian Tett and Alexandra Harney, "Forging a Mega-Marriage," *Financial Times*, August 23, 1999.

to lessen the consequences of its own self-indulgence. In the process, the depreciating dollar has blunted the competitive strength of others. These observations have helped to confirm the view that global money markets dance to the trumpets of mercantilist power rather than to the bagpipes of classic liberal equilibrium.

EMU was Europe's solution. Its internal money stabilized, Europe would be in a better position to protect itself against the volatile dollar in particular and the unpredictable violence of globalizing financial markets in general. EMU was also expected to reinforce a common macroeconomic discipline against excessive debt and inflation. Within Europe, EMU was meant to lower costs and favor more rational long-term investments. Some Europeans also hoped that EMU might ultimately encourage a more stable dollar and more stability for world exchange rates generally. In short, by the end of the twentieth century, global money markets were not disintegrating Europe. On the contrary, they appeared to be providing a powerful incentive for more intense European integration.

GLOBAL TRADE: BLOCS?

Arguably, a world made up of large monetary blocs would fit closely the actual patterns of international trade, which can easily be seen as more regional than global. World trade appears to center on three poles: Europe, East Asia, and North America. Such patterns, of course, are always in the eye of the beholder, but each is at least partially structured by formal regional organizations. The figures are impressive. Roughly 31 percent of all the world's foreign trade takes place inside Western Europe; another 11.2 percent takes place within East Asia; and 7.5 percent within North America. In other words, roughly 50 percent of the world's trade takes place inside one of these three blocs. Another quarter takes place among them.[21]

There is, of course, a major anomaly in the way such bloc figures are presented. Since trade among the members of the European Union

---

[21] See *Direction of Trade Statistics Yearbook* (Washington, DC: International Monetary Fund, 1999), pp. 34, 70, 71, 152–156, 326, 467–469.

has traditionally been demarcated as "foreign," European economies seem much more involved in external trade than the American economy. In reality, the external sectors of the EU and the United States are roughly equivalent. In 1995, for example, the United States exported 15.4 percent of the world's merchandise exports, and the EU 19.4 percent, not counting intra-EU trade. This amounted to 8.4 percent of GDP for the United States and 8.7 percent of GDP for the EU.[22] The import patterns and overall balance, however, are very different. America's trade is highly unbalanced overall, with very large bilateral deficits, large in absolute size with Japan and China and large in proportion to exports with several smaller Asian countries (see table 12.1). By contrast, Europe's overall trade is roughly in balance, and its trade accounts with North America show a comfortable surplus (see table 12.2).[23] Obviously, there is nothing wrong with large bilateral deficits with one part of the world if there are compensating surpluses in another. In the American case, however, there are not.

The basic picture is not much altered by comparing current account balances rather than merchandise trade alone. The current account includes trade in "services," a category that includes foreign investment income as well as payments for "nonfactor services." In 1998, for example, the United States ran a current account deficit of $220.6 billion, while the EU ran a surplus of $83.1 billion (see table 12.3). In subsequent years, up to 2001, the current account balances of both the

[22] *OECD Economic Outlook, June 1998* (Paris: OECD, 1998), pp. 207, 288. Half the foreign trade conducted by the EU countries is with each other, inside the EU. As the EU deepens, and particularly with a common currency in place, it grows increasingly dubious that internal European trade should be considered foreign at all. It is like counting interstate trade in the United States as foreign. Similarly, typically half the foreign investments made by EU member states are in other EU countries. In 1995, for example, 49.6 percent of all EU foreign direct investment was in the EU and 6.8 percent went to non-EU European countries. Calculated from *OECD International Direct Investment Statistics Yearbook* (Paris: OECD, 1997) and *OECD Economic Outlook, June 1998*, op. cit.

[23] In 1998, EU exports totaled USD 2.22 trillion, while its imports from the rest of the world came to USD 2.17 trillion. Its trade with the United States was in rough balance; it ran considerable deficits with Asia, offset by surpluses with Latin America, the Middle East and Eastern Europe. *IMF Direction of Trade Statistics, 1999* (Washington, DC: International Monetary Fund, 1999), pp. 70–75. For 1999 figures, see tables 12.1 and 12.2.

TABLE 12.1

1999 U.S. Merchandise Trade Balance (billions of U.S. dollars)

U.S. balance with . . .	Exports	Imports	Exports as % of imports	Trade balance
World	702	1059	66	−357
Japan	57.7	134	43	−76
China	12.9	86.5	15	−73
Malaysia	8.8	21.7	41	−12.9
Indonesia	1.9	10.2	20	−8.3
Hong Kong	12.7	11	112	11.6
EU	151.9	200	76	−49
NAFTA	248	308.3	81	−60

Source: International Monetary Fund, *Direction of Trade Statistics Yearbook 2000* (Washington: IMF, 2000), pp. 474–475.

TABLE 12.2

1999 EU Merchandise Trade Balance (billions of dollars)

EU balance with . . .	Exports	Imports	Exports as % of imports	Trade balance
World	811.59	830.54	102	+52
Japan	38	79	48	−41
China	21	49	42	−28
Malaysia	6.8	13.7	50	−6.9
Indonesia	3.5	9.4	44	−5.9
Hong Kong	17	18	94	−1
U.S.	193	176	110	18
Mexico	11	5	220	6
Canada	17	15	113	2

Source: International Monetary Fund, *Direction of Trade Statistics Yearbook 2000* (Washington: IMF, 2000), pp. 70–74. The World figures exclude intra-European trade. Including intra-European trade, EU total exports and imports would be $2,179 billion and $2,127.4 billion, respectively.

TABLE 12.3
2000 Estimated Current Account Balances, Elements

	Trade, net	Nonfactors, net	Investment income, net	Current account
U.S.	−450.9	+86.7	−19.9	−432.8
EU	52.4	2.9	−15.5	−15.0

Source: OECD Economic Outlook, December 2000 (Paris: OECD, 2000), pp. 256–259.

United States and the EU have tended to deteriorate. Nevertheless, the EU has maintained at least a small surplus, while the U.S. deficit has continued to grow rapidly. In 2001, for example, the EU current account surplus was expected to be $37.1 billion, while the U.S. deficit was expected to reach a record $421.8 billion.[24]

America's overall deficit puts heavy political pressure on U.S. trade relations generally. Japanese-American trade diplomacy has been highly acrimonious for decades, but without bringing the bilateral account anywhere near balance. In recent years, American-Chinese trade relations have fallen into the same pattern. There is, moreover, a recurring American tendency to try to compensate for the habitually large deficits with Asia by a surplus with Europe. Since the 1960s, successive U.S. governments have half imagined they might balance America's global trade at the expense of European farming. For years, the United States conducted a stubborn campaign to kill off the Community's Common Agricultural Policy (CAP) before it could take root. Policies of this sort are not popular among European producers, who often react violently when their governments or the European Commission seem insufficiently ardent in defense of their interests. While it is easy enough to fault the CAP on grounds of economic efficiency, it must be admitted that the United States also greatly subsidizes its agriculture.[25] Given the cultural and political significance of farming and the countryside in most European countries, not to men-

[24] Ibid., p. 243.
[25] In May 2000, Congress approved $15 billion in aid to U.S. farmers for the third year in a row. See "$15 Billion for Farmers Is Approved by Congress," *New York Times*, May 26, 2000, p. A17.

tion cuisine in various national cultures, it seems unrealistic to imagine Europe's widely abandoning its own food production to the United States.

Arguably, America's trade deficits faithfully reflect its government's long-standing commercial strategy. Like most other advanced countries, the United States often subsidizes and protects not only its agriculture but also its weaker industrial firms, often those that produce traditional products. But the government generally does not discourage such firms from moving their production abroad, where they can find cheaper labor to restore their competitiveness and profits. By contrast, federal policy does positively favor home investment in those technologically advanced industries and services in which the United States is thought to have, or wishes to have, a strong comparative advantage—for example, aircraft, biochemicals, telecommunications, financial services, computer software, and audiovisual materials. And throughout the 1990s, a great deal of diplomatic effort was devoted to prying open foreign markets for such products and services.

Inconveniently, America's European and Japanese competitors often pursue similar strategies. The EU and the United States have strikingly similar export profiles in manufacturing.[26] Their similar export profiles reflect their shared enthusiasm for advanced industries—presumably because only such industries can earn sufficient profits to sustain the high wage costs, levels of education, research, and general infrastructure typical of advanced countries.[27] Thus, everyone favors a similar cluster of industries: high technology, computers and software, aerospace, defense, biomedicine, financial services, and so on. Governments subsidize the scientific research and education that bolster such industries. Governments often subsidize production as well. Top-

---

[26] *OECD World Economic Outlook, June 98* (Paris: OECD, 1998), p. 211.

[27] These industries are also commonly supposed to be "high value-added." As Paul Krugman has pointed out, however, this is not necessarily the case. High-technology industries such as electronics and aircraft have value added per worker that is not much above the average for all manufacturing, while the highest value-added industries tend to be the most capital-intensive, such as oil refining. See Paul Krugman and Maurice Obstfeld, *International Economics: Theory and Policy* (Reading, MA: Addison Wesley Longman, 1997), pp. 276–277.

level diplomatic interventions to promote sales are commonplace. This high-tech strategy, pursued by all advanced countries together, naturally causes political friction among them. Ironically, what presents itself as the preferred liberal remedy, dictated by the enlightened pursuit of comparative advantage, ends up generating a good deal of old-fashioned mercantilist conflict among governments. In recent years, the political nature of commercial conflict has grown increasingly open and unrestrained. Many governments, including the American, seem deeply involved in industrial espionage.[28] American trade diplomacy has grown increasingly unilateral and imperious. Numerous disputes have created a remarkably acrimonious relationship with the EU in recent years, as well as with Japan and China.

Another major source of transatlantic commercial acrimony is the increasing American inclination to invoke economic sanctions against various "rogue states" for their involvement with international terrorism or human rights violations. European countries have important trade relations and investments with some of these states: Iran, Iraq, and Libya, for example. American legislation seeks nevertheless to punish foreign firms that ignore the American restrictions. In recent years, not only Congress but individual American states and even local communities have taken to imposing sanctions on foreign firms.[29]

---

[28] A particularly egregious incident occurred in 1995, when the maladroit attempts of the U.S. Central Intelligence Agency to bribe French officials produced a major scandal. See Frank Viviano, "Five Americans Accused of Spying by France," *San Francisco Chronicle*, February 23, 1995. In July 2000, superior U.S. capacities for electronic eavesdropping on phone traffic in Europe and around the world generally prompted a French inquiry into America's "Echelon" network. See Joseph Fitchett, "French Start Industrial Spy Probe of U.S. Network," *International Herald Tribune*, July 5, 2000, p. 1. The French themselves doubtless have high expertise in this ancient mercantilist skill. For an entertaining fictional treatment that faithfully captures American paranoia and self-justification, see David Ignatius, *A Firing Offence* (New York: Random House, 1997).

[29] Perhaps the most widely publicized instance of this related to the passage of an amendment to the 1992 Cuban Democracy Act in March 1996 (also known as Helms-Burton), which provided, inter alia, for legal proceedings against foreign companies or persons deemed to be "trafficking" in property deemed to have been expropriated by Cuba from U.S. nationals. For the European reaction, see Pascal Fletcher, "Spain Threatens US over Cuba," *Financial Times*, September 3, 1999; Guy de Jon-

Needless to say, these imperial legal pretensions are not welcomed by the Europeans and indeed have been forcefully resisted. On balance, America's aggressive commercial diplomacy has provided a powerful inducement for Europeans to consolidate and intensify their own economic bloc. The advantages for European states are clear. The Brussels bureaucracy has proved a highly effective champion of European interests. EU partners, represented collectively by the Commission, have been able to negotiate with a tenacity and toughness that would be difficult for many of them individually.

GLOBALIZATION AND FOREIGN DIRECT INVESTMENT

By definition, globalization means not only selling home-produced products in markets around the world, but also easy use of foreign factors of production—including foreign labor and technology. This globalized use of factors implies a high level of foreign direct investment (FDI)—to build facilities in foreign economies, to merge with or otherwise control foreign firms, to participate in networks of agreements to license production, and to share research and development costs. There are numerous signs of increasing globalist production. Since the late 1980s, sales from foreign affiliates have been growing more rapidly than exports of goods and services.[30] By 1997, exports from foreign affiliates were one-third of world exports and were valued at some $2 trillion, while overall sales of foreign affiliates were reckoned to be $9.5 trillion, or 7 percent of global GDP. Of all global payments of royalties and fees, 70 percent were between parent firms and their foreign subsidiaries.[31]

As might be expected, the accumulated stock of foreign direct investments has burgeoned. In 1997, it was equivalent to 21 percent of

---

quieres "U.S. and EU Try to Square Sanctions Circle," *Financial Times*, October 14, 1997; and Tom Buerkle, "Bitterness over U.S.-EU Trade Deal Proves It a Truce, Not a Settlement," *International Herald Tribune*, April 15, 1997.

[30] UN Conference on Trade and Development (UNCTAD), *World Investment Report: Trends and Determinants* (New York, Geneva: United Nations, 1998), p. 1.

[31] Ibid., p. 2. Capital for investment, other than that contributed by the transnational corporations (TNCs) themselves, increased by $1.6 trillion.

global GDP. In that same year, new FDI flows reached $400 billion. Cross-border agreements among firms proliferated, along with bilateral investment treaties among states. Much of this globalist production is concentrated in relatively few firms. The world's one hundred largest transnational corporations (TNCs) are said to control one-fifth of global foreign assets.[32] In 1995, these firms had foreign sales of $2 trillion and employed close to six million people. Twenty-five American corporations control half their country's outward foreign direct investment. The same pattern of concentrated globalization is visible in developing countries, whose own top fifty transnational firms are not only rapidly increasing their global investments but, in respect to their size, are already substantially more transnational in their holdings than big TNCs based in the developed countries.[33]

The United States, the EU, and Japan together are home to eighty-seven of the world's top one hundred transnational firms and account for 88 percent of their foreign assets. Not surprisingly, the three are responsible for most of the foreign direct investment that goes on in the world. Among individual countries, the United States has been both the largest single recipient of FDI and also its largest single source. Collectively, however, the EU countries are substantially larger sources and recipients. Per capita, the United States is a somewhat bigger recipient, but the EU is a much larger source. Together, the United States and the EU regularly absorb one-half to two-thirds of the world's FDI and are sources for roughly three-quarters of it. Each, moreover, is a major investor in the other. In 1998, for example, 80 percent of inflows to the United States came from the EU, and 31 percent of the EU's inflows came from the United States. In recent years, the United States has been absorbing much more FDI than it generates, whereas the reverse is true of the EU (see table 12.4).[34]

[32] UNCTAD, *Transnational Corporations, Market Structure and Competition Policy* (New York, Geneva: United Nations, 1997), p. 83.

[33] UNCTAD, *World Investment Report: Trends and Determinants*, op. cit., p. 2.

[34] Japan resumed heavy investing abroad by the mid-1990s, after falling sharply from a peak of $41 billion in 1989–1991. The figures above do not include, however, the reinvested earnings of earlier Japanese FDI—reckoned in 1994 to be $14 billion in the manufacturing sector alone. Japan's outflows are mostly directed toward the

225

TABLE 12.4

Total Foreign Direct Investment, 1999 (in billions of dollars)

	Inflows	Outflows
U.S.	275	150
EU	305	509
Japan	12	22

Source: United Nations Conference on Trade and Development (UNCTAD), Handbook of Statistics (New York, Geneva: United Nations, 2000), pp. 246–247.

Nearly half the European outward investments in the 1990s took the form of mergers and acquisitions of foreign firms. The inflow for mergers and acquisitions within Europe, however, has generally been much lower than in the United States, thanks perhaps to regulatory barriers that have been slow to erode in countries like Italy and Germany. European patterns do vary considerably from one country to another. Among European states, Britain was both the largest investor and the largest recipient. Germany was a large investor but a small recipient. France was a considerable investor but a larger recipient than Germany, though not so large as Britain (see table 12.5).

Europe's unbalanced FDI flows contrast sharply with its balanced performance in exports and imports. The investment imbalance is said to be a principal cause of the relative weakness of the euro against the dollar and the yen in the last years of the century, a weakness that otherwise might seem surprising, given Europe's well-balanced trade and very low inflation.[35] What is the significance of Europe's invest-

---

United States and developing Asia. Inflows have generally been negligible. Ibid., pp. 42–45.

[35] See Martin Wolf, "A Continent's Weak Currency," Financial Times, April 26, 2000, p. 13, and Michael R. Sesit, "Overseas Investors Pour Money into U.S., Bolstering the Dollar: Europeans Lead the Charge—Hurting the Euro," Wall Street Journal Europe, June 27, 2000, p. 1. The latter article features another dimension of Europe's outflow to the United States: purchasing of U.S. securities for portfolio investment. According to Mr. Sesit, who cites figures from the Securities Industry Association, foreign purchases of U.S. securities were $141 billion net in the first quarter of 2000—far more than enough to compensate for the U.S. current account deficit of $102.3 billion in the same quarter. Of the $141 billion in net purchases, Europeans

TABLE 12.5

Direct Investment Flows in Selected European Economies 1997–1999
($ million)

	Inflows			Outflows		
	1997	1998	1999	1997	1998	1999
Austria	2,654	4,567	2,813	1,987	2,765	2,797
France	23,178	29,495	39,101	35,591	45,471	107,952
Germany	11,097	21,163	26,822	40,733	91,159	50,596
Italy	3,700	3,065	4,901	10,414	14,096	2,958
Spain	6,375	11,863	9,355	12,652	24,365	19,549
United Kingdom	33,227	63,649	82,182	61,586	119,018	199,289

Source: UNCTAD, Handbook of Statistics 2000 (New York and Geneva, 2000), pp. 246–247.

ment deficit? In a global economy, it seems logical for a group of rich and highly developed economies, with a moderate current account surplus, to invest heavily abroad and thus run a net deficit on FDI. The American pattern—a huge current account deficit financed in good part by an investment inflow—is harder to understand. There are several possible explanations. The United States, it is said, is a far more open and dynamic economy than a Europe still bogged down in sclerotic corporatism. Thus, as Germany appears to illustrate, European firms with global possibilities vigorously plant themselves in America and Asia, while no one seems interested in making comparable investments in Germany. A further explanation is that much of Europe does not really welcome foreign investment. While European firms are heavily involved in mergers and acquisitions abroad, the continental business climate is hostile to corresponding foreign takeovers within Europe. Indeed, European states often still resist takeovers of national firms by other European firms. In effect, European states and firms seem to have become globalist neomercantilists, eager to penetrate other economies through FDI but sometimes reluctant

---

were responsible for $93.3 billion, and for 94 percent of foreign purchases of U.S. stocks. Germans were the biggest single buyers. For comparative trade statistics, see table 12.1 and note 23 above.

to see a corresponding penetration of their own.[36] Big European firms invest in other countries and regions as a strategy for surviving and flourishing. They nevertheless cling to the national states that nourish and protect them and thereby remain enmeshed in the corporatist bargaining networks typical of those states. Being global as well as European helps big firms to maintain competitiveness by lowering costs, and it also enhances their bargaining position at home. Labor-intensive goods can be produced abroad while production at home can concentrate on goods whose large profits and dynamic markets justify the home country's high costs and elaborate infrastructure. Pursuing a globalist strategy of specialization, however, often requires major changes in the location of production, a volatility that upsets older and more comfortable patterns of employment. To retain good jobs, workers need frequent retraining and great flexibility, often mobility as well. In recent years, new technology has brought a similar volatility to employment in many service industries. Telecommunications is an obvious illustration. Labor resists these changes, and its resistance threatens the traditional bargains on which postwar corporatist cooperation has based itself. In effect, the pace of technological change and access to global markets is increasing the tension between Europe's neomercantilism, oriented toward aggressive competitiveness, and its welfare states, oriented toward social peace. The continuing clash promises a prolonged period of social and economic tension—in Europe and, indeed, in all advanced parts of the world.

One way to reconcile competitiveness and welfare is to practice protectionism at home together with heavy direct investment abroad. But the combination is a dysfunctional remedy insofar as it relieves the pressure to eliminate uncompetitive practices at home and thereby encourages the migration of firms to global sources of cheaper and more tractable labor. Ideally, neomercantilist competitiveness and the welfare state should be complementary. Europe's generous benefits and high standard of living depend ultimately on its remaining competitive. But competitiveness in rich societies depends not only on a high level of skills and infrastructure, but also on social peace. In

---

[36] Naturally, generalizations about European FDI need to be qualified according to country and industry. See table 12.5 and note 35.

many European states, social cooperation is closely linked to the smooth functioning of various corporatist structures that compel a broad consensus. At times, such structures seem a serious handicap, particularly for welfare states in need of reform. Nevertheless, Europe's overall postwar experience suggests that the effort needed to cultivate and sustain a broad national consensus is worth the trouble. Given reasonable political leadership and a long history of successful cooperation, reaching consensus on reform is hardly a hopeless task. Europe's are not zero-sum societies, where harsh economic alternatives make class warfare inevitable. For rich and well-endowed Europe, the optimal strategy for attracting investment and sustaining competitiveness should be not to degrade home labor, but to increase its quality, as well as to enhance further the continent's already highly cultivated physical, social, and cultural environment. Continental Europe's high unemployment throughout the 1990s, however, indicated that a successful balance between competitiveness and welfare had remained elusive.

The quickening pace of reform in the new century, together with significant drops in unemployment, suggests that Europe's welfare states are beginning to adapt more successfully and, in the process, to attract more investment.[37] But what is the price—for Europe's nation states and for the EU's collective solidarity and integration?

While patterns of FDI vary significantly among EU members, Europe's experience does not provide a prima facie case that globalization erodes the role of states in promoting national economic competitiveness. Quite the contrary. Much of the competition for investment concerns assets where the state's role is critical—a well-trained workforce, social peace and discipline, infrastructure, technological research facilities, transparent property rights, laws and regulations

---

[37] See Frédéric Lemaître, "Les Surprises des 35 heures," p. 1; Philippe Ricard, "L'Allemagne baisse l'impôt de 291 milliard de francs en sept ans," p. 2; and "Reforme à l'allemande," p. 15, *Le Monde*, July 16–17, 2000; also "Chômage: Le Medef fait la révolution," pp. 1, 8, and "Nouveau modèle social," p. 17, *Le Monde*, June 15, 2000. See also John Schmidt, "Schroeder Triumphs in Battle over Taxes," *International Herald Tribune*, July 15–16, 2000, p. 1, and "Europe Goes Back to Work," *Financial Times*, July 17, 2000, p. 12. For a more skeptical view, see Wolfgang Munchau, "Germany Takes a Small Step in the Right Direction," ibid., p. 13.

without arbitrary interference, tax holidays and other direct or indirect subventions, and diplomatic assistance to secure favorable treatment. Competition for direct investment—from national or foreign firms—is very much a neomercantilist exercise. Obviously, competition for investment also limits the neomercantilist state. To succeed, a state cannot follow macroeconomic policies that harm local firms or impede their trade. In general, erratic and arbitrary government policies grow more and more costly. But limiting states in this fashion seems more a healthy disciplining or rectification of the state's role than a diminishing of it. Indeed, global competition for investment may strengthen the mercantilist state, by providing a convenient rationale for resisting populist policies injurious to competitiveness.[38] As EMU has illustrated, European integration seems to many people the best way to break free of the Eurosclerosis deeply implanted in Europe's postwar national economies—the inflexible labor markets, high unemployment, runaway fiscal spending, high taxes, and uncompetitive regulation. In short, globalization does not appear to offer a vision that undermines or even competes with Europeanization. Instead, more integration is often promoted as the best way for Europe's national economies to sustain their global competitiveness. These views,

---

[38] Robert Skidelsky writes here, "My impression is that you use mercantilism so broadly that you obscure the distinction between the mercantilist state and the liberal state based on rule of law." My answer is that there is perforce a large area of overlap. To succeed in their avowed aim of improving national competitiveness, proper neomercantilists have to learn how to channel independent market forces efficaciously. This requires a rule of law. When neomercantilists are also communitarian nationalists, they seek to improve competitiveness by avoiding conflict by structures that encourage cooperation and solidarity. And when they are also "good Europeans," they extend that cooperative ambit to their neighbors. Similar adjustments can obviously be made to the liberal state so that practical liberal politicians arrive at similar positions—those that elicit enough cooperation and consensus to make a liberal state possible. Both traditions—the liberal and the neomercantilist communitarian—are deeply implanted in Western political and economic culture. The latter has been predominant on the continent since World War II, with the consequences discussed in chapter 9. Hence, the liberal counterattack, now reinforced by the "global" economy. Continental states will adjust—but probably driven more by neomercantilist and communitarian concerns than by enthusiasm for libertarian individuality and competition per se.

of course, are not universally held. Europeanization can also be counted as a way to generalize Europe's dysfunctional habits—a view popular, for example, among the many British neo-liberals who remain skeptical of the EU.

EUROPEAN CHAMPIONS?

European integration, working in tandem with the dynamics of globalization, has been a strong influence pressing for a restructuring of industry within the EU. European firms have seen a broad wave of acquisitions, mergers, and alliances among themselves, as well as with U.S., Japanese, and other non-European firms. National governments are often the midwives of deals to concentrate producers, particularly in industries concerned with defense, high technology, and banking. The pattern of integration among European firms has some obvious parallels with the pattern of integration among European states. Increased competition has, first of all, encouraged a consolidation of national firms to produce national champions. Britain seems the major exception, where foreign takeovers—European, American, or Japanese—have seldom been discouraged. By contrast, Germany and Italy, while investing significantly abroad, have strongly resisted takeovers of their own firms by foreigners, European or otherwise. France, while notorious for its state-backed national champions, has, in fact, also avidly and successfully courted very significant foreign direct investment.[39]

Federal or neoliberal enthusiasts have eagerly been awaiting a further phase, with genuinely "European" firms—not tied to any one nation state and thereby implying the erosion of national political authority—either to the benefit of "market forces" or to the EU's own political structures. Logically, EMU should encourage such a development. It is too early to say to what extent this further European phase is actually occurring. Europe's industrial consolidation shows all the complexity and ambiguity that characterizes its political integration. Despite the single market, it is not so clear that the different national

[39] See table 12.5.

markets have grown homogenous. European national firms thus operate in what appear to be several distinct national markets. To do so,
they acquire distribution and production facilities in several countries.
Naturally, more transnational activity encourages more regulation at
the EU level, but that regulation is still qualified by subsidiarity and
by the confederal nature of the EU's policymaking. A great many
trans-European direct investments, mergers, and strategic agreements
have occurred. To what extent do trans-European firms become ana-
tional or "European" in their ownership, management, and general
culture, as well as in their marketing and production?

In some critical industries with heavy costs, global competition
might be expected to generate genuinely "European" corporations. In
aerospace, for example, a European group, Airbus Industrie, has
achieved marked success against its principal global competitor, the
American giant Boeing. But Airbus has traditionally been a consortium of national firms in partnership rather than an integrated firm.[40]
Each partner, moreover, has had intimate relations with its own national government—as has Boeing with the U.S. government. Recent

[40] Headquartered in France, Airbus Industrie was for several years a consortium of
four national firms: Aerospatiale Matra (France) with a 37.9 percent shareholding,
Daimler Chrysler Aerospace (Germany) also with 37.9 percent, BAE Systems (UK)
with 20 percent, and CASA (Spain) with a 4.2 percent stake. Airbus is also associated
with Alenia (Italy), Fokker (The Netherlands), and Belairbus (Belgium). In May
2000, the national partners in Airbus agreed in principle to establish it as a single
company under French law. This was to take place through a merger of Aerospatiale
Matra, Daimler Chrysler Aerospace, and CASA into European Aeronautics Defense
and Space (EADS). See "Airbus Integrated Company to Be Set Up under French
Law," *AFX European Focus*, May 11, 2000, and Graham Dunn, "EC Clears EADS
Merger," *Air Transport Intelligence*, May 11, 2000. Formal agreement was announced on June 23, 2000, to form a single private company, under French law.
EADS would hold 80 percent of the new Airbus Industrie. At the same time, Airbus
announced plans to go ahead with a new giant airliner, the A3XX, designed, among
other things, to challenge Boeing's dominance in the market for large airliners. See
"Airbus A3XX, le géant des airs," *Le Monde*, June 23, 2000, pp. 1, 18, 19; Joseph
Fitchett, "Airbus Clears Last Hurdle for Launching Superjumbo," *International Herald Tribune*, June 19, 2000; *International Herald Tribune*, June 24–25, 2000, pp. 1,
11; and Kevin Done, "Airbus Partners Unite for Boeing Challenge," *Financial Times*,
June 24–25, 2000, pp. 1, 10. The EADS merger took place on July 10, 2000. See
<http//:www.eads-nv.com/eads/en/index.htm>.

years, however, have seen great pressure to transform Airbus into an integrated private firm. Formal arrangements to do so were announced in June 2000. It remains to be seen what kind of actual structure finally evolves.

Similar pressure favors trans-European mergers in defense firms. For a long time, however, the results have been more strategic partnerships with ad hoc arrangements than genuine corporate mergers. The big nation states, generally the principal funders and customers for such industries, remain reluctant to have their roles marginalized by Europeanization. Presumably, any "European" firm would be dominated either by one leading country or by private interests acting through the market. Neither alternative is really acceptable. Arguably, real progress will require further political evolution among the major states—not only toward a common foreign and security policy in the EU, but also toward more genuinely integrated military forces. Whether such progress will be a further elaboration of confederal arrangements or will represent a mutation to federal structures remains to be seen. If the past is any guide, prospects for the former are more promising than for the latter.

Will a confederal pattern also continue to characterize other industries with strong traditions of state involvement, like telecommunications, nuclear power, older public utilities, and even, as in some countries, banking? Here again, the answer is unclear. Obviously, there has been a great deal of mutual investment as well as trading across Europe's borders. Nevertheless, attempts by firms from one European country to take over major firms in another often meet powerful resistance, official or otherwise. Every European country has its own structures of ownership and power, with public and private sectors, woven together in unique ways. Europe's different national technostructures have certainly learned to operate in each other's territory, and to cooperate in mutual interest. But they resist losing control of their own patch. Ownership and self-determination are too closely related. Foreign owners are probably tolerated more easily in industries that seem anyway to be in decline, but even then reluctantly. In short, Europe's ancient national and neomercantilist structures are highly imaginative in learning how to cooperate efficiently but do not thereby disappear.

233

Some analysts suggest that the only real European companies are American. Europe's firms, of course, also tie up with American partners, often to acquire advanced technology or management skills. Smaller countries, in particular, are tempted to find some profitable niche with the Americans rather than to band together to produce a European champion. Perhaps these reciprocal patterns do suggest a globalist future, where big European firms, increasingly heedless of national roots, will not so much Europeanize as Americanize. But the already huge scale of America's firms, the peremptory and intrusive character of America's commercial diplomacy, and the global pretensions of its courts, all work to discourage the more advanced and ambitious European firms from linking themselves too tightly to American partners. In certain critical industries, much of the pressure to Europeanize comes from the need to remain competitive globally, or to become so. The desire to give European business the scale and support enjoyed by its American competitors thus contributes to a more integrated European economy. As has so often been the case, it is the American challenge that drives the Europeans together. By the turn of the century, Europe seemed poised for a major restructuring of its industries, on the heels of a great wave of mergers and acquisitions. But how European firms coalesce reflects, in a commercial idiom, the same hybrid and volatile mixture of national, confederal and federal elements that characterizes the European Union politically.[41]

---

[41] Although national consolidation remains a strong pattern, the French themselves are moving away from total adherence to the concept of national champions in defense as well as other fields, as note 40 describes with Airbus Industrie. French authorities did not oppose, for instance, plans for a merger between the German Hoechst and the French Rhône-Poulenc. See Geoffrey Owen, "The Americanization of European Business," *Wall Street Journal Europe*, July 27, 1999, p. 14. See also plans for promoting a Franco-German nuclear power group out of Framatome and Siemens. "Framatome: Vers un pôle nucléaire européen," *Le Monde*, July 30, 1999, p. 1. The American example was also a major impetus behind the sustained drive in the EU to deregulate. Despite some successes, however—among them the takeover of Germany's Mannesmann by Vodafone AirTouch and France's CCF by HSBC—the bulk of merger activity continues to be domestic. See Alex Skorecki, "M & A Bandwagon Swerves on Regardless," *Financial Times*, May 12, 2000. Chancellor Schroeder's successful tax reform, passed in July 2000, promised major changes in Ger-

GLOBAL LABOR?

The increasing global migration of capital and technology suggests that labor markets have grown more linked internationally. Since firms are increasingly free to invest their capital and technology wherever conditions favor their competitiveness, a major element in their decision making is the relative cost, productivity, and flexibility of labor. The growing significance of foreign trade in domestic economies also seems noteworthy, particularly because a very large part of international trade—one-third according to some experts—is carried on among different branches or subcontractors of the same business firm. Common sense suggests that such trade has often been driven significantly by the search for cheap labor. Western firms, using foreign subsidiaries or subcontractors, export technology that can be employed more profitably abroad than at home. Many factors influence their decision. But all other things being equal, labor cost is likely to weigh heavily. In effect, labor abroad is competing with labor at home. Liberal economists encourage this practice as a rational adaptation to the inevitable evolution of technology and comparative advantage. When firms in advanced countries hive off older products and technology to suitable less-developed countries with cheaper labor, both sides should benefit. The poorer country advances its industrial development and itself becomes a growing market for the exports of others. The rich country imports older products for less than they could be produced at home and so increases its real income. It frees resources for expanding its more advanced industries. The advanced society thereby perpetuates its competitiveness and prosperity.[42]

---

many's corporate structures and culture by phasing out capital gains taxes for crossholdings of corporate shares. See Christopher Rhoads, "Tax Breakthrough in Germany Opens Window of Opportunity: Change Is Expected to Unleash a Wave of Divestiture, Spin-Offs and Acquisitions," *Wall Street Journal Europe*, July 17, 2000, p. 1.

[42] See Raymond Vernon, "International Investment and International Trade in the Product Cycle," *Quarterly Journal of Economics* (May 1966), pp. 190–207. For my more skeptical view, see, David P. Calleo, *The Bankrupting of America* (New York: William Morrow, 1992), pp. 165–167.

The net effect on employment in advanced countries is, however, hotly disputed, above all in continental Europe, which clings to its postwar ideal of stable and protected employment. Globalist economists argue that exporting old jobs from declining industries creates new jobs in advancing industries. Logically, the new jobs should be well paid, moreover, because they should be in industries where the advanced country has a continuing comparative advantage—the sorts of industries and services requiring well-trained and therefore higher priced labor. By contrast, labor entrapped in declining industries has an unpromising future. Such reasoning depends on complex technological, educational, social, and political assumptions about the dynamics and consequences of innovation. Protectionists and many mercantilists doubt that such assumptions are sufficiently credible to justify the globalist's enthusiasm for exporting production. From the mercantilist's nationalist perspective, it may be better to preserve a wide range of industries and services as a sort of genetic pool for future innovation, now unforeseeable. Subsidizing new technology can revolutionize and recapture old industries as well as create new ones. And the belief that exporting jobs creates compensating new employment at home is, skeptics would say, an expectation more religious than economic in character.

The empirical evidence is ambiguous. As noted earlier, the United States has probably gone farther than most other advanced countries in downsizing, exporting, or simply eliminating unfashionable industries. New industries and services proliferate, and new jobs have been created in abundance. Many undoubtedly have been in advanced sectors of the economy and pay high salaries. More, however, have been in services where wages and job security are low and benefits minimal.[43] In many working-class families, to sustain the family income

---

[43] For a discussion of the relationship between trade, unemployment and wages, see Richard Freeman, "Are Your Wages Set in Beijing?" *Journal of Economic Perspectives* (Summer 1995); Adrian Wood, "How Trade Hurt Unskilled Workers," *Journal of Economic Perspectives* (Summer 1995), pp. 57–80; Matthew Slaughter and Phillip Swagel, "The Effect of Globalization on Wages in the Advanced Economies," *IMF Working Paper WP/97/43, 1997*; Donald R. Davis, "Does European Unemployment Prop Up American Wages? National Labor Markets and Global Trade," *American Economic Review*, vol. 88, no. 3 (June 1998), pp. 478–494.

once earned by one wage earner, two are now required. Recent decades record a startling increase in the inequality of earnings and wealth among Americans.[44] The same shift is found among the British.[45] Both countries follow a similar liberal and globalist economic strategy, and the radical shift of wealth and income within them seems a logical outcome of that strategy.

As liberal economists often point out, this process, whereby the remuneration paid to capital and expert training increases disproportionately to that paid to unskilled labor, does not really depend on a globalized economy. It will occur in any dynamic national economy whether or not its firms are investing heavily abroad. In such an economy's advanced and lucrative sectors, demand for capital and skills increases naturally, and the returns paid to these factors will grow correspondingly. Appropriately trained workers and professional people will be better paid, and rapidly growing new industries should provide handsome returns to the capital invested in them. Similarly, in any such dynamic economy, where labor is well paid, firms seeking to compete successfully are drawn to technology that reduces labor costs, whether or not these firms are exporting jobs abroad. Insofar as this labor-saving process does not occur, the economy loses its dynamism and probably grows less competitive. The most likely result is declining overall growth and living standards, together with higher unemployment. Similarly, if firms do not export their older technology to countries with cheaper labor, they are more likely to lose revenue abroad than to save jobs at home.

---

[44] According to Department of Commerce figures, the overall incidence of poverty in the United States declined from 22.4 percent in 1959 to a plateau of around 11.6 percent during 1973–1979. It then rose again to 15.1 percent in 1993. The trend was especially marked among ethnic minorities and children. At the same time, there was a very noticeable increase in wealth inequality. While the average wealth of all U.S. households increased by 23 percent in real terms between 1983 and 1989, that of the superrich grew by 47 percent. This trend may have abated in the first half of the 1990s. See William R. Cline, *Trade and Income Distribution*, (Washington, DC: Institute for International Economics, 1997), pp. 4–14.

[45] The majority of OECD countries experienced an increase in income inequality during the 1980s. Aside from the United States, the trend was most marked in the Netherlands, Sweden, and the United Kingdom. See *Income Distribution in OECD Countries* (Paris: OECD, 1995), pp. 47–58.

Globalization does, of course, intensify the process. Insofar as cheap unskilled labor becomes easily available abroad, the demand for similar laborers at home falls, and their market position deteriorates. Even highly trained workers may suffer the same fate if the production to which their skill applies migrates abroad. In globalist logic, their best strategy is to retrain to acquire skills needed in still growing industries and to move to where those industries are located. Government should foster worker retraining, improve infrastructure and education generally, and encourage competitive new industries. Welfare for workers and companies should be used to ease transitions, but not to impede them.

For laborers, the adjustment process is frequently not as facile as globalist logic implies. In the globalist vision, workers are tirelessly adaptive, protean in their skills, and mobile in their residences, pulling up and putting down roots with ease. Husbands, wives, and children are equally enterprising breadwinners, attentively attuned to market opportunities. Human nature balks. When big industries downsize drastically, workers cannot so easily retrain, and in any case, older workers often have difficulty finding comparable jobs. Moving populations to new regions obviously has collective costs, especially if it means abandoning infrastructure in one place and having to re-create it in others. Migration disrupts local economies and disintegrates old patterns of community relationships. For some, the consequences are liberating, but for others, they are demoralizing.

To a greater extent than in the United States and Britain, continental Europeans have resisted playing their parts in the globalist scenario. But much of continental Europe has also had record unemployment and, as a consequence, intense fiscal pressure throughout most of the 1990s. Globalists are not surprised. As they see it, the power of today's market economy is relentless and unforgiving. Resistance to the market's logic does not reduce the painfulness of change; it merely reduces its benefits. Many liberal economists would therefore prefer to subsidize poorly paid workers directly rather than otherwise impede firms from hiring and firing at will or migrating to cheaper labor abroad.[46]

---

[46] For a discussion of the superiority of subsidies over tariffs as instruments of policy, see Melvin B. Krauss, *The New Protectionism and Industrial Trade* (New York: New York University Press, 1978).

Not surprisingly, workers and others adversely affected by technology and globalist trends look to the state to assert a different logic, that of community and collective power. It is the state's duty, they affirm, to ensure that communities are kept vital and that the right to work in tolerable conditions is protected. New generations of citizens should be trained and employed in a fashion that develops their minds and spirits and permits them to earn a decent living in reasonable security. To fulfill such duties, the state will need to foster new industries and services and often to shelter and rejuvenate old ones. In short, much of continental Europe wants to keep the postwar era's neomercantilist welfare state. Such ideas are deeply implanted in Western societies. The more brutally these ideas are assaulted, the more violent will be the reactions.

One way or another, however, Europeans will have to come to terms with the new world economy.[47] Through most of the 1990s, globalist ideas were on the offensive, in Europe as elsewhere. They played a large role in promoting further European integration, EMU in particular. But opposition, intellectual and political, was gathering force. Some of that opposition turned against the EU itself. But there is no intrinsic reason why neomercantilist communitarians who resist global liberalism should oppose a European bloc. Quite the contrary. Protectionism on a collective European scale should be more effective and less costly than individual national protectionism. How far European neomercantilists and communitarians actually do embrace protectionism is likely to depend on how disruptive and traumatic the consequences of technology and globalization turn out to be in coming decades.

GLOBALIZATION: LIBERAL AND MALTHUSIAN VERSIONS

The spread of industrialization to new countries and regions has been going on for at least a couple of centuries. So has the intensive application of new technology. Shifting patterns of comparative advantage,

---

[47] By the end of the century, both France and Germany were apparently making progress toward a more efficient version of their traditional welfare states. See notes 37 and 41 above.

investment, trade, and employment have often been traumatic for particular industries, individuals, and regions. But it is difficult to argue that the results have not been overwhelmingly positive, above all for Western working classes and societies in general.[48] Why should the current situation be different? Today's technological change may be rapid but is probably no more traumatic in its effects than, for example, the invention of steam power, the telephone, the internal combustion engine, or the electric motor. Nor is today's global trade more significant, in proportion to national economies, than during many periods in the past. Since Ricardo, liberal market theory has taught that when each of two trading partners concentrates on what it does best, greater economic efficiency will result for both.[49] Subsequent elaborations of the theory state that standards of living will tend to equalize. Incomes of workers in the poorer partner will rise toward those of the richer, while workers generally will also benefit from cheaper prices for the products they buy. Both sides will gain as greater specialization results in greater productive efficiency all around. Some workers, of course, may benefit more than others, and particular interests will be disrupted and forced to adjust. This is globalization's benign paradigm.

By the same logic, however, wages in the high-wage country also move downward toward the levels of the low-wage country. Advantages to workers in the more prosperous partner would be harder to perceive if improvement in the poorer country's living standards was relatively modest, while the decline in the richer country's standards was comparatively major. All other things being equal, the actual balance presumably depends not only on the collective gains in effi-

---

[48] For a classic statement of the benefits to Western workers and societies of capitalist creative destruction, see Joseph Schumpeter, *Business Cycles: A Theoretical, Historical and Statistical Analysis of the Capitalist Process*, vols. 1–2 (New York and London: Macmillan, 1939).

[49] For the original statement of this argument, see David Ricardo, *Principles of Political Economy and Taxation* (London and Melbourne: Everyman Edition, 1973), pp. 81–82. The later refinements, and specifically the theory of factor equalization, flow essentially from the Heckscher-Ohlin and product-cycle models. See E. F. Heckscher and B. Ohlin, *Heckscher-Ohlin Trade Theory*, ed. and trans. H. Flam and J. Flanders (Cambridge, MA: MIT Press, 1991).

ciency, but also on the relative size and income levels of the two labor pools that trade is bringing into competition.[50] So long as the high-wage pool is much larger, capital is available for the poorer country, and its politics are not too dysfunctional, wage levels in the poorer country can be expected to rise relatively quickly toward the high levels of the richer country. The tendency for the rich country's high wages to decline will be relatively slight and more easily compensated by the cheaper prices for goods and greater productivity resulting from increased competition and efficiency in a larger market.

By and large, globalization during the postwar era fitted the benign paradigm. In the 1960s and 1970s, the countries being integrated internationally were Japan, followed by newly industrialized countries, mostly in Asia—countries like Korea, Hong Kong, Singapore, and Taiwan. Japan soon enjoyed Western wage levels, and several other Asian countries were approaching or surpassing them by the 1980s.[51] The asymmetry of labor pools, together with the abundance of new products and services being produced in the West, protected Western living standards. In other words, the shock to the Western labor supply was small, and there was ample opportunity to develop capital-intensive products in the West, with jobs to match. Thus, while there were dislocations and some losers in the West, the overall consequences were favorable, for Western as well as Asian countries.

The future, however, may not be the same as this benign past. The major change is that China has now become an eager participant in the global economy, a development that began before the end of the Cold War. The effective entry of this giant labor force into the world

---

[50] The phrase "all other things being equal" covers, as usual, a multitude of assumptions. For wage equalization to occur, capital and transfers of appropriate technology have to be available for the smaller, poorer economies, along with entrepreneurial talent, a well-structured and flexible labor market, a benign political atmosphere, open markets for exports, access to needed raw materials, and so on. As the text notes, these conditions were met in many places in the postwar Pax Americana, particularly in the rapidly developing Asian economies. Globalization of investment went hand in hand with globalization of trade. See also note 29.

[51] By 1985, per capita income in Singapore and Hong Kong equaled or exceeded that in Spain, Ireland, and Italy. *World Development Report, 1985* (New York: Oxford University Press, 1985), pp. 174–175.

economy can reverse radically the relative size of globalized Western and Asian labor pools. Formerly, globalization meant Western living standards for workers in smaller Asian countries. Now, assuming that capital is available to develop China and Asia's other giant economies, globalization is more likely to mean a significant deflation of high Western wage levels toward low Asian wage levels.[52] For the Western laborer, or the Westernized laborer elsewhere, globalization of labor markets has turned malignant. Logically, among the early victims should be workers and firms in Asia's smaller, semi-Westernized economies, as appears to have been the case in the severe Asian recession that struck in 1997.[53]

The shift from benign to malignant paradigms for international integration is reminiscent of the brutal change of mood between two masterworks of classic liberal theory: Adam Smith's *The Wealth of Nations* (1776) and David Ricardo's *Principles of Economics and Taxation* (1817). In between, Thomas Malthus published his *Essay on the Principle of Population* (1778), which imposed a much gloomier view of the future, reminiscent of the view of today's environmentalists. Malthus's message, that population tends to expand until it reaches the limits of the resources available, transformed Smith's liberal economics, with its cheerful faith in a benign natural balance, into Ricardo's gloomy science, where overpopulated economies eventually stagnate in misery. For Ricardo, Malthus's relentless pressure of rising population made achieving the maximum of economic efficiency a desperate imperative. As Ricardo saw things, interfering with

[52] To put this into more formal economic analysis: If the globalized labor force is suddenly and massively increased by very cheap labor of quite high quality (e.g., the Chinese workforce), the price of world labor will fall, other things being equal. Output will doubtless go up and prices will fall, but not enough to compensate the displaced Western workers subject to the new competitive conditions. Given the huge numbers involved, the shock of the new cheap labor will disrupt the world economy to such an extent that a timely reallocation of high-priced Western labor to new specialized products and services becomes impossible. A major constraint will be the environmental cost of the greatly increased production needed to raise living standards in China to Western levels.

[53] For a discussion of the Asian crisis as the outcome of capitalist overproduction, see Benedict Anderson, "From Miracle to Crash," *London Review of Books*, vol. 20, no. 8 (1998).

free trade, or trying to alleviate the suffering of impoverished workers through welfare and government subsidies, merely eroded profits further and hastened the onset of capitalist decline.[54]

Integrating Asia's giant populations into the world economy threatens a severe Malthusian shock, likely to rehabilitate not only Malthus but Marx, since China and India can provide Western capital with a reserve army of the unemployed of dizzying proportions.[55] It is comforting to recall, however, that Malthus, Ricardo, and Marx have so far proved bad prophets. All three underestimated capitalism's stupendous growth of productivity over the nineteenth and twentieth centuries. The historical record therefore encourages diffidence toward apocalyptic forecasts. Many factors may intervene to prevent the rapid unfolding of the Malthusian scenario, including, of course, protectionism in the West or the East. It is worth noting, for example, that today's Chinese planners themselves emphasize internal development and are relatively skeptical about export-led growth.[56] What does seem clear, however, is that trade and technology will not quickly raise living standards in the populous Asian countries to Western levels. Given China's population, not to mention that of India or Indonesia, achieving the old benign paradigm for globalization would require a rate of world industrial growth, and an environmental tolerance for it, that seems improbable with any technology now known.[57] As a result, prosperous Western labor is likely to grow increasingly vulnerable as globalization proceeds.

---

[54] See David Ricardo, *The Principles of Political Economy and Taxation*, op. cit., pp. 94–97.

[55] For Marx's classic analysis of the role of the reserve army of the unemployed in holding down wages and bolstering profits, see Robert Tucker, ed., *The Marx-Engels Reader* (New York: Norton, 1978), pp. 426–427. See also note 8, chapter 5.

[56] For a comprehensive overview of Chinese policy options and growth prospects see World Bank, *China 2020: Development Challenges in the New Century* (Washington, DC: World Bank, 1997).

[57] For a discussion of the environmental policy challenges facing Asia, see Asian Development Bank, *Energy End-Use: An Environmentally Sound Development Path* (Manila: Asian Development Bank, 1993); also see Asian Development Bank, *Economic Policies for Sustainable Development* (Manila: Asian Development Bank, 1990).

PROTECTIONISM AN OPTION?

If globalism does turn Malthusian, the consequences for Western societies and nation states seem so grim that some kind of protectionist response appears inevitable. For Europe, the need to accommodate East European labor is an important complication adding further opportunities and problems. Ultimately, Europe will also have to find some accommodation for the rapidly growing populations of Turkey and North Africa. The basic question is whether West European economies can protect their high-priced labor without a self-defeating sacrifice of economic efficiency. Liberal economists of the present generation have been taught to hate protectionism with a truly Calvinist passion, and so they are better disposed to analyze its costs than its benefits. Protectionism, they note, subsidizes relatively uncompetitive industries and diverts entrepreneurial energy into the political rather than the economic marketplace.[58] Protectionism thus retards the productivity growth on which economic and social progress ultimately depends. Moreover, a tolerant attitude toward political interference with the marketplace often seems to go hand in hand with a self-indulgent view toward fiscal deficits and inflation. These fears are hardly without foundation. Neo-Keynesian economists, for example, were often notoriously complacent about the high inflation of the 1970s. Their insensitivity to the outrage of capitalist savers helped to provoke the new fashion for Hayekian views in the 1980s and 1990s. But neoliberals, in turn, have been too complacent about global trends impoverishing a significant part of their own working population and leading to a grotesque imbalance of wealth within their own societies. Powerful mercantilist and protectionist reactions on behalf of communitarian values should have been expected. Such reactions are clearly visible at the beginning of the twenty-first century.[59]

---

[58] Certain forms of protection particularly encourage rent seeking. For example, a system where the government auctions off quotas impels firms to compete to secure them. Firms expend resources on gaining political influence as opposed to economic efficiency. For a detailed exposition, see Anne Krueger, *The Political Economy of Trade Protection* (Chicago: University of Chicago Press, 1996).

[59] Examples were the riots against the World Trade Organization in Seattle in November 1999 and the Washington demonstrations against the World Bank and Interna-

For the historian of ideas who remains agnostic before these rival economic dogmas, trends toward neomercantilism and protectionism are not, in themselves, occasions for regret or bad conscience. Modern states have always been mercantilist and protectionist to some degree. Indeed, even the current fashionable liberal strategy of shifting to advanced industries requires in practice a high degree of direct or indirect state involvement. States have an inescapable role in economic life, which carries not only the right but the duty to protect the welfare of their people. When states are weak, and the collective values they are meant to defend are neglected, national economies suffer. So, in due course, does the global economy. Under present circumstances, with Western living standards threatened by global labor markets, not only is an increase in protectionism and neomercantilism probable, but arguably, it is also desirable. An efficacious mix of protection for older industries and neomercantilist subsidies for new ones seems very much in order. And if mainstream politicians fail to protect Western living standards, they will predictably be shoved aside by less conventional political forces. Indeed, signs of rising political extremism are easily found in almost every West European country. The trend is undoubtedly a just cause for disquiet, but not for surprise. How long, for example, can traditional elites stay in power when unemployment rates over 10 percent are commonplace, or when youth unemployment is 25 percent, as in France throughout much of the 1990s?

In short, to predict a general drift toward neomercantilism and protectionism is merely to state the obvious. The real task is to make the resulting policies successful in their legitimate aims and limited in their complementary damage. In a Europe already weakened by Eurosclerosis, a drift toward more protection and subsidy can be disastrous in the absence of countervailing liberal policies and institutions. The goal of a sensible neomercantilist policy should be to preserve living standards and social peace in Western countries without compromis-

---

tional Monetary Fund in April 2000. For an account of the former, see "The New Trade War," *The Economist*, December 4, 1999, and Gerard Baker, "Starbucks Wars," *Financial Times*, December 4, 1999; for the latter, see also "Seattle Comes to Washington," *The Economist*, April 15, 2000, and Alan Beattie and Dan Lerner, "Ragtag Army Takes Battle to 'Unholy Trinity,'" *Financial Times,* April 15, 2000.

ing the long-term competitiveness of their economies or causing unbearable tensions in interstate relations. For the EU, there is the additional problem of accommodating cheap labor among close neighbors in Eastern Europe and, increasingly, in Turkey and North Africa as well. Finding the right mix between social and industrial protection and international competition raises difficult and elusive questions that need to be examined dispassionately. Unfortunately, contemporary public discourse over economic questions has developed a dogmatic, pseudoreligious quality that discourages serious and balanced analysis. Achieving effective policies and disciplining them in the interest of international comity requires a broad philosophical framework, one that honors economic values but synthesizes them with the moral, political, and geopolitical values that are certainly no less relevant to public policy, or indeed to lasting economic success itself.

LISTIAN EUROPE AND THE WORLD POLITICAL ECONOMY

Under current circumstances, it is perhaps useful to recall what Friedrich List was preaching in the middle of the nineteenth century. List, it may be remembered, was a liberal as well as a communitarian nationalist. He believed in the market as an essential mechanism not only for economic efficiency but also for maximizing individual liberty and initiative. At the same time, he did not believe that the market could, by itself, guarantee the broad development required for a good society or even for a successful economy.[60] Durable success, he believed, would come from a balanced national economic development that fostered freedom and initiative, while protecting other common interests and values. List had, moreover, a sophisticated view of the international dimension of political economy. Free trade was good for the national economy, List believed, provided the country had developed enough so that its own nascent industries would not be overwhelmed, particularly in those advanced sectors vital for the broader evolution of the society and culture. A good global system was one that respected and guarded the general right of nations to develop in a

---

[60] See chapter 5 above for further discussion of List.

balanced fashion. In other words, a global system should be judged on whether or not it encourages the best potential of the national societies that compose it. Unlike many economic liberals today, List neither expected nor wished that global integration would progressively enfeeble and atomize nation states. A truly liberal international order would, he thought, base itself on the cooperation of national governments that recognized each other's vital functions and respected every nation's right to have its own space to develop.

List was also an early prophet of Europe's Common Market. As the United States developed, he expected Europe's nation states to band together to match its scale and to hold their own in competition against it. As a communitarian nationalist, List was naturally drawn to a confederalist model of European unity. Europe's nation states would not disappear. They would remain the sources of political legitimacy and the mobilizers of common will. But they would cooperate intimately, while respecting each other's rights and dignity. They would build together a continental framework that would maintain liberty and vitality by fostering competition among member countries at convergent stages of development. But that framework would also balance their competition by a shared sense of social justice, humane values, mutual respect, and common geopolitical interests. Today's European Union qualifies, more or less, as List's vision realized.

If confronted with Europe's current problems, List would presumably agree that if heavy structural unemployment persists, neomercantilism and protectionism should have their place among the remedies. He would probably agree, for example, that European states should protect their agriculture and their labor, and he would almost certainly favor state support for high-technology industries. But List would presumably also insist that these policies would be much more effective if applied within a European Union of common rules and liberal internal markets, rather than within single nation states separately. Trying to find common policies to protect diverse national interests can, of course, break up any confederal union. But the need for collective protection can also be an incentive to reinforce rather than undermine political cohesion. List would almost certainly argue that putative sacrifices in immediate economic efficiency could be justified as legitimate costs for preserving Europe's technological future, its social and cultural values, and its domestic peace, all vital elements of longer-term economic success. At the same time, List hated heavy-handed authoritarian governments. Presumably, he would have found the European Union's diversity and liberal internal rules important safe-guards against the inherent excesses of state action in the economy. List knew the United States of his day intimately and admired it greatly and wanted Europe to find its own way to imitate it. America's formula was to be very large and diverse, liberal internally but relatively autarkic externally. The EU puts Europe in a position to achieve these features collectively, as List imagined it would.

This Listian sort of reasoning has many implications for global order. Protectionist responses orchestrated by so diverse a confederacy are almost certainly more responsible and porous and less damaging to economic efficiency than separate and rival national protectionist policies would be in a fragmented Europe. The very size and power of a European bloc should impel its members to think in responsible geopolitical terms, whereas individual European nation states in isolation would be more inclined toward free riding as a natural and attractive option. Heightened global influence and geopolitical self-consciousness almost certainly press EU members to accommodate their numerous Eurasian, Middle Eastern, and North African neighbors. Leading from a position of collective strength, they should want to preserve access to Asia's rapidly growing markets and therefore be more inclined to reach some kind of generous but balanced trading arrangements. A strong European bloc should also favor open trade and intimate collaboration with the United States—for all the usual cultural and military reasons, not to mention the immense reciprocal business investment. With broadly similar living standards, tastes, and levels of development, neither should be in a position to overwhelm the other. A powerful European Union, making Europe an advanced and formidable competitor, should encourage balanced transatlantic agreements to prevent governments from clashing too brutally and directly over technological trade. Similarly, a strong European monetary bloc, sporting its own reserve currency as an alternative to the dollar, ought to help stabilize the global system. Making it harder for anyone to abuse reserve currency status should bring greater stability and discipline to world finance, a common interest, after all, of Europeans, Asians, and Americans alike.

GLOBALIZATION AND WORLD PEACE

Whatever liberals may believe, globalization is not, in itself, a prescription for greater international harmony. Quite the contrary. Given the widespread social and economic dislocation that may be expected around the world in the twenty-first century, advanced states should be particularly attentive that their national solutions to global problems do not give rise to unbearable international tensions. It is widely assumed that democratic nation states cannot go to war with each other. We may hope this proves true, even if the argument seems to be based on simplistic and ahistorical reasoning.[61] There is certainly no lack of historical evidence that capitalist states can drift easily into economic conflicts, especially during hard and uncertain times. Given the domestic politics of trade in every country today, it seems critical to develop better rules and structures to harmonize policies and to adjudicate the inevitable disputes. To make such machinery effective, there needs to be a basic balance of power that discourages aggressive and domineering behavior and encourages all parties to assume their proper geopolitical responsibilities. Such a world balance is unlikely without a strong and cohesive European bloc. Fortunately, the economic trends promoting globalization also favor creating that bloc.

Before the European Union can become a durable feature of the twenty-first century, however, it first needs to address two fundamental challenges. One is its constitutional problem: What states should be in the union and how should that union be organized? Should the EU be only part of a larger pan-European system, or should it expand itself until ultimately it becomes, itself, the pan-European system? The other basic challenge is Europe's security problem, obviously closely related to its constitutional problem: How should the EU organize itself to maintain order in Pan-Europe? How should it collaborate with America and Russia to do so? The next two chapters take up these challenges in turn.

---

[61] The democratic peace argument, building on Kant, is discussed at greater length in chapter 16.

Unfinished Business I: Constitutional Projects

THE FEDERALIST HOUR

THE MAASTRICHT TREATY formally transformed the European Community into the European Union. The change reflected Europe's wider ambitions, generated in part to preclude its rekindled fears. But the ambitions lay in diverse directions. The EU wanted to fill its new pan-European space by expanding its own membership to newly liberated Central and Eastern Europe, including the Balkans and perhaps even Turkey. In effect, the EU was bidding to replace the bipolar system with a European system. At the same time, the EU wanted to enlarge its scope and intensify its integration. Hence, monetary union and common security and defense, together with various efforts to reform constitutional procedures and structures. In effect, the EU wanted both to complete the old projects of the 1980s, which meant deepening integration and extending common action to new spheres, and also to meet the new pan-European challenges of the 1990s, which meant expanding its membership. The goals seemed complementary. Enlarging the membership would require a stronger core—with a full range of statelike functions and a streamlining of decision making and administration.

Following Maastricht, the EU set out in all directions at once. Scope was extended dramatically as Maastricht scheduled Economic and Monetary Union for 1999. According to the treaty, there was also to be, in due course, a common foreign and defense policy, a "social chapter," and common immigration control, as well as close police and judicial cooperation. Deepening was to proceed in tandem. Administrative apparatus and decision-making procedures were to be streamlined and various "democratic deficits" addressed. Meanwhile, officials proclaimed an open-ended expansion of the membership, expected to result eventually in an EU of twenty-five or more countries.[1]

[1] See, for example, Jacques Santer, "The Union's Agenda—Madrid and Beyond,"

Austria, Finland, and Sweden were admitted in 1995; a Europe of Twelve became a Europe of Fifteen. Already in 1993, at the Copenhagen summit, the Commission had announced plans to open negotiations with the Czech Republic, Estonia, Hungary, Poland, and Slovenia.[2] By the turn of the century, Bulgaria, Cyprus, Latvia, Lithuania, Malta, Romania, Slovakia, and Turkey had been added to the list of those with a "vocation to join." It became commonplace to speak of a "Europe of Thirty."

The Treaty of Amsterdam, the follow-up to Maastricht, was signed on schedule in 1997 but showed only limited movement toward broadening the EU's scope and still less toward reforming its constitution.[3] Amsterdam's disappointments were assuaged in 1999, when the Economic and Monetary Union was born on schedule. Achieving EMU, however, required splitting the membership. Alongside the new Europe of Fifteen grew up a more ardent "Euroland" of Eleven. Ex-

---

speech at the 70th anniversary of the Foreign Press Association, The Hague, December 7, 1995.

[2] Declaration at Copenhagen on membership. Copenhagen European Council, June 21–22, June 1993, conclusion of the presidency, SN 180/93.

[3] Amsterdam developed the EU in four main areas: It strengthened the powers of the European Parliament and also of the Commission's president. It extended qualified majority voting to further areas in the Council, and it developed mechanisms for Common Foreign and Security Policy (CFSP). A summary and early discussion of the provisions of the Amsterdam Treaty may be found in *Initial Analysis of the Treaty of Amsterdam* (Brussels: European Parliament Directorate-General for Committees and Delegations, Committee on Institutional Affairs, Conference 4001/97 of June 19, 1997). Amsterdam was generally perceived as having failed to live up to its goals: preparing the way for enlargement, answering concerns about the democratic legitimacy of EU institutions, and improving the efficiency of their decision-making process. See Tom Buerkle, "Amsterdam Treaty Scorned as Mediocre," *International Herald Tribune*, June 27, 1997; Philip Stephens, "The Ragbag Treaty," *Financial Times*, June 10, 1997, p. 12; and Frank Vibert, "Maastricht II Misses the Mark," *Wall Street Journal Europe*, June 17, 1997, p. 10. See below in this chapter for more discussion of the constitutional and security reforms undertaken at Amsterdam. For the official line, see the European Council's *Press Release on Intergovernmental Conference* of June 18, 1997 (Brussels: European Council, 1997). For a similarly positive view of enlargement, see Michael Nentwich and Gerda Falkner, "The Treaty of Amsterdam: Toward a New Institutional Balance," *European Integration Online Papers*, vol. 1, no. 15 (1997), <http://www.eiop.or.at/eiop/texte/1997-015.htm>.

panding the EU membership would predictably widen the split still further. None of the prospective new member states from Central and Eastern Europe had much chance of meeting EMU's membership criteria within the foreseeable future.

Juxtaposing the formation of EMU with the opening of negotiations for a much more diverse pan-European membership highlighted the constitutional issue that Amsterdam had done little to resolve: how to govern an EU that was expanding and diversifying its membership while simultaneously widening the range of its common policies and collective decision making. The answer presumably lay with constitutional reform that would permit more rapid and democratic policymaking, together with more efficient and transparent administration. Amsterdam's slow progress in these directions suggested that the EU's basic confederal character was not going to be easy to change. This, in turn, suggested rather sharp alternatives. One was that a union determined to deepen its integration and enlarge its scope should keep its membership as homogenous as possible, in other words, should expand its membership only very selectively, if at all. The alternative was that a union fated to expand its membership would have to back off from Maastricht's ambitions for enlarging its scope, perhaps even from EMU itself.

Those alternatives may impose themselves in the long run. But if the usual postwar pattern continues, Europe's union, however illogically constituted, will find a way to expand its membership, enlarge its scope, and adjust its constitution accordingly. Progress will be dialectical rather than linear, with numerous crises, false starts, and failures along the way.

The Nice summit in December 2000, scheduled to pursue Amsterdam's unfinished constitutional business, easily lent itself to such a prognosis. With the ambiguous exception of the British, few of the major participants professed wholehearted satisfaction with the results. The French, holding the presidency, had sought to avoid "theological" disputes over ultimate goals and, instead, to concentrate on achieving Europe's "common objectives": "develop fully the euro, the common foreign and security policy and a strengthened European role in the world." This required institutional changes. Nice was to result in a Europe "able to work"—arrangements strong enough to prevent the risk of paralysis that an EU of thirty members could cause."[4] The agenda called for streamlining the European Commission and extending the practice of qualified-majority voting in the Council of Ministers, reweighting national votes in the Council and the European Parliament to be more in accord with relative populations, and clarifying and simplifying the mechanisms for closer extended cooperation among the more "proactive" member states.

After months of desultory preliminaries, the culminating summit was intense, prolonged, and acrimonious. Like Amsterdam three years before, Nice did produce considerable reforms, but they were clearly incomplete.[5] Least satisfactory was the reform of the Commission, which was mostly put off. Big countries renounced their right to a second commissioner starting in 2006. But each member would still have one commissioner, until membership reached twenty-seven, whereupon further reform would be attempted. This would presumably involve a reduction of the number of commissioners. National "representation" would henceforth be achieved by rotation.[6]

Reforms of the Council were more significant. Roughly, votes of the big countries were tripled, whereas votes of the smaller members were merely doubled. Candidate states were also assigned their putative voting weights.[7] The principal issue was the reluctance of small states to see their influence lessened to the advantage of the more populous big states. A further issue was united Germany's demand for a larger vote than other big states, refused by France. In compensation, Germany received a substantially larger representation in the European Parliament than France, Britain, or Italy (ninety-nine votes versus seventy-two for each of the others). An elaborate balance-of-power system was nevertheless left in place. After Nice, proposals in the Council face a triple hurdle: 73.29 percent of the weighted votes, a

---

[4] Hubert Vedrine, "A Greater Europe by Reform," *Financial Times*, September 7, 2000, p. 15.

[5] Draft approved by the Conference of Representatives of the Governments of the Member States at <http://ue.eu.int/cig/nice/>.

[6] European Parliament Notice to Members, "Overview of the Results of the Intergovernmental Conference," December 19, 2000.

[7] For the new and old weights of members and candidates, see *Le Monde, Selection Heldomadaire*, December 16, 2000, p. 3.

two-thirds majority among the member states, and a majority that collectively represents at least 62 percent of the Union's total population. Requiring a two-thirds majority of states serves to protect the smaller countries, while requiring 62 percent of the EU's population serves the interests of the large states—Germany in particular.[8] In effect, a typical hybrid formula was found.

Nice also significantly limited the issues on which a national veto might still be invoked. Newly excluded from the veto were such questions as choosing senior officials, streamlining the European Court of Justice, immigration and asylum issues (but not before 2004), and most trade in services. Significant derogations were, nevertheless, left in place. The British excluded matters of taxation and social security. The Germans excluded the free movement of professionals. The French excluded trade in culture, audiovisual services, education, health, and social services. And the Spanish excluded alterations in structural funds until 2007.

Nice also eliminated national vetoes on "reinforced cooperation." After Nice, any eight or more member states may band together to integrate more rapidly in one sphere or another, provided that the Commission validates that the initiative does not endanger the single market or the Union's acquis communautaire in general. At the same time, in response to strong American warnings against European defense structures outside NATO, Prime Minister Tony Blair, on his return from Nice, stressed that the EU's new defense arrangements would be based on "sovereign national discussions" and that "collective defense will remain the responsibility of NATO," with whom the EU was aiming "to develop a strategic partnership."[9]

Taken all in all, Nice can easily be read simply as another milepost along postwar Europe's contentious but successful progress toward integration. As usual, new challenges have brought new integration. The changes are gradual and consent among the members is wary and

---

[8] See "So That's All Agreed, Then," in *The Economist*, December 16, 2000, pp. 25–28.

[9] Prime Minister Tony Blair's Statement on the Nice Summit, December 11, 2000 <http://www.number-10.gov.uk/default.asp?PageId = 2992>.

grudging. And despite the changes, the Union's traditional hybrid character remains. Today, as before, the EU is Atlantic, federal, confederal, and anarchic. The balances shift, but the elements remain. Seen in this complacent perspective, Nice revealed not only the European Union's continuity and stability but also its capacity for adaptation and progress. Like Amsterdam and Maastricht before it, Nice was another defining moment in postwar Europe's complex but highly successful pattern of progressive integration. It showed that the end of the Cold War had brought out confederal Europe's strength rather than its weakness.

There are, to be sure, darker and more radical views of the future. As Europe entered the year 2001, popular support for the EU was at an all-time low in most countries. Ratification of the Nice Treaty in national parliaments could hardly be taken for granted. There was, therefore, no compelling reason to assume that the successful postwar pattern must continue. The environment for European integration may have so worsened after the Cold War that Europe's great experiment with integration will finally fail, or at least enter a long period of stagnation and weakness. Under such circumstances, enlargement may overstretch the Union fatally. Conversely, some crisis may provoke a successful federalist mutation at last. The desire for more fundamental reform emerged at Nice in the agreement to hold, by 2004, a new intergovernmental conference, demanded by the Germans to establish the relative rights and duties of the EU, the member states, and Europe's "regions." Such an agenda will presumably give an opening for the more radical constitutional innovations proposed by the German foreign minister Joschka Fischer and occasionally echoed by the French president Jacques Chirac.[10]

To assess the prospects for more radical constitutional change requires grasping the essence and interdependence of the EU's three major constitutional issues: membership, scope, and governing struc-

---

[10] "From Confederacy to Federation—Thoughts on the Finality of European Integration," speech by Joschka Fischer at the Humbolt University in Berlin, May 12, 2000 <http://www.germanembassy/org/au/eu-fisch.htm>. For Chirac's speech to the German Bundestag, see note 55 below.

ture. Each issue has its own vocabulary and theoretical framework and poses its own choices. But failure or success with one issue is likely to impact significantly on the others.

EXPANDING EU MEMBERSHIP

Boundaries and size are critical issues for any state. They determine demographic and economic resources, as well as the problems and prospects for security. For communitarian nation states, boundaries are even more critical, since they determine the cohesion of the state's political culture and civil society and thereby its prospects for sustaining a government by consensus. What is true of a single communitarian nation state is probably even more true of a confederal grouping of such states. Boundaries of the bloc determine not only its collective resources but also the diversity of cultures, situations, and interests among its member states, all of which greatly affect their potential for consensus and common action.

In the history of political thought, the link between a state's diversity and its prospects for consensual government has been a source of great argument. As chapter 4 has already discussed, one position is the nationalist approach of Jean-Jacques Rousseau, prophet and inspiration for the French Revolution and the nation states that it spawned. Another is the federalist approach of James Madison. Their differences seem significant for analyzing the prospects of an expanding European Union. Rousseau taught that the larger and more diverse the state, the more difficult it would be to hold it together by agreement. A big and heterogenous state would therefore require a powerful centralized government with authoritarian leadership. By contrast, in smaller and more homogenous states, the interests of citizens should be less dissimilar and therefore public consensus easier to sustain. Citizens should find it easier to generate a true general will and concert their actions around it. Such states could permit themselves to be governed more loosely and with more real participation by the citizenry.[11]

---

[11] Rousseau noted, however, that states might be too small and democracy too direct,

Madison's different approach led him to opposite prescriptions. Like Rousseau, he was concerned that "factions"—special interests—would monopolize government and exploit the general public for private gain. To prevent any such exploiting monopoly power, Madison thought it best to enlarge the "orbit" of the state to create such diversity that no single faction, or amalgam of factions, would be strong enough to form a stable majority and thus be able to appropriate public power for private purposes. In effect, Madison was a sort of political Adam Smith. He assumed that the political marketplace works like an ideal liberal economy. Competition leads to decisions that favor the general interest, unless colluding special interests form a monopoly power (majority) that distorts the market's decisions.[12]

The approach of either writer has its vulnerabilities. Rousseau can be called totalitarian because he seems obsessed by the need to promote an active consensus and convergence of interests. The temptation for his followers is to impose that consensus and convergence by dictatorship and state terrorism, as was done soon after his death by his fanatical Jacobin disciples in the French Revolution's Reign of Terror.[13] Madison can be accused of fatuous optimism because he downplays the need for active leadership to sustain unity. Madisonian politics can lead to "imbecility" in government, a recurring problem with America's constitutional checks and balances.[14] Both charges, of course, are caricatures. Rousseau was passionately committed to individual self-determination, and Madison, prodded by Hamilton, agreed on the necessity for a strong executive within his balanced constitu-

---

in which case the general will might easily be lost as the people fragmented into interest groups, quarreling over their own particular shares of public goods. See Jean-Jacques Rousseau, *The Social Contract*, book 3, ch. 4, in *Political Writings*, ed. and trans. Frederick Watkins (New York: Nelson, 1953).

[12] James Madison, Alexander Hamilton, and John Jay, *The Federalist Papers* (Baltimore: Johns Hopkins University Press, 1981). See especially paper number 10, written by Madison.

[13] For analysis of such tendencies, see, for example, J. W. Chapman, *Rousseau: Totalitarian or Liberal?* (New York: Columbia University Press, 1956).

[14] For a disillusioned "federalist" view of America's constitutional debility, see Brooks Adams, *The Degradation of Democratic Dogma* (Cleveland: Frontin Press, 1956; originally published 1919).

tion. Nevertheless, the two approaches imply radically different prescriptions for the European Union. Rousseau's approach indicates slow
expansion with relatively strict criteria for convergence; Madison's approach opens the way, in theory at least, to expand rapidly, even to very
diverse neighbors. Arguably, however, Madisonian expansion remains
compatible with democracy only where Rousseauist consensus is, in
fact, present.[15] Without consensus, maintaining a union requires force.
Madison had hoped that sufficient consensus could be built around a
widely shared interest in maintaining the Constitution itself, with its
balances and rights. But as America's terrible Civil War indicated, in
troubled times deeper and darker sources of loyalty are needed.

For today's European Union, the issue of size versus consensus is
suddenly critical. Formerly, the Soviet Empire limited the nascent European Community to democratic Western Europe, including a trun-
cated and Westernized Germany. Now, however, the EU seems to
have no natural boundaries with the Slavic east and southeast. The
Union's declared policy, moreover, has been increasingly Madisonian.
The European Commission's *Agenda 2000*, published in 1997, eluci-
dated how the prospective members could meet the acquis communautaire of membership. *Agenda 2000* not only promised negotiations
for the ten states mentioned earlier but also explicitly left the door
open to Bulgaria, Romania, Latvia, and Lithuania.[16] Membership, according to the Commission president of the time, Jacques Santer, was
a permanent process of inclusion. Some officials even mentioned
Ukraine, Belarus, and Moldova as future prospects.

Ardor cooled thereafter, as the West European leaders began to
anticipate the large costs to the EU's budget, arising primarily from
the EU's own requirements. These estimates reflected how new members had been accommodated in the past.[17] When Spain and Portugal

---

[15] For a classical "neo-Hegelian" synthesis of the two traditions, see Bernard Bosanquet, *The Philosophical Theory of the State* (London: Macmillan, 1920; originally
published 1899).

[16] See H. G. Krenzler, *Preparing for the Acquis Communautaire* (Florence: Robert
Schuman Center, 1998). See also note 15.

[17] After a limited transition period, new members were expected to converge on the
Union's uniform regulations and economic norms, a policy tailored to protect employment and agriculture among existing members. For differences and inequalities

joined, for example, they were required to accept, over time, all the acquis communautaire, including the Common Agricultural Policy (CAP), as well as legal norms for the treatment of workers and the environment. In addition, labor unions from the older member countries actively encouraged and subsidized union militancy in the new. As a result, the newcomers lost some part of their initial market advantage, which lay in their relatively cheap labor as well as less stringent regulations.[18] In compensation, both Iberian countries received not only large inflows of private investment capital but also large transfers from Brussels to subsidize the costs of transition. These included "structural funds" and "cohesion funds"—to help restructure agriculture or upgrade educational and physical infrastructure, steps needed so that the newcomers could compete successfully as their labor and other costs rose toward EC levels.[19]

In effect, the EU's past policy might be called more Rousseauist than Madisonian. The priority was to bring new members as rapidly as possible to levels of productivity, living, and welfare roughly similar to those of older members. Convergence, moreover, was to "level up" rather than to "level down." Success required a consensus among the older rich members that it was in their interest not only to incorporate the poor new members but to subsidize their rapid development. The feasibility of the strategy depended on there not being too big an economic gap and too many poor countries at once. Cultural predispositions, work habits, standards and practices of public admin-

---

between northern and southern Europe and how they were dealt with in earlier accessions, see G. Kourvetaris and A. Moschonas, eds., *The Impact of European Integration* (Westport, CT: Praeger, 1996).

[18] Accepting the CAP, for example, meant rising food prices, which pushed up wages. See *The Development and Future of the CAP*, Bulletin of the European Community, supplement 5, 1991.

[19] The EU's Structural Funds are to develop its poorer regions to meet Community standards and compete successfully within the Common Market. Most transfers go to Ireland, Greece, Spain, and Portugal and amounted to more than 161 billion European Currency Units (ECU) between 1993 and 1999. The Cohesion Fund is for transportation infrastructure in poorer regions. Most of its transfers go to Ireland and the Mediterranean countries and amounted to 15.1 billion ECU between 1993 and 1999. W. Weidenfeld and W. Wessels, eds., *Europa von A–Z* (Bonn: Bundeszentrale für politische Bildung, 1997), pp. 387–400.

istration, and legal and political institutions had to be near enough to close the gap over a reasonable period of time. With Spain at least, the strategy, albeit expensive, produced satisfactory results.[20] Expansion to Eastern Europe, however, is a much more ambitious undertaking. Subsidizing the transition costs for the Visegrad countries (Czech Republic, Poland, and Hungary) was initially estimated to cost 75 billion European Currency Units (ECU) from the EU's budget by 2002. Even before the Russian financial debacle had reduced East European economic prospects, these estimates seemed highly optimistic.[21]

By the later 1990s, German reunification had already amply demonstrated how hugely expensive a policy of rapid convergence might be in former communist countries. To pursue a convergence policy for the old GDR, the Federal Republic had radically unbalanced its budget and thereby plunged the whole continent into a deep recession. Despite the huge spending, the progress of East Germany was disappointing. In other former communist countries, the transformation to market economies soon encountered manifold and intractable problems. Western countries grew cautious about their commitments to

---

[20] By the early 1990s, the agricultural sector was reduced to employing 13 percent of the Spanish labor force and contributing 6.1 percent to GDP. Success was somewhat more ambiguous for Greece and Portugal. By the early 1990s, almost a decade and a half after accession, the agricultural sector still employed 25.3 percent of the labor force in Greece and 19.0 percent in Portugal against an EC average of 6.6 percent. The agricultural share of GDP for Greece and Portugal stood, respectively, at 16.6 percent and 8.9 percent against a Community average of 2.4 percent. In the agricultural sector, Greece and Portugal seem developing rather than advanced countries. Similarly, in the industrial sector, both, unlike northern community members, tend to specialize in resource-intensive products rather than skill- and capital-intensive ones. See Eleftherious N. Bothas,"The Socioeconomic Structure of the European Union," in G. Kourvetaris and A. Moschonas, eds., *The Impact of European Integration*, op. cit., pp. 39–52.

[21] *European Community Relations with the Countries of Central and Eastern Europe* (Brussels: European Commission, 1995). See also P. Van Ham, *The EC and Eastern Europe: Collaboration and Integration since 1947* (London: Pinter, 1994). For an understanding of the general approach of the EU toward enlargement to Central and Eastern Europe, see Agenda 2000 <http://europa.eu.int/comm/agenda2000/index_en.htm>. See also *Agenda 2000*, op. cit.

aid. At the Dublin summit in December 1996, the rich Western states controlling the Council had formally frozen the EU's budget ceiling at 1.27 percent of GNP until 1999.[22] At the Berlin summit in March 1999, Germany, long the "milk cow" for the EU budget, tried to reduce its own outsized net contribution. Money for expanding the membership was supposed to come from savings in the existing budget, including a major reform of the Common Agricultural Policy. By the spring of 1999, after intensive negotiations, only very limited agreement had been reached.[23] Europe's farmers were mobilized to resist deep cuts in the CAP, and they had powerful support in both France and Germany. Poorer countries that were already members, like Greece, Ireland, and Spain, were resisting any sharp decline in their own structural and cohesion subsidies. The Union's non-European associates, particularly in Africa and the Middle East, were fighting to preserve their own long-standing subventions. By the summer of 1999, the costs of the war in Kosovo and the huge reconstruction needs after it seemed a further major constraint on financing rapid enlargement.[24]

Expanding membership would certainly be easier if the Union not only cut back its CAP and structural and cohesion funds to older members but also downplayed convergence around the acquis communautaire. In an EU that was more a free-trade area and less a confederacy of corporatist national economies, poor countries could enjoy their natural advantages and thus require lesser subsidies. In other words, they could pay their workers less and pollute their environment more freely. This "British" option has great rhetorical and intel-

---

[22] Conclusion of the presidency, European Council meeting, Dublin, December 13–14, 1996, Bulletin of the European Union, 1/2 1997.

[23] Conclusion of the presidency, European Council meeting, Berlin, March 24–25, 1999, Bulletin of the European Union, 2/3 1999.

[24] The costs of the seventy-eight-day air campaign against Kosovo, estimated at around $2.3 billion, were borne mainly by the United States. The costs of rebuilding Kosovo's schools, homes, health care facilities, and electrical and water systems are to be borne mainly by Europe and are estimated by the World Bank to reach $1.23 billion. See <http://www.worldbank.org/thlm/extdr/kosovo/>. For a more general account of the rebuilding of the Balkan region, see Michael Emerson, *Redrawing the Map of Europe* (Basingstoke, UK: Macmillan, 1998).

lectual appeal among liberal politicians, journalists, and professors. In theory, it could help competitiveness in all European economies by permitting businesses more flexibility and cost cutting. But the European Union is unlikely to proceed far enough toward this laissez-aller of Thatcherite dreams to make the absorption of numerous poor new members easy. To do so would radically disrupt politics in the old continental member countries, whose corporatist and mercantilist traditions resist accepting the primacy of the market over other social and political values. And of course, it would wreak havoc among the new poorer entrants from the East, whose labor is organized and steeped in corporatist ideology, and whose own agriculture and industry could easily be crushed by Western competition.[25] In short, absorbing new members rapidly would still require heavy subsidies. Even so, the EU's expansion can be expected to require long transition periods.

EMU further complicates expansion. Even the most successful among the former communist countries have high inflation rates by the West European standards of the 1990s.[26] For some, hyperinflation has been a constant threat. Squeezing such countries into a Western monetary framework can be expected to cause serious political reactions. Inflation helps to mask the brutal changes that switching to a market economy entails. Partisans of "shock therapy" argue, of course, that an EMU compelling tight macroeconomic discipline in former Soviet economies would greatly speed their transformation. Skeptics, however, note that the historical evidence linking rapid growth to low inflation is far from clear. When, for example, Western Europe's economies were growing rapidly and successfully transforming themselves in the 1950s, their inflation rates tended to be quite high, as their real interest rates were relatively low.[27]

---

[25] See *Second Regular Report on Progress toward Accession of Poland* (Brussels: Commission of the European Communities, October 13, 1999).

[26] *World Economic Outlook, May 1997* (Washington, DC: International Monetary Fund, 1997), pp. 133, 127.

[27] After World War I, the modernization of German industry was certainly aided by inflation, whereas British industrial modernization was not encouraged by the tight monetary policy instituted by Churchill to sustain the pound's prewar parity. Studies of the period after World War II indicate, however, that low growth and very high

At the very least, having East European members in the EU will greatly complicate finding an appropriate common monetary policy. But whether the new members join the EMU or not, they will be powerfully influenced by the prevailing monetary climate. They cannot expect to tailor EU or EMU policies to suit their relatively unstable and inflationary economies. Richer Western members will dominate policy. For candidate countries, struggling to enter the EU will mean prolonged tutelage, very possibly without even nominal voting rights. Whether such tutelage will prove acceptable will doubtless depend on the generosity and success of the compensation. Insofar as that compensation is likely to be more limited than formerly, candidates may come to wonder whether EU membership is worth the economic struggle and political humiliation. Disgruntled East Europeans may feel themselves entrapped in an imperium dominated by others, the recurring melancholy theme running throughout their histories.

Expansion's difficulties are obviously not solely economic. Adding new members also threatens geopolitical cohesion among the older partners. Initially, it was the Germans and the British who pressed most energetically for the EU to expand eastward. British motives were transparent. The bigger and more diverse the membership, the more diluted integration was likely to be. The same reasoning made the British diffident toward NATO enlargement, since they wanted NATO to remain an effective military alliance. German motives were more complicated. During the Kohl chancellorship, Germans argued that enlarging both the EU and NATO was vital for their own national

---

inflation have often gone together. A study comparing 109 countries during the period from 1960 to 1989 shows that the relatively slow growers had, on average, inflation rates of 31 percent, whereas fast growers had inflation rates of 12 percent per annum. See R. Levine and D. Renelt, *A Sensitivity Analysis of Cross-Country Growth Regression* (Washington, DC: Worldbank, 1990). For additional evidence, see M. Bruno, *Crisis, Stabilization, and Economic Reform* (Oxford, UK: Clarendon Press, 1993). But 12 percent is a far cry from the 2 percent average of EMU countries in 2000. For a long-range perspective on German growth, see Henry Christopher Wallich, *Mainsprings of the German Recovery* (New Haven: Yale University Press, 1955). For a critical view of the consequences of very tight money on European growth in the 1990s, see Jean-Paul Fitoussi, *Le Débat Interdit* (Paris: Arlea, 1995).

security. Germany wished no longer to be the exposed eastern frontier of the West. Instead, it wanted a belt of friendly, stable, and dependent surrounding states—the Czechs, the Poles, perhaps the Balts as well. But while seeking security, the Germans risked reviving ancient quarrels instead. NATO expansion has threatened German relations with Russia. The accession of Austria, Finland, and Sweden in 1994 significantly augmented the number of northern and Central European members of Germanic character. Further expansion of the EU eastward will greatly increase the weight of Germanic Middle Europe at the expense of Latin southern Europe—a trend that risks straining the Franco-German partnership, while, at the same time, making it even more critical for the EU's cohesion. An Eastern policy that alienates Germany from both Russia and France has an ominous historical resonance.

DEMANDS OF HISTORY

Do all these difficulties mean that EU membership should not be expanded? Quite apart from questions of historic justice, powerful geopolitical, political, and economic reasons bolster the claims of Central and Eastern European countries to be included in some pan-European system. Secure peace and prosperity are unlikely so long as the former communist states do not find a comfortable place for themselves in the new European order. Including them may revive old tensions in the West, but arguably, such tendencies are unavoidable, and it is better to domesticate them inside the European Union. And while the Eastern countries will have major problems for a long time, they also bring serious assets to the West. It should not harm Western Europe to have its own nearby pools of cheaper and perhaps more flexible labor, among well-educated neighbors with close cultural affinities, and populations on a scale that can be expected to reach Western living standards relatively quickly. For an overcapitalized and oversaturated EU, it will do no harm to have new members that need investment and have a healthy appetite for new consumption.[28] In short, arguments for enlarging the Union are not merely altruistic.

[28] For Europe's low return on capital, see chapter 9, note 23.

Security problems—in particular, events in Yugoslavia—have added new pressure for EU enlargement. West Europeans, aghast at the murderous conflicts on their doorstep, often directed at whole civilian populations, have grown disillusioned with the practical limitations of the United Nations and leery of American pretensions to global peacekeeping. Pushed to develop an alternative, they have tended to envision a "Greater Europe," where collective action is based on principles that grow out of a common civilization and organized by institutions of a consentient community of states. "European" states would share a code for human rights and diplomatic behavior, with machinery for protecting individuals and minorities, settling ethnic and national disputes and generating common interests. Ideas of this sort were much discussed in elections to the European Parliament in June 1999. Such a pan-European construction was, of course, a very old idea. All things considered, it was not an unreasonable hope that the early twenty-first century might see it realized. Western Europe's major powers would presumably favor it. Arguably, it would also be an ideal environment for a rejuvenated and democratic Russia. The United States, like everyone else, might have hesitations and mixed feelings but would not oppose a determined Europe.

As always, the problem was giving European aspirations practical form. One obstacle throughout the 1990s was the inability to distinguish the project of a pan-European diplomatic, legal, and security system from the project of expanding membership of the European Union itself.[29] Early in the decade, the French president, François Mitterrand, had tried to distinguish between the two by floating the idea of a broad "European Confederation."[30] But it was angrily rejected by

[29] For my more extended views on this topic, see chapter 15 and "Europe, Pan Europe and the New World Order," *National Interest*, no. 63 (Spring 2001).

[30] Mitterrand's original concept, proposed in December 1989, was that of a "common and permanent organization," based on the thirty-five signatories of the 1975 Helsinki Accords on European cooperation and security. Such a confederation, he emphasized, would have depended on the political union of an inner core, comprising the then twelve member states of the European Union. See John Phillips, "Mitterrand Calls for Confederation of Europe," *United Press International*, December 31, 1989; also William Dawkins, "Mitterrand Calls for a European Confederation," *Financial Times*, January 2, 1990, p. 3.

East European leaders as a transparent and unworthy ruse to deny their countries a rightful place in the European Union.[31]

As a result, by the end of the century, the perfect had seemingly become the enemy of the good. That economic reasons made it risky to expand the EU rapidly should have been obvious to all. The EU's member states, poised at last to complete the single market with monetary union, would not abandon these fruits of several decades of economic integration in order to indulge the East Europeans with an easy path to membership. But since the former communist states angrily rejected any arrangement with the EU states other than full membership, the stage was set for a severe crisis within Pan-Europe and within the EU itself. At the same time, and partly as an alternative to their stalled EU candidacies, East European governments, encouraged by the Americans and the Germans, pressed for the expansion of NATO. Predictably, enlarging the Western alliance alienated the Russians and preempted any genuine pan-European security system. NATO's advance into old Soviet Europe made it look as if American hegemony was to be substituted for Russian, at least until the distracted Americans grew preoccupied with other matters. In the background was the specter of a reborn German Mitteleuropa. Thanks to a lack of vision all around, Europe seemed to be walking backward into the nineteenth century.[32]

---

[31] For the East European reaction, see Henry Kamm, "Havel, in Rebuff to Paris, Backs U.S.-Europe Ties," *New York Times*, June 12, 1991, p. 17; also Ian Davidson, "Ambiguity Clouds Idea of Pan-Europe Confederation," *Financial Times*, June 12, 1991, p. 4. Americans, suspicious of any European grouping with a European rather than transatlantic focus, joined in the criticism. As a reflection of the mood of the time, George Bush told the Europeans in 1991 that "if your ultimate aim is to provide independently for your own defense, the time to tell us is today"—the implication being that the United States was unhappy with West European attempts to organize Pan-Europe without intimate American participation and might well withdraw in pique. Quoted in Robert Mauthner and Lionel Barber, "U.S. seeks EC Defence Pledge," *Financial Times*, November 8, 1991, p. 1, and cited in Elizabeth Pond, *The Rebirth of Europe* (Washington, DC: Brookings Institution, 1999), p. 57.

[32] For a particularly gloomy view on Europe's future in the post–Cold War world, see J. J. Mearsheimer, "Back to the Future: Instability in Europe after the Cold War," *International Security*, vol. 15, no. 1 (1990). See also Michael Mandelbaum, *NATO Expansion: A Bridge to the Nineteenth Century* (Chevy Chase, MD: Center for Political and Strategic Studies, 1997).

Perhaps our new twenty-first century will evolve a less emotional and more pragmatic approach to establishing a larger European order. Before the larger pan-European order can be built successfully, however, there must be a realistic assessment of the limits as well as the potential of the European Union. These limits are set not only by economic realities but also by the inner constitutional character of the European Union itself. The limits of that character were well exposed during the Cold War and did not disappear when the Cold War ended.

CONSTITUTIONAL REFORM

Even before the issue of enlargement came to the fore, the constitution of the European Union was widely criticized for being politically and administratively dysfunctional—inefficient, indecisive, arbitrary, and suffering from a series of "democratic deficits" undermining its legitimacy. Arguments about how to remedy these structural insufficiencies already formed the substance of a long-standing and highly stylized constitutional debate. Woven through that debate was the old antagonism between Brussels federalism and Gaullist confederalism.

By the 1990s, a good deal of criticism was being directed at the inefficiency of the European Commission. The issue came to a head in March 1999, when the European Parliament issued a report that questioned not only the Commission's competence but also its integrity and impelled the entire Commission to resign. So drastic a remedy seemed anomalous, given the Commission's extraordinary achievements over the years, including its role in launching EMU successfully in 1998. But although there have obviously been highly competent and dedicated officials in the EU bureaucracy from the start, they have been forced to work through a preposterously cumbersome quota system providing every member state with at least one commissioner, together with a goodly share of parking slots for surplus bureaucrats. Under the circumstances, it is surprising that the system has worked as well as it has. What would happen with expansion to thirty or more members—several with bureaucracies inherited from the old Soviet system—can only be imagined.

The Amsterdam Treaty did try to remedy the situation. It gave the Commission's president greater formal authority internally, including a bigger voice in choosing and assigning the other commissioners.[33] In its fashion, Amsterdam also addressed the issue of the Commission's size and enlargement. According to a protocol annexed to the treaty, before the next enlargement of membership, states with two commissioners would have to give up one, provided that agreement had been reached on new voting arrangements in the Council. That agreement was reached at Nice. Hence, the big states are scheduled to lose their second commissioner in 2006. But Nice postponed further reform of the Commission until the membership reached twenty-seven.[34]

The Commission has been widely criticized for being not only inefficient and venal but also undemocratic and arbitrary. In practice, critics say, it has been largely unaccountable for how it implements the Council's decisions. The Commission's natural bureaucratic ten-

[33] As revised at Amsterdam, Article 158(2) of the *Treaty Establishing the European Community* reads, "The governments of the Member States shall nominate by common accord the person they intend to appoint as President of the Commission; the nomination shall be approved by the European Parliament. The governments of the Member States shall, by common accord with the nominee for President, nominate the other persons whom they intend to appoint as Member of the Commission." Article 163 was revised to state that "the Commission shall work under the political guidance of its President." *Treaty of Amsterdam amending the Treaty on European Union, the Treaties establishing the European Communities and Certain Related Acts: Part One: Substantive Amendments* <http://ue.eu.int/Amsterdam/en/...c/en/treaty/Partone/amst11.htm>. The Amsterdam Intergovernmental Conference (June 1997) also called for a reorganization of commissioners' portfolios to eliminate some of the more peculiar bundlings, for example, the notorious portfolio of Fisheries and Humanitarian Affairs. See Michael Nentwich and Gerda Falkner, "The Treaty of Amsterdam: Toward a New Institutional Balance," *European Integration Online Papers*, vol. 1, no. 15 (1997), <http://www.eiop.or.at/eiop/texte/1997-015.htm>, p. 5. See also C. Giering, "Vertrag von Amsterdam," in W. Weidenfeld and W. Wessels, eds., *Europa von A–Z* (Bonn: Bundeszentrale für politische Bildung, 1997), pp. 326–333. Romano Prodi, nominated as Commission president in April 1999, after the scandals that had led the Santer Commission to resign, insisted that the European Parliament, rather than pass on individual commissioners, accept his "government" as a whole and secured from each potential commissioner a promise to resign if asked by him to do so. See Peter Norman, "Great Expectations," *Financial Times*, July 12, 1999, p. 13.

[34] Draft approved by the Conference of Representatives of the Governments of the Member States at <http://ue.eu.int/cig/nice/nicefr.asp?lang=en>.

dency to standardize regulations and procedures favors a uniformity often offensive to national sensibilities and in many instances unnecessary. This has been a favorite topic for anti-European politicians, whose grotesque illustrations, frequently spurious, have nevertheless reflected sentiments widely felt.[35] How to reconcile the need for uniform standards in a single market with a healthy and stimulating degree of diversity is a real enough issue. To respond, Maastricht introduced the principle of subsidiarity, designed to locate more regulatory decision making at national or subnational levels whenever possible.[36] The principle was doubtless salutary, but so long as the Union advances, nothing is likely to stop the flow of administrative competence to its Commission. The problem is to find the means to keep the Commission sensitive to public feelings, as well as able to build public backing for desirable policies.

Here the European Parliament clearly has a critical role as an investigative watchdog against administrative arbitrariness, incompetence, and corruption and also as a forum through which the Commission can rally support. The Parliament, which can refuse to appoint the Council's president and slate of commissioners or reject the Union's budget, has ample powers for getting the Commission's attention and forcing a more open style of administration. The Parliament's problem is to organize itself.

The major constitutional issues, however, lie not in the Commission or even the Parliament, but in the Council of Ministers. The

[35] For a scathing critique from a disgruntled Commission bureaucrat, see Bernard Connolly, *The Rotten Heart of Europe* (London: Faber & Faber, 1996).

[36] According to the Maastricht Treaty, *subsidiarity* means that the European Commission should act only when a desired objective can be achieved better at a supranational level; the means employed should be proportional to the desired objective. For various studies of the principle of subsidiarity, see N. A. Neuwald, "A Europe Close to the Citizen? The Trinity Concepts of Subsidiarity, Transparency and Democracy," in A. Rosas and E. Atola, eds., *A Citizens' Europe: In Search of a New Order* (London: Sage Publications, 1995), and P. Bianchi, "Subsidiarity and Its Significance," in P. Devine, Y. Katsoulacos, and R. Sugden, eds., *Competitiveness, Subsidiarity and Industrial Policy* (New York: Routledge, 1996). For a detailed description of the intricacies of "mutual recognition," see John Van Oudenaren, *Uniting Europe: European Integration and the Post-Cold War World* (Lanham: Rowman & Littlefield, 2000), pp. 105–107.

Council, like the Commission, is criticized for its "democratic deficit." National politicians complain that their governments regularly invoke intergovernmental agreements in Brussels to override or ignore parliamentary opposition at home. In effect, governments are inclined to decide basic policies among themselves in the European Council and thereby to escape the normal checks and balances of their national political systems. No doubt, this happens often enough. But since no important EU policy can be carried against the firm opposition of a major state, the solution is that electorates should begin to judge national governments for what they permit Brussels to do.

Here, the European Parliament should also play a critical role—exposing, analyzing, and correcting the Council's legislation, even without pretending to usurp its ultimate legislative function.[37] A Parliament that played such a role would not only make it harder for national governments to evade accountability at home for what they do in Brussels but also raise, throughout Europe, the level of public awareness of European interdependence. Even if the European Parliament plays only the role of an elected House of Lords, its debates could clarify to the public key issues before the Council—with effects reverberating into national parliaments, thus generating real political pressure on the member governments. Whether making Council debates more open would improve the quality of governance is, of course, debatable. Discrete decision making, dominated by expert advisers, has its advantages, especially in periods of prolonged economic difficulty. From this perspective, the supposed impotence of

[37] Amsterdam greatly extended the range of "codecision procedures"—introduced at Maastricht—whereby the Parliament can veto acts passed by the Council in areas such as employment, social policy, health, freedom of movement, the single market, and the environment. Codecision has now become the most frequently used legislative procedure. Presumably, Parliament now has greater influence in designing the acts themselves. To exercise that influence constructively, however, requires the Parliament to organize itself coherently—difficult, given the heterogeneity and political marginalization of the deputies themselves. For a listing and analysis of the changes after Amsterdam, see Renaud Dehousse "European Institutional Architecture after Amsterdam: Parliamentary System or Regulatory Structure?" (European University Institute, Working Paper RSC No 98/11).

national governments before the omnipotence of Brussels is a "noble lie" that allows those governments to cope more successfully with their problems. Arguably, more transparency in the Council could reduce its effectiveness. In compensation, however, it could also help European electorates to realize the extent to which national policies require the cooperation of neighboring states. This would help to dispel the less than noble lie that Europe's "sovereign" states could easily do whatever their electorates please, were it not for the pusillanimity of their leaders. Obliviousness to their interdependence is a democratic deficit among the publics themselves. It is dangerous, since it leaves the door open to populist demagogues who promise what no national government can deliver.

The most serious criticism of the Council, however, is not that its decision making is obscure and undemocratic, but that it is dilatory and indecisive. In principle, there is widespread agreement that some new formula is urgently required to speed up regular business. In constitutional questions, or in intergovernmental spheres like foreign and defense policy, voting procedures are still subject to a *liberum veto*. Leaving such arrangements in place while expanding the Union's membership and scope threaten to bring the Council to a standstill. So blocked a system, its pretensions steadily augmenting, would be increasingly dangerous. States would be robbed of their individual power and initiative, while no effective confederal authority would substitute. Federalists, of course, have their traditional solution: National voting power should be adjusted for population and decisions taken by weighted majority. A version of that formula has, in fact, long been used for a great deal of routine decision making in the EU's "First Pillar," where day-to-day affairs of economic integration are dealt with.[38] The relative voting power of member states remained greatly disproportionate to population.[39] Amsterdam was sup-

[38] At Amsterdam, qualified majority voting was extended from the First Pillar core both to the Second Pillar fields discussed below and to Third Pillar areas in justice and home affairs. These last included incentive measures in employment and social policy, public health, and fraud prevention. See the European Council's *Press Release on Intergovernmental Conference* of June 18, 1997 (Brussels: European Council, 1997). See also <http://europa.eu.int/scadplus/leg/en/cig/g4000c.htm>.

[39] Before Nice, Luxembourg, with 450,000 inhabitants, had two votes, while Ger-

271

posed to remedy the disproportionality as well as to extend weighted majority voting to "Second Pillar" (intergovernmental) matters— including CFSP. But its preparatory intergovernmental conference (IGC) failed to live up to expectations. Smaller states feared that giving up their outsized voting power would leave them at the mercy of the big states. The big states, preposterously underrepresented in formal voting power, clung to the veto to protect themselves from being coerced by an artificial majority of small states. Even Germany, the most populous state and traditionally the most federally minded, flatly refused to drop the veto.[40] Three years later, at Nice, the EU did agree on a complex new system for weighted voting that appeared to give more power to the big states. Nevertheless, many issues beyond the First Pillar remained intergovernmental and not subject to weighted voting.

Important initiatives, however, had been taken earlier at Amsterdam to elaborate intergovernmental structures for the formulation and conduct of common foreign and security policy (CFSP). The Amsterdam Treaty provided for a "Monsieur PESC"—a high representative speaking for the Council in CFSP matters—who was also to serve as the Council's secretary-general, and whose staff was to include military and diplomatic planning and early-warning groups. The distinguished first appointment, Javier de Solana, previously secretary-general of NATO, suggested that the new post could greatly change the environment for the Council's decision making in diplomatic and security issues.[41] But Amsterdam's actual provisions for decision mak-

---

many, with 80 million, had only ten. Britain, France, Germany, and Italy, home to nearly 80 percent of the EU's total population, had only 55 percent of the Council's votes. When the Community had only six members, the distribution of voting weights ensured that decisions could be taken only if supported by countries representing 70 percent of the bloc's population. Later the figure dropped to 58.3 percent. See Emma Tucker and Lionel Barber, "EU Tones Down Most Ambitious Plans," *Financial Times*, June 18, 1997, p. 2.

[40] At Amsterdam, Germany took the lead in opposing any surrender of national veto power over immigration, borders, and other sensitive policy areas. See Tom Buerkle, "Amsterdam Treaty Scorned as Mediocre," *International Herald Tribune*, June 27, 1997, p. 5.

[41] For an assessment of the effects of Amsterdam on CFSP, see Jörg Monar, "The

ing were tortuous. States unwilling to go along with common action in foreign and security matters but reluctant to impose a veto were allowed to retreat to "constructive abstention." The abstaining state thereby recognizes the decision as committing the Union in general but not itself. Once such a general decision about a CFSP matter is taken, moreover, further implementing decisions require only a weighted majority. There is, however, an "emergency brake" that allows a member to hold up a subsequent decision for "important and stated reasons of national policy." A qualified majority can then refer the blocked decision back to the Council, where it once more requires unanimous approval to go forward. While Nice simplified procedures and eliminated the veto for "enhanced cooperation" in general, Britain insisted on retaining the national veto for CFSP and defense questions.[42]

The complexity and apparent futility of this formal procedure only underscores how difficult it is to leave the veto in place for some questions but not for others. If the veto is to mean anything, each member has to decide for itself when its own veto should apply. A Council reform that really eliminated the national veto would be, in effect, a mutation to federalism. At the same time, in a matter of vital interest, where big states agreed, particularly if Monsieur PESC's planning and early-warning groups had permitted ample discussion beforehand, small states might find it difficult to block actions, whatever their formal rights.

PERSISTING FEDERAL AND CONFEDERAL PERSPECTIVES

The shortcomings of such incremental reforms suggest more radical alternatives. Federalists, of course, have always advocated cutting the Gordian knot by installing a supranational government responsible to a federal European Parliament. Since the 1950s, Brussels federalists have proposed a scenario in which the European Commission, chosen

---

European Union's Foreign Affairs System after the Treaty of Amsterdam: A Strengthened Capacity for External Action?" *European Foreign Affairs Review*, vol. 2 (1997), pp. 435ff.

[42] See Blair statement, December 11, 2000 <http://www.number-10gov.uk/default. asp?Page1d-2992>.

by the European Parliament, is installed as the Union's executive power, while the Council of Ministers becomes a second chamber representing the member states, much as the German Bundesrat represents the German Länder—able to block but not to initiate legislation. The Commission's first president, Walter Hallstein, attempted to precipitate such a revolution in 1967 and thereby provoked de Gaulle's boycott of the European Council of Ministers. The ensuing "Luxembourg Compromise" confirmed the hybrid constitution, including the Council's primacy, and resulted in Hallstein's downfall.[43] But the old federalist hopes have never died. In 1998, for example, the Commission's former president, Jacques Delors, suggested that the major party groupings in the European Parliament should name their candidate for the Commission's presidency before European Parliamentary elections. Any president of the Commission chosen thereafter would be more likely to have a committed majority behind him in the Parliament and would be endowed, at least indirectly, with a high degree of popular legitimacy. Arguably, when the European Parliament forced the Santer Commission to resign in 1999, it was a significant step in this direction.[44]

Confederalists, of course, have always rejected such schemes out of hand. Parliamentary democracy, they argue, cannot be established on

[43] For Hallstein's proposals to augment the importance of the Commission-Parliament, see Commission of the EEC, *Ninth General Report of the Activities of the Community: 1 April 1965 to 31 March 1966* (Brussels, 1965), ch. 1. See also Maurice Couve de Murville, *Une Politique étrangère, 1958–1969* (Paris: Plou, 1971), ch. 8, especially pp. 329–339. For my analysis near the time, as well as further sources, see D. P. Calleo, *Europe's Future: The Grand Alternatives* (New York: W. W. Norton, 1967), pp. 69–78, and D. P. Calleo and B. M. Rowland, *America and the World Political Economy* (Bloomington: Indiana University Press, 1973), pp. 127ff., note 26, and pp. 307ff. For an analysis of the relevance of the Luxembourg Compromise to EU decision making, see "Use of the Luxembourg Compromise in the Council," *Official Journal of the European Communities*, vol. 39, no. 217 (1996).

[44] After a scathing parliamentary report induced the Santer Commission to resign in March 1999, the incoming new Commission, headed by Romano Prodi, took the parliamentary hearings and confirmation much more seriously than its predecessor. See "Incoming Commissioners Prepare for a Grilling," *Financial Times*, August 30, 1999, p. 2. See also "Brussels Goes Back to School," *Financial Times*, September 17, 1999, p. 13.

a European scale merely by mimicking the constitutional machinery of Europe's nation states. To make a parliamentary system work requires political parties that can form majorities unified enough to sustain a disciplined and coherent government. To have a political system of such parties requires a reasonably integrated political culture. Such cultures do exist within most European nation states, but they are the fruit of a long historical development, generally within a shared language and culture, as any good nationalist theorist of the nineteenth century would have been quick to point out. A similarly unified political culture is clearly missing on a European scale, confederalists argue, and cannot simply be ordered to measure. The European Union, therefore, cannot expect to transform itself rapidly into a single European nation state. Thus, assuming that the federal European Parliament can be analogous to a national parliament, and expecting to base a European government on it, is a vain exercise, harmful because it distracts from pursuing more realistic reforms. The point at issue is hardly new. Rousseau is answering Madison: A modern state must be based on an active consensus of its citizens. And Herder would add that consensus is unlikely unless the state is also a nation. De Gaulle would conclude that, since Europe is not a nation, it should not attempt to be a state. It should remain a confederacy—a Europe of States.

This Gaullist conclusion fits well the observation, common among analysts familiar with the EU's inner workings, that the real managing power in the Council lies with its Committee of Permanent Representatives (COREPER).[45] This is the crown of the sizable group of national civil servants posted in Brussels to prepare the work of their ministers in the Council. These civil servants represent their respective national bureaucracies and constantly negotiate with each other and with the Commission. These informal networks are what has

[45] For further discussion of COREPER, see Martin Westlake, *The Council of the European Union* (London and New York: Routledge, 1998), and Fiona Hayes-Renshaw and Helen Wallace, *The Council of Ministers* (New York: St. Martin's Press, 1997). For discussion of the functioning of the European Union in the wake of Maastricht, and in particular the enhanced role of COREPER, see Peter Ludlow, "Beyond Maastricht: Recasting the European Political and Economic System," *Centre for European Policy Studies Working Document 79* (Brussels: Centre for European Policy Studies, 1993).

275

made the Union work as well as it has. The great increase in the number of member states envisaged in EU enlargement may be expected to burden these networks substantively and physically.

A BURKEAN PERSPECTIVE

Europeans have been debating their constitutions since the days of Plato and Aristotle. Among the most insightful of the modern analysts was Edmund Burke, whose writings span the dramatic mutations of the French and American Revolutions. Burke forcefully defended the proposition that successful constitutions cannot simply be cast but must grow naturally through history—through a process of trial, error, and habit formation. Innumerable factors are in play—unconscious as well as conscious, emotional as well as "rational." No one's particular constitutional scheme can capture all the vital factors. Reformers should therefore approach constitutional reform, however necessary, with humility, caution, and tenderness—as to "the wounds of a father." Even the most well-intentioned reforms risk rending the fabric of legitimacy and loyalty and turning loose a swarm of unimagined and often violent consequences.[46]

Reflecting on COREPER suggests a Burkean observation: The functioning of the European Council of Ministers, and of the EU in general, depends less on formal institutional arrangements than on the accumulated habits and organizational culture shared by members interacting within the institutions. In the Council, for example, majority voting procedures are almost never used—unless a country has reason to want to see itself formally outvoted.[47] Instead, members go on

[46] For the classic statement of Burke's views on revolution, see Edmund Burke, *Reflections on the Revolution in France* (Oxford and New York: Oxford University Press, 1999).

[47] Since the 1966 Luxembourg Compromise, if core national interests of any one state are involved, Council members keep negotiating until an acceptable compromise can be found. This practice was reemphasized when the distribution of Council votes was reshuffled during the enlargement round of 1994 that brought Austria, Finland, and Sweden into the Union. The "Ioannina Compromise," reached during the negotiations, states that if twenty-three of the Council's total of eighty-seven votes are

bargaining until they reach workable compromises. In the words of one seasoned observer, the EU is a bazaar with the rules of a club, or perhaps a club that is really a bazaar.[48] What matters is that the members are willing and able to make concessions to each other until they can reach a balanced agreement. Over the years, this bargaining among the states—within the Council, among the national bureaucracies, or with the Commission—has evolved elaborate rules of the game. A good deal depends on networks of informal contacts at every level. All in all, the system works surprisingly well. It is complex, but so are most of the national systems in Western Europe. The government of a continent of advanced democratic states can hardly be made simple. The American system, although much more centralized and "federal" than the EU, is hardly less complex—given the volatile balances and informal networks that exist among the federal government's three independent branches and their bureaucracies, or between the states and the federal government.

The vital significance of the EU's intergovernmental culture complicates its enlargement. New members have to learn to play the game. Above all, they have to be willing and able to redefine national interests in the search for more general European interests. In the past, some new members have been quick to learn, some less so. Many of the candidates being considered early in the twenty-first century are not particularly promising in this respect. Many are former communist states jealous of their new-won freedom and caught up in heroic efforts to learn the habits of democratic cooperation within their own national systems. They are still burdened with the usages,

---

against a decision, the members must keep negotiating until a compromise is found. Thus, the Council is commonly described as a consensus-making machine, and a member state is seldom formally outvoted in a final Council decision. See C. Engel, "Rat der Europaeischen Union," in W. Weidenfeld and W. Wessel, eds., *Europa von A–Z* (Bonn: Bundeszentrale für politische Bildung, 1997), pp. 284–289. It remains to be seen how much the reweighting of votes at Nice in 2000 will change the Council's preference for consensus. Over time, with many more members, formal voting procedures may well be invoked more often. Nevertheless, the old consensual habits are likely to persist, particularly since the mechanisms for enforcement of contested majority decisions are unlikely to be greatly developed.

[48] Professor Michael Stürmer, in conversation with the author, August 1999.

TABLE 13.1
GDP per Capita in 1999 (in U.S. dollars)

Germany	25,372	Slovenia	10,425
Spain	14,266	Hungary	4,802
Greece	11,763	Poland	3,983
Portugal	10,782	Estonia	3,536

Source: World Bank Indicators Data Base, 1999 <http://devdata.worldbank.org>.

and indeed the personnel, of the old order. Such states are not likely to be easy partners for the EU.[49] And with the best will in the world, they are likely to lack the national resources needed to play the community game. Western Europe's corporatist states have elaborate systems of political, social, and economic dialogue that make them quickly aware of interests damaged by EU decisions. Governments are skilled in cosseting and outmaneuvering the damaged interests and have the resources to compensate them in one way or another. The national patronage network offers an overall package of benefits and subventions sufficient to disincline corporate groups from serious rebellion. But the former communist countries lack anything like the same means to grease the wheels of national consensus. Even the relatively poor former new members—Spain, Portugal, and Greece— were much more developed and prosperous when they entered the Community than almost any of the East European candidates of the 1990s (see table 13.1).[50] This underdevelopment of former communist

[49] See the remarks of a former German ambassador to the EU (1985–1990), Werner Ungerer, noting that heterogenous newcomers "might have difficulties adapting to the political culture in Brussels where compromise seeking has developed into an art. . . . a refined form of defending national interests." Quoted in J. Lewis, "Is the 'Hard-Bargaining' Image of the Council Misleading? The Committee of Permanent Representatives and the Local Elections Directive," *Journal of Common Market Studies*, vol. 36, no. 4 (December 1998), p. 485.

[50] In 1977, GDP per capita in Spain, Greece, and Portugal was respectively $3,150, $2,830, and $1,670—far below that in Denmark ($9,040) and West Germany ($8,140), but not so distant from the UK ($4,370), Italy ($3,470), or Ireland ($2,950). D. Seers and C. Vaitsos, eds., *The Second Enlargement of the EEC: The Integration of Unequal Partners* (New York: St. Martin's Press, 1982), p. 69. Table 13.1 suggests the magnitude of current problems with enlargement.

countries—in national habits and resources as well as intergovernmental culture—is a formidable handicap for playing the role of EU partner. In short, if it is not easy to change the way the EU has learned to function, neither is it easy to incorporate the new East European applicants into that way of functioning.

Conflicting Democratic Traditions

A further complication troubles the EU's constitutional debate: Europe's nation states do not, in fact, share a democratic model. What seems normal in some may seem undemocratic to others. In particular, there is a fundamental distinction between adversarial systems, based on a clearly defined parliamentary majority and opposition, and "corporatist" or "constitutionalist" systems, based on a broad consensus negotiated among a wide variety of distinct political groups and institutions. Britain has traditionally provided a relatively pure version of the adversarial system. Between elections—if the majority holds together—the prime minister is a sort of elected dictator, with the power to pass the legislation needed to carry out an electoral program. Such a system requires highly disciplined parties. Its advantage is that an election appears to offer voters a clear-cut choice between comprehensive programs. The corporatist or constitutionalist model does not. Instead, it offers voters the power to choose the players who will negotiate policies in the future. These players will presumably give the voters some idea of their predispositions, but once they are elected, there is no guarantee that they will be able to implement their programs, since they may well not have the power to do so. Throughout the postwar years, the Italian system was probably the purest version of such a system among the big European states. The United States, with its constitutional "separation of powers," offers another version. In the United States, federal legislation requires the assent of the president and both houses of Congress. It is entirely possible that the president's party will lack a majority in one or both houses. In recent years, that has been the case more often than not. In any event, the American president does not control even his own party, nor does his constitutional power or continuation in office depend on his party's support. The same trend toward divided plural government has been visible in France, where cohabitation was the rule throughout most of the 1990s, and even in Germany, where the chancellor's party did not control the upper house of parliament through most of the 1990s.[51]

In pluralist "constitutional" systems of this sort, with no clear political chain of command, consensus obviously requires a high degree of bargaining among a multiplicity of political actors and forces. As a result, the majority of voters, per se, exercises less direct power on the outcome of political decision making than in an adversarial system, where voters presumably can choose between two clear-cut alternatives. Deciding which sort of system is preferable, in the abstract, depends on a variety of complicated philosophical assumptions. In practice, the success of one model or the other depends on a country's political culture and general situation. Broadly speaking, a well-functioning adversarial system requires a relatively high degree of consensus throughout the society and no deep differences between major parties that make the victory of one intolerable to the other. A constitutional system seems more appropriate to a country with multiple "cleavages" in its society—with diverse regions and ethnic groups and strong private institutions that represent this diversity.

Whether conceived of as a permanent confederacy or as a federation in the making, the EU is obviously a constitutionalist rather than an adversarial construction. Traditionally, it lacks even the independent and popularly elected "royal" executive that characterizes the American and French systems. As a result, the EU must perennially disappoint those who favor the direct—if episodic—popular democracy of the British adversarial model. The chances of ever removing this discontent seem slight. Europe as a whole seems irremediably constitutionalist. At the same time, the EU has had the advantages of

---

[51] One consequence was that the SPD-controlled Bundesrat blocked the Kohl government's reforms of the German tax system and thereby prolonged Germany's economic disarray in the 1990s. France has now shortened the presidential term from seven to five years, which aligns presidential and parliamentary elections and, arguably, makes cohabitation less likely. See Robert Graham, "Election Change Urged after French Vote: France's Constitution Approval of Shorter Presidential Term," *Financial Times*, September 26, 2000, p. 2.

its constitutional form. The European Commission, for all its structural flaws and occasional bad habits, is a highly competent technocracy. It collaborates easily and intimately with the national bureaucracies gathered in COREPER. Moreover, the Council's opaque decision making seems well suited to finding diplomatic compromises that avoid sharp conflicts and long-standing grievances among the member states. This sort of administration and decision making seem acceptable enough so long as the issues are not intensely ideological and therefore remain amenable to expert technocratic manipulation. However, as an enlarging EU progresses into monetary union, along with common diplomacy, security, and defense, the old tricks for keeping mass politics and politicians at bay are bound to be tested more severely. In 1999, for example, election campaigns for the European Parliament were strongly inclined to politicize EU issues along national party lines. EU policy may well play an increasing role in national elections or in the formation of national governing coalitions. If so, the Council and the Commission may grow more "political." A majority of Social Democratic governments on the Council, for example, or of deputies in the Parliament, might press for "Social Democratic" policies on a European scale, and possibly for a Social Democratic Commission to carry them out.

The degree to which this takes place presumably will depend on the extent of political convergence among Europe's nation states. If Social Democracy comes to mean the same thing in Britain, France, and Germany, then it may make sense to speak of a Social Democratic Party in the European Council or Parliament. Such convergence may, in time, be a natural outcome of the economic convergence that is expected to follow from EMU. But with the enlarged membership that is also widely expected, such a close degree of economic convergence seems unlikely for the EU as a whole, at least for a decade or two.[52] And even among the old members, despite their remarkable economic convergence, real political convergence seems a remote

---

[52] On the expected economic impact of enlargement, see the European Commission's "Impact Study," cited in G. Avery and F. Cameron, *The Enlargement of the EU* (Sheffield, UK: Sheffield Academic Press, 1999), ch. 8.

prospect.[53] So long as this is the case, the EU's hybrid system will not easily lend itself to mass pan-European politics, Europeans, for better or worse, will continue to complain of the EU's democratic deficits.

In many respects, Europe's constitutional debates have scarcely advanced since the 1960s. In the special conditions of the Cold War, there probably was no real need to do so. But now that a stronger constitution is indicated, Europe still seems unready for radical federalist solutions. In May 2000, Germany's Green foreign minister, Joschka Fischer, speaking in an unofficial capacity, proposed an inner core of EU members that would participate in all aspects of the EU, including EMU and CSFP, and that would adopt various federal arrangements for governing their common business. Fischer's scheme called for a clear differentiation between European and national functions. At the European level, Fischer suggested a parliament of two houses—the lower chamber consisting of members of national parliaments, with representation based on population, and an upper house where national delegations would be equal—as in the German Bundesrat or the U.S. Senate. Fischer also suggested a directly elected European "president"—either of the Council or of the Commission, or both. In some respects, Fischer's proposals seemed an updating of a famous Lamers-Schäuble paper of 1994.[54] But it also followed on

---

[53] Prime Minister Tony Blair and Chancellor Gerhard Schroeder have together espoused a "third way" to adapting the European welfare state to a globalized world. Their vision was widely rejected within France's ruling Socialist Party, because of its "liberal" tone. In Germany itself, the vision was also resisted by strong forces in the Red/Green government and particularly viewed with suspicion in the Eastern Länder, more inclined to believe their development requires an interventionist state. See Tony Blair and Gerhard Schroeder, *Europe's Third Way*, June 8, 1999, discussed in "Schroeder backs Blair . . . ," *Financial Times*, June 9, 1999, p. 28. For the German text, see statement on June 8 at <http://www.spd.de>. For the reception of the paper in France, see "Europa's Dritter Weg," *Die Zeit*, vol. 39 (1999) and Jospin Compares French Socialism, Blair's Third Way," *Le Monde*, April 27, 1999. For an authoritative East German reaction, see interview with R. Hoeppner, prime minister of Sachsen-Anhalt, *Die Zeit*, vol. 31 (1999).

[54] Karl Lamers, *Strengthening the Hard Core*, first published as *Reflections on European Policy* by the Christian Democratic Union and Christian Social Union (CDU/CSU) parliamentary group in the Bundestag on September 7, 1994. A paper of fifteen pages, it urged France and Germany, together with the Benelux countries, to create a genuine federal core for the rest of the EU.

the heels of a similar proposal from former Commission president Jacques Delors, and a joint proposal from former French and German leaders, Giscard d'Estaing and Helmut Schmidt. Governments, as usual, reacted with polite caution. In due course, French president Jacques Chirac launched a grand design before the German Parliament.[55] All these proposals indicated a growing awareness that enlargement was a major and intractable challenge. Anxiety was mounting, but neither politicians nor publics at large seemed ready for radical reforms. Instead, political leaders began to muse privately that enlargement would take a long time and would certainly bring major changes, but these would have to evolve slowly. Under such circumstances, it is natural to look for some clever innovation that could continue Europe's success with hybrid arrangements. Amsterdam had reached for such a solution by introducing a "flexibility clause" permitting closer cooperation among members who wished it. In effect, Amsterdam sanctioned the principle of variable geometry.[56] Given the unsettled and intractable constitutional issues facing the EU, the principle seems destined for thorough exploration.

VARIABLE GEOMETRY

Variable geometry is a concept with wide and diffuse appeal. It offers something to federalists and technocratic functionalists, as well as to the political descendants of General de Gaulle. Federalists, for example, can embrace variable geometry because they hope it means a federal core with a confederal periphery. As mentioned a moment ago, the idea was floated in a famous paper circulated in 1994, issued by Karl Lamers and Wolfgang Schäuble, two distinguished leaders of the West German Christian Democratic Party. The paper was also

---

[55] "Our Europe," speech by President Jacques Chirac to the German Bundestag, Berlin, June 27, 2000 <http://www.info-france-usa.org/EU2000/bundesta.htm>.

[56] The Amsterdam Treaty introduced a general flexibility clause (Titel VIa, Art. K.15–K.17 EUT) that allows a group of states to move ahead of the rest in specific areas of cooperation provided their cooperation serves the fundamental goals of the EU and is open to other member states if they wish to join. See W. Weidenfeld and W. Wessels, eds., *Europa von A–Z* (Bonn: Bundeszentrale für politische Bildung, 1997), pp. 213–215.

thought to reflect the thinking of Chancellor Kohl. It proposed a powerful inner core of states, accepting a much greater degree of supranational decision making among themselves. As Kohl's behavior three years later at Amsterdam illustrated, however, Germany was not prepared, any more than any other European state, to surrender its national self-determination to a federal body. Nevertheless, the idea of a federal inner core persists. As Jacques Delors has insisted, enlargement will make it imperative.[57]

Variable geometry also offers possibilities for the more functionalist approach of the supranational Europe's classic promoter, Jean Monnet. The approach is to depoliticize critical dimensions of European interaction and leave them to be run by supranational experts. EMU seems to fit and advance this pattern. It puts monetary policy, and to some extent fiscal policy, in the hands of an independent European Central Bank (ECB) run by experts. The assumption is that monetary policy should and can be protected from mass politics. Economic policies do, of course, have an obvious technocratic aspect. Economists of one school or another are seldom shy about prescribing what they believe is the scientifically correct course to follow. Monetarist economists tend to believe there is a right monetary policy for any given situation. Some would reincarnate the classic gold standard. Others believe the money supply has to be more actively managed, since it is the "loose joint" of the market economy, as Hayek once said. But, according to Hayek, the creation of money should be as stable, predictable, and automatic as possible. Monetary conditions should not be manipulated for the sake of short-term improvements in the general economy—a view also vigorously advocated by Milton Friedman.[58]

Devotion to monetary stability is deeply implanted in the German Bundesbank. That outlook, of course, is not universally admired among economists, even in Germany. The American Federal Reserve, for example, presented a different model for the 1990s. Its manage-

[57] For Delors's pronouncement, see "L'Européen Delors critique l'Europe," *Le Monde*, January 19, 2000. Delors admitted, however, that the core would still consist of nation states and would be, in effect, a federation of nation states.

[58] Milton Friedman. *Capitalism and Freedom* (Chicago: University of Chicago Press).

ment of the money supply was aggressively discretionary and seemed much more successful than that of the Bundesbank—if creating jobs and sustaining growth without inflation are the criteria. For many Europeans, one of EMU's great attractions has been that it might enable the new European Central Bank to imitate the Federal Reserve. In short, even among the technocratic experts, there have been sharp and fundamental differences of opinion about monetary policy.

To succeed with EMU, those in charge will have to find the right balance of priorities for Europe as a whole, and to know how to achieve them. This will depend not only on their formal economic expertise and conjunctural luck, but also on their judgment, imagination, and persuasiveness. These are hardly technocratic rather than political virtues. It seems scarcely conceivable that Europe's national politicians will leave these issues in the hands of technocrats, particularly if things start to go wrong, as seems almost inevitable in the course of things. This ultimate primacy of politics in setting economic policy is nicely embodied in the "illogical" way the European Central Bank is supposed both to govern the monetary union and, at the same time, to fit its directives within the EU's general economic policy. The bank's day-to-day operations are directed by its central managing board of six professionals, all meant to be independent of any national control. ECB thus seems a perfect areopagus for technocratic management. Its perfection, however, is marred by a larger governing board, which sets basic monetary policy and where the six managing directors are joined by the heads of the national central banks of the participating states. These national banks remain in existence under EMU and are the institutions charged with actually implementing ECB policies in each country. How their boards and heads are selected, and what degree of independence they enjoy, varies from one country to another, although there has been a general trend toward more autonomy. While, as ECB board members, these national central bank heads are charged to maintain a European perspective and not to take national instructions, they will not find it easy to ignore the particular interests and situations of their own national economies. In short, even the technocratic ECB has a significant confederal character. Alongside the ECB, moreover, is the EU's Council of Finance Ministers (ECOFIN), charged with setting the Union's economic policy generally, and in particular its exchange rate policy. It is difficult to imagine how exchange rate policy can be set without control of short-term interest rates and hence monetary policy. The anomalies of the situation are glaring, but probably no more illogical or ambiguous than the relationship between the government and the central bank in most national states, where the real locus of initiative is constantly moving and depends heavily on general political and economic conditions, as well as on shifting fashions of economic orthodoxy.

The imbroglio over the appointment of the first chairman of the ECB in 1998 made clear that Europe's politicians were not prepared to abdicate to its technocrats. As the French government spelled out rather brutally, it would not accept a European Central Bank appropriated by the Bundesbank's technocrats, nor by the Germans in general. The new ECB was to have its functional independence, but like everything else in the EU, it would ultimately be responsible to Europe's nation states and would reflect a balance among them. The German government, still led by Chancellor Kohl, did not really appear to disagree.[59] And within a few months, the Red-Green coalition that succeeded Kohl in Germany was vigorously asserting the primacy of governments in setting the EU's overall economic policy. While the new German finance minister, Oskar Lafontaine, ultimately left the Schroeder government, presumably for his flamboyant advocacy of growth over monetary stability, the ECB soon lowered interest rates and watched the euro depreciate with remarkable equanimity.[60] In effect, EMU reaffirms the EU's traditional hybrid constitu-

---

[59] French president Jacques Chirac, during the Brussels Summit in May 1998, threatened to veto the appointment of Wim Duisenberg, the European central bankers' choice for the presidency of the ECB. The squabble ended in a compromise in which Duisenberg allegedly pledged to step back before the end of his eight-year term to leave the job to the French candidate, Jean-Claude Trichet. Some later comments from Duisenberg, once installed, cast doubt on his intentions. By pushing the French candidate so insistently, Chirac did make clear, however, that the final decision about the appointment was to be made by Europe's political leaders and not by the central bankers themselves. Not everyone was pleased. For French, German, and British reactions to the compromise, see "An Uneasy Compromise," and "The Germans Attack 'Lazy Compromise,'" *Financial Times*, May 4, 1998, pp. 2, 17.

[60] The euro, after touching a high of 1.19 against the dollar soon after its launch in

tion. Technocratic expertise is recognized as a vital tool for formulating and implementing collective policies, but legitimacy depends ultimately on the political will of the member states.

The same complex pattern is likely to repeat itself as Europeans grow serious about Maastricht's goal of a Common Foreign and Security Policy (CFSP). The effectiveness of the Treaty of Amsterdam's Monsieur PESC will depend on the degree to which the big member states can reach a consensus for him to represent. No matter what voting arrangements emerge, big states will weigh more than small states, and no state will reliably support a foreign policy that it perceives does serious harm to its own interests. Looked at from this perspective, the tortuous arrangements that effectively preserve the national veto seem realistic. What really matters is not the formal voting rules but whether the new arrangements for CFSP foster a political and institutional culture that pushes states to define their own national interests in a European perspective.

The same caveat is equally true for developing actual military cooperation. Like monetary integration, it is a sphere with an obvious technocratic dimension that lends itself to apolitical expertise. But the limitations of technocratic leadership will grow manifest whenever actual military action is required. Soldiers cannot be put at risk unless their nation state is willing to commit them. Jointly managed arrangements, like the Franco-German Brigade or the Eurocorps, remain a military Potemkin village so long as major participating states are unwilling to commit themselves to fighting side by side on behalf of Europe. Here again, the formula of variable geometry can allow things to move forward. Those who are ready can act. The real challenge, for CFSP and for common defense, is not merely to create an effective technocratic structure, but also to animate it with a political will shared by Europe's major states, a will to pool their fates and act together—in the military sphere as already in the monetary sphere. Technocratic institutions can help to precipitate such a consensus, as

---

January 1999, had dropped to dollar 0.91 by March 2000. With inflationary pressures apparently absent, Germans seemed not overly averse to a weaker currency to improve their competitiveness and prompt their lagging economy.

well as give it practical effectiveness. But technocracy cannot, by itself, substitute for the political will to take common action.

Variable Geometry: Gaullist Style

Arguably, the real inventor of variable geometry was General de Gaulle. As a license to form coalitions of the willing, it seems implicit in the very idea of a Europe of States. De Gaulle took for granted that Europe's old nation states would continue to have sharply distinct perspectives, capabilities, and interests. Given those divisions, the right to abstain or dissociate from one common course or another would be essential to building and sustaining consensus for union in general. The contributions and commitments of individual states would inevitably vary from one sphere of common action to another. To insist that all states proceed in lockstep would only guarantee paralysis. But willing states should also have the right to go ahead with new forms of cooperation. If they succeeded, they would create new realities that would alter the future calculations of their abstaining partners, which might well be drawn in eventually. This was the way de Gaulle explained the Franco-German Treaty of 1963, in part as a response to the failure of his earlier "Fouchet Plan" for a broader-based European confederacy.[61] Twenty-five years later, the same rationale permitted an EMU that left out four of the fifteen EU members.

The great strength of the confederal approach is that it exposes the real foundations of interstate cooperation, namely, the will and capacity of the member states to sustain and advance it. Other approaches search for a shortcut through some structural formula. Some federalists, for example, want to dismember national power to reapportion it between regional governments and a European federal center. Others—"functionalists"—emphasize how national sovereignty should be devolved to autonomous professional agencies whose scale is tailored to the needs of the function itself. Economic liberals, by contrast, "deregu-

[61] Charles de Gaulle, *Major Addresses, Statements and Press Conferences of General Charles de Gaulle, May 19, 1958–January 31, 1964* (New York: French Embassy Press and Information Division, 1964), pp. 219–221, 238–240.

late," to leave as many decisions as possible to a European or global capitalist marketplace. Confederalists, of course, have their own version of structuralism. They expect that institutions that engage nation states in continuous mutual study and bargaining can promote harmonious definitions of national interest and lead to effective common action. But their basic approach, oriented to the nation state, makes them unlikely to lose sight of the essential players, namely, the states that remain the genuine sources of popular legitimacy. It is these states that possess the political machinery for determining the different national interests, and it is these states that do much of the bargaining to harmonize those different interests. Thus, for example, while federalists in the 1960s hoped to build "Europe" by strengthening the supranational institutions of the EEC, de Gaulle emphasized instead the need for European states to change their mentality—to opt for a European rather than an Atlantic identity. Each school, of course, could fault the other for a lack of realism. Gaullists criticized supranationalists for assuming that federal structures could be efficacious without mobilizing political will through mass politics. Federalists criticized Gaullists for assuming that a political will shared by Europe's nation states could be mobilized without federal structures. Over time, as the European Union has gathered substance, the two schools have moved closer together.

De Gaulle's approach led him to focus sharply on the capacity of the French and the Germans to compose their differences and lead the others. In 1963, he and Adenauer set up the elaborate machinery of the Franco-German Treaty to root a practical partnership deeply throughout the two governments. As both statesmen anticipated, France and Germany have jointly taken the lead to develop the collective actions needed to hold Europe together and advance its common interests. Whenever the two powers have cooperated closely, Europe has tended to move forward. Whenever they have been at odds, Europe has stalled. Meanwhile, Italy has been integration's free rider and Britain its opponent. In practical terms, therefore, a European Union built on the model of variable geometry has depended on the intensity and durability of Franco-German partnership.

What are the prospects that their joint leadership will continue after the Cold War? Often depicted as the "Franco-German couple," they seem an old pair firmly settled in a marriage of convenience, both determined not to let petty differences poison their life together. Governments and bureaucracies do cooperate closely and effectively at many levels and have continued to do so through a variety of leaders. Polls indicate considerable mutual trust between the two publics, if not entirely among their elites. Nevertheless, the two governments and cultures show few signs of converging.[62] Respective views of national interest have probably grown more rather than less distinct in recent years. Reunification has created a new Germany, its population and economy roughly a third larger than France's.[63] With their capital reinstalled in imperial Berlin, some revival among Germans of their old Middle European daydreams is widely anticipated and expected to make the French marriage less convenient. In effect, the Soviet collapse has gradually returned the Germans to their whole modern history—with its old possibilities and dangers. As they grow once more dominant in Central Europe, Germans glimpse a fateful historical choice. One way leads toward traditional dreams of a Germanic *Mitteleuropa* stretching eastward; the other way leaves Germany an essentially West European country, sharing the lead in building a Westernized European Union. Naturally, Germans try to balance and conflate both aims. Inevitably, this attempt leads to contradictory tendencies in their policies and feeds French apprehensions. Probably, the French will guard their American ties more carefully as a result. Possibly, they may be more inclined to cultivate the Russians, who after NATO enlargement feel betrayed and threatened by the West. De Gaulle himself, after all, once thought the Franco-German alliance only a second-best solution. More fundamental, he once believed, was the Franco-Russian alliance, "which though repeatedly betrayed and

---

[62] For a shrewd study of the two political and cultural traditions, see Patrick McCarthy, "The Franco-German Axis from de Gaulle to Chirac," in D. P. Calleo and E. R. Staal, eds., *Europe's Franco-German Engine* (Washington, DC: SAIS, Brookings Institution, 1998). See also H. Schauer, *Europäische Identität und demokratische Tradition: Zum Staatsverständnis in Deutschland, Frankreich und Grossbritannien* (München: Olzog Verlag, 1996).

[63] For an interesting series of views on evolving Franco-German relations, see Patrick McCarthy, ed., *France-Germany in the Twenty-First Century* (New York: Palgrave, 2001).

repudiated, remained no less a part of the natural order of things, as much in relation to the German menace as to the endeavors of Anglo-American hegemony."[64]

History has moved on since de Gaulle's ruminations. Several decades of close Franco-German cooperation have obviously left their mark. Nevertheless, under present and future circumstances, differences and suspicions could easily multiply. France and Germany are economic competitors with sometimes conflicting interests. Half-suppressed but lingering dislikes and resentments are still there among their populations, perhaps especially among their elites. In Germany, a traditional Atlanticist element in the Protestant north, but also in parts of the Bavarian ruling party, the Christian Social Union (CSU), remains cynical and uneasy about the French connection.[65] Among East Germans, the French partnership, forged during the Cold War, has yet to develop much appeal. As the new eastern Länder find their voice in shaping German politics, the consequences remain to be seen. In summary, Franco-German ties are well developed and resilient and are constantly reinforced by the trends that favor European integration generally. But they are also subject to erosion and not unbreakable.

VARIABLE GEOMETRY AND EUROPEAN DEFENSE

By the late 1990s, the Franco-German couple was showing some signs of becoming a ménage à trois. Unlike the French or Germans, the British were traditionally reluctant to see a stronger European bloc. After the Soviet collapse, the British government quickly favored the Union's rapid expansion to the East, not least because of the

---

[64] Charles de Gaulle, *Salvation* (New York: Simon & Schuster, 1960), p. 728.
[65] On the diffident Franco-German couple, see Michael Stürmer, "Deux rêves dans un seul lit: Franco-German security cooperation," in D. P. Calleo and E. R. Staal, eds., *Europe's Franco-German Engine* (Washington, DC: SAIS, Brookings Institution, 1998), and Hans Peter Schwarz, "United Germany and European Integration," in D. P. Calleo and Markus Jelitto, eds., *The New Germany in the New Europe* (Washington, DC: Johns Hopkins Foreign Policy Institute, 1995).

damage it would do to integration in the West.[66] Britain's customary anti-European views had always had considerable appeal in some German circles. In the later 1990s, a pattern of Anglo-German cooperation was occasionally noticeable in financial and defense industries and sometimes seemed ostentatiously designed to exclude the French.[67] The British posture toward Europe began to change in 1997, when the Labour Party, led by Tony Blair, finally returned to power, and with a strong majority. Blair felt the country was unready to join the EMU but was concerned to end Britain's traditionally isolated and unproductive position toward the EU in general. Pressing for the Common Foreign and Security Policy was his method. Among its advantages, it capitalized on Britain's military prowess. Blair's proposals for the EU and NATO are discussed in the next chapter. Little was new about such proposals except their sudden support from the British.

---

[66] For a cogent and frank exposition of British perspectives on the prospects for European integration after German reunification, see Margaret Thatcher, *The Downing Street Years* (New York: HarperCollins, 1993), ch. 25, 26.

[67] British, French, and German relations grew tense during the various moves in 1998–1999 toward concentrating Europe's aerospace and defense industries. British Aerospace (BA) and German DASA refused to let the French government-owned Aerospatiale join them in a projected European defense alliance. Ultimately, however, the British-German merger foundered, and instead, in October 1999, Germany's Daimler Chrysler Aerospace AG merged with France's Aerospatiale Matra AS. Chancellor Schroeder and French prime minister Jospin were present at the signing of the deal in Strasbourg. Eventually, a new firm, European Aeronautic Defence and Space Company (EADS), was formed and made its first public offering in June 2000. German and French interests were 30 percent each, along with a 5.5 percent share for SEPI, the Spanish state holding company. For a time, BA remained aloof and instead merged with another British defense firm, General Electric Co., Marconi Electronics, in November 1999. See "America in Its Sights: BAE Systems Needs a US Deal to Fulfil Its Aim of Becoming the Defense Industry Leader," *Financial Times*, December 14, 1999: "British Aerospace Buying Marconi Electronics," *Newsweek*, January 19, 1999; "European Firms to Form Defense Giant," *Washington Post*, October 14, 1999; and "Pentagon Targets Europe," *CNN*, July 7, 1999. By the summer of 2000, Britain's BAE Systems joined EADS to create a new private company out of Airbus Industrie. EADS held 80 percent of the shares and BAE 20 percent, but with certain minority rights. See chapter 12, note 38; also, Kevin Done, "Partners in Adversity Get Set to Take Off," *Financial Times*, June 24–25, 2000, p. 10.

The British initiative found a warm response in France and Germany. Only time could tell whether it reflected a resolute British turning, sustainable against deep-seated domestic opposition and perhaps strong American displeasure. Doubts notwithstanding, the potential significance of such a British shift was difficult to overestimate. Of all the major spheres of collective European policy, CFSP seems the most confederal, and therefore the most dependent on variable geometry. Collective military effectiveness depends on the willingness of Europe's major governments to commit themselves to joint action. Not the least of Europe's difficulties with CFSP has been the quite different postwar military capabilities and perspectives of its major states. As discussed earlier, Britain and France emerged from the Cold War as minisuperpowers, with significant nuclear, naval and air forces. Both had professional armies capable of rapid interventions and backed up by general staffs able to act on their own. Following the Cold War, both began seriously augmenting these capabilities.[68] Germany, by contrast, came out of the Cold War with a large and well-equipped conscript army, but hobbled by various constitutional inhibitions and without a professional general staff capable of planning or conducting independent operations. As the next chapter discusses, these arrangements were deeply rooted in the postwar political culture and made it difficult for Germany to adapt to new circumstances.

Before Blair, progress toward CFSP, as well as toward actual cooperation among military forces, naturally depended heavily on the French and the Germans. Given the basic differences in their military structures and cultures, the two found it inherently difficult to develop a common policy to impose on the rest of the EU, particularly in the face of continued British opposition and recurring American diffi-

---

[68] France, Great Britain, Belgium, the Netherlands, and Luxembourg all moved toward professional armies in the 1990s, whereas the restructuring and reequipment of the German "Bundeswehr" lagged behind. Britain was a particularly vocal proponent of upgrading European defense capabilities and, with the backing of France and Italy, proposed a set of "defense convergence criteria" to concert and accelerate defense restructuring in the WEU countries. See Matthias Geiss, "Marsch ins Ungewisse," *Die Zeit*, July 29, 1999, and Theo Sommer, "Wehrpflicht oder Berufsheer?" <http://www.archiv.zeit.de/zeit-archiv/daten/pages/titel.txt.19960301.html>.

dence. German governments could expect strong resistance from large sections of the German public and also within their own military establishment. As a result, despite several Franco-German initiatives announced with great fanfare over the years, Kohl's Germany remained ambivalent about pushing the EU into a serious security role, particularly if it meant a quarrel with the Americans in NATO. After the Soviet collapse, Germany's heavy political-economic presence in Eastern Europe made it seem impolitic to feature a higher German military profile. NATO enlargement, led by the Americans, offered a plausible alternative. It seemed better that friction should develop between Russians and Americans and leave Germany to play a soothing role between the two. With Russia's future direction so uncertain, moreover, antagonizing the Americans and depending on France for nuclear protection were not particularly attractive options.

By the end of the 1990s, after the wars in Bosnia and Kosovo, a more autonomous capacity for collective security seemed increasingly significant for the EU's overall cohesion and momentum. Given the leading role of the Franco-German partnership, Germany's structured difficulties in the military sphere became a greater and greater liability for the EU in general. Defense, in other words, was becoming the Achilles' heel of Franco-German Europe. The British initiative suggested a major constitutional breakthrough, not only by bringing Britain more seriously into the confederacy, but also by taking pressure off the weakest link in Franco-German cooperation. The extent to which Blair's initiative can succeed depends, ultimately, on the evolution of the pan-European security system itself, of which more in the next chapter.

EUROPE'S CONSTITUTIONAL PROSPECTS: A SUMMARY VIEW

Since Maastricht, the European Union has been trying to widen its scope, extend its membership, and streamline its institutions, all at the same time. In the 1990s, the priority went to widening the Union's functions. At the end of the decade, EMU and CFSP were greatly advanced, if far from completed. But basic constitutional reform—the streamlining of institutions—had not greatly progressed. It remained difficult to abandon the EU's traditional hybrid structure, despite its inherent limitations. A genuinely federal Europe still seemed difficult to imagine without some overwhelming crisis, a crisis as likely to shatter unity as to advance it. Europe thus seemed fated to remain, at most, a confederacy where nation states were still the key players. The interaction of these states has, however, been growing more and more structured, and federal elements of various sorts have had an increasing place in that structure. Nevertheless, the cohesion and effectiveness of the confederacy continues to depend ultimately on consensus among its member states. The confederacy's capacity to sustain new tasks depends on how adding those tasks affect the consensus of the whole. If the new tasks serve important national interests, consensus will strengthen. But attempting ambitious common tasks can also make the limits of consensus more visible and disrupt the integration already achieved. As the EU continues into the new century, it is unclear how expanding its scope to monetary and macroeconomic policy generally will affect the consensus among its states. The ultimate consequences of pursuing common defense are still more uncertain. Whereas Europe's cohesion has traditionally depended heavily on a close working relationship between France and Germany, developing common foreign and security policies should increase Britain's role as well. It remains to be seen whether a more important role for Britain will strengthen or weaken the European Union. But doubts notwithstanding, a powerful logic seems to press the West European states into more and more intimate confederacy. In effect, they are moving to fill out the old agenda of European unity, set forth in the 1980s and enshrined in Maastricht.

At Maastricht, however, the EU also pledged to widen its membership. The list of candidates has grown steadily. Countries in Eastern and Central Europe are said to need quick and full membership in order to stabilize themselves and their neighborhoods. To argue in this way, however, risks confusing cause and effect. EU countries are stable collectively insofar as they willingly accept and fulfill common or converging policies. They do so, by and large, when these policies appear to serve their national interests and when pursuing them collectively—with constant negotiation and adjustment of differences—seems more efficacious than pursuing them separately. But the fit between the national interest of most new members and the collective interest of most old members is not at all self-evident, even for countries as advanced in transformation as Poland, the Czech Republic, and Hungary. All are still far from Western standards. Quick membership would require heavy subsidies that seem improbable and could, themselves, prove disruptive to cohesion and morale, and hence harmful to transformation, as seems to have been the case in East Germany.[69] Meanwhile, several obvious candidate states, like those of the former Yugoslavia, still have smoldering security problems. While the reward of ultimate EU membership can encourage countries to settle their differences peacefully, the EU's hybrid constitution, where differences are settled by consensus, is hardly adequate for containing severe internal conflicts. For enforcing peace in the Balkans, a more imperial structure, presumably the outcome of the CFSP and the reformed NATO to come, seems a more appropriate instrument than EU membership.[70]

In short, it seems unreasonable to expect the old forms of European Union, suitable for converging Western states, to be extended indefinitely to the East. The delicately balanced machinery seems unlikely to function with too many diverse new members. The EU will not be doing the rest of Europe any good by destroying its own cohesion. The intrinsic problems of administrative harmonization and political consensus are difficult enough without obstinately pursuing quasi-universalist policies that cannot be expected to succeed. Widening, therefore, seems likely to assume a different form from a simple extending of membership, as in the past. A tacit consensus seems to be developing that the whole process will take a long time and will require more heterogeneous structures of participation and governance.

---

[69] Transfers of more than a trillion DM in the aftermath of unification, though aimed at promoting the transformation of the East German economy and raising the living standard in the new Länder, has, perversely, eliminated the competitive advantage of East German products and led to a partial deindustrialization of the region. See P. J. Smith, ed., *After the Wall* (Boulder, CO: Westview Press, 1998), pp. 109–139. Bringing in West German owners and managers has alienated and demoralized many people in the East.

[70] For intimations of a permanent occupation, see, for example, David Rohde, "Kosovo Seething," *Foreign Affairs*, vol. 79, no. 3, May–June 2000, pp. 65–79.

These stubborn realities suggest some obvious practical conclusions. The EU in its present form cannot stretch itself to include countries like Turkey and Ukraine. It certainly cannot include Russia. If it cannot include Russia, it should be careful about how it includes the Baltic states. These prohibitions have nothing to do with the worthiness of the peoples in question, or with their intrinsic capacity for a liberal and prosperous future. They have to do with the limits of the consensus-building powers of the West European confederacy. For those countries whose economic, cultural, and strategic attributes make them possible candidates for the EU, realistic economic and political criteria should be set. Aid, investment, market access, and political persuasion should obviously be targeted toward reaching those criteria. For nearly all candidates, success will not come quickly. Nor should full membership.[71] Expansion will undoubtedly change the EU. As it grows more heterogenous, it will either disintegrate or grow more imperial in character. As Jacques Delors has rather belatedly observed, the bigger the periphery, the greater the need for a strong core.[72] Whatever the apparent forms, few if any of the new members—and indeed not all present members—will ever belong to the EU's inner governing core.

---

[71] Firm institutional connections can nevertheless exist throughout a long transition, or indefinitely. Following the Rome Treaty, Art. 228, 238, the European Economic Community concluded numerous association agreements with groups of third countries— former overseas dependencies of Union members, Mediterranean countries, and, most recently, Central and East European countries. The agreements establish privileged economic relations between the Union and the associated countries and aim to promote political, economic, and societal transformation toward democracy and a market economy. See F. Algieri, "Assoziierungspolitik," in W. Weidenfeld and W. Wessels, eds., *Europa von A–Z* (Bonn: Bundeszentrale für politische Bildung, 1997), pp. 69–71. Association agreements have been conceived of either as a preparatory step toward full membership in the Union or as compensation for nonmembership. The form of association could be elaborated to provide a real alternative to full membership. A council of association with the right to review and be heard on all the Union's internal directives would be an obvious practical step. The idea of such a council was suggested long ago in Georges Berthoin, "The European Union in a Changing World: New Perspectives and Challenges," in David P. Calleo and Philip H. Gordon, eds., *From the Atlantic to the Urals* (Arlington, VA: Seven Lakes Press, 1992).

[72] See note 57 above.

Meanwhile, Pan-Europe has its own imperatives, which the states of the European Union share, and for which they have major responsibilities. While a larger pan-European structure may well be needed, it seems unlikely that the European Union can, itself, become that Eurasian system. It seems not the European Union's destiny to rule Eurasia. Rather, it is to rule itself, and thereby to make its own vital contribution to a larger Eurasian system. In short, the EU's primordial task is to solidify Western Europe, failing which there can be no satisfactory Pan-Europe.

By pretending to an expansion of its own membership that seems implausible, the EU not only risks its own hard-won cohesion but it also risks impeding progress toward building further institutions for Pan-Europe. These institutions will also take time. Not only must the EU itself evolve further, but so must Russia, the United States, and the transatlantic relationship generally. Arguably, Russia will have to become a more normal country and certainly the EU must complete itself sufficiently to permit a more equal military alliance with the United States. The latter seems the obvious purpose of Europe's current drive to achieve a Common Foreign and Security Policy, as well as the European Security and Defense Project (ESDP) that has followed in due course. Here again, the EU is conditioned by the need to sustain its confederal consensus. New functions should be clearly in the interest of the member states and thereby should strengthen the confederacy's inner cohesion. The present case for CFSP is that Europe's interest now requires it, in other words, that Europe is no longer adequately served by remaining an American military protectorate. Whether that is really so, and what kind of European security system should emerge, is the subject of the next chapter.

Unfinished Business II:
Security after the Cold War

COLD WAR ANOMALIES

A CONFEDERACY WHOSE members are unwilling to defend each other's territory seems hard to take seriously. Yet the founding document of Europe's postwar confederacy, the Treaty of Rome, carried no security obligations.[1] In reality, the creators of the EEC were profoundly concerned with security. But their focus was not on the current threat—the Soviet Union—but on what was considered the perennial threat: the risk that Europe's major states might turn on each other once more. The early Community was particularly anxious about a renewal of Franco-German conflict. Meanwhile, the original six EEC partners were all members of NATO and covered by an American protectorate. Europeans felt free to let the Americans manage the Soviet threat of the present, while they built a community of their own to preclude the fratricidal threats of their past. This division of labor also left the EEC free to concentrate on advancing Europe's economic security, not least against its American military protector. Given the nature of the Soviet threat and the availability of the Americans, this otherwise schizophrenic specialization seemed to Europeans an optimal arrangement, even if the anomalies periodically troubled Europeans and Americans alike.

The whole arrangement worked well enough, but the end result was a marked asymmetry in postwar transatlantic development. Western Europe's confederal economic bloc, under Franco-German leadership, became a major force in the world economy, rivaling the United States and not afraid to contend with it. But Europe's collective secu-

---

[1] On the Treaty of Rome and the early institutional development of the Community, see Paul Minet, *Full Text of the Rome Treaty and an ABC of the Common Market* (London: Christopher Johnson, 1962), and Richard Mayne, *Postwar: The Dawn of Today's Europe* (London: Thames & Hudson, 1983).

rity remained under the Americans in NATO, even though several European states had substantial military forces of their own.[2] As discussed in chapter 10, military asymmetry developed among the major European states as well. Britain and France became serious nuclear powers with conventional forces capable of acting beyond Europe. Germany had no nuclear forces and, while possessing an impressive conscript army, lacked a general staff to give it the capacity for independent use outside NATO. In any event, Germany's federal constitution appeared to inhibit using military forces for purposes beyond the direct defense of home territory.[3]

EARLY REACTIONS TO SOVIET WITHDRAWAL

When the Soviets withdrew from the middle of Europe, they also negotiated arms agreements that made it impossible for them to return rapidly. Shortly thereafter, the Soviet Union collapsed entirely.[4] Its successor, the Russian Federation, inherited most of the still huge if progressively dilapidated Soviet nuclear arsenal, along with an increasingly demoralized army. This new Russia was very different

[2] In 1985, for example, French military forces totaled 464,300, British 327,100, and German 478,000. The United States had 2,151,600. See *The Military Balance, 1999–2000* (Oxford: Oxford University Press for the International Institute of Strategic Studies, 1999), p. 300, and also David P. Calleo, *Beyond American Hegemony* (A Twentieth Century Fund Book; New York: Basic Books, 1987), pp. 153, 162.

[3] Starting with the recruitment of 1955, the traditional interpretation of Germany's Basic Law restricted German forces from any activities except defense obligations under NATO. See Stephen F. Szabo, "Security Implications of a Unified Germany," in William D. Wharton, ed., *Security Arrangements for a New Europe* (Washington, DC: National Defense University, 1992).

[4] On November 19, 1990, at the CSCE meeting in Paris, NATO and Warsaw Pact members signed a major treaty on conventional armed forces in Europe. This Conventional Forces in Europe (CFE) agreement limited the deployment and equipment of the two alliances and entered into force on July 17, 1992, after verification procedures had been agreed on. In September 1991, the Soviet Union itself was dissolved. See Michael Mandelbaum, *The Dawn of Peace in Europe* (A Twentieth Century Fund Book; New York: 20th Century Fund Press, 1996).

from the old. It was at least protodemocratic; its government was relatively friendly to the West and heavily dependent on its aid. Under the circumstances, the need and legitimacy of an American military protector for Europe was no longer self-evident.[5] A large part of America's European forces withdrew during the Gulf War and did not return thereafter. United States forces stationed in Europe dropped from over 400,000 in 1990 to roughly 120,000 in 1998 and remained at that level for the rest of the decade. United States defense budgets also began falling rapidly—by roughly one-third in real terms in the decade after 1988.[6] Some American analysts questioned the need for continuing NATO at all.[7] Many suggested major alterations in its character—away from its rigidly hierarchical command structure to one designed to accommodate an autonomous European "pillar."[8] Europeans seemed to be preparing themselves for some such arrange-

[5] NATO's Alliance Strategic Concept, adopted in November 1991 at Rome, invited East European countries to meet regularly with NATO members in a North Atlantic Cooperation Council (NAAC) and also in meetings on civil defense and environmental issues. Even though it was recognized implicitly that the Soviet threat had disappeared, the new Alliance Strategic Concept continued to support NATO's integrated defense, substantial U.S. forces in Europe, and reliance on nuclear weapons "to make aggression incalculable." France complained that NATO was impeding the building of a European Security and Defense Identity. Tensions ran high and President Bush declared at one point, "If you don't want us in Europe, tell us now and the US will leave." See Stanley R. Sloan, *NATO's Future: Beyond Collective Defense*, McNair Paper 46 (Washington, DC: National Defense University, 1995).

[6] In 1985, U.S. defense spending was $403 billion dollars; in 1998, it was $259 billion (in constant 1998 dollars). *The Military Balance 1998–1999* (Oxford: Oxford University Press, 1998), p. 16. For my own earlier analysis, see David P. Calleo, "A New Era of Overstretch?" *World Policy Journal*, vol. 15, no. 1 (Spring 1998), pp. 11–26.

[7] See, for instance, Richard Ullman, *Securing Europe* (A Twentieth Century Fund Book; Princeton: Princeton University Press), especially pp. 54–62. For a general discussion, see Michael Mandelbaum, op cit., especially ch. 9.

[8] See, for example, David P. Calleo, *NATO: Reconstruction or Dissolution?* (Washington, DC: Johns Hopkins Foreign Policy Institute, 1992). For the likelihood of a European pillar see David G. Haglund, *Alliance within the Alliance? Franco-German Military Co-operation and European Pillar of Defense* (Boulder, CO: Westview Press, 1991), and William C. Cromwell, *The US and the European Pillar: The Strained Alliance* (Houndsmill, UK: Macmillan Academic and Professional, 1992).

ment. The 1980s had seen various experiments with European military cooperation—leading eventually to a Eurocorps outside NATO.[9] The Treaty of Maastricht, unlike the Treaty of Rome, set collective security as a specific goal for the European Union.[10] Generally, Europeans cut military spending less than the Americans, although European levels were, of course, lower to begin with (see table 14.1).

Meanwhile, President Bush's failure to win reelection in 1992 appeared to confirm America's declining interest in foreign policy and

[9] The heart of the Eurocorps was a Franco-German brigade established in 1988, which became operational in 1990 with roughly 4,000 troops. Troops from Belgium, Spain, and Luxembourg were added over the next six years. The Eurocorps reflected the French view of a two-pillared NATO. Assigned to NATO for Article V contingencies, the Eurocorps was also intended to be the basis for a European army to address security issues without depending on NATO or the United States. Eurocorps' relationship to NATO was formalized in December 1992, and its role as a multinational force under the auspices of the Western European Union was confirmed in May 1993. See Vigleik Eide, "The Military Dimension in the Transformed Alliance," *NATO Review*, vol 2, no. 4 (1994).

[10] At Maastricht, it was agreed on to establish a Common Foreign and Security Policy (CFSP), although Title V and Article J of the treaty both promised more than was actually produced. The CFSP was to be one of the pillars of the European Union, although Article J1 is careful to refer to "the Union and the member states" defining and implementing a CFSP, a clue to its intergovernmental nature. The objects (Article J1) were not surprising: promoting common values, interests, and the independence of the Union; strengthening security; promoting international cooperation; and enhancing democracy. These were to be pursued by systematic cooperation between member states and the gradual implementation of "joint actions," where the member states have common interests. Perhaps the crucial section is Article J4, in which it was agreed that CFSP "shall include all questions related to the security of the Union, including the eventual framing of a common defense policy, which might in time lead to a common defense." This section implicitly distinguishes between a common defense policy and the more expansive idea of common defense envisaged by Jacques Delors. "Decisions and actions of the Union which have defense implications" were subcontracted to the WEU, which is to "elaborate and implement" decisions of the Union. This arrangement could be read to separate CFSP among the twelve from defense in the WEU or NATO. But since the WEU is also described as an integral part of the EU, the separation seems limited. See Trevor Salmon, "The Union, the CFSP and the European Security Debate," in Juliet Lodge, ed., *The EC and the Challenge of the Future* (New York: St. Martin's Press, 1994), p. 265.

TABLE 14.1
Defense Spending as Percentage of GDP

	U.S.	France	Germany	Italy	United Kingdom
1985	6.5	4	3.2	2.3	5.2
1995	3.8	3.1	2	1.8	3.1

Source: The Military Balance 1998–1999 (Oxford: Oxford University Press for the International Institute for Strategic Studies, 1998), p. 306.

new priority for domestic rejuvenation.[11] Falling military outlays played a large part in America's rapid progress toward a balanced budget, which turned out to be the principal achievement of the Clinton administration's first term.[12] Given the overall direction of American policy, devolving responsibility for European defense to the Europeans themselves seemed a logical American geopolitical strategy. That logic was reinforced by the developing strategic picture in Asia, where rising Chinese power seemed bound to increase U.S. involvement.[13] While the Pentagon's official defense planning showed little sign of any such coherent strategy, Clinton's own speech before the French National Assembly in June 1994 blessed efforts to create more autonomous European structures, and appeared to open the way for a more European NATO.[14]

[11] See Pamela Constable, "The Issues of the Campaign of 1992: Foreign Policy," Boston Globe, October 7, 1992. See also David P. Calleo, "A New Era of Overstretch? American Policy in Europe and Asia," World Policy Journal, vol. 15, no. 1 (Spring 1998).

[12] See chapter 11, note 34.

[13] For a general discussion, see Michael Mandelbaum, The Strategic Quadrangle: Russia, China, Japan and the United States in East Asia (New York: Council on Foreign Relations Press, 1995). See also David P. Calleo, "A New Era of Overstretch?" World Policy Journal, op. cit.

[14] In Paris, Clinton said the United States supported Europe's autonomous efforts to curb the rise of "militant nationalism" in Bosnia and elsewhere and, in general, approved European attempts at integration, noting that "America wishes a strong Europe, and Europe should wish a strong America," and encouraged its leaders to enlarge the European Union eastward. See <http://www.pub.whitehouse.gov/urires/ I2R?urn:pdi://oma.eop.gov.us/1994/6/7/16.text.1>. See also Maureen Dowd, "Clinton

THE YUGOSLAV CRISIS

Ending the Cold War did not end Europe's security problems, but it transformed their character. After the Soviets withdrew and collapsed, many parts of Eastern Europe and Central Asia experienced an efflorescence of ethnic conflicts, banditry, organized international criminality, and general lawlessness. For Europeans, the most spectacular new security problems occurred in the multiethnic federation of Yugoslavia—created after World War I to connect Serbia with Slovenia, Croatia, and various other south Slavic and Muslim pieces of the disintegrated Habsburg Empire, including Bosnia-Herzogovina.[15] During World War II, the Yugoslav federation split between those who resisted and those who supported the Germans. After World War II, Marshall Tito, one of the wartime communist resistance leaders, reinvigorated federal unity, broke with Stalin, and kept the Soviets at bay.[16] In the early 1990s, after Tito had died and the Soviet Union had collapsed, the Yugoslav federation itself disintegrated. Slovenia and Croatia, both German-oriented, declared themselves independent states, their independence justified on ethnic principles. After strong pressure from Germany, the EU recognized both states. Croatia's declaration of independence led it to a showdown with Serbia. It also left Bosnia the choice of seceding or accepting vassal status within a Greater Serbia. The choice was highly divisive, since Bosnia had a Muslim majority but a large Serb population unwilling to become

---

Warns of Violent Nationalism," *New York Times*, June 8, 1994, and Charles Bremner, "Clinton Asks Europe to Join Crusade for Security," *New York Times*, June 8, 1994.

[15] For the origins of the Yugoslav wars, see Laura Silber and Allan Little, *Yugoslavia: Death of a Nation* (New York: TV Books, 1996), and Noel Malcolm, *A Short History of Yugoslavia* (London: Macmillan, 1994). Both reject the view, argued influentially by Robert Kaplan in *Balkan Ghosts* (New York: Vintage, 1994), that the wars represent primarily the revival of ancient ethnic hatreds rather than the machinations of post-Tito politics. Kaplan's argument is alleged to have shaped President Clinton's perspective on the conflict. See Richard Holbrooke, *To End a War* (New York: Random House, 1998), p. 22.

[16] For a general overview of Yugoslavia under Tito, see Richard West, *Tito and the Rise and Fall of Yugoslavia* (New York: Carroll & Graf, 1995), and Nora Beloff, *Tito's Flawed Legacy* (Boulder, CO: Westview Press, 1986).

a minority in a new state. As a consequence, the Muslim leadership's decision to hold a referendum on independence led the Serbian leadership in Bosnia to launch a ruthless war of ethnic cleansing, backed by the Yugoslav army. Bosnia's Croats, backed in turn by Zagreb, joined in Bosnia's dismemberment. The large Muslim population, lacking an armed state of its own, was relatively helpless. Atrocities were widespread and flagrant.

By August 1992, European political leaders had decided to intervene. Within a few months, roughly 6,000 foreign troops were in Yugoslavia, mostly British and French soldiers in Bosnia. The European intervention did undoubtedly save many lives and lead toward an eventual settlement, but it appeared painfully inept, mainly because Europeans were unwilling to establish the military ascendancy needed to catalyze a diplomatic breakthrough. Indeed, European troops came close to being treated as hostages by the local warring parties, in particular by the Serbs. Meanwhile, unspeakable barbarity prevailed under the noses of the forces sent to prevent it.

There were numerous causes for Europe's weak performance.[17] European forces were acting under a problematic UN mandate that imposed numerous inhibitions.[18] The major European states were con-

[17] For critical American interpretations of the European performance in Bosnia, see Warren Zimmerman, *Origins of a Catastrophe* (New York: Times Books, 1996), and Richard Holbrooke, *To End a War* (New York: Random House, 1998). For European perspectives, see David Owen, *Balkan Odyssey* (Orlando, FL: Harcourt Brace, 1995); Jonathan Eyal, *Europe and Yugoslavia: Lessons from a Failure* (London: Royal United Services Institute for Defence Studies, 1993); and Carl Bildt's review of Holbrooke's book: "The Search for Peace," *Financial Times*, July 2, 1998, p. 16. For indictments of the response of the international community as a whole, see James Gow, *Triumph of the Lack of Will: International Diplomacy and the Yugoslav War* (New York: Columbia University Press, 1997), and Mark Dunner's series of articles in the *New York Review of Books* on November 20, 1997; December 4, 1997; December 18, 1997; February 19, 1998; March 26, 1998; and April 23, 1998. For the later stages of the war, see David Rhode, *Endgame* (New York: Farrar, Straus & Giroux, 1998), and *Unfinished Business: Report of the International Commission on the Balkans* (New York: Carnegie Endowment for International Peace, 1996).

[18] Established in February 1992 as an interim arrangement in Croatia, the United Nations Protection Force (UNPROFOR) had as its initial mandate to secure UN-protected areas and later, as the conflict spread to Bosnia-Herzegovina, to monitor

fused about their own purposes and divided among themselves. Britain, for example, committed a substantial number of troops but was ambivalent about using them forcefully, particularly under European or UN rather than NATO auspices. The Germans, mindful of their excesses in the region during World War II, and eager to affirm their reformed identity as a civilian power, refused to send combat forces at all. With the British diffident and the Germans absent, the French, despite considerable forces and mounting chagrin, were not prepared militarily, politically, or economically to attempt to impose a solution on their own. European forces were thus not in Bosnia to fight, but to get in the way of the real combatants, by providing relief services and ambiguous protection to hapless civilians caught in the middle. The best hope for such a policy was that the warring groups would tire of the killing and agree on how to divide the territory. Europeans could speed the process with a combination of bullying and bribery.

The United States played an unhelpful role, one that displayed the ambivalence of its post–Cold War foreign policy in its worst light. While absent militarily, the United States was very much present diplomatically. American propaganda encouraged Muslims to reject any settlement based on partitioning Bosnia. This did little to help resolve the situation, since it was soon obvious that an integrated Bosnia could only be imposed and sustained by *force majeure*. No one was prepared to provide such force, least of all the Americans. But the Europeans, undermined by their own divisions as well as by American meddling, could not broker an agreement for partition. Meanwhile, the position of their troops began to deteriorate to the point where they were unable to ensure their own safety, paralyzed as they were by conflicting mandates and national policies. Prodded by an exasperated Chirac, the Americans finally sent ground forces, mobilized NATO, and took charge.[19] Led by the Americans, NATO mar-

---

ceasefires and ensure the delivery of humanitarian aid. Authorized to use force in self-defense and to coordinate with NATO over the use of airpower, its lack of appropriate combat capabilities, small size, and emphasis on neutrality rendered it incapable of carrying out its commitments. In March 1995, the UN Security Council replaced UNPROFOR with three independent peacekeeping forces. <http://www.un.org/Depts/dpko>. See also Warren Zimmermann, op. cit., p. 224.

[19] Clinton's decision to commit serious American forces to Yugoslavia came indi-

shaled an impressive display of force; the fighting in Bosnia was halted, and the Dayton Accords imposed de facto partition, dressed up as a Bosnian federation.[20]

Europeans grumbled that Dayton's solution was not substantially different from the partition they had themselves proposed a couple of years earlier in the Vance-Owen Plan.[21] At the time, American misgiv-

---

rectly, in the form of a pledge that American troops would help extricate the lightly armed UN peacekeepers if necessary. After the hostage crisis at the end of May 1995 (and reconfiguration of the UN force in Bosnia), the United States realized the growing likelihood that the United Kingdom and France might withdraw in November. Newly elected French president, Jacques Chirac, publicly indicated that French troops would not remain in Bosnia for another winter without a more positive mandate. Clinton finally realized that the imminent breakdown of the UNPROFOR mission meant that U.S. ground forces would, in fact, have to go in to Yugoslavia. See Richard Holbrooke, *To End a War*, op. cit., pp. 65–68.

[20] The Dayton Agreement (November 21, 1995) marked the end of four years of war. According to the treaty, Bosnia remained a sovereign state with internationally recognized borders but was divided into two entities—the (Muslim-Croat) Federation of Bosnia and Herzegovina, with 51 percent of the territory, and the Serb Republic, with the rest, except for Sarajevo, which attained the status of a unified city. The central government consisted of a collective presidency of three persons elected by direct vote—one in the Serb Republic and two in the federation, with a bicameral parliament, consisting of a fifteen-person upper chamber and a forty-two-person lower house. Representatives in the former were to be selected from the assemblies in the districts and in the latter by direct elections from the two parts of the country. The Dayton Agreement provided for a peace implementation force (IFOR), consisting of a sixty-thousand-member NATO-led international force. In contrast to the limited rules of engagement that regulated the UN's peacekeeping operation in Bosnia during the war, IFOR could use decisive force against anyone violating the ceasefire agreement. See Ed Vulliamy, *Season in Hell: Understanding Bosnia's War* (New York: St. Martin's Press, 1994).

[21] The Vance-Owen plan, unveiled in January 1993, proposed that Bosnia-Herzegovina would retain the outward form of a republic but would be divided up into ten autonomous provinces, loosely bound and under a weak central government. The provinces would be ethnically based—Serb, Croat, and Muslim—but would not have any "international legal personality" enabling them to "enter into agreements with foreign states"; that is, Croat provinces could not accede to Zagreb nor Serbian provinces to Belgrade. The country was defined as a "decentralized state" made up of "constituent peoples," with "most government functions carried out by the provinces." The republic "would be progressively demilitarized under UN/EC supervision." The plan was praised by its supporters as a workable compromise between the

ings had stiffened the Muslims to oppose it, although they did acquiesce in the end. The delay, however, undermined the European strategy for isolating and pressuring the Serbs, who never did accept the European scheme. There were, however, some critical differences in the later American plan agreed to at Dayton. Dayton preserved a veneer of Bosnian unity that was easier for the Muslims and their American supporters to accept. Two years of ethnic cleansing, moreover, had simplified the boundary questions. Dayton's actual ethnic divisions were large blocks of contiguous territory rather than the checkerboard of cantons proposed by the earlier Vance-Owen Plan. Dayton's agreement was also significantly favored by military developments. Just before Dayton, the Croats, loosely allied with the Muslims, had taken the offensive and were in the process of decisively defeating the Bosnian Serbs, who consequently were ready for a settlement.[22] When the Americans and NATO entered the fray, moreover, they used impressive air strikes on the reluctant Serbs. These, together with sustained artillery pounding by an Anglo-French Rapid Reaction Corps, helped create a sense of overwhelming military dominance. This sense, no doubt, greatly speeded up the settlement. By contrast, before the United States entered the scene militarily, the European forces presented as the United Nations Protection Force (UNPROFOR), had never made an impressive display of power. Consequently, the European mediation was never taken seriously.

Each side took away different lessons. Europeans had vivid evidence of their need for an effective Common Foreign and Security Policy but also a forceful reminder of the difficulties among themselves in agreeing on one. Although greatly irritated by the Ameri-

---

declared aims of the international community and what was politely called "recognizing the realities on the ground." Its critics said it legitimized past ethnic cleansing and cleared the way for more. The Vance-Owen plan is described and defended in David Owen, *Balkan Odyssey* (Orlando, FL: Harcourt Brace, 1995), pp. 89–149.

[22] On August 4, 1995, Croatian troops, blessed by the U.S. government, conducted a successful blitzkrieg to drive the Serbs out of the Krajina. For a description of the events leading up to Dayton, in which U.S. bombing combined with substantial gains by the Croats and Muslims at the expense of the Bosnian Serbs, see Richard Holbrooke, *To End a War*, op. cit., ch. 3.

cans, Europeans also realized the conveniences of having them around. Among the Americans, success at Dayton seemed to swell a new wave of triumphalism. Only Americans, it was said, could lead a Western coalition to success.[23] The Clinton administration had always sported a low-grade Wilsonian rhetoric that implied hegemonic ambitions. But given the country's apparently low priority for foreign policy and its inhibitions about the use of its own troops, the rhetoric was hard to take seriously. After Dayton, however, the policy began to imitate the rhetoric. Gradually, American hegemony was forcefully reasserted in NATO. American misgivings about an independent European pillar strengthened and NATO failed to devolve more of its commands to the Europeans. The French, who had earlier seemed ready to reenter NATO's military structures, remained formally aloof from them.[24] Meanwhile, American triumphalism took on an economic as well as a military dimension. Europe's economies were in particular difficulty during the early and middle years of the 1990s. As the American economy boomed, the president began lecturing the world on its comparative virtues.[25]

NATO ENLARGEMENT

Probably the most significant sign of new assertiveness in American foreign policy was the American decision to press for extending NATO membership to East European countries, despite vehement Russian opposition. Initially, the Americans had been reserved about opening NATO membership to East Europeans. Although prolific with schemes for associating former Soviet states with the alliance,

---

[23] See Richard Holbrooke, *To End a War*, op. cit., p. 215.

[24] See Elizabeth Pond, *The Rebirth of Europe* (Washington, DC: Brookings Institution, 1999), p. 83, and also Jonathan Marcus, "Adjustment, Recrimination: Franco-U.S. Relations and the New World Disorder," *Washington Quarterly*, vol. 21, no. 2 (Spring 1998), pp. 17–32.

[25] See, for example, President Clinton's statement during the G7 meeting in Nova Scotia, Canada, in June 1995, <http://www.pub.whitehouse.gov/uri-res/I2R?urn:pdi://oma.eop.gov.us/1995/6/16/2.text.1>, or "A Balkanisation of the Group of 7," *New York Times*, June 18, 1995.

like Partnership for Peace, early schemes had been careful to include the Russians themselves. The mood shifted in 1993 and was signaled in President Clinton's July 1994 Warsaw visit, where he spoke favorably of Poland's NATO aspirations.[26] After Dayton, and particularly during the presidential campaign of 1996, Clinton made early NATO enlargement a major administration project.[27]

From without, U.S. proposals seemed almost calculated to outrage the Russians. Even assuming that some form of NATO enlargement was required, there were several options. To begin with, if the alliance was to be expanded, there was a logical case for inviting Russia itself to join. NATO would thereby become a cooperative European "security community" including Russia, rather than a Western alliance opposing Russia.[28] Short of this, inviting Poland, the Czech Republic, and Hungary to join could be presented as a simple rectifying of Stalin's historic mistakes—a once-for-all restoration of East-West borders artificially altered by the Cold War. The West would merely be reclaiming the old crown lands of Austria, together with a Poland whose postwar borders had already been shifted radically westward. Conceivably, Slovenia, Slovakia, and even Croatia could eventually follow, with the same rationale. Sooner or later, Romania and Bulgaria, and even the rest of former Yugoslavia and Albania might also be construed into membership, on the grounds that they needed stabilizing and were of little interest to the Russians.

[26] In an anxiously awaited speech before the Polish Sejm on July 7 1994, President Clinton said, "[NATO] expansion will not depend upon the appearance of a new threat in Europe. . . . We are working with you . . . in part because the United States believes that when NATO does expand, as it will, a democratic Poland will have placed itself among those already ready and able to join . . . we will not let the Iron Curtain be replaced with a veil of indifference." See *USIS WF*, July 8, 1994.

[27] On October 22, 1996, President Clinton announced "America's goal": "By 1999, NATO's 50th anniversary and ten years after the fall of the Berlin Wall, the first group of countries we invite to join should be full-fledged members of NATO." See *USIS WF*, October 22, 1996.

[28] See, for instance, Richard Ullman, *Securing Europe*, op. cit. For a general discussion, see Michael Mandelbaum, op. cit., especially ch. 7. For the Clinton administration's attitude, see, inter alia, President Clinton's "Statement on NATO Expansion," <http://www.pub.whitehouse.gov/uri-res/I2R?urn:pdi://oma.eop.gov.us/1997/5/14/5.text. 1>. American policy was that Russia might eventually join but meanwhile be a partner with "a voice in, but not a veto over NATO's business."

To have any chance of soothing the Russians, however, such a policy would presumably have to renounce explicitly expansion to countries the Russians have historically regarded as vital to themselves. Such countries include most former territories of the Soviet Union, notably the Baltic States, Belarus, and Ukraine. Far from issuing any such reassurances, President Clinton, after inviting in the Czechs, Hungarians, and Poles, himself toured Eastern Europe to promise further openings and went out of his way to signal his enthusiasm for including the Baltic States.[29] The American government, meanwhile, was ostentatiously cultivating close military relations with Ukraine and several Central Asian states and was also embroiled in schemes for oil pipelines in the Caucasus and Central Asia, all more-or-less designed to reduce Russia's influence in regions where it had been predominant since the eighteenth century.[30]

Once taken up by the Americans, NATO expansion proved difficult for anyone else in the West to oppose. Like EU expansion, it was a

---

[29] "Clinton Promises to Seek NATO Membership for Baltics," *Washington Post*, January 17, 1998.

[30] The United States signed a range of defense cooperation agreements with Central Asian states that have been the basis for arms sales and military exercises, including U.S. participation in CENTRAZBAT, the Central Asian peacekeeping battalion. See, for example, the agreement signed with Kazakhstan in November 1997, reported by Linda D. Kozaryn in "U.S., Kazakhstan Increase Military Ties," *American Armed Forces Information Services*, November 1997, <www.defenselink.mil.news/news/Nov1997/n11261997_9711262.html>. Catherine McArdle Kelleher, then deputy assistant Secretary of Defense for Russia, Ukraine, and Eurasia, stated during Exercise Central Asian Battalion '97, "The United States' interest in this area is a recognition of the need for its independence, sovereignty and stability. The Partnership for Peace gave a framework and justification for having more direct and extensive contacts." Quoted in Douglas J. Gillert, "U.S. Ventures Cautiously into Former Soviet Territory," *American Armed Forces Information Services*, September 1997 <www.defenselink.mil.news/news/Sep1997/n10061997_9710063.html>. For authoritative defenses of Western incursions into Russia's near abroad, see, inter alia, F. Stephen Larrabee, *Ukraine's Place in European and Regional Security* (Santa Monica, CA: RAND, 1998, RAND reprints, RAND/RP-748), reprinted from Lubomyr A. Hajda, ed., *Ukraine in the World: Studies in the International Relations and Security Structures of a Newly Independent State* (Cambridge: Ukrainian Research Institute, Harvard Papers in Ukrainian Studies Series, 1998), and Wolfgang Ischinger, "Not against Russia: Security and Cooperation in the Baltic Region," *Internationale Politik* (February 1998).

policy with wide if superficial appeal. East European governments were pressing hard to be included, and Western countries felt benevolent toward the East Europeans and more than a little guilty about their harsh fate throughout the twentieth century. The Germans seemed particularly insistent on rolling NATO's "carpet of stability" eastward.[31] The French, whatever their real thoughts, felt they could not afford to seem less enthusiastic.[32] As West European countries began to calculate the costs and other difficulties of EU expansion, enlarging NATO began to seem a providential diversion.

ALIENATING RUSSIA

NATO expansion was bound to outrage the historic sensibilities of Russians and make them afraid for the future. No historic great power could be expected to react otherwise to such a military intrusion into its adjacent areas. To make matters worse, Russians were bound to see these moves as a direct violation of promises made at the time of German reunification.[33] The Russians, after all, had withdrawn from

---

[31] The first major Western political figure to advocate NATO enlargement openly was the German defense minister, Volker Rühe, who declared in early 1993, "Eastern Europe must not become a conceptual 'no-man's land.' . . . I cannot see one good reason for denying future members of the European Union membership in NATO"— and argued, furthermore, that NATO membership could even precede EU membership. Volker Rühe, "Shaping Euro-Atlantic Policies—A Grand Strategy for a New Era," Alastair Buchan Memorial Lecture at the International Institute for Strategic Studies, London, March 26, 1993. Kohl took longer to be persuaded. See Elizabeth Pond, *The Rebirth of Europe*, op. cit., pp. 65–69.

[32] France showed marked coolness toward enlargement of the alliance—particularly just prior to NATO's Brussels summit of January 1994, where enlargement was accepted by all sixteen heads of state and government. This opposition continued but was perhaps mellowed by the prospect that the European Security and Defensive Initiative (ESDI) would change the nature of NATO. See Pascal Boniface, "NATO's Enlargement, France's Dilemma," in David G. Haglund, ed., *Will NATO Go East?* (Washington, DC: CSIS, 1998).

[33] The issues of whether a united Germany would continue to remain in NATO, whether NATO forces would be stationed in the old GDR, and how the NATO and Warsaw Pact confrontation of the Cold War might be transformed into a cooperative

their empire voluntarily. For the United States and Germany to act thereafter as victors forced the Russians to acknowledge that they had been defeated. The Russians were thus denied a useful myth, not altogether false, that they had themselves created the new Europe by freeing their empire abroad at the same time as they had freed themselves at home. Presumably, such a myth would make it easier for them to accept the new Europe that had resulted. Arguably, this would have been a better basis for Europe's long-term security than an enlarged NATO. Instead, the West seemed intent on collecting its gains, like Stalin after World War II.

Whatever their feelings, Russians in the 1990s were in no position to confront the West head-on. Any serious show of force, even if they had been capable of it, would have been counterproductive, as it would merely have rejuvenated the Cold War's old anti-Russian alliance. Russia's would-be reformers desperately wanted Western credits and investment. But NATO's enlargement nevertheless created rankling grievances.[34] Over time, the West could only lose by antagonizing Russia. Even in its weakened state, it remained a nuclear superpower. Extending NATO guarantees to Eastern Europe after the Cold War was potentially a more formidable commitment than defending West Germany during the Cold War, when NATO's boundaries in

---

pan-European security system ran all through the various talks leading to German reunification in 1990. Much of the discussion was over whether, after reunification, NATO troops could be stationed on the territory of what had been the GDR. It was in the context of these discussions about a broader mutual security system that Gorbachev ultimately accepted that united Germany should have full sovereignty and remain in NATO if it wished. Agreement was announced at the end of bilateral negotiations between Kohl and Gorbachev during July 1990. See Stephen F. Szabo, *The Diplomacy of German Unification* (New York: St. Martin's Press, 1992), ch. 7; also, Philip Zelikow and Condoleezza Rice, *Germany Unified and Europe Transformed* (Cambridge: Harvard University Press, 1995), p. 270.

[34] Even in the short term, there were formidable opportunity costs to the West. The Russian Duma, for example, began to hold back approval of arms control treaties highly advantageous to the West—far more so, some experts thought, than any putative advantage from adding new members to NATO and modernizing their armies. See Michael E. Brown, "Minimalist NATO: A Wise Alliance Knows When to Retrench," *Foreign Affairs*, vol. 78, no. 3 (May–June 1999), pp. 204–218.

Central Europe were relatively short and precisely defined.[35] Only a modest Russian economic and political recovery could easily render NATO's extended military position in Eastern Europe overexposed and vulnerable. A responsible American foreign policy would presumably not undertake such commitments unless prepared to create a military structure to make them effective. To act otherwise would run unbearable risks of future wars, quite possibly nuclear. Was NATO really prepared to launch a nuclear war over a disputed Polish border, a civil war in Ukraine, or a Russian intervention to stop ethnic fighting in Latvia? Or did NATO plan to maintain sufficient conventional capabilities to overawe the Russians in their own neighborhood? American policy seemed based on the assumption that Russia was finished as a great power, a dubious historical wager.[36]

The way NATO enlargement was conducted not only threatened to create a major long-term security problem with Russia but also greatly reduced the West's capacity to manage Europe's more immediate security problems, for which Russian cooperation was hard to dispense with. This grew clear in the second Yugoslav war of the 1990s—NATO's conflict with Serbia over Kosovo. Before returning to the later Yugoslav crisis, however, it seems useful to consider the global implications of NATO enlargement—in particular its "strategic dissonance" with American and European security interests in Asia.

ASIAN REPERCUSSIONS OF NATO ENLARGEMENT

Traditionally, Russia is not only a great power in Europe but also a great power in Asia. NATO enlargement thus carried significant im-

---

[35] Even the cost of modernizing the armies of the new NATO members is considerable. Countries in the throes of economic transformation presumably have other urgent uses for their scarce resources. In its zeal for boosting NATO enlargement, however, the Clinton administration assumed not only that the military implications would be slight but that the West Europeans would, in any event, bear a large part of the costs. Neither assumption was plausible. See David G. Haglund, *Will NATO Go East?* (Ottawa: Center for International Relations, 1996).

[36] For a discussion of the U.S. lead in land forces, see Colonel Volney J. Warner, "Technology Favors Future Land Forces," *Strategic Review* (Summer 1998), pp. 40ff.

plications for American policy in East Asia. As in Western Europe after World War II, America's leading strategic role in the Asian region was partly explained by the need to prevent the malignant revival of an indigenous great power. Japan, like Germany, was coaxed to renounce nuclear weapons by American promises to extend its own deterrent.[37] As in Europe, extending deterrence in Asia was seen to require "flexible response"—providing conventional options—and was expensive. Indeed, the United States actually fought two conventional wars in Asia. It was only partly successful in Korea and failed in Vietnam. Matters grew easier for the United States in the 1970s, as China and the Soviet Union were quarrelling and the United States was able to play one off against the other.

With the ascendancy of Deng Xiaoping in the 1970s, however, China partially opened its economy and began growing very rapidly, according to its own singular model of authoritarianism tempered by

[37] In 1951, the United States led forty-seven other nations into signing a formal peace treaty that restored Japan's sovereignty but imposed a "Peace Constitution" that bars Japan from waging war or maintaining a standing army. During the same year, the United States also negotiated the U.S.-Japan Treaty of Mutual Security and Cooperation, which entered into force in 1952 and committed the United States to protecting Japan in case of war, while providing for the continuation of U.S. military bases in Japan. The Japanese have frequently invoked their imposed "Peace Constitution" to resist building up or contributing military forces for peacekeeping missions. Nevertheless, Japan was one of the last countries to sign the Nuclear Non-Proliferation Treaty in 1970 and did not ratify it until six years later, after the United States promised not to interfere with Tokyo's pursuit of independent reprocessing capabilities in its civilian nuclear power programs. Japan's level of military spending remains well below the international average, however. In 1998, Japan spent just 1 percent of GDP on defense, a lower proportion than any NATO country with the exception of Luxembourg. See Selig S. Harrison, *Japan's Nuclear Future* (Washington, DC: Carnegie Endowment Foundation, 1996), and Lauren Wylie, *Destinies Shared* (San Francisco: Westview Press, 1989), p. 23; see also *The Military Balance, 1999–2000* (Oxford: Oxford University Press for the International Institute of Strategic Studies, 1999), pp. 300, 302. In absolute accounts, however, Japanese expenditure, at $36.99 billion, was reckoned to be slightly larger than that of China ($36.709 billion), Britain ($36.613 billion), or Germany ($32.387 billion) and only slightly below that of France ($39.807 billion). For a general assessment of Japanese policy, see "Japan Still Floundering," *Strategic Survey, 1999/2000* (Oxford: Oxford University Press for the International Institute of Strategic Studies, 2000), p. 205.

anarchy. By the end of the twentieth century, China had become a giant on the move—full of conflicting forces and tendencies. Within the early decades of the twenty-first century, it could become the world's largest economy.[38] The frenetic social changes that accompany such growth raise questions about China's political stability. Many analysts are also worried about its growing military spending and technological capacity.[39] There nevertheless seems no reason to assume, a priori, an implacable Chinese hostility to the West, let alone a mindless and self-destructive expansionism. But the potential threat is sufficient to require reasonable precautions. China seems more likely to develop in a fashion benign for its neighbors, and for itself, if contained within a balanced regional security system. The aim of an American containment policy is presumably not to threaten China, but to encourage it to follow a path of peaceful engagement with its neighbors. Arguably, it is in China's interest to be reliably "contained." A mutual security system with Russia, Japan, India, and the United States ought to allow China enough room for maneuvers to protect its own interests. From a Chinese perspective, of course, a satisfactory regional system must deter not only China but the United States and Japan. Accordingly, China has been developing an increasingly formidable strategic nuclear force, aimed presumably at containing the United States. By the start of the new century, American plans

[38] China, growing steadily at a rate of 8–9 percent annually, tripled its GNP in less than two decades. Some observers believe that China's total economy will surpass that of the U.S. early in this century. See Dwight Perkins, "How China's Economic Transformation Shapes Its Future," in Ezra Vogel, ed., *China-US Relations in the Twentieth Century* (New York: American Assembly, 1994), ch. 4, and William Overholt, *The Rise of China* (New York: Norton, 1993), p. 54.

[39] Analyses of Chinese military power are contentious since the country does not fully divulge its defense-related military expenditure. The official military budget does not account for the 600,000-strong People's Armed Police, nuclear weapons procurement, some defense-related research and development, and soldiers' pensions. The International Institute for Strategic Studies (IISS) concludes that the actual defense spending is at least four times greater than the official figure. By this reckoning, China's military spending is equivalent to Britain's. China's official budget for 1999 was 105 billion yuan ($12.6 billion), an increase in real terms of 13 percent over 1996. IISS, *The Military Balance, 1999–2000* (Oxford: Oxford University Press, 1999), p. 175. See also note 37 above.

for a significant antimissile defense system (National Missile Defense) against "rogue states" threatened to lead to a more rapid Chinese strategic buildup.[40]

Assuming that China does sustain an effective nuclear deterrent, America's regional strategy should logically shift from nuclear to conventional forces—from strategic deterrence to flexible response. The United States will not want to be constrained to rely primarily on its strategic deterrent in order to protect its regional interests in Asia. But containing China through conventional forces will grow progressively more expensive for the United States, and impossible without major regional allies. During the Cold War in Europe, it was Germany that provided the manpower for flexible response. Like Germany, Japan is without nuclear weapons. Nevertheless, Japan seems unlikely to risk alienating China by replicating Germany's Cold War role.[41] Geopolitically, Russia seems America's natural Asian ally, all the more useful because it has a long history of close relations with India. Russia's position in Asia is highly vulnerable. Its huge territorial acquisitions of the eighteenth and nineteenth centuries are populated mostly by people of Sinic or Turkish origin, with only a thin veneer of indigenous Russians. The Chinese population in these Russian domains has been increasing rapidly, fed by migration.[42] If

[40] China has consistently opposed such a U.S. national missile defense system (NMD) on the grounds that it would undermine China's deterrent capability. See Erik Eckholm, "China Warns of a Buildup if U.S. Erects Missile Shield," *International Herald Tribune*, May 12, 2000. For discussion of a possible U.S. alternative to NMD, see also Theodore Postol, "Hitting Them Where It Works," *Foreign Policy*, no. 117 (Winter 1999–2000).

[41] As the two largest democracies and market economies in the Asia-Pacific, the United States and Japan presumably share basic security objectives. Nevertheless, Washington and Tokyo are bound to reconsider their long-standing arrangements, especially if Korea unifies and China continues to grow. A security arrangement based primarily on American troops in exchange for Japanese money is unlikely to be sustainable, and the Japanese have begun to debate their security options. See Mike M. Mochizuki, "The Strategic Quadrangle and Japan," in Michael Mandelbaum, ed., *The Strategic Quadrangle: Russia, China, Japan, and the United States in East Asia* (New York: Council on Foreign Relations Press, 1995).

[42] The population on the Russian side of the border is 6 to 8 million, and on the Chinese side up to 120 million. For the view that demography makes a reconstruction

Russia's weakness makes Siberia a huge prize for whoever can grab it, stable peace in the region will be elusive.

Whereas Russian-Chinese relations were openly hostile in the 1970s, by the 1990s the two were aligning together against the United States. Better Sino-Russian relations are not, in themselves, harmful to Western interests. What is not helpful to Western interests is good Sino-Russian relations stemming from their mutual hostility to the United States. A Russian-American entente in Asia is unlikely if there is serious conflict between the two powers elsewhere. If it is a priority for the United States to balance China in Asia, then it should also be a priority not to antagonize Russia unnecessarily in Europe. In short, aggressive NATO enlargement seems counterproductive for America's East Asian policy. This is not to say that American policy should give Asian security priority over European. If the Russians were ready to overrun Western Europe, the United States would have little choice but to defend its NATO allies. But after the Soviet retreat and collapse, embodied in the arms agreements of the Gorbachev era, Russia in the 1990s did not and, realistically, could not pose any immediate military threat to its West and Central European neighbors. In short, it remains difficult to understand the rationale for American policy toward Russia in the 1990s. To have carelessly alienated Russia seems a profound mistake. It also seems unworthy. The post–Cold War era began with an exceptional act of creative and generous statesmanship from the Russians themselves. It is difficult to take pride in the American response. American statesmanship seems to have been a good deal more enlightened at the beginning of the Cold War than after its end.

While Europe's states are only marginally involved in East Asian security arrangements, Europe nevertheless has a vital interest in their success. It would be hard for Europe to escape the unhappy consequences of a general Asian war involving the United States and China. Nor can Europe easily detach itself from the strategic fate of

---

of the China-Russia anti-U.S. alliance of the 1950s unrealistic, see Joseph S. Nye, "China's Re-emergence and the Future of the Asia-Pacific," *Survival* (Winter 1997–1998), and Richard Bernstein and Ross H. Munro, *The Coming Conflict with China* (New York: Knopf, 1997).

Russia. A liberal, prosperous, friendly, and cooperative Russia in Europe seems unlikely if its Asian regions are in turmoil.

EUROPEAN REACTIONS: REJUVENATING CSFP

Europe's maladroit handling of the Bosnian crisis, coupled with America's maladroit handling of Russia, powerfully reinforced European motives for creating the machinery for a Common Foreign and Security Policy (CFSP). As described in the last chapter, the Amsterdam Treaty of 1997 called for establishing a single spokesman for the foreign policy of the EU states—a Monsieur PESC—who would be endowed with a planning staff and also serve as the European Council's secretary-general. In September 1998, a fresh advance for CFSP came from an unexpected source: the British. Prime Minister Blair met with the new German chancellor, Gerhard Schroeder, and they issued a joint declaration favoring an autonomous European defense capability within NATO. A few weeks later, Blair's intensive conversations with President Chirac at the Channel port of St. Malo resulted in a joint declaration along similar lines. British and French governments thereafter began intensive consultations to develop proposals for both the EU and NATO. The war in Kosovo appeared to increase support for such proposals. Among European governments, the security issue was coming to the fore.

The ideas Blair was promoting had been around for a long time. The European Union was to endow itself with machinery for collective decision making in foreign and security policy, as well as its own mechanism for planning military operations and coordinating military forces. This European machinery would generally operate as the "European pillar" within NATO, where it would be under the formal command of the American Supreme Allied Commander (SACEUR). But the European forces would also be capable of acting either within the NATO framework or outside it in cases where the Europeans wished to act and the Americans did not care to involve themselves; NATO's assets might be "borrowed" for such purposes.[43] NATO,

---

[43] Tony Blair and Jacques Chirac, *Declaration on European Defense, UK-French Summit, Saint-Malo, 3–4 December 1998* (available from the French Embassy in the

meanwhile, would change its own structures according to the European Strategic Defense Initiative (ESDI), designed to modify the old hierarchical command structure in order to facilitate ad hoc coalitions.[44] Europe's defense apparatus might also contribute to peacekeeping efforts of the UN Security Council—where Britain and France are, of course, permanent members—or of the Organization for Security Cooperation in Europe (OSCE). The British initiatives also emphasized the need to consolidate Europe's defense industries, so that they could compete successfully with the American giants in the tighter armaments market after the Cold War.[45]

UK <http://www.ambafrance.org.uk>). EU foreign and security policy also dominated the Cologne Summit, held on June 3–4, 1999, at which Javier Solana, former NATO secretary-general, was appointed High Representative for Common Foreign and Security Policy. The summit made little other progress, however, beyond an agreement to incorporate the WEU into the EU by the end of 2000. See Martin Walker, "Cologne Summit Ducks the Big Issues," *Manchester Guardian Weekly*, June 5, 1999.

[44] The concept of a European Security and Defense Identity (ESDI) has never been fully defined. It encompasses both a political concept and new operational capabilities and arrangements. As a concept, ESDI implies the end of the Cold War's closely integrated and hierarchical command structure. It means a bifurcated NATO structure, with European members empowered to consider problems together, formulate their own distinctive collective policies, and act together to carry them out—with or without American participation. Ostensibly, this more autonomous European capability is not meant to weaken NATO's military solidarity. Thus, the United States formally supports ESDI, as the means to upgrade the European component of the North Atlantic Alliance, as agreed on in NATO's ministerial meeting in Berlin in 1996. Whether the EU can create an effective military capability for carrying out collective military interventions without American leadership and assets, or indeed, whether such a melange of diverse states can express an effective security "identity" at all, remains to be seen. See Holly Wyatt-Walter, *The European Community and the Security Dilemma, 1979–1992* (London: Macmillan, 1993), and Philip Gordon, *The US and the European Security and Defense Identity in the New NATO* (Paris: Institut Français de Relations Internationales, 1998).

[45] In recent years, the U.S. government has encouraged a series of mergers in the American defense industry. For an analysis, see Amy J. Boatner, "Consolidation of the Aerospace and Defense Industries: The Effect of the Big Three Mergers in the United States Defense Industry," *Journal of Air Law and Commerce*, vol. 64, no. 3 (Summer 1999), and, Ann R. Markusen, *The Economics of Defense Industry Mergers and Divestitures* (New Brunswick, NJ: Rutgers University Center for Urban Policy Research, 1997). Europeans together spend roughly 60 percent of the American de-

European Trends Reinforced: War in Kosovo

The final year of the 1990s saw another outburst of large-scale ethnic persecution in Yugoslavia—this time in the Serbian province of Kosovo. Serbs considered Kosovo the cradle of their national identity. For generations, however, its population has been predominantly Albanian and the province had enjoyed an autonomous status within Serbia and the Yugoslav federation. By the 1980s, the demagogic Serbian politician Slobodan Milosevic was using the grievances of Kosovo's Serbian minority to bring himself to power in Serbia and Yugoslavia. Once installed in Belgrade, Milosevic abolished Kosovo's autonomy, sent in troops to discourage resistance, and ran the province for the next ten years as a virtual colony. Albanians were dismissed en masse from state jobs, and the Albanian-language university was shut down. For most of this time, Kosovar Albanians resisted nonviolently, under the direction of their pacifist "president," Ibrahim Rugova. By late 1997, however, a guerrilla movement had emerged. In response, the Serbs began systematically terrorizing Albanian villages. The rationale was that the Kosovo Liberation Force (KLA), nourished from Albania, was threatening the Serbian minority and planning to detach the province. Serbian repression soon drove even moderate Albanian leaders to demand independent status.

---

fense budget, but their capabilities for projecting power are proportionately much less. Nominally, the Europeans have collectively more soldiers, ships, and combat aircraft than the United States. But several countries—Germany and Italy are notable—have large draft armies that are difficult to use for external interventions and whose cost precludes the development of professional forces. European procurement policies would presumably be more efficient if coordinated, and European defense industries could be more competitive if consolidated and merged. Efforts in this direction have been under way for several years, with some impressive results toward the end of the 1990s, but also many disappointments. See John Deutch, Arnold Kanter, and Brent Scowcroft, "Saving NATO's Foundation," *Foreign Affairs*, vol. 78, no. 6 (November–December 1999); "Europe Gets a Defence Giant," *The Economist*, October 16, 1999; "Make Us One but Not Now," *The Economist*, April 25, 1998; also "European Industrial Restructuring," *Armed Forces Journal International*, vol. 136, no. 1 (1998). For Europe's burst of defense industry mergers in mid-2000, see chapter 12, note 40.

Western governments had long been aware of the situation's explosive potential among neighboring states and regions—not only in chaotic Albania but also in Macedonia, another fragment of the Yugoslav federation with a delicate ethnic balance. As the situation continued to deteriorate, British and French governments, collaborating closely with the Americans, attempted to impose a settlement at the Rambouillet Conference of February 6, 1999.[46] The idea was to leave the province nominally part of Serbia but to restore local autonomy and to station Western forces there to protect the inhabitants. The Serbs rejected the arrangement and continued to terrorize the local Muslim population. As it had threatened to do, NATO opened an aerial campaign against all of Serbia.[47]

The immediate results were not what NATO planners had hoped for. The Serbian army stepped up its terrorism, which sent a million Kosovar Muslims flooding into surrounding countries: Albania, Macedonia, and the Yugoslav republic of Montenegro. Civilian mass suffering reminiscent of World War II forced the West to mount a colossal relief effort. As NATO intensified the bombing and attacked civilian as well as military targets throughout Serbia, there was widespread public unease in most Western countries. But whatever their private misgivings, major NATO governments remained firmly in support of the intervention, although against strong public protests in Germany and Italy. Other states in the Balkan region, notably Hungary, Romania, and Bulgaria, also supported NATO, again against strong domestic opposi-

---

[46] The plan drawn up by the West insisted that Kosovo remain part of Yugoslavia for at least three years and be run by "democratically accountable institutions" with a legislature, executive, and judiciary of its own. The cultural and religious rights of all communities would be guaranteed, although Kosovo would be under the control of ethnic Albanians. An international force of twenty- to thirty-thousand peacekeepers would enforce the agreement. On the legacies of the Rambouillet conference for the future of Kosovo, see Michael Mandelbaum, "A Perfect Failure," *Foreign Affairs*, vol. 78, no. 5 (September–October 1999).

[47] The Americans mainly conducted the air campaign, with significant British and French participation. The European air force deployed in Kosovo was estimated to be around 20 percent of the total. The French contribution alone was 14 percent. See David Owen, "France Backs Defense Criteria," *New York Times*, June 17, 1999. For interallied and internal U.S. differences, see Wesley K. Clark, *Waging Modern War* (New York: Public Affairs, 2001).

tion.[48] Professional criticism of the military intervention sprouted on all sides. Even among many firmly convinced that the West should not tolerate Serbian behavior in Kosovo, the air campaign, with its random destruction of civilian targets, not only in Kosovo but also in Serbia, was seen as repugnant and all the more grotesque because it seemed unable to stop the Serbian terror against the Kosovo Muslims. Many critics of the exclusive air campaign, including several members of the American Congress, called for NATO to send ground troops to Kosovo. But despite months of preparation, NATO seemed to lack either the plans or the forces for such an action. It was clear that the Clinton administration was reluctant to use its own ground forces and was resisting any NATO ground campaign.[49] Instead, the official American position was that the air bombardment would break Serbian military power and morale and thereby permit the return of the Muslim Kosovars to their homes. The British government, while faithfully supporting the air campaign, also began publicly demanding a forcible ground intervention. West European troops began massing on Kosovo's external borders.

Differences among the allies reflected a diffuse undercurrent of anti-Americanism all along the political spectrum, not only in Western Europe but elsewhere as well. Russian public opinion was angrily opposed to the whole intervention. So were the Chinese.[50] Russia's unease began to have tangible consequences, as the Yeltsin government began vigorously trying to mediate a settlement between the Serbs and NATO. On June 10, 1999, the Serbs, prodded by the Russians, agreed to withdraw their military forces from Kosovo. Western troops began to occupy the province. These troops included an American contingent,

---

[48] For repercussions of the Kosovo war on bordering states, see John Tagliabue, "Crisis in the Balkans: Repercussions," *New York Times*, May 12, 1999, and Gustav Niehbur, "NATO and the New Loyalties in the Balkans," *New York Times*, April 12, 1999.

[49] On the debate over ground troops in Kosovo, see Paul Rogers, "Lessons to Learn," *World Today* (August–September 1999) and Wesley K. Clark, *Waging Modern War*, op. cit.

[50] For a lucid and informed analysis of the Chinese response to the Kosovo crisis, see Lanxin Xiang, *The Chinese Military: Problems of Modernization*, PSIS Occasional Paper No. 3 (Geneva, 1999).

and all were under NATO military command. The Russians insisted on a military role for themselves but balked at NATO command. Complicated separate arrangements were agreed on. The Serbian armed forces left as promised, but the Western forces pledged to replace them were slow to arrive. Albanian refugees, however, returned much more rapidly than expected, while the Serbian inhabitants mostly fled. The beleaguered UN was meant to be overseeing care for the refugees and was in charge of civil administration, including police forces to protect the remaining Serbs. But the UN's police and civil administrators were scarce, in good part because many of the countries that had promised to pay for them, in particular the United States, did not do so. As a result, the Muslim guerrillas had their way in much of Kosovo. Reprisals were common, while Western forces that tried to intervene were often attacked. As in Bosnia, de facto partition began to seem more and more likely.[51]

The EU, meanwhile, began discussing various plans for reconstructing the whole Balkan region. Preliminary estimates of the costs were high, and the United States had made it clear that EU countries would be expected to bear the major share.[52] The prospects were uncertain at best. Serbia's President Milosevic was under indictment as a war criminal, and the United States balked at aid plans including Serbia until Milosevic was gone.[53] Serbia's central position in the regional economy, however, greatly limited the relevance of development plans that left it out. By the fall of 2000, the Serbian electorate was ready to vote Milosevic and his party out of power. His successor, Vojislav Kostunica, was himself a vigorous nationalist but seemed a considerable improvement. Nevertheless, the future was filled with difficulty. For a start, relations had deteriorated badly between Serbia and Montenegro, the other remaining member of the federation. Meanwhile, UN authority was not established firmly in Kosovo. Many European states were

---

[51] See Jane Perlez, "Kosovo's Unquenched Violence Dividing U.S. and NATO Allies," *New York Times*, March 12, 2000.

[52] For a discussion, see Michael Emerson, *Redrawing the Map of Europe* (New York: St. Martin's Press, 1998).

[53] On May 23, 1999, the International War Crimes Tribunal indicted Milosevic on charges of "crimes versus humanity and violation of the laws or customs of war." See <www.state.gov/www/regions/eur990527_Kosovo_indictment.html>.

apparently reneging on their commitments of forces and aid, while many other countries, including the United States, were sharply restricting the use of the forces they did provide. The Clinton administration had seemed bent on keeping Kosovo out of the headlines until after the November 2000 election. The new president, George W. Bush, had talked during the campaign of removing American forces from the Balkans. Very possibly, the wars of Yugoslav succession are not yet over.

Lessons of Kosovo

In many respects, the whole Kosovo episode seems a cautionary tale for American pretensions to continuing military hegemony in Europe. Despite the apparent success of NATO's bombing campaign, a general deterioration of transatlantic relations seems to have followed. Arguably, the Clinton administration made two fundamental errors, one military and one diplomatic. Militarily, it engaged American forces and credibility without adequately analyzing the probable consequences of the instruments it chose. Using excessive means, unable, by their very nature, to achieve the limited ends being sought, was bound to displease and alarm publics in Europe and all around the world. Bombing from the air and refusing to engage on the ground were widely seen to reflect triumphalist America's technological and military arrogance, combined with its lack of organic attachment to European affairs. Diplomatically, the administration made another fundamental error. It allowed the United States to appear in charge of what ought properly to have been presented as a European initiative. Americans resisted justifying the intervention as a pan-European project, in part because this would have implied a greater role for the Russians. Some European leaders, notably Javier Solana, NATO secretary-general, did try to portray the intervention as a European regional initiative.[54] But such efforts were studiously ignored by the Americans and, more sur-

---

[54] See Javier Solana, "Kosovo Is a Defining Moment for Europe's Future," *International Herald Tribune*, April 17–18, 1999, p. 6.

prisingly, by the British as well.[55] In dismissing a European regional justification for intervention, the United States seemed itself to be asserting a new hegemonic right—to intervene wherever and whenever it pleased, on behalf of an international community and code of conduct whose definition was America's own special prerogative.[56] Prime Minister Blair's Gladstonian language reinforced these global pretensions, while neglecting the opportunity to make any kind of European regional case instead. In short, the Kosovo intervention was presented by friend and foe alike within the framework of triumphalist American globalism. Strong reactions from Russia and China, and from among the Europeans themselves, were hardly surprising.

Both these military and diplomatic errors were typically American. The military campaign reflected recurrent professional fantasies where invincible airpower and high-tech weaponry permit interventions with low risk to American forces themselves. The accompanying diplomatic rationale reflected the administration's own triumphalist neo-Wilsonian rhetoric about the indispensability of American leadership. Thanks to this maladroit diplomatic presentation, NATO's courageous intervention to stop barbarous genocide in Europe, initially pressed on the Americans by the British and the French, was widely depicted as an essentially American project, reflecting the universalist pretensions of the world's "hyperpower."[57] Both the military and the diplomatic mis-

---

[55] For an account of Blair's call for a new international structure for global crises and his declaration that NATO was to become the military wing of the new world order, see Hugo Gordon, "America Wowed by a 'Tony' Blair," *Daily Telegraph*, April 24, 1999.

[56] The unilateral claims were all the more galling to some since they followed the American campaign to block the creation of the International Criminal Court—thus showing, it seemed, U.S. disdain for multilateral attempts to define the international community and its codes. See Michael Mandelbaum, "A Perfect Failure," op. cit.

[57] In a speech at the Institut Français des Relations Internationales, the French foreign minister Hubert Vedrine described the United States as a hyperpower, whose supremacy extended to every aspect of the world's economy, technology, language, and culture. The United States now saw itself as the victor of history, chosen to propagate democracy everywhere. Not surprisingly, the rest of the world might see this as a pretention to global hegemony. See Lara Marlowe, "A Greater UN Role to Counter the US Hyperpower," *Irish Times*, June 13, 1995. For another version of the same speech, see Hubert Vedrine, *Speech at Franco-Indian Conference*, New Delhi, Febru-

takes reflected characteristics of current American institutions and political culture that limit the capacity of the United States to conduct an appropriate foreign policy.

The Kosovo intervention revealed a further basic defect of American and European diplomacy in the 1990s: the failure to construct a pan-European security system with a secure place for Russia. Ironically, it was Russia's diplomatic intervention that allowed the Serbs to withdraw and the Western bombing campaign to end. Thus, the whole Kosovo experience suggested the West's need for Russian cooperation in creating a stable new European system. Unfortunately, it also suggested how much NATO enlargement had alienated Russia from the West.

EUROPEAN SECURITY: LONGER TRENDS

NATO's Kosovo intervention may well prove a significant moment in the evolution of European security cooperation. Several critical appointments in 1999 suggested that the adaptation of European institutions was entering a more decisive phase. NATO's secretary-general during the Kosovo intervention, the able Spanish Socialist politician Javier Solana, was named the European Union's Monsieur PESC. He was succeeded at NATO by Britain's secretary of state for defense, George Robertson—a forceful figure closely identified with Blair's proposals for a serious European pillar in the alliance. The European Commission itself installed a new president, Romano Prodi, the prime minister who, in 1998, had skillfully led Italy into EMU. A number of major trends were pushing European states toward more military coordination among themselves and a more self-reliant position in relation to the Americans. Typically, Europe's integration advances in spheres where states find collaboration enhancing their national prospects and their real sovereignty. Intra-European military cooperation developed very little during the Cold War because European states found the Atlantic Alliance a superior alternative. The Soviet threat from Eurasia

---

ary 17, 2000 <http://www.doc.diplomatie.fr>. Vedrine argues that the fault lies less with American strength than with European weakness and disorganization.

legitimated the heavy American presence, among Americans and Europeans both. The Soviet collapse naturally changed the whole security environment in a fashion that lessened the value of American hegemony. Europe's new security problems—terrorism, drugs, gangsterism, and ethnic guerrilla warfare—were more internal police problems than the traditional military challenges of the Cold War.[58] They were internal to Europe, increasingly so as the EU enlarged. It is uncomfortable to have the management of the EU's internal security problems directed by an outside power, however friendly. Without the Soviet threat, the legitimacy of American leadership is no longer self-evident. As Kosovo suggests, the United States will probably not be very good at managing Europe's new problems. Coping with them successfully requires a broader range of resources—political, economic, diplomatic, and cultural—than the United States is likely to make available.

Not only does the United States lack the assets needed to continue its hegemonic role in European security, but it also increasingly lacks the national constitutional arrangements that would permit such a role to be exercised with success. Domestically, the United States is not organizing itself for a hegemonic world role. America's domestic politics give little encouragement to those who expect its leadership abroad to be professional, constant, and oriented toward long-term perspectives. Exercising America's world role successfully depends heavily on a strong presidency. The attacks on the presidency during Clinton's second term were part of a pattern recurring since the late 1960s. The earlier Reagan and Bush administrations were also handicapped by multifarious legal investigations challenging them for unconstitutional behavior—usually over foreign policy.[59] Starting with Franklin Delano Roosevelt, the United States has had a long cycle of presidential ascendancy in the constitutional balance—a cycle greatly prolonged by the Cold War.

[58] See Alessandro Politi, *European Security: The New Transnational Risks*, Chaillot Paper no. 29 (Paris: Western European Union Institute for Security Studies, October 1997).

[59] On Bush and Reagan Iran-Contra problems see David C. Phillips, *Foreign Policy Failure in the White House: Reappraising the Fall of the Shah and the Iran-Contra Affairs* (Lanham, MD: University Press of America, 1993), and Cynthia J. Arrison, *Crossroads: Congress, the Reagan Administration and a United America* (New York: Pantheon, 1989).

Since Vietnam, the rest of the American political system has seemed driven to strip the presidency of those lingering wartime powers that go with the exercise of world hegemony. Without the Soviets, the American political system is merely returning to normal. The circumstances of the election of 2000 do not indicate a reversal of presidential decline.

A resurgent Russian threat would, of course, soon reverse this trend within the United States and would certainly rekindle European ardor for keeping the Americans around. Threats from the Middle East might well have the same effect. In short, while Europe's domesticated security problems are not suitable for American direction, Europe would presumably need American power to deal militarily with Soviet missile threats or a rejuvenated Saddam Hussein. But this reasoning has its limits. Europe cannot successfully resolve its security relations with the Russians simply by invoking the old Cold War alliance, even if it is still available. Now that Russia has, in its fashion, entered the world economy, it is no longer so isolated from the European system itself. Not only is the American Constitution returning to normal, but so is European geography. Europe and Russia once more discover themselves to be intimate neighbors. For many of the real security problems that confront Europe after the Cold War, Russia's political and military cooperation seems at least as useful as America's. Permitting an American-run NATO to dominate relations with Russia will be, for Europe, a strategy that carries a high risk of self-defeat. Over the long run, moreover, Russia's own economic and political success seems vital to Europe's security and prosperity. Unless Russia goes completely off the rails domestically, Europeans are likely to believe their security better served by finding a modus vivendi with Russia than by emphasizing an abrasive military preponderance. But so long as NATO's rolling enlargement and America's own exuberant military presence in Russia's "Near Abroad" are constant irritants, Europeans are likely to see the United States as more a part of their problem with Russia than as the solution to it.

Europeans are likely to entertain similar conclusions about their relations with Middle Eastern countries, which are also close neighbors geographically. America's inability to engage constructively with either Iran or Iraq, or to broker a basic deal among Israelis, Palestinians, and their neighbors, encourages Europeans to dissociate themselves from

American hegemony in the Middle East. Here again, the United States can sometimes seem less a solution to Europe's security problems than a major cause of them.

Behind all these particular considerations, a transatlantic cultural difference appears to be growing wider. Europeans, with the possible exception of the British, take a comparatively civilian view of security. In their own societies, they go to great lengths to avoid violence. When confronted with it, their usual reaction is to conciliate—to soothe away the frictions that cause it. Despite their current economic strains, Europeans continue to give priority to social consensus. When Europeans look at American society and institutions, they are deeply disturbed by the violence, institutional as well as random, that they perceive. When they consider American diplomatic and military leadership, they find it all too easy to infer a preference for force over conciliation, particularly as America's leadership in Europe is mainly structured through a military alliance. The Cold War made America's militarized leadership legitimate and appreciated. The end of the Cold War makes it less and less so.

Under such circumstances, continuing the old American hegemonic role in NATO risks growing increasingly dysfunctional. It not only promotes an unattractive stereotype of the Americans, unfair but powerful, but also encourages Europeans to avoid facing the military requirements of their new situation. America's fitful hegemony perpetuates Europe's disgruntled weakness and also its moral free riding. This mutual posturing has gone on for a long time, but without the Cold War, its potential for undermining transatlantic relations is much greater. Ideally, before the deterioration gets too serious, European states will feel pushed to take the primary responsibility for their own security.

Prospects for European security cooperation will be greatly enhanced by success with EMU. Not only is monetary union a giant step forward in integration, but managing it successfully will also require a further general streamlining of collective institutions and decision making. That process should make it easier to develop effective institutions for security cooperation as well.[60] Insofar as EMU mobilizes an economic

[60] Emma Bonino, Commissioner for Consumer Policy, EC Humanitarian Offices and Fishery in the Santer presidency, suggested a DMU—Defense and Military Union—

and financial superpower, it seems highly anomalous for the EU to remain militarily dependent on America—its principal ally but also its principal competitor. The euro also has probable consequences for America's tolerance of hegemonic burdens. A successful euro will almost certainly be the world's other major reserve currency. For international firms and investors, the size of the EU's economy and financial markets makes holding euros an obvious alternative as well as a complement to holding dollars. As the euro takes hold, it seems likely to constrain the ease with which the United States can go on finding cheap money to cover its economy's habitual deficits. It will cost the United States more to borrow on a large scale from abroad. There should therefore be increased pressure to reduce America's deficits.

During the Cold War, America's habitual external and fiscal deficits were often thought to reflect the outsized burdens of a benevolent hegemony, the heavy geopolitical burden borne on behalf of free-riding allies. As successive American administrations saw things, the United States provided the public good of common defense for the Europeans and Japanese, who failed either to provide otherwise for their own defense or to compensate the United States adequately, a view that fed the perennial debate over "burden sharing." John Connally, Nixon's secretary of the treasury in 1971, used to point out how the American "basic" balance-of-payments deficit was about equal to the exchange costs incurred by United States troops in Europe. The economics were dubious, but the political rationale was clear. The reserve role of the dollar should be used to compensate the United States for its outsized role in the common defense. Manipulating the dollar, as Nixon did, was an indirect imperial tax, needed to keep the bipolar system going.[61]

---

proceeding along formalized and incremental lines similar to EMU. While her proposals were greeted coolly, British and Italian prime ministers Tony Blair and Massimo d'Alema suggested in July 1999 that EU member states should set "convergence" criteria for defense spending, in a fashion akin to the criteria agreed on at Maastricht in the economic sphere. See Emma Bonino, "A Single European Army," *Financial Times*, February 3, 1999; also, Tom Buerkle, "A Maastricht Approach to EU Defense?" *International Herald Tribune*, July 21, 1999.

[61] See David P. Calleo, *The Imperious Economy* (Cambridge: Harvard University Press, 1982), ch. 4, and *The Bankrupting of America*, op. cit., ch. 6; and "The Strategic Implications of the Euro," *Survival* (Oxford: Oxford University Press for the

Europe's interest in monetary union dates from that era. Three decades later, the success of the euro is expected to limit America's capacity to go on imposing indirect taxation through manipulation of the dollar. Americans will increasingly demand more military burden sharing. Europeans, assuming more burdens, will also take back more power. In short, a Europe whose money is successfully challenging the dollar around the world is unlikely to remain indefinitely a U.S. military protectorate.

Do these long-term trends mean the end of the postwar Atlantic Alliance? They could, but should not, since the primordial interests and instincts of both Europeans and Americans favor continuation. The problem is to take the Alliance out of its Cold War framework and refit it for a new pan-European system, a system in which the American role is no longer so baldly hegemonic and from which the Russians are no longer excluded. Not surprisingly, however, many people's imaginations cling still to the Cold War formula. Bringing the United States into Europe kept the peace there for more than four decades. It also allowed the West European states to flourish and form today's European Union. States in Western Europe would like to continue enjoying these advantages, and states in Eastern Europe are desperately eager to share them at last. But the Soviet collapse took away the rationale for the Cold War structure. To continue the old formula now, without the Soviet threat, is to transform the alliance into something different from what it was— less stable and less desirable. Nevertheless, an alliance is still needed. While the old Soviet threat is gone, Russia and America still remain in Europe, together with the prosperous states of the European Union and the stunted states disgorged from the old Soviet Empire. Together they form Pan-Europe, within which the principal Western institutions that grew up during the Cold War—the EU and NATO—must now be redefined. The challenge is to keep the advantages that bipolar Europe made possible for the West, but without failing the challenge of Pan-Europe.

This means recasting the American alliance and also building a new cooperative relationship with Russia. To construct such a balanced

---

International Institute for Strategic Studies, Spring 1999), pp. 5–19. For the concept of the basic balance of payments, see chapter 9, note 17.

system, without endangering its own security, Europe needs autonomous and effective capabilities for managing security problems within its own neighborhood. These capabilities should permit Europe to hold up its end in a "tripolar" security system for Pan-Europe. The next chapter spells out that system further. It is a strategic model that seems in harmony with the broader economic and political trends of recent decades. On balance, these trends point toward a more plural world— the topic of chapter 16. At present, however, pluralist visions of the future are not much entertained in official Washington. There, among America's neoimperialists, the prevailing fashion is a unipolar world order, dressed up in the neoliberal rhetoric of globalism. High technology is the World Spirit driving history, and America is its agent. In recent years, this vision has been developing an important military dimension—one whose implications are a unipolar world indefinitely extended. It seems worth exploring this military vision before considering the various models for Pan-Europe presented in the next chapter.

MISSILE DEFENSE

American triumphalism of the 1990s fed itself on the belief that the United States dominated the high technology of the new era. Those who believe they possess such dominance are naturally tempted to convert it into military power, even if doing so upsets the existing geopolitical foundations for peace. Already by the 1980s, the Reagan administration's "Star Wars" antimissile defense was attempting to overturn "mutually assured destruction"—the strategic foundation of the Cold War balance. The Reagan project aimed for a protective "bubble" able to shield the United States from even a large-scale Soviet missile attack.[62] While the votaries of Star Wars were, at best, premature in their strategic expectations, the project did spawn a large number of "smart weap-

---

[62] For various contemporary views on the Reagan SDI debate, see Robert W. Tucker, George Liska, Robert E. Osgood, and David P. Calleo, *SDI and U.S. Foreign Policy*, Johns Hopkins Foreign Policy Institute (Boulder, CO: Westview Press, 1987), and Paul H. Nitze, *The Impact of SDI on U.S.-Soviet Relations* (Washington, DC: U.S. Department of State, 1986). For spending on, see Harry Waldman, *The Dictionary of SDI* (Wilmington, DE: Scholarly Resources, 1988).

ons" as ancillary by-products. These greatly augmented American capabilities in conventional warfare, an improvement demonstrated in the Gulf War and then against Serbia. Research for missile defense continued during the Clinton administration, which in its last year launched an intensive diplomatic campaign to prepare the way for deploying some kind of minimal system. Years of research had not produced anything close to the initial "bubble," and indeed, there was widespread skepticism that any defensive system could ever be effective—given the fertile possibilities for evasion. In any event, the Clinton administration was thinking about deploying only a minimal "national missile defense" (NMD). Its purpose would be to protect America's homeland against a small-scale attack from one of the various "rogue states" alleged to be developing intercontinental missiles, notably, North Korea, Iran, and Iraq. Many experts doubted that even so minimal a system would ever be reliable; many also doubted whether the various "rogues" were attempting, or could ever achieve, the capabilities alleged to be developing among them. By 2001, however, the incoming Bush administration was strongly asserting its intention to pursue the missile defense project—technically and diplomatically—with much greater resolution than its predecessor.

While the technical fate of America's NMD will probably remain undetermined for a long time, the hypothetical issues it raises have an almost infinite capacity for disturbing strategic relations between the United States, China, Russia, and Europe. To begin with, the project, once launched, can never be laid to rest. No matter how often it fails its current tests, it can always be argued that if only enough more money is spent, success will eventually follow—a view highly congenial to the Pentagon and its defense contractors, and therefore to a good part of the Congress as well. Not only is it impossible to put NMD to rest, but it also seems impossible to limit the dangers it poses to others. To foreign governments, it seems highly unlikely that NMD, once developed and deployed, will remain the minimal system envisaged in the Clinton scenarios. Many Republicans have long advocated a more ambitious system. Should the technology actually ever be developed, it seems unlikely that a Republican administration will refrain from deploying it.[63]

---

[63] In May 2000, George W. Bush, the then Republican presidential nominee, called

Even the limited system considered by the Clinton administration would significantly impair the deterrent power of China's small strategic force. Given the unstable character of geopolitical relations in the Far East, the Chinese would undertake intensive efforts to restore their deterrent. Whether America's Asian protectorates would actually be safer under these circumstances is, at best, uncertain. With the strategic nuclear balance challenged in so tense a region of the world, the risk of a nuclear war—brought on through miscalculation, desperation, or generalized paranoia—could easily escalate.

An effective large-scale American antimissile system could also sharply devalue the strategic nuclear deterrents of other major powers. It is only natural that these powers be concerned about the effects on American foreign policy. An effective strategic defense, combined with conventional superiority, conjures up visions of an all-powerful America. What would the United States do with such power? While some fear a new American isolationism, many others see a unilateralist hyperpower, able to intervene anywhere with impunity. For America's allies, as well as potential antagonists, these are disturbing fantasies. Europeans and Japanese, for example, might become geostrategic hostages—substitute targets used to deter an otherwise invulnerable United States. The Clinton administration tried to assuage anxieties of this sort by suggesting a cooperative "theater defense"— for Europe, perhaps Russia, and, in theory, even China. The technology for theater defense is different, and perhaps easier, but no one, Europeans included, relishes being dependent on technology controlled by the Americans.[64] Most share a sense of irritation and alarm

---

for a much broader version of NMD than that proposed by the Clinton administration, accompanied by large—and possibly unilateral cuts—in America's nuclear arsenal. Administration officials criticized his proposals on the grounds that extension of NMD would stimulate an arms race with Russia and China and make negotiated reductions in nuclear weaponry far less likely. See Alison Mitchell, "Bush Says U.S Should Reduce Nuclear Arms," *New York Times*, May 24, 2000, p. 1; also, Steven Lee Myers, "Defense Chief Invites Bush to Pentagon for Briefing," *New York Times*, May 29, 2000, p. A10.

[64] For the distinction between a regional "boost-phase" system and the mid-flight interceptors of the Clinton project, see Theodore Postal, "Hitting Them Where It Works," *Foreign Policy*, no. 117 (Winter 1999–2000). For a survey of the debate, see

that the Americans have shaken the relatively benign strategic climate of the 1990s, for reasons that seem frivolous or worse. For those inclined to see an increasingly hubristic character to American triumphalism, the need for a new global balance seems all the more compelling. Europeans are well aware of how much NMD is tied to technological competition in the new world economy, a struggle in which they are America's only genuine rivals.

Since the prospects for defensive missile technology are uncertain, and likely to remain so for many years, it is difficult to draw out the practical consequences for European security. In the short run, NMD will probably not have a great effect on European plans for common defense. The needs driving European states toward CSFP are immediate and much less hypothetical. After living with American reluctance to commit ground troops throughout the 1990s, Europeans are unlikely to believe that NMD will result in a new American enthusiasm for committing troops on behalf of allies. Hence, they will proceed with their own plans for CSFP, ESDI, and common defense forces. Beyond, the Europeans will hedge their bets. They will continue to link their own defense initiatives with NATO. If, however, NMD leads to a severe deterioration of relations between the United States and Russia, European reactions may be more radical. Much will depend on how the Russians play their cards. All in all, NMD seems more likely to reinforce than to diminish Europe's interest in more autonomous military capabilities, and perhaps also in a wider and more inclusive pan-European security system. The next chapter considers the possibilities for such a system.

Steven Mufson, "Threat of 'Rogue' States: Is It Reality or Rhetoric?" *Washington Post*, May 29, 2000, p. A1.

Unfinished Business III:
Organizing Pan-Europe[1]

VISIONS OF THE NEW WORLD ORDER

THE FADING AWAY of the bipolar world has sent many states into a sort of identity crisis. The travails of "transformation" have been obvious in former Soviet countries and in China and also in the West. Some Americans believe the "new world order" confers on them a protracted vocation for world hegemony. The American Century is to become the American Millennium. The public reacts with an unstable mixture of indifference, satisfaction, skepticism, and resentment. While America's political imagination is bemused by its "unipolar" scenario, many Europeans are attracted by plans for a more cohesive and independent Europe. Some Europeans are openly skeptical that American hegemony guarantees their interests now that the Cold War is over and want to reform NATO and give themselves more autonomous military capabilities. How Europe itself evolves is widely recognized to be among the major determinants of the world order that does eventually emerge. A stronger and more self-reliant Europe, together with a rapidly growing China, possibly India, and perhaps even a reinvigorated Russia, also implies a more balanced or "plural" order in the world. A pluralist paradigm thus challenges the unipolar.

These ruminations have familiar theoretical and philosophical underpinnings. The unipolar paradigm reflects a hegemonic view of global politics, according to which a benign leading power is required to bring order to an anarchic world. The pluralist vision, by contrast, shuns hegemonic "hyperpowers" and favors a variety of regional systems with a global balance and a division of responsibilities among several clusters of power. Both paradigms are infused with globalism but define it differently. Unipolar globalism emphasizes how an open

[1] A somewhat different version of this chapter was published as "Europe, Pan Europe and the New World Order," in *National Interest*, no. 63 (Spring 2001).

and democratic world often thrives in company with political, economic, and cultural hegemony—as in the Pax Britannica of the nineteenth century or the Pax Americana of the twentieth. Pluralists, by contrast, prefer what might be called a constitutionalist form of globalism, one that emphasizes the diversity of an interdependent world—with proliferating centers of economic growth, initiative, and power. Pluralists favor that diversity for its own sake and are leery of global centralization and cultural homogeneity.

In practice, the paradigms coexist and blend. And each flourishes on both sides of the Atlantic. Which vision appeals more is often a matter of historical taste and imagination—linked, of course, to all sorts of national and group interests and identities. Abstract predispositions, however, have to come to terms with geopolitical realities.

COUNTERVAILING REALITIES

The most obvious geopolitical reality at the turn of the century is the economic and military preeminence of the United States. Convinced pluralists discount that primacy and focus on longer-term trends that seem to imply a broader dispersal of power. No one really knows what the future will bring. Today's world is too complex and uncertain. Either paradigm has obvious explanatory strengths but also particular vulnerabilities. America's inner limitations as a hegemonic power bring the unipolar paradigm into question. American economic strength seems undermined by the country's big and rising external deficit. The growing significance of the euro suggests that financing that deficit in the future may be more costly and disabling. The size and longevity of the deficit suggest that America's economy is structured so that it habitually absorbs more than it produces. Earlier, this apparent structural imbalance could be explained by the heavy military burdens of the Cold War. Now it can only be ascribed to chronic low saving and excessive consumption, frequently topped up by excessive investment at home or overseas. These habits are hard to give up, and others depend on them. Not only does lowering consumption and investment lower living standards and growth, but much of Asia's prosperity depends on America's trade deficit. The United States is said to be the world's "buyer of last resort." Continuing the U.S. deficit addiction requires regular heavy financing from abroad. Thanks in good part to the international role of the dollar, the financing has generally been easy to arrange. Most recently, it has been provided by a huge influx of foreign capital investing in the United States. The pricking of the stock market bubble early in 2001 suggests the impermanence of this particular form of easy finance.[2]

The United States also has broader handicaps for the role of world hegemon.[3] Impulses toward "isolationism" and "unilateralism" are deeply rooted in the political culture. Constitutional arrangements, which limit the power of the federal executive and the professional civil service, make it difficult to sustain balanced, coherent, and well-administered long-term policies, sensitive to the needs of other countries. The United States, of course, has conducted a hegemonic foreign policy with notable success through a good part of the past half century. But this policy required a severe distortion of the American Constitution—a dramatic extension of presidential power, provoked by the shocks of two world wars and the prolonged Cold War that followed. Since the late 1960s, the country has been drifting back to its traditional balance. Doubtless, the problems of the Clinton presidency were rather special, but nearly every other presidency since the days of Lyndon Johnson and Richard Nixon has had its own variety of constitutional imbroglio. The other constitutional elements—the Congress, the courts, and the states—have been banding together to cut the imperial presidency down to size. Given the circumstances of the recent presidential election, the new Bush administration seems unlikely to reverse a trend that reaches back over seven of its predecessors. In short, although visions of world hegemony may beguile large sections of America's political elites, the country generally has less and less tolerance for the burdens and discipline needed to exercise such a role. In such circumstances, it is all too easy for enthusias-

---

[2] For the author's more extensive discussion, see "The Strategic Implications of the Euro," *Survival* (Oxford: Oxford University Press for the International Institute for Strategic Studies, Spring 1999), pp. 5–19.

[3] See the author's "The U.S. Post-Imperial Presidency and Transatlantic Relations," *International Spectator*, Istituto Affari Internazionale (Rome: Fratelli Palombi), vol. 35, no. 3 (July–September 2000), pp. 69–79.

tic elites to get overextended, with commitments that the country will prove unwilling to sustain.

Overextension, of course, is the fatal vice of any hegemony. America's long-term strategy for avoiding it has been to build up a genuine European "partner." In effect, this strategy is a way of synthesizing unipolar and pluralist visions of the future. A strong European Union, able to take primary responsibility for maintaining peace in its own space, could relieve the United States of a heavy burden and free resources for maintaining order elsewhere, most notably in Asia. This is not because Asia is more important to the United States but because Europe has the makings of an indigenous balance, whereas Asia does not. Arguably, the principal impediment to this hegemonic-pluralist synthesis has been not America's opposition but Europe's own lingering disunity. The end of the Cold War, however, has created a new Europe, waiting to be pulled together. The European Union has ambitious plans to do the pulling. But like America in the world, the European Union risks overextending itself in Europe with commitments that its own political structure will not sustain. Various American interests, meanwhile, have started worrying about losing military hegemony in NATO and show signs of a growing hostility to these European initiatives. If the West is not careful, its American and European halves, both overextended, will end up defeating each other. The alliance will suffer accordingly. The way to avoid such a tragically stupid outcome is to devise a new European system with realistic roles for the European Union and for the United States. *Realistic* means in harmony with the essential characteristics and interests of each. America has its limitations but so, of course, does Europe.

THE NEW EUROPE'S VULNERABLE STRENGTH

Rivalries among the European states have dominated most of modern history—never more than in the first half of the twentieth century. Supposedly, today's European Union has put an end to the old quarreling Europe. But the EU has a very particular constitutional character, formed within the bipolar system of the Cold War. A realistic view of the EU's future role depends on a realistic view of its inner character.

As chapter 8 discusses at length, from the beginning there have been four models for Western Europe's constitution: "Atlantic Europe," "Federal Europe," "Gaullist Europe," and "Nobody's Europe." Today's European Union has evolved as a hybrid product of all four. With the EU, Europe has given birth to a new political form, a sort of Hegelian synthesis between a centralized continental government and a multinational state system. Europe's states have created this union not to give up their national sovereignty but to enhance it. Since these states are intimately interdependent, their national domestic or foreign policies are unlikely to succeed if at cross purposes. National states have more real sovereignty—more capacity to achieve what their populations want—by constantly negotiating and compromising. But Europe's states impose this collective regime on themselves only when doing so clearly seems to increase their capacity for achieving national goals. Hence, during the Cold War, European states ardently pursued "integration" in the economic sphere but not in defense, where, under an American protectorate in NATO, they could find greater safety with less constraint.

Europe's hybrid community was greatly helped by the Cold War, and the end of the Cold War greatly disturbed it. German reunification upset the balance between France and Germany. With the Soviet collapse and a weak Russia, the liberated states of Central and Eastern Europe not only threatened to generate a swarm of troubles—as Yugoslavia soon demonstrated—but were also a vacuum threatening to draw in Germany and arouse hostile British and French reactions. In other words, the end of the Cold War promised a return to Europe's anarchical state system and its traditional German problem. A post-Soviet crisis of transformation struck Europe in the West as well as in the East.

MAASTRICHT: EUROPE'S BOLD AND AMBIVALENT RESPONSE

France and Germany met this challenge boldly at Maastricht in 1991. Their solution was a radical double expansion of the postwar confed-

341

eracy, newly rechristened the European Union. Along with a great broadening of functions, the EU also planned to enlarge its membership radically. At the Copenhagen summit in 1993, the EU committed itself to negotiate with a wide range of prospective members, including several former communist countries. The number kept growing and ultimately stretched to Cyprus, Malta, and Turkey. By 1995, the former Cold War "neutrals"—Austria, Finland, and Sweden—had joined. It became commonplace to speak of an EU of thirty members. In effect, the EU was setting out to turn itself into the new pan-European system. The concomitant expansion of function and membership naturally implied a significant reform of internal governing arrangements. Accordingly, streamlining the union's decision making was an integral part of Maastricht's grand strategy. In principle, this streamlining could be accomplished by a turn toward genuine federalism. The union might move away from its intergovernmental character toward a real central government on German or American models, perhaps with a French- or American-style presidency. If the union's history is any guide, the most likely outcome is not a federal Europe but a further adaptation of the hybrid confederal model evolving since the 1950s. But even this course will demand significant changes. The fierce resistance and limited success demonstrated at Nice suggest that these reforms will take a long time. Nice thus suggests disagreeable alternatives. The EU will have either to curtail expanding its functions or to limit its membership.

For those who do not want a strong European Union, like the British, enlargement without successful federal reform is quite acceptable. It means a weaker union. But given the unlikelihood of federal reform, why do those who want a stronger and more cohesive Europe not oppose enlargement? At this juncture, they are mesmerized by what is undoubtedly a compelling geopolitical reality. The Europe they are dealing with today is Pan-Europe. It includes not only Central and Eastern Europe, but Russia. In many respects, it also includes the United States. What it requires, therefore, is not merely an updated West European system but a replacement for the Soviet and bipolar systems as well. Unfortunately, this appears to be a task beyond the consensus-building powers of a confederal European Union. To fulfill such a pan-European role, the EU must turn itself into an imperial federation—a hyperpower on its own, strong and centralized enough to dominate the Russians and replace the Americans. Since Europe's modern history—from Philip II to Hitler—richly demonstrates the futility and danger of attempting to subjugate Europe's states to a single centralizing power, perhaps it is time to begin seriously exploring schemes that do not start by presuming what seems impossible: either a strong and cohesive EU that stretches itself to cover Pan-Europe or a Europe run from America.

THREE PAN-EUROPEAN MODELS

How should Pan-Europe be organized? Logically, three models present themselves: bipolar, unified, and tripolar.

In bipolar Pan-Europe, the West claims its Cold War victories, and Western institutions enlarge; NATO and the EU eventually include most of the countries liberated by the Soviet collapse, except for Russia itself. A crippled Russia receives compensatory aid and perhaps diplomatic respect but is kept at arm's length.

In the second model, unified Pan-Europe, the old East and West of Europe join intimately to create a closely integrated Eurasian system. The European Union and NATO extend eastward—and eventually embrace rather than exclude Russia.

In the third model, tripolar Pan-Europe, the EU, Russia, and the United States form three distinct but articulated poles. Each, while tied to the others, remains sufficiently distinct so as not to undermine its own cohesion. Neither the EU nor NATO becomes, itself, pan-European. Instead, each remains a critical Western element within a larger and looser pan-European superstructure. The European Union, for example, extends full membership only to Central and East European countries whose political economies are sufficiently convergent with the West to be absorbed successfully. The EU does not imagine including Russia but nevertheless develops close economic relations with it, and also with the other former Soviet states. The United States remains present in Pan-Europe through NATO, but less as the active manager of European security than as the ultimate guarantor of Western Europe against a resumption of Russian (or German) aggression or an explosion of violence in the Near and Middle East. The United States and Russia cultivate their common security interests in the Far East. NATO thus grows more European and less American-dominated, as the EU develops autonomous diplomatic and defense institutions, capable of acting efficaciously either inside or outside NATO. Russia does not actually join this more European NATO but cooperates closely with it through some overarching pan-European security structure.

MODELS: BIPOLAR EUROPE REBORN?

Of the three models, which is preferable? The first model, reconstituting bipolar Europe, implies not only Russia's permanent estrangement from an Atlanticized Europe but also its enfeeblement and even dissolution, presumably for the benefit of its East European or Central Asian neighbors. Such a course hardly seems in anyone's long-term interest. The vision of an anarchical Russia, with its old nuclear arsenal and expertise privatized, should provoke deep caution among us all. Many people in America and Europe do, of course, dream of a weak, dependent, perhaps dismembered Russia and would like to see Ukraine, Central Asia, and the Baltic states bound tightly to the West. Old German fantasies of Middle Europe flicker into half-life. But these fantasies of Russian dissolution flirt with hubris on a grand scale, for the United States as well as for Germany. The volatile boundaries of Eastern and Central Europe have, again and again, been fault lines for modern Europe's political and military earthquakes. No one should begrudge the nations along this fault line their newfound freedom. But the West should be careful that this new liberty is not allowed to lead to a fresh cycle of conflict between Russia and the West, or among the Western powers themselves.

The Russians, after all, are in the midst of a heroic effort to transform themselves into a modern nation state, a transformation that implies not only democracy at home but also a less intrusive relationship with surrounding states. Chechnya notwithstanding, it is nowadays possible to imagine a Russian hegemony over its near neighbors that is not crushingly oppressive. In the interests of wider Eurasian order, the West should encourage these civilizing trends—not least by refusing to take advantage of Russia's apparent weakness. The West has no real interest in replacing Russian influence in Ukraine or authority in the trans-Caucuses and Central Asia. Seriously meddling to defeat Russian interests in these neighboring places risks unloosing a swarm of demons that Western powers have neither the means nor the vocation to master.

The resulting Eurasian vacuum would be not only a fertile breeding ground for organized crime, neighborhood genocide, and stampedes of terrified populations but also a highly counterproductive environment for West European integration. It cannot be healthy to have the German government back in Berlin, with Moscow enfeebled and Eastern Europe weak. It would be hard for Germany to resist being drawn into that revisionist vortex. Germany unbalanced in Middle Europe would alarm France and Britain and undermine the foundations of the European Union. At the same time, a weak Russia, with only a feeble hold on its huge Siberian empire, would be a menace to stability in Asia as well as in Europe.

A reborn bipolar model with a weak Russia would very likely also undermine transatlantic relations. Expanding NATO and keeping Russia at arm's length implies continuing American domination of the alliance. But with Russia isolated as well as weak, the United States would be too strong for the Europeans to welcome as hegemon. In any event, Europe's new security problems are such that close Russian cooperation is needed to manage many of them. Such cooperation seems unlikely if the Americans, playing an active hegemonic role in NATO, are contending with Russia in its own "near abroad." A not unlikely consequence is that Europeans would begin to take their distance from the United States. The principal danger is probably not that the United States will dedicate itself seriously to pan-European hegemony. Provoking a desperate Russia is too dangerous, and the regional problems are too intractable and too marginal to America's own vital interests. In any case, America's enthusiasm or capability for actually playing an extended hegemonic role is too inconstant. But the United States may well allow itself to drift toward such a policy sufficiently to embitter the Russians and provoke new waves of paranoia and imperialism among them. The same could be said about any revival of German ambitions for Mitteleuropa.

In summary, the old bipolar model cannot be patched up to suit the new pan-European future. Pan-Europe cannot be built around the vision of an American protectorate and Europe's acquis communautaire extended to all and sundry except for Russia. Given the geographical realities, a successful pan-European system is unlikely without a strong and benign Russia—preferably a federal nation state that is peaceful, democratic, multiethnic, and prosperous. If such a well-intentioned Russia does not evolve, Europe's future will be grim. Bipolar Pan-Europe favors this worst outcome by anticipating it. For better, or for worse, Russia is a great power with a major role in European security and prosperity—both in its own near abroad and in Middle Europe generally. But Russia's role, like that of the United States, or indeed of the EU, should be contained within a cooperative pan-European framework with a structured bias toward collective rather than unilateral action.

INTEGRATED PAN-EUROPE?

If Russia does become a reasonable European country, why not aim for our second formula: a closely integrated Pan-Europe? Logically, such a model implies Russian membership in NATO and the EU. Making Russia comfortable with such an arrangement would require profound internal changes in both organizations. In the alliance, it would mean turning away not only from American hegemony but also from NATO's essential character as a transatlantic counterbalance to Russia. While this might suit Russia, it would not suit the West. It would be foolish for the Western states to throw away their own transatlantic alliance, even if Russia does become a model European citizen. Few countries, presented with weak neighbors, are safe from the imperial virus. Russia seems unlikely to be an exception. In short, while any stable pan-European system will require Russian cooperation, it will also require insurance against a resurgent Russian threat. Not only does the Atlantic Alliance still seem the most secure way to deter that threat, but it also continues the other advantages of the old bipolar system. American presence deters aggressive behavior by West European states toward each other, as well as toward Russia or the United States itself. And it also gives European states considerable control over American policy.

It could be argued that Russia would be contained even better if it were taken into the Western alliance, as was done with Germany in the 1950s. The parallel, however, is not very exact. Nazi Germany surrendered unconditionally. Thereafter, it was menaced by the Soviets and occupied—in both west and east. Even the Federal Republic's constitution and government were largely imposed by its new Western allies. It is hard to see how these conditions could fit Russia. Today's Russia is certainly weak, but it is not occupied, nor has it been brought to its present condition by a Western conquest. The Soviet retreat was, after all, voluntary. Arguably, it was mainly brought about by essentially beneficent forces within Russia itself.[4] It seems unwise, as well as ungenerous, to regard today's weakened Russia as a defeated power, easily malleable to Western designs and fated to remain a negligible force in Europe's future. A reliable pan-European order seems unlikely to be built on such assumptions. Militarily and geopolitically, Russia remains too big either to be kept out of Pan-Europe or to be incorporated into Western Europe.

The economic side of the integrated pan-European model seems even less plausible than the military. Trying to include Russia in the European Union seems a forlorn cause, unless the EU abandons its pursuit of economic and political integration. It is questionable whether such a bloated and denatured EU could survive its own centrifugal impulses.

---

[4] It seems inaccurate historically and imprudent geopolitically to assume that East European resistance brought down the Soviets. The persistent courage of those who kept defying the Soviets and their collaborators, above all in Poland, did demoralize the "satellite" communist regimes and inspire opposition forces within the Soviet Union itself. But it did not actually throw the Soviets out of their empire. The retreat from Central Europe, the liquidation of that part of Stalin's World War II legacy, was something the Soviets, under Gorbachev, themselves decided to do.

TRI-POLAR PAN-EUROPE

By a process of elimination, our third model seems the most reasonable: an articulated or tripolar Pan-Europe. Essentially, it adapts and rearranges the parts of the old European and bipolar systems to suit a more cooperative coexistence with the Russians, as well as a more balanced Atlantic Alliance. It builds new pan-European institutions, as opposed to weakening old institutions by giving them impossibly overextended new roles. Thus, NATO remains essentially Western, preserving something of its old bipolar, hegemonic, implicitly anti-Russian character. But this anti-Russian aspect of NATO remains dormant unless needed. Meanwhile, the West European states, their own security cooperation intensified around EU institutions, assume primary responsibility for managing their own near abroad. They remain still in alliance with the Americans, but also in close collaboration with the Russians. NATO, while remaining a Western construction, evolves a cooperative superstructure that includes the Russians— arrangements continuing along the lines of the NATO-Russia Charter and Partnership for Peace. The institutional linkage for a broad pan-European security might develop through a refashioned Organization for Security and Cooperation in Europe (OSCE), perhaps endowed with a regional security council of major states—a structure analogous to the "contact group" that proved the way to organize pan-European cooperation in the Yugoslav wars.[5] An OSCE framework,

---

[5] The Contact Group, formed in April 1994, comprised five powers (the United States, Russia, France, Germany, and the United Kingdom), working in conjunction with the cochairmen of the Steering Committee of the International Conference on the Former Yugoslavia. Its main achievement, and one that laid the basis for an eventual settlement, was the mid-1994 "Contact Group Plan" that allowed the Serbs to retain 49 percent of Bosnia (as opposed to 70 percent under Vance-Owen) and assigned the rest to the Bosnian-Croat federation. The plan also had the unforeseen consequence of driving a wedge between Milosevic, who supported it, and the Bosnian Serbs, who did not. See Warren Zimmermann, op. cit., p. 231. See also chapter 14, note 21. An OSCE security council would presumably include the same five states and perhaps also Italy, Spain, Poland, and Turkey—possibly some on a rotating

encouraging multilateral and rule-based interventions, should help to soften and civilize Russian predominance in its own near abroad. In due course, the OSCE structure could even be extended to the Middle East and North Africa. The United States and Russia would cultivate their common security interests in the Far East. The European Union and the United States would remain bound by a broad Atlantic Alliance, not only to sustain a more European NATO but also to collaborate to define and promote a global economic agenda.

The EU itself remains an essentially West European construction but adds a new superstructure of formal pan-European economic arrangements, reaching out to all the EU's neighbors. Ideally, Russia should be progressively integrated into the looser pan-European economy. Russia and other Central Asian states could well become Western Europe's privileged long-term suppliers of energy and raw materials. With a decent political and legal framework, parts of Russian industry could become competitive and attractive for foreign investors. And should Russia rejuvenate its high-technology sector, its firms could become interesting partners for European and American firms alike.

The tripolar approach to Pan-Europe assumes that the United States, the European Union, and Russia are each too large and too different to merge together within a single closely integrated system. Their respective capacities for democratic politics and harmonious economic and social development are better served by their remaining distinct entities, sharing a new regional superstructure. This means that NATO and the EU remain Western rather than pan-European. Such deliberate self-limitation runs counter to the natural tendency to build the future on organizations that have proved themselves in the past. Both institutions have been hugely successful, but trying now to extend either one to all of pan-Europe is to misunderstand their essential character and the reasons for their postwar success. To imagine using the EU as the pan-European framework is to see it as a nascent federation, or a new Napoleonic (or German) empire, rather than as

---

basis. Perhaps, like ESDI in NATO, ad hoc task forces could be formed, coopting different members for different problems.

the confederacy of nation states that it is. Similarly, trying to extend NATO to Pan-Europe is to misunderstand NATO's character as a defensive alliance, to see it as a nascent Atlantic empire—something neither Americans nor Europeans would long sustain. By contrast, an articulated pan-European system preserves both the essential EU and the essential NATO, without destroying them by overextension. Rather, it uses both as building blocks within a larger and looser regional framework.

BOUNDARIES

An articulated pan-European model that presupposes continuing Western and Eastern cores poses the delicate question of boundaries between them. The Russians objected strongly to NATO's expansion, presumably because they saw it as a way of reconstituting the bipolar system on worse terms for themselves. The putative eastward expansion of the European Union has not aroused the same immediately hostile Russian reaction. But an enlargement of EU membership would eventually raise the issue of what security guarantees were involved and how they would be met in practice. The model would probably work better if the major centers kept themselves concentrated and held back from filling all the available spaces. The European Union, wary of giving the Russians legitimate grounds for antagonism, or of destabilizing its own institutions by too rapid growth, would expand only slowly and selectively. A Europeanized NATO might parallel the EU's eastward growth but not lead the way. While the EU's association agreements would proliferate and intensify within Eurasia and would include Russia in some fashion or other, the former communist states would also be encouraged to develop special ties among themselves. East Europeans would be cautioned not to neglect links with the Russians.

Behind the tripolar model lies a broad pluralist perspective. It envisages an interstate structure that acknowledges and values the distinctiveness of nation states, while creating machinery for their cooperation—arrangements that presuppose an assignment and sharing of regional responsibilities among the great powers, but are also infused with concern for the balance of power. Herder's nationalism contributes respect for the cultural limits of democratic political consensus, together with his optimistic and developmental view of the capacity of democratic nation states to coexist in peaceful cooperation. Balance-of-power theory supplies the necessary realist caution: Peaceful coexistence grows more probable within a balanced system, self-consciously constructed to constrain everyone—above all, the powerful. Without such a structured balance, the big states will not be inclined to honor the rights and living space of the small. Nor will they acquire the good habits typical of postwar European statecraft. Those postwar good habits, as I have tried to show, have been the product not only of structured cooperation but of an implicit balance. It has been that balance, together with the EU and NATO, that has made sympathy for the needs and views of neighbors a practical necessity for the politician, rather than a worthy but improbable dream. At the same time, big states have to be able to act in concert, when rules are clearly being broken.

WHY PAN-EUROPE?

If the heterogeneity of the constituent pan-European elements so limits their integration, why envisage pan-European structures at all? Beyond the EU and NATO, why not rely on the existing global organizations: the UN Security Council, IMF, World Bank or Groups of Seven or Eight. Why is a pan-European layer of organizations needed? There are several answers.

To begin with, many countries in Central or Eastern Europe, or even in Central Asia or the Middle East, passionately desire to join the EU or NATO but do not fit—economically, militarily, or politically. Economically, it is important that these countries be included in structures that promote whatever degree of pan-European economic assistance and intercourse is sustainable. Politically, former Soviet countries are reinforced in their new democratic habits by belonging to a fellowship of advanced democratic societies. Militarily, as Russia revives, some of these countries may have to accept de facto Russian hegemony, as indeed others, like Serbia, may have to accept Western hegemony, even if they do not like it. It is important that such countries belong to some pan-European organization that sets common principles for the rights of states and individuals and provides collective institutions to foster those rights. In practice, of course, the efficacy of such institutions must depend on whether the three major poles actually subscribe to the self-limiting principles of pan-European cooperation.

This brings us to perhaps the real reason for pan-European institutions. The ideal of "Europe," for all the ambiguous and bloody history behind it, retains a powerful capacity for promoting consensus around a variety of humane political values—not only among the members of the EU and their would-be partners in Central Europe, but also in Eastern Europe, in Russia itself, perhaps even in nearby parts of the Muslim world, and certainly in America. The concept of Europe is therefore a powerful asset to promote ideals that ought to be universal but cannot be reliably sustained on a global basis. This is not to say that the humane ideals associated with Europe should not be promoted and defended globally. But it is to acknowledge a special obligation to make these ideals prevail in Europe—an obligation shared by all the children of European civilization, Americans and Russians included.

There is no reason to throw away such a powerful asset on the grounds that it seems less ambitious than the pursuit of a universal world order. The real truth is that the world can progress toward anything like a rule of law only by consolidating such islands of humane order, sustained by pride in shared cultural values. Europeans, thanks to the horrors and accomplishments of their history, enjoy a special consciousness of the rights of individuals, societies, and states. They ought to be able to act in their own space according to that consciousness without having to rely on the United Nations, whose own consensus and capacity for action are necessarily of a lower intensity. In effect, Pan-Europe should become an efficacious example of the possibilities of variable geometry on a global scale. Entrusting the application of universal values to the regional structure of Pan-Europe, moreover, has another particular advantage. It unhooks European support for these values from American pretensions to world hegemony, pretensions that greatly divide Europeans and threaten world order.

While the intellectual case for articulated Pan-Europe may be powerful, there are also serious reasons for skepticism about its practical prospects. Success will require resolute reasonableness from Russians, Europeans, and Americans alike. Russia must overcome its brutal and dysfunctional past and must find a worthy modern version of itself. The United States will need to steel itself for a long period of attentive self-restraint. As for Europeans, they may be expected often to disappoint their own expectations, or to take longer and more circuitous routes to realizing them. Britain's enthusiasm for European cooperation may prove as unreliable in the future as in the past. As the Kosovo intervention seemed to illustrate, the British moral imagination does not naturally find a standard for its values in Europe. Like the Americans, the British have a natural taste for global universalism. Before Wilson, there was Gladstone. And even the Franco-German partnership may be in for a difficult period. Both partners need to adapt their own national systems to a more ruthlessly competitive world. Reunified Germany, its future increasingly mortgaged and its government back in imperial Berlin, may prove a more restless and ungenerous partner than formerly. Italy, too, after its heroic drive to meet the EMU criteria, has had great difficulty achieving the constitutional changes needed to complete its adaptation to a strong and stable currency.

Still, the difficulties of European states should not be exaggerated. We are speaking of nations whose civilizations ennoble mankind and whose creativity and humanity are far from exhausted. Europeans will always have divisions among themselves. They are too talented and energetic for things to be otherwise. But their problems should be considered against the magnitude of what they are attempting, and what they have already accomplished.

Nor should we forget that the rest of the world has a good deal riding on their success. A strong, balanced, and stable pan-European system will immeasurably strengthen the West and enrich its values. As the next chapter suggests, it would be a giant step forward toward a world whose problems are manageable. Without such a Europe in the new century, a happy new world order is difficult to imagine, and America's unipolar fate is likely to prove a curse laid on its future.

Europe in the New World Order

How WOULD a more united and powerful Europe fit within the likely global order of the twenty-first century? How it might fit depends not only on its own character but on the likely nature of the rest of the global system. A major question is whether that system will continue to be "unipolar"—dominated by the United States, the unique "indispensable nation." Certainly, no one else at the turn of the century seems in a position to supplant the United States—still the greatest military power by far and also endowed with a highly dynamic national economy, still the world's largest. But even if there is no new pretender to hegemony, the distribution of power and wealth may nevertheless be growing more "plural," and with significant consequences for global order. In any event, the strength of the United States may well be less enduring than it seems. Americans may be growing weary of hegemony and may no longer be disciplined enough politically to run the world successfully. America's superior military power may be less and less capable of being applied efficiently. The economic and military rise of Asian states may be making the world less manageable; a more independent European Union may portend a brewing geopolitical conflict within the West itself. Or the world's economic life may be growing too complex and anarchical to be regulated by any state. This last consideration points to another familiar set of issues: the perennially tense relations between nation states and capitalism. Is globalized capitalism growing more impervious to political regulation? Is it also increasingly unstable?

Obviously, no one can answer such questions with any great assurance. We sense that Europe, America, Russia, and the Asian states are moving toward a new dispensation, within which old questions about hegemony, nation states, and capitalism may well need fresh answers. How should we now think about these questions? What can the past tell us about them?

AMERICAN HEGEMONY IN A UNIPOLAR WORLD?

Throughout the 1990s, Americans were still enjoying the Indian summer of their global hegemony. Balance as a precondition for world order was not a view strongly favored in Washington. The abrupt end of the Cold War had left behind a large bureaucracy and intellectual establishment, together with extensive economic interests—all oriented toward America's exercise of international power. After the Cold War, these elements were naturally disposed to see the world as unipolar and the United States as its unique and indispensable superpower. Events often conspired to confirm that perspective. European states were embarrassingly ineffective in the long Yugoslav crisis of the 1990s. And Europe's economies floundered while the American economy continued to steam ahead.

As a mood of military and economic triumphalism grew rampant in the American government, American policy often grew increasingly assertive and unilateral, loath to submit to multilateral decision making. American behavior in trade disputes grew increasingly imperious and quarrelsome, while projects to strengthen Europe in the world economy, like EMU, aroused widespread American suspicion and animosity.[1] Militarily, the United States was also in an assertive mood. Within Europe, it pressed a maximalist view of NATO's future missions and membership and dragged its feet on internal reforms relaxing American hegemony. The United States was instead emphasizing its own predominance in Eurasian affairs. American military advisers, using the machinery of NATO's Partnership for Peace, were ubiquitous and active throughout Eastern Europe and Central Asia.[2] In the Middle East, ten years after the Gulf War, the Clinton administration was still insisting on an embargo against Iraq, punctuated by desultory bombing and missile attacks, despite strong opposition among most of the European allies. Similarly, American diplomacy frowned on European efforts to return to more normal relationships with Iran. By the turn of the century, the United States was pressing strategic projects,

[1] See chapter 12, notes 28 and 29.
[2] See chapter 14, note 30.

355

in particular national missile defense, that seemed designed to perpetuate American military and technological predominance, even at the cost of upsetting the world's underlying strategic stability.[3] The Clinton administration, which had begun with a modest geopolitical agenda and a determination to focus on domestic rejuvenation, ended up bemused by a neo-Wilsonian globalist vision, with America the world's indispensable leader.

IMPERIAL LIBERALISM

The early twenty-first century is often said to resemble the beginning of the last century. Both were periods of triumphant liberalism when international capitalism was rapidly integrating economies. But even if national societies were growing more cosmopolitan and integrated economically in 1900, there was no equivalent to the United States today. No single national culture was threatening to dominate all the others. In this respect, a more instructive parallel is between our own time and the eighteenth and early nineteenth centuries. This was a period when Europe saw the progressive integration of its national cultures under the aegis of France—the continental superpower of the day.

French culture and language, backed by French power, seemed poised to fulfill the Enlightenment dream of a progressively more rational and homogenous world. Then, as now, cultural uniformity did not please everyone. Chapter 4 discusses how German Romantics rose in revolt against what they regarded as the superficiality and banality of Germany's Francophone Enlightenment—an importation they saw threatening German culture and identity. Outraged at the universalist pretensions of *la grande nation*, Herder's nationalism proclaimed the right of all peoples to have a culture and identity of their own. Progress, in Herder's vision, was not the homogenization of the world according to one model, but the separate, if mutually stimulating, elaboration of many models—a plural world full of en-

---

[3] See the end of chapter 14.

ergy and diversity, whose history showed the ceaseless clash and reconciliation of opposite forces.

Today, the world has seemingly entered a new liberal Enlightenment—a new season of rapid economic growth and cultural homogenization. Once more, a highly advanced and outsized power seems the engine of the world's improvement, the indispensable international manager, its hegemony the natural outcome of the world's integration and progress. The temptation that such ideas dangle before American global ambition seems all too clear. Moreover, as French, British, and American historical experience all suggest, liberalism can easily be infiltrated with imperialist purposes. Recent years have seen this old predilection amply displayed.

"DEMOCRATIC PEACE THEORY"

Democratic peace theory poses a view of the future much in vogue during the latter years of the Clinton presidency. It provides a particularly apposite example of the liberal affinity to hegemonic power. Peace theory has a highly respectable provenance, one that goes back—appropriately enough—to the Enlightenment. Kant's vision of "Perpetual Peace" (1795) is a particularly favored source.[4] Kant's towering stature in modern philosophy lends plausibility to the theory's key tenet: Republics, where ordinary citizens ultimately decide policy, seldom go to war with each other. Progress toward republican government is also therefore progress toward perpetual peace.[5] Peace theory also draws from another key Enlightenment source: liberal economics. As liberal politics brings perpetual peace, so liberal eco-

---

[4] Kant's essay was published shortly after the French Revolution's Reign of Terror. A great admirer of Rousseau, Kant looked with sympathy on the revolution, although he would never permit himself to admit the right of revolution in his native Prussia.

[5] Tom Paine, the great popular apologist for the American Revolution, made the same point more concretely: Kings enjoy making wars because they do not actually have to fight them. The ordinary people who are plunged into the pain and gore of battle, and who are ruined by the crushing expense, have much less enthusiasm for the whole experience. Democracies, it follows, are much less inclined than absolute states toward unnecessary quarrels with their neighbors.

357

nomics brings perpetual prosperity. Each reinforces the other. The optimism of Kant joins the optimism of Smith. Both philosophers share the Enlightenment's overriding goal: to improve mankind's lot through the steady and cumulative application of reason.[6] What, then, is wrong with such a benevolent theory?

It may well be that liberal democracies are less warlike than authoritarian dictatorships. Nevertheless, there are some disquieting problems with the argument. Some of the shortcomings should probably be traced to Kant himself. Kant radiates a strong faith in the benefits to be gained from the circumscribed application of formal democratic practices. But his republic is a very elusive construction, based on the ethical imperative that all laws must be subject to the categorical imperative that governs individual morality: Prescribe for others only what you are willing to have applied to yourself. Citizens, however, are explicitly prohibited from using their voting power for any collective pursuit of "happiness." In other words, politics is not to interfere with economics. This prohibition abstracts from politics most of the sources of civil conflict. So denatured a view of politics makes it easy to ignore the feebleness of liberal democratic forms when unsupported by a deep political consensus or by a viable economy. Without these underpinnings, liberal institutions tend to be short-lived, and therefore not much of a barrier to international conflict.

Democratic peace theory, in short, lacks an adequate sense of context—political or economic. It seems naive, for example, to assume that a liberal economic market, once installed, will automatically guarantee prosperity. There is, after all, a great deal of experience to the contrary over the past few centuries. The recent history of Eastern Europe's transformation to capitalism should illustrate the futility of

---

[6] True to its Enlightenment roots, Smith's liberal economics offered up a confident vision of linear progress. Not surprisingly, Romantic conservatives thought liberal economics fatally flawed by its materialist view of human nature and utilitarian view of society. The critique grew more vehement as British economics progressed from the eclectic richness and general optimism of Adam Smith to the more rigorous but straitened logic of Ricardo, whose "gloomy science" reflected the discouraging logic of Malthus plus the particularly barren view of individuals and societies typical of Benthamite Utilitarianism. Romantic poets—from Blake onward—kept reminding their compatriots of the inadequacies of such a liberal worldview.

importing mechanical formulas and ignoring the context within which they are applied. It seems equally questionable to use the experience of NATO countries to prove that democracies do not go to war with each other. Arguably, there are more convincing explanations—the sobering consequences of sharing a major common enemy, or of having their military forces enthralled to a major common protector.

No theory of international relations is, of course, free from its inadequacies. Liberal peace theory is surely no worse than many others. For Americans at this moment in history, however, it poses a particular danger. Arguments based on peace theory have, for example, been widely used to urge extensive NATO enlargement—despite vehement Russian opposition. Realists tend to recognize a wide expanding of NATO as the natural but probably unwise American reaction to Russian weakness. For peace theorists, however, NATO's enlargement becomes a way of stabilizing nascent liberal democracies. American power is dressed up as the globalization of liberal values. American power is not like that of other nations but is intrinsically benign—the instrument for history's benevolent progress. This is a line of reasoning that grows more dangerous when it is sincerely believed.

Given America's prosperity and military preponderance in the late twentieth century, these imperious tendencies might easily have been stronger. But despite a shared taste for pretentious rhetoric, neither the Clinton administration nor the Republican-dominated Congress of the late 1990s had a stable enthusiasm for filling the role of global hegemon.[7] Both insisted that the United States should go on running the world, but without devoting much attention to the world's affairs or expecting to pay any outsized price, human or economic, for leadership. While the United States was embarrassingly sensitive to any sign of demotion from superpower status, it nevertheless seemed to have no viable or even coherent strategy for exercising hegemony in Europe or around the globe. Thus, for example, while America's low-grade war with Iraq kept alive the image of the United States as the world's police force and undoubtedly contributed to the misery of the hapless Iraqi population, it had no genuine strategic purpose, since it

---

[7] See, for example, Charles William Maynes, "Pax Americana: The Impossible Dream," *Foreign Service Journal* (March 2000), pp. 20–25.

was not seriously designed to topple the regime and had little chance of doing so. And while the administration clung tenaciously to America's hegemonic role in NATO, it showed little talent or stomach for actually exercising sustained and responsible military leadership in the alliance. Its basic approach to the exercise of military power was "hegemony on the cheap." Following the Cold War, the United States never conducted a serious reconsideration of military doctrines and force structures. Instead, it took refuge in doctrines, popular among the American military since the Vietnam debacle, according to which technology would obviate the need for soldiers on the ground. This allowed the administration's military spending, much reduced in any case, to be targeted to sustain the economy's leadership in high technology.

After its success at Dayton, however, the Clinton administration grew not only more extravagant in its rhetoric but more careless in its promises. The result was a growing risk that its bluff might be called. The Kosovo intervention of 1999 proved a moment of considerable revelation. The cause of the intervention—to stop the Serbian government's systematic ethnic cleansing—was certainly worthy. Most European governments, in particular the British and the French, strongly supported it. In many respects, the intervention was their initiative. Nevertheless, it had to be conducted through a NATO dominated by the United States. The Europeans were lucky to have their American hegemon, since they themselves were still woefully unprepared for collective military action. But NATO's air campaign reflected the fabulosity of Pentagon military doctrine and revealed the perils of American leadership. The Kosovo experience also indicated the risks to Europeans of alienating the Russians. Given Russia's displeasure, it was important for Europe to have the Americans involved. But America's maladroit handling of NATO enlargement was the initial cause of Russian disaffection. Having the Kosovo intervention conducted by an alliance so dominated by America compounded Russian fear and anger.

The Russians were not alone in their hostility. Perhaps the most instructive lesson from the Kosovo intervention was the popular reaction against it in many parts of the world—surprising, given the odiousness of the Serbian cause. But the reaction had little to do with international support for Serbian oppression. Rather it reflected the widespread unpopularity of American pretensions to world leadership. With Russia alienated and hostile, and backed by China, the West had either to abandon the intervention or go ahead without asking for a mandate from the UN Security Council. But bypassing the UN triggered fears on all sides of a United States unrestrained by international law, a hyperpower out of control.[8] The vehement Chinese popular reaction was of particular interest.[9] In short, from a European perspective, American leadership may have been indispensable militarily, but it was a liability politically. Thus, while the Kosovo intervention may have demonstrated the continuing benefits of the transatlantic alliance for both Europe and America, it did not encourage hopes for a stable European system built on American hegemony.

ANOTHER AMERICAN CENTURY?

It is difficult to look back over the 1990s without sensing a deterioration of transatlantic relations, one manifested less in open confrontation than in quiet mutual alienation. The deterioration continues. The prospect of a Europe growing stronger—economically, politically, and militarily—clashes with those visions of a unipolar world popular with certain parts of America's political elites. Having had one American century, these elites are now preparing themselves for another. This imperial American vision of the future is not very well founded. To begin with, it misreads the nation's own basic character. Most Americans do not see the United States as the Roman Empire reborn, nor does America's peacetime political system easily adapt itself to a Roman future. The imperial vision also misunderstands the sources of America's postwar success in Europe. America's postwar strategy was

---

[8] European misgivings over U.S. unilateralism were especially strong among the French. See John Vinocur, "Going It Alone, US Upsets France," *International Herald Tribune*, February 3, 1999, p. 1, and "France Has a Hard Sell to Rein in US Power," *International Herald Tribune*, February 6, 1999, p. 2. For balanced statements of French misgivings, see Foreign Minister Hubert Vedrine's various speeches on the subject. See chapter 14, note 57.

[9] See chapter 14, note 50.

not Roman. Its aim was not to annex Europe to America, but to set Europe on its own feet as a partner rather than as a dependency.

That American strategy not only helped to restore Europe's pride but also aroused America's own best instincts. Dragged into Europe's balance-of-power system, the United States proved different from the typical European power at its apogee. The United States did not act like a republican version of the Habsburgs or the Bourbons, or even of the British Empire. America's greatest successes were at the outset of the postwar era—from the Marshall Plan to the consolidation of the German Federal Republic and the launching of the European Economic Community. American leaders were notable in Europe not only for their steadfast resistance to the Soviets, but also for their reticence and restraint toward their allies. American leaders succeeded not least because of their sophisticated and generous sympathy with Europe and, in many cases, their capacity for genuine friendship with Europe's leaders.

It is interesting to speculate on the roots of this American better self—its sympathy, generosity, and respect for other countries. History has perhaps been kinder to the United States than to Europe's great powers. As a nation state, the United States was planted in a bounteous, spacious, and isolated continent. It united its polyglot and restless population around universal ideals of liberty, opportunity, and equality before the law. It is pleasing to think that America's idealism, diversity, and good fortune have produced a national character generous toward the outside world.[10] But, postwar America's better instincts toward its allies were undoubtedly helped by sharing with them a particularly sinister, threatening, and clumsy enemy. Ironically, the demise of that enemy seems to have brought forward a meaner and smaller America, a place where bombastic imperial visions mingle with dangerously moralistic, self-righteous, and simplistic views of past and future.

Tomorrow's global system, however, does not seem hospitable to

---

[10] Early America's virtues coexisted with slavery, the dark side of the American heritage—a caution against assuming an exceptional virtue that somehow frees Americans from the baser tendencies that generally affect other powerful peoples, whenever their power is excessive and inadequately restrained.

facile imperial visions. The new Asia promises great turmoil, and Americans will almost inevitably be drawn deeply into trying to channel and accommodate its rising powers. For the United States, the Asian challenge in the new century is likely to be no less demanding than the European challenge in the last. Logically, this Asian challenge should make it in America's interest to have Europe be a serious ally rather than a costly dependency. In other words, the Asian challenge should encourage the United States to welcome a Europe that is strong and self-sufficient, one that is able to take the primary initiative for maintaining order in its own space, and one that engages generously and constructively with Russia. That sort of Europe is far more likely to be a positive world force than a fragmented Europe whose schizophrenic quarrels render it impotent and sullen, its pusillanimous nation states perennially attracted to free riding. Under the circumstances, triumphalist American diffidence toward European unity and independence in the 1990s was, for the longer term, a dysfunctional reaction for the Americans themselves. Fortunately, instead of discouraging the Europeans, it spurred them to greater efforts.

Uncontrollable Capitalism?

American triumphalism after the Cold War was not only military but economic. Throughout most of the 1990s, the huge American economy was almost uniquely successful among advanced nations. Nevertheless, many analysts were increasingly troubled by what seemed dangerous flaws in the economy's foundations: a basic disequilibrium evidenced by large and expanding trade and current account deficits, together with a low, even negative, rate of personal saving, heavy foreign borrowing, and a stock market whose values seemed crazily overvalued. These flaws, moreover, seem intimately related to basic problems of the world economy as a whole.

For most parts of the world economy, the 1990s were a troubled decade. The Soviet collapse at the outset was followed by a prolonged slump in Western Europe and a brutal deterioration of conditions in Japan. Most other Asian economies had fallen into severe trouble by 1998, with consequences that helped to blight the still fragile Russian recovery, then spread to Latin America and reverberated in the West itself. In this rolling global crisis, trouble began typically in currency and financial markets and then spread to production, trade, and employment. The common explanation combined the raucous volatility of world financial markets with the weakened condition of many financial institutions exposed to that volatility. In addition, a powerful deflationary trend in commodity prices, including oil, ran through much of the decade and depressed conditions in many countries, Russia included. A parallel deflationary tendency in manufactures, visible by 1996, also made trade competition increasingly sharp.[11]

Dysfunctional legacies from the Cold War were often at the bottom of these difficulties. Arguably, the enormous pool of mobile capital that made it so easy to destabilize foreign-exchange and financial markets was a natural result of the decades of systematic monetary inflation and exploitation of the dollar, consequences related, in turn, to the West's chronic overspending for "guns and butter" and skewed burden sharing. The pitiful disarray of former Soviet economies reflected their own decades of malinvestment in war-oriented production. The later deflationary trends in manufactured goods were fed by large increases of production exported by countries with low costs and low consumption. Probably the greatest deflationary shock was the rapid entry of Chinese goods and labor into world markets in the 1980s, after decades of absence resulting from the warfare, chaos, and lunatic tyranny that had been China's fate throughout most of the twentieth century.[12]

With Asian conditions so deflationary, the principal obstacle to a world depression lay, it seemed, in the capacity of the United States to go on absorbing the surplus products of others, while attracting for-

[11] The world dollar prices of manufactures fell by a cumulative 12 percent between 1996 and 1998, nonoil commodities fell by 19 percent and oil by 41 percent. *World Economic Outlook, May 1999* (Washington, DC; International Monetary Fund, 1998), p. 167.

[12] Between 1980 and 1997, China's share of world exports rose from 1.0 percent to 5.1 percent. *Direction of Trade Statistics, 1998* (Washington, DC: International Monetary Fund, 1998). For more discussion of the implications for the global economy of the entry of the Chinese labor force, see Benedict Anderson, "South-East Asia: From Miracle to Crash," *London Review of Books*, vol. 20, no. 8 (April 16, 1998).

eign capital to finance its consequent very large trade deficits. By the later 1990s, American officials noted how the United States had become the world's "consumer of last resort," a major feature of America's lingering hegemonic role in the world economy.[13] Initially, it was the outsized American appetite for imports that helped call into being the rapidly growing export industries of Asia's "little tigers" in the 1970s, just as it had greatly facilitated the rapid growth of Japanese exports earlier in the 1960s.[14] America's trade and current account deficits grew still larger in the 1980s. By the 1990s, they were swelling to new records and, in the process, underwriting China's explosive entry into the global economy.[15] With deflationist trends menacing the international economy, any serious improvement in America's trade balance threatened to collapse what was left of Asia's "export-led" growth and reinforce a spiral of deflation around the world.

America's ability to continue absorbing the rest of the world's surplus production depended on its own habitual high consumption and low saving, together with its capacity to finance the consequent current account deficits easily and cheaply.[16] By the late 1990s, America's heavy consuming habits seemed to depend on the wealth effects

---

[13] On the U.S. role as consumer of last resort, see David E. Sanger, "Clinton Toughens Stance on Trade," *International Herald Tribune*, November 12, 1998, p. 13; Martin Crutsinger, "Administration Warns of Fragility of Global Economic Recovery," *Associated Press*, April 29, 1998; "Rubin Says U.S. Cannot Be 'Consumer of Last Resort,'" *AFX News*, February 1, 1999. See also Robert Rubin, *Remarks before the World Economic Conference, Davos, January 30, 1999* <http://www.ustreas.gov/press/releases/pr2920.htm>.

[14] For Asian growth, see The World Bank, *The East Asian Miracle* (New York: Oxford University Press, 1993); for an early analysis of Japan's postwar commercial and political relations with the United States, see David P. Calleo and Benjamin M. Rowland, *America and the World Political Economy* (Bloomington: Indiana University Press, 1973), ch. 8.

[15] See chapter 9, note 20. The U.S. share of Chinese exports rose from 8.6 percent in 1991 to 18.0 percent in 1997. *Direction of Trade Statistics, 1998* (Washington, DC: International Monetary Fund, 1998), p. 158.

[16] In the 1980s, the U.S. current account deficit was financed largely through foreign purchases of government bonds; by the mid-1990s the largest sources of external finance were foreign direct investment in the U.S. and foreign purchases of U.S. corporate securities. See *The Economic Report of the President, February 1999* (Washington, DC: U.S. Government Printing Office, 1999), pp. 263, 449.

of what many feared was an already vastly inflated stock market.[17] At the same time, EMU's launching of the euro, fated to rival the dollar as a reserve currency, cast doubt on whether America's habitual easy financing of external deficits could continue indefinitely. Arguably, a global economy whose prosperity appeared to rest on such uncertain foundations needed serious structural adjustment. The old forms of American economic hegemony were no longer adequate.

From an American perspective, an obvious solution was for the EU to start absorbing a larger share of the world's bloated production. In 1997, for example, with a GDP roughly the same size as the American GDP, the EU's current account surplus was roughly $117 billion, and its trade with Asia was approximately in balance. The United States, by contrast, had an overall current account deficit close to $155 billion and a trade deficit with Asia of around $141 billion.[18] With Europe's growth sluggish and its unemployment high, boosting its demand seemed an obvious prescription. Doing so would presumably stimulate not only domestic production and employment but also imports. Fear that such a course would lead to inflation seemed unreasonable; the EU's overall rate of price increases was low throughout most of the decade and well below 2 percent per annum by the end.[19] Moreover, as U.S. practice seemed to demonstrate, opening trade with Asia was the best way to pursue a growth-oriented domestic policy while avoiding the inflationary consequences. More open Asian trade would not only keep down European prices but also pressure European governments, unions, and business firms to accelerate long-overdue reforms of the labor market. A more flexible labor market, as in the United States, would open the way to a rapid growth of employment in services, despite the increased importing of manufactures.[20]

Europeans resisted this new version of "locomotive" economics, as

---

[17] For early anticipations of the risks and implications of a U.S. stock market crash, see Floyd Norris, "Greenspan Seeks to Cast Himself as a Small Player," *International Herald Tribune*, January 22, 2000; "Greenspan and the Markets," *Financial Times*, October 16, 1999, leader p. 16; and Martin Wolf, "Watch Out for the Fireworks," *Financial Times*, January 27, 1999, p. 23.

[18] For more detailed figures see chapter 12, note 25.

[19] *OECD Economic Outlook: December 1998* (Paris: OECD, 1998), pp. 240, 242.

[20] See *The OECD Jobs Study* (Paris: OECD, 1994), especially pp. 17–20, 33–36.

they had resisted the old version in the late 1970s. With the EU's unemployment over 10 percent throughout most of the decade, governments were leery of actively promoting more imports from Asia, let alone of justifying such imports as a means of breaking resistance to labor market reform. In any event, it was not self-evident that Europe was more "protectionist" toward Asian imports than the United States.[21] As for stimulating consumption in general, European governments shied away from a prescription that they feared would simply exchange one disequilibrium (unemployment) for another (a trade deficit). Instead, the EU was struggling to find its own combination of microeconomic structural reform and macroeconomic equilibrium that would permit low inflation, high employment, balanced trade, and reasonable growth—shared equitably throughout the population. To achieve these balanced aims would require not only reforming the labor markets but also sustaining the macroeconomic discipline that had been the fruit of achieving EMU.

European policies in the 1990s seemed informed by a fundamentally different economic worldview from American policies: Europeans seemed influenced by a more classic vision of economic balance. Instead of a world economy where one radical imbalance (the American deficit) sustains another (the Asian surplus), Europeans favored a global regime where all countries and regions stay in external equilibrium because they guard their own internal balances.[22] A

---

[21] The principal evidence for this view came from the relative rates of growth of U.S. imports, which expanded by 8.0 percent a year in real terms between 1990 and 1997, while those of the EU grew by only 4.9 percent. However, the ratio of exports to GDP in the United States was fairly similar to that of extra-European trade to combined GDP in the EU, that is, around 11 percent. *OECD Economic Outlook, December 1998* (Paris: OECD, 1998), p. 200. For a discussion of the causes of the widening of the U.S. trade deficit, see *OECD Economic Outlook, June 1999* (Paris: OECD, 1999), pp. 198–206. Both the EU and the United States reached major trade agreements with China in the spring of 2000. For a discussion of the U.S.-China agreement, see Deborah McGregor, "House Hands Clinton Policy Triumph on China," *Financial Times,* May 25, 2000, p. 14; also, "China's Challenge," *Financial Times,* May 26, 2000, p. 20. The consequences for Europe's Asian trade and current account balance remain to be seen. Past experience suggests that while EU trade may grow strongly, it will not be sharply unbalanced.

[22] Even in this classic perspective, however, a rapidly developing country can legit-

United States adopting such a regimen would cut its external deficit to manageable proportions. This reduction would presumably require restoring macroeconomic balance, a regimen broadly similar to what European states had adopted for EMU. Consumption would have to be reduced, savings increased, and excessive credit brought under control. Applied to Asia, the European perspective would prescribe drastically reducing dependence on Western markets by developing domestic markets. To do so, Asia should presumably imitate the West by enriching its own population, as opposed to relying on America's capacity to absorb cheap imports ad infinitum, thanks to inflated domestic demand and hegemonic forms of foreign borrowing. In other words, Asian economies should increase public and private consumption and reduce saving, or at least cut borrowing from abroad, in order to keep investment and growth to a rate sustainable without an outsized trade surplus. One obvious way to increase Asia's domestic and regional absorption is by improving public infrastructure and amenities and sharing more wealth with workers. Europe's enthusiasm for restoring a global system of stable exchange rates reflects a similar priority for domestic and regional equilibrium. To make a world with stable exchange rates, constituent units should converge on domestic policies conducive to equilibrium, as Europe did during its long struggle for EMU.[23]

Behind these economic preferences are major philosophical differences that run all through modern culture. European policymakers in the 1990s hoped to unite their economies around a shared notion of equilibrium and how to maintain it. This was that pensée unique of German provenance that had come to dominate the imaginations of

---

imately be a net importer of capital—a sound practice if the capital is well invested, that is, if it will generate a reasonable return and if the debt can be financed. Similarly, a rich and mature economy should be a net exporter of capital, provided that its external earnings or reserves can compensate for the outflow.

[23] For evidence of European, and especially French, thinking on exchange rate management under the euro, see Peter Norman, "France Proposes Forex Stability Plan," *Financial Times*, February 9, 1999, p. 2; "France Unveils Plan to Stabilize World Market," *Financial Times*, September 23, 1998, p. 3; and David Owen and Ralph Atkins, "European Calls for Reform of Global Financial System," *Financial Times*, September 15, 1998, p. 6.

European policymakers in the 1970s, as they struggled with runaway inflation and welfare spending. By contrast, the United States was still boldly using its hegemonic power to impose American preferences on a malleable world. The preferences, often benevolent in intent, nevertheless presumed an indefinite continuation of America's unbalanced hegemonic habits. From the reigning European perspective, these habits represented a world order imposed by an alien and superior power rather than a natural and self-sustaining equilibrium based on rules applicable to all. America was, in truth, a "hyperpower." It was only a short step to regarding America as itself a menace to world order. But the fault lay as much with the unnatural weakness and dependency of Europe as with the excessive strength and aggressiveness of the Americans.

In the conditions of the 1990s, the American government felt little compulsion to take European views seriously. Discussions were mostly a dialogue of the deaf. Economic quarrels multiplied, and a basic erosion of transatlantic trust and cooperation was apparent. Europe's principal reaction was to press ahead with the Economic and Monetary Union. In a global system with shaky rules and precarious stability, Europe's states felt they needed a solid monetary and trading bloc to defend their own prosperity and social peace. If they succeeded, they might ultimately be able to force the Americans to negotiate more seriously about a stable global regime. In other words, achieving a better framework of global rules and balances would first require a global balance of power. A European bloc seemed the necessary precondition for such a global balance. In effect, Europeans were pursuing the global strategy List had foretold in the mid-nineteenth century and that the Imperial Germans, in their fashion, had proclaimed in World War I.

EMU was thus an implicit challenge to American economic hegemony; the advent of the euro was, in itself, a sign that the world economy was outgrowing the old patterns of the Pax Americana. This basic trend toward a more plural dispensation of wealth and power reflected not so much American failure as American success. For over half a century, a liberal world economy, inspired and largely managed by the Americans, had spread prosperity, investment, and growth throughout the world. One consequence had been predictable from the start: a more plural distribution of global wealth, power, and initiative. As a result, the Americans, by themselves, increasingly lacked the means, imagination, or will to dominate the system as a whole. In such a situation, the alternative to mounting chaos is either a fresh or renewed hegemony or a cooperative multilateral system, based on rules and with an effective balance of power to sustain those rules.[24]

A new hegemon to replace the United States seems unlikely in the present state of the world. For the reasons I have been suggesting, clinging to the old postwar American hegemony is a policy also likely to fail. But while American global hegemony may show numerous signs of flagging, a balanced and cooperative plural system to replace it still seems far away. Ideally, such a system could be constructed from a group of major powers and regional blocs that, committed to stabilizing their own countries and regions, could also converge on rules for stabilizing the world system as a whole. Creating regional blocs and global structures requires effective multilateral institutions to encourage the search for common interests and perspectives. The twentieth century, of course, spawned many such regional and global

---

[24] The Great Depression of the 1930s has often been ascribed to the failure of the United States to play a hegemonic role in stabilizing the international monetary system; see, for example, Charles Kindleberger, "International Economic Organization," in D. P. Calleo, ed., *Money and the Coming World Order* (New York: Lehrman Institute, 1976), especially pp. 34–35. A contrary view, however, blames the Depression on hegemonic abuse of reserve currency status and believes the appropriate remedy was restoring an equilibrium based on the gold standard. The latter argument was particularly well articulated by Jacques Rueff (see bibliography to chapter 9). For an introduction, see Judith Kooker's chapter in D. P. Calleo, ed., *Money and the Coming World Order*, op. cit. See also Charles de Gaulle's press conference on the world monetary system in 1965, in *Major Addresses, Statements and Press Conferences* (New York: French Embassy and Information Division, 1967), vol. 2, pp. 179–181. For my own reflections, see my "De Gaulle and the Monetary System: The Golden Rule," in Robert O. Paxton and Nicholas Wahl, eds., *De Gaulle and the United States: A Centennial Reappraisal* (Oxford, UK: Berg, 1994); also my chapter, "The Decline and Rebuilding of an International Economic System: Some General Considerations," in David P. Calleo, ed., *Money and the Coming World Order*, ibid. For a discussion of the role of the IMF in the contemporary international economy, see Michel Camdessus, *An Agenda for the IMF at the Start of the 21st Century*, speech at the Council on Foreign Relations, New York, February 1, 2000 <http://www.imf.org/external/np/speeches>.

institutions.[25] Of these, the European Union was by far the most intensive and significant.

Perversely, taming Europe's own self-destructive power struggles might, in the end, lead to a new conflict between Europe and America. But Europe's new strength could also make possible a more efficacious form of cooperation across the Atlantic—one that results in a broad strengthening of the West in the world. Instead of quarreling over definitions of "burden sharing" that tend to presume a continuing special hegemonic exceptionalism for the United States, the two Western giants might work out a more balanced and comprehensive view of their global roles and responsibilities. And just as France and Germany have created a civilized form of joint hegemony for Europe, the EU and the United States may one day build a similar form of joint and balanced leadership for the emerging new global system.

The basis for renewed Western partnership will not be, we can hope, a shared determination to suppress the Asians for another century or two.[26] Rich and liberal Western nations do, however, share a legitimate interest in avoiding self-destructive quarrels among themselves and bloody chaos in the rest of the world. And it is also in their interest to foster the sort of growth needed to reduce the desperate poverty that still afflicts a great proportion of the world's population.

---

[25] The number of intergovernmental organizations rose dramatically following World War II—from seventy in 1940 to over one thousand by 1981. See Robert Keohane, "International Institutions: Can Interdependence Work?" *Foreign Policy*, vol. 110 (Spring 1998), pp. 82–97.

[26] See Samuel Huntington, *The Clash of Civilizations and the Remaking of World Order* (New York: Simon & Schuster, 1996). Like Herder, Huntington is skeptical that one single culture, or way of life, can be long imposed on the rest of the world. Huntington is, of course, also a realist. There is no *Kraft* in Huntington's world to guarantee a happy coexistence of rival cultures, as there is in Herder's world. Huntington expects conflict. But his skepticism about the ability of one culture to dominate the others suggests that hegemony is not an enduring solution to that conflict. The alternative is presumably a reasonable balance of power. This will come, Huntington rightly believes, not from the automatic processes so beloved by the neoliberals, but perhaps from enlightened statesmanship, representing collectively the world's diverse interests, aware that clashes among those interests are inevitable and that peace depends on statesmen resolutely exercising self-restraint, searching for shared interests, and seeking a reasonable balance among all parties.

A rejuvenated Western partnership would, of course, draw on long-standing habits of institutionalized transatlantic cooperation, based initially on American hegemony and European need during the Cold War. A rebalancing of responsibility and power might prolong those ties indefinitely. Europe and America could re-create on a global scale the postwar accommodation of France and Germany on a regional scale. Both sides of the Atlantic would have learned enough from the past to avoid repeating the old mistake of refusing mutual accommodation.

Ideally, Europe would contribute not only its economic weight to a Western global partnership but also its "civilian" mentality. Europe, lacking America's legacy of oversized military power, should be more inclined toward conciliation than confrontation. In the recurring struggle between the worldviews of Herder and Hobbes, Europeans might be more naturally inclined to Herder—to the principle that nations and regions can live peacefully together and develop in their own ways, so long as they respect the right of others to do the same. Since time has made us sadder and wiser historians than Herder, we know that international harmony seldom comes without great effort—requiring both enlightened leadership and balanced power. A genuinely "Euro-American" form of global leadership should be more acceptable to the rest of the world than the American hyperpower. Euro-American leadership might be more efficacious in prompting the difficult adjustments that the twenty-first century's rapidly expanding global system will require. For ordering a new and more plural global economy, Europe's preference for economic equilibrium might prove a more durable and appealing intellectual foundation than the voluntarist and ad hoc economics popular in hegemonic America. As America came to rescue Europe in the twentieth century, a rejuvenated Europe may come to save the Pax Americana in the twenty-first.

Before such a balanced global system emerges in any reliable form, however, Europe must strengthen its own structures. In particular, the EU must adopt the constitutional reforms and achieve the security arrangements needed to consolidate a coherent European bloc. And the European Union must recast its relations with both the United States and Russia. A pan-European order that is genuinely tripolar, rather than hyper-American or hyper-European, seems the soundest long-term basis for Eurasian peace. Only within such a pan-European structure does it seem likely that Russia can be brought back into the European family and that the United States can be comfortably kept there. And only within such a frame can the European Union be saved from its own temptation toward Eurasian overstretch.

As I noted in chapter 1, it is tempting to see a balanced and cohesive Europe as the harbinger not only of a more plural world—arguably a mixed blessing—but also of a world with reasonable hopes for peaceful stability. Europe may once more be ready to give political lessons to others. In the nineteenth century, the European nation state proved the best formula for reconciling the conflicting domestic needs of democratic Western societies. But in crowded, interdependent Europe, the nation state formula was unable to resolve the old problem of interstate order. Since World War II, Europe has pushed the nation state formula to a new confederal plane, one that preserves the accomplishments of the nation state while it seeks to overcome its limitations. Europe's hybrid confederacy is, in effect, a highly creative evolution of the nation state, a genuinely new political form. Thanks to it, European states have converted their interdependence into a strength rather than a liability. And with this new strength, Europeans have gone a long way toward reconciling the democratic politics of communitarian nation states and the efficiencies of international capitalism. With luck, Western Europe's experience may provide the inspiration for a stable order in Pan-Europe as well. And perhaps, just as Europe's nineteenth-century nation state became the political formula adopted throughout the world in the twentieth century, Europe's twentieth-century hybrid confederacy may become the model for the new regional systems needed elsewhere in the twenty-first century.

Dynamic and deeply rooted trends—military, political, cultural, and economic—are pushing European states to consolidate their union and take charge of their own collective security. In doing so, they will naturally recast the Atlantic relationship on a more plural basis. While nothing in such matters is reliably certain, the plural direction in the West itself seems part of an unfolding historical pattern across the globe. A contemporary Herder should rejoice in the new and richer palate of cultures and energies that such a world implies. But Herder's happy ending seems more likely if the West itself, managing its own maturity with grace and imagination, presents a rational model for the rest of the world. A strong, humane, and cohesive Europe—linked to Russia as well as America, and helping to give balance to both East and West—seems a vision of the future in harmony with the better parts of our nature and the most promising trends in our history.

Index